THE JUST SOCIETY

THE JUST SOCIETY

Edited by

Ellen Frankel Paul, Fred D. Miller, Jr.,
and Jeffrey Paul

CAMBRIDGE
UNIVERSITY PRESS

Published by the Press Syndicate of the University of Cambridge
The Pitt Building, Trumpington Street, Cambridge CB2 1RP, England
40 West 20th Street, New York, NY 10011, USA
10 Stamford Road, Oakleigh, Melbourne, Victoria 3166, Australia

First published 1995

Printed in the United States of America

Library of Congress Cataloging-in-Publication Data

The just society / edited by Ellen Frankel Paul, Fred D. Miller, Jr.,
and Jeffrey Paul. p. cm.
Includes bibliographical references and index.
ISBN 0-521-55857-3
1. Justice. 2. Equality. I. Paul, Ellen Frankel. II. Miller,
Fred Dycus, 1944– . III. Paul, Jeffrey.
JC578.J83 1995
320.01'1–dc20 95-13173
CIP

ISBN 0-521-55857-3 paperback

The essays in this book have also been published,
without introduction and index, in the semiannual journal
Social Philosophy & Policy, Volume 12, Number 2,
which is available by subscription.

CONTENTS

INTRODUCTION

"Justice," observes Aristotle, "is a social virtue, which necessarily brings all the other virtues in its train."* The obligations that societies owe to their citizens as a matter of justice, and the arrangement of social institutions to fulfill those obligations, are among the central concerns of contemporary political philosophy. But what is justice and how should societies attempt to secure it? What values should social institutions be designed to promote, and when should governments step back and leave their citizens to manage their own affairs?

The twelve essays in this collection—written from a range of perspectives by prominent philosophers and political theorists—address these questions and examine related issues. Some explore the relationship between justice and equality, asking whether societies should strive to eliminate inequalities in their citizens' levels of opportunity or welfare. Some consider whether societies are obligated to provide their less fortunate citizens with some minimum level of subsistence, or whether the provision of such relief is best left to private charitable organizations. Some essays look at the relationship between justice and other values, such as mutual consent, the protection of property rights, or the elimination of exploitation. Others deal with the rules governing specific practices, such as the distribution of health care, the pursuit of academic inquiry and research, or the assignment of punishments. Still others propose and defend principles for designing and assessing social institutions.

In the collection's opening essay, "Immanent Liberalism: The Politics of Mutual Consent," Roderick T. Long explores the liberal ideal of the just society, in which social interactions are based on the mutual consent of individuals. Long notes that the dominant varieties of liberalism today seek to realize this ideal only vicariously, through (actual or imputed) consent *to* a political structure, while a dissenting minority of liberals seek instead to realize this ideal immanently, through everyday consensual relations *within* a political structure. He argues that the immanent-liberal strategy is a more faithful embodiment of the liberal ideal, while the vicarious-liberal strategy (as found, for example, in the work of John Rawls) represents a triumph of communitarian values in liberal guise. Long contends, further, that the immanent/vicarious distinction is more significant than the capitalist/socialist one: decentralist socialists and free-market libertarians take an immanent approach and have much in common with one another, he claims, while advocates of central planning, and of corporate capitalism, share a vicarious approach. Immanent liberals—

* Aristotle, *Politics* III.13.1283b38–40 (trans. H. Rackham).

whether capitalist or socialist—seek to put the individual in control of his everyday life, while vicarious liberals content themselves with giving the individual a voice in determining what sorts of institutions he will live under.

The primacy of the individual is also a central theme of Loren E. Lomasky's contribution to this volume, "Justice to Charity." Lomasky argues that charity is a virtue to be practiced by individuals, rather than an obligation that society owes to the unfortunate. He embraces the widely held belief that the misfortunes of others matter, and that moral people should be willing, when possible, to contribute to the relief of others' distress. Yet he rejects, at least for the most part, the idea that people have rights to welfare or duties to provide for the welfare of others; such rights and duties, he argues, are justifiable only within strict limits. The tendency to cast charity in terms of rights and duties is, Lomasky claims, a symptom of the "jurisprudential paradigm," in which all moral issues are reframed in legalistic language. A better way to approach the issue, he suggests, is to ask, "How may I live well?" On this approach, the approach of many premodern moral philosophers, charity is one virtue among the many that make up a good life—a life lived among other people, in which one recognizes their needs as well as one's own. Rights and duties, on Lomasky's view, form a kind of "shell" protecting the individual's freedom of action; virtues such as charity are exercised within that shell, at the discretion of the individual. Nevertheless, Lomasky maintains that his view leaves room for minimal welfare rights, rights which societies must guarantee to their citizens (though these cannot properly be called "rights to charity"). Such rights, he argues, are limited by a number of conditions: one has a right only to be provided with the minimum aid necessary to sustain a decent life, and one has a claim only against the surplus of others—a claim which, furthermore, is valid only if one is genuinely unable to provide for oneself, and only if voluntary charity is not forthcoming.

Like Lomasky, Alexander Rosenberg is concerned about the extent of societies' obligations toward their citizens. In "Equality, Sufficiency, and Opportunity in the Just Society," Rosenberg argues that the moral obligations of a society do not extend to the provision of equality of welfare or other outcomes, or even to the provision of equality of opportunity. Equality of outcome, he contends, is unattainable: even if we could identify the myriad sources of inequality, any attempt to compensate for them would require a kind of pervasive interference in everyday life that would prove unsustainable in practice. The attempt to implement equality of opportunity faces similar difficulties and would lead, in practice, to demands for equality of outcome—for any difference in outcomes among identifiable groups would be seen as evidence that opportunities had not yet been equalized. As an alternative to equality, Rosenberg defends the view that society is at most obligated to provide sufficiency: each citizen is entitled to a level of resources sufficient to enable him to discover and pursue what he really cares about (or ought to care about). The doctrine of sufficiency avoids a number of problems associated with the pursuit of equality. It eliminates the need to measure a society's total wealth and to find ways of comparing the various goods that are to be equalized; moreover, it eliminates or minimizes various destructive incentives, such as the incentive to conceal one's wealth or advantages, and to exaggerate one's disadvantages. Rosenberg concludes that sufficiency is worthy of investigation as an alternative to government-imposed equality.

Larry S. Temkin takes a more favorable view of the idea that societies should be concerned about promoting equality. His contribution to this volume, "Justice and Equality: Some Questions about Scope," explores the extent to which we should care about inequality between different societies or across different generations. Temkin sets out to categorize various types of egalitarianism—from the most extreme form, which strives for equality across societies and across time, to the least extreme form, which limits the concern for equality to contemporaries within a single society. In the course of his discussion, he touches on a number of important topics, including the relative importance of natural and social injustice, the role of equality under contractarian systems of morality, and the significance of "special" obligations toward one's family and friends. He also considers whether the pursuit of equality within a single generation is compatible with the pursuit of equality between generations, challenging the idea that redistribution designed to achieve equality within a generation tends to reduce the overall amount of wealth available to future generations. He concludes that our views on the scope of equality will have wide-ranging consequences in practice—affecting, for example, our views on the morality of aiding the poor in other societies, on the preservation of natural resources, on the proper allocation of aid to the disabled, and on the permissibility of burdening future generations with debt.

While Temkin focuses on questions about the scope of equality, and their impact on efforts to achieve justice, Allen Buchanan addresses the impact of technological change. In "Equal Opportunity and Genetic Intervention," Buchanan explores the ways in which genetic manipulation might be used to either enhance or reduce equality of opportunity. He begins by noting that under some influential theories of justice, especially Rawls's theory, genetic differences which contribute to differences in ability are considered "morally arbitrary"; under these theories, such characteristics are not to be allowed to influence individuals' life-prospects. Those individuals whose genetic make-up causes them to have lower life-prospects are to receive special consideration, so that each may have an equal opportunity to pursue his own conception of the good life. Buchanan identifies two principles that might underlie this approach: the Resource Redress Principle, requiring compensation for disadvantages caused by natural endowments; and the Resource Equality Principle, requiring that all resources, natural and social, be distributed equally. He considers a pair of arguments which purport to justify these principles—one based on a formal principle of equal treatment, the other based on an analysis of the concept of equal opportunity itself—and finds that neither argument is sound. Nevertheless, he argues that a principle of equal opportunity may have a role to play in efforts to prevent genetically based deprivations, such as severe disabilities, and to limit attempts at genetic enhancements, such as the development of superior cognitive skills or resistance to disease.

Allen W. Wood shares Buchanan's concern with inequality and its effects on individuals' life-prospects. In his essay "Exploitation," Wood approaches the issue of exploitation in terms of inequality: to exploit someone is to take advantage of his weakness or vulnerability, where that vulnerability involves an inequality of wealth or status between the exploiter and the person being exploited. Wood argues that, on this view, exploitation is not a moral concept: it is not part of the very meaning of the concept that exploitation is wrong or bad. He believes that exploitation is usually thought to be wrong not because it is wrong by definition, but because it violates a moral principle that most of us hold: the principle that it is dishonorable to use the weaknesses of others to further one's own ends, and degrading to have one's own weaknesses used by others. Wood employs his analysis to explicate and defend both the traditional Marxian claim that wage labor is exploitative and the more recent claim that contracts for surrogate motherhood are exploitative. In each case, the typically vast inequalities in bargaining position—between worker and capitalist, or between birth mother and adopting parents—render the transaction exploitative. Nevertheless, Wood acknowledges that such relationships, while exploitative, can be mutually beneficial. In some cases, such relationships may be just and may violate no one's rights, even though we may find them morally objectionable on other grounds.

The next three essays examine issues of justice that arise in other areas of life: in the delivery of health care, in educational institutions, and in the penal system. Dan W. Brock addresses discrimination and equal access in health care in his contribution to this volume, "Justice and the ADA: Does Prioritizing and Rationing Health Care Discriminate against the Disabled?" Brock focuses on the state of Oregon's attempt to control health-care costs by prioritizing various services according to their costs and benefits—an attempt which has been criticized as unjustly discriminating against disabled persons in violation of the Americans with Disabilities Act (ADA). He uses this example to illustrate some of the problems that arise in situations of this kind, when societies attempt to find a rational way of allocating scarce resources. Brock notes that Oregon's proposed program used quality-of-life measures to evaluate the benefits of various treatments, and that these measures appear to devalue disabled persons' lives in comparison with the lives of nondisabled persons. He argues that this proposal raises at least three serious and difficult problems regarding the prioritization and rationing of scarce health-care resources. There is a fundamental conflict between attempting to maximize the overall benefits that health-care services can provide for all, and attempting to give each individual a fair chance of receiving the care he needs. There is the question of whether special consideration or compensation should be given to individuals suffering from disabilities through no fault of their own. Finally, there is what Brock calls the "perspective problem": whether, in evaluating the quality of life with a disability, one should adopt the perspective of a person with that disability, or that of a nondisabled person. Brock discusses each of these problems in turn, emphasizing that these issues become increasingly important as governments and private insurers attempt to rein in escalating health-care costs.

Elizabeth S. Anderson's essay on justice in education deals not with the distribution of resources but with the distribution of cognitive authority: the ability to take part in inquiry, to have one's ideas taken seriously, and to participate in decisions about what subjects are worthy of study. In "The Democratic University: The Role of Justice in the Production of Knowledge," Anderson examines the egalitarian critique of higher education, which claims that universities systematically deny cognitive authority to marginalized groups on the basis of race, class, and gender. She also considers the claims of conservatives and libertarians who view the egalitarian movement as a threat to freedom of speech, and who advocate the model of a "free market of ideas." These rival views of trends in higher education, she argues, express distinctive political epistemologies—accounts of the social relations among inquirers that best promote research and learning. Anderson defends a democratic model of inquiry in opposition to the market model, claiming that, in cultures marked by entrenched inequalities, "free markets of ideas" enable dominant groups to devalue or silence the speech of subordinate groups, violating their academic freedom and impairing the quality of research. She argues that a liberal-democratic culture of inquiry promotes academic freedom and sound research through informal speech norms that recognize the equality of inquirers, granting them effective access to the floor, and respectful attention and response, regardless of inequalities based on ascribed social identity. To secure this equality, many egalitarians recommend formal codes restricting offensive speech, but while Anderson believes that highly limited codes are defensible, she emphasizes the need for a democratic *culture* of equality, which cannot be secured by legalistic means.

The allocation of health-care resources, or of opportunities to participate in inquiry, can plausibly be thought of in terms of distributive justice. The practice of meting out punishments, in contrast, is typically justified not by appeal to principles of distribution, but by appeal to principles of retribution, or to the practice's utility as a means of deterrence. Daniel M. Farrell challenges this way of thinking about punishment in his contribution to this volume, "Deterrence and the Just Distribution of Harm." Farrell explores the possibility that a deterrence-based theory of punishment may appeal to certain nonutilitarian principles governing the distribution of harm. The central principle that he discusses states that, when one is confronted with the possibility of being harmed by another person's wrongful conduct, one is entitled to choose that the other person shall be harmed, rather than allowing oneself to be harmed. Farrell argues that this principle, in conjunction with other principles governing the degree of harm that may be inflicted on the offending party, can justify our practice of making and carrying out deterrent threats, including formal threats of punishment for criminal conduct. The same principles, he argues, underlie our belief that the intended victims of violence are justified in using (or threatening to use) violence in self-defense. By appealing to principles of just distribution, he concludes, we can develop a theory of punishment that avoids the standard objections raised against utilitarian and retributive theories.

Both Farrell and Anderson explore the justice of practices or "rules of the game" that govern people's dealings with one another; in a sense, their essays reflect a shift in contemporary moral and political philosophy from the analysis of individual actions to the analysis of the social and legal institutions that govern interaction. This shift is the subject of Thomas W. Pogge's essay "Three Problems with Contractarian-Consequentialist Ways of Assessing Social Institutions." Pogge notes that it is tempting to assess institutional schemes in broadly consequentialist terms: by reference to their comparative impact on the quality of life of prospective participants. While this approach seems initially plausible, Pogge argues that it has troubling implications. It entails excessive attention to certain natural inequalities (for example, in cheerfulness and good looks) that affect quality of life. It fails to support equality of opportunity, since it assumes that prospective participants will care only about the benefits they can expect to receive under various schemes, and not about how a particular distribution of benefits comes about—leaving open the possibility that arbitrary factors such as race and gender could influence distributions. Finally, Pogge contends, this approach might require draconian revisions of our legal system, including the relaxation of standards of evidence, and the elimination of proportionality in sentencing, in order to reduce levels of criminal activity. In light of these disturbing implications, Pogge concludes, it is time to consider alternatives to the prevailing prospective-participant approach—and, perhaps, time to reexamine political philosophy's concentration on the justice of institutions.

Among the central institutions that concern political philosophers are institutions governing property, and these are the focus of Michael Gorr's contribution to this volume, "Justice, Self-Ownership, and Natural Assets." Gorr begins with a strategy for defending property rights that can be traced back to John Locke: the attempt to ground property rights in self-ownership. After evaluating a number of efforts to explicate a principle of self-ownership, Gorr proposes a moderate principle which states that each person has a right to have "a significantly stronger say than anyone else" in determining how he lives his life and in restricting what others may do to him. Armed with this conception of self-ownership, Gorr takes up the charge, made most prominently by Robert Nozick and Michael Sandel, that Rawls's theory of justice is premised upon a rejection of self-ownership. This charge arises out of Rawls's insistence that, rather than assigning each individual a right to his natural talents, a society should treat the distribution of natural talents as a collective asset. Gorr argues that the critique of Rawls's treatment of this issue involves some serious misunderstandings, and that Rawls's theory (particularly in its most recent, avowedly "political" interpretation) carries with it a deep commitment to an important form of self-ownership. Gorr concludes with some observations on the rationale for recognizing a right to self-ownership and on the extent to which it is useful or illuminating to premise an account of justice on claims about the moral relations people bear to themselves.

The collection's final essay examines the influence that the Western liberal tradition of property rights and limited government has had on Chinese political thought. In "Designing Democratic Institutions and the Problem of Evil: A Liberal Chinese Perspective," Baogang He explores the thought of a number of Chinese liberals whose views on the design of just social institutions have been influenced by Western political theorists such as John Locke, David Hume, and James Madison. These Chinese liberals call for a distinctive approach to the design of institutions—an approach based on the assumption that all citizens, and especially those who hold power, have the potential to do evil. Baogang He describes the emergence of this approach and contrasts it with the Maoist approach, which emphasizes the perfectibility of human nature and the virtue of political leaders. He argues that Chinese liberals implicitly conceive of evil in terms of the violation of rights, and shows how they would design democratic institutions to control the problem of evil by limiting opportunities for corruption. Such democratic arrangements would include an institutional guarantee of individual rights, a separation of political powers, and institutions designed to channel political ambitions so that they may be made to serve the public good. Baogang He believes that Chinese liberals have made an important breakthrough in linking the problem of evil with institutional design, and that democratic institutions, with their built-in checks and balances and self-correcting mechanisms, hold the key to resolving China's political troubles.

Assessing the justice of societies and their institutions is one of the defining tasks of political philosophy. The twelve essays in this volume offer valuable insights into the theories and principles that underlie such assessments.

ACKNOWLEDGMENTS

The editors wish to acknowledge several individuals at the Social Philosophy and Policy Center, Bowling Green State University, who provided invaluable assistance in the preparation of this volume. They include Mary Dilsaver, Terrie Weaver, Carrie-Ann Zinaich, and Pamela Phillips.

The editors would like to extend special thanks to Executive Manager Kory Swanson, for offering invaluable administrative support; to Publication Specialist Tamara Sharp, for attending to innumerable day-to-day details of the book's preparation; and to Managing Editor Harry Dolan, for providing dedicated assistance throughout the editorial and production processes.

CONTRIBUTORS

Roderick T. Long is Assistant Professor of Philosophy at the University of North Carolina at Chapel Hill. He received his Ph.D. in philosophy from Cornell in 1992. He has published in *Utilitas* and *Social Philosophy and Policy*, and has recently completed a book tentatively titled *Aristotle on Fate and Freedom*. His current project is a study of Socrates' theory of moral psychology in the Socratic works of Plato and Xenophon.

Loren E. Lomasky is Professor of Philosophy at Bowling Green State University. He was educated at Michigan State University, Harvard University, and the University of Connecticut, and has taught at the University of Minnesota, Duluth, and at the University of Connecticut at both the Hartford and Storrs branches. He is the author of *Persons, Rights, and the Moral Community* (1987), the coauthor, with Geoffrey Brennan, of *Democracy and Decision: The Pure Theory of Electoral Preference* (1993), and the coeditor with Brennan of a volume of essays titled *Politics and Process: New Essays in Democratic Theory* (1989).

Alexander Rosenberg is Professor of Philosophy and Director of the University Honors Program at the University of California, Riverside. He has received fellowships from the American Council of Learned Societies, the National Science Foundation, and the John Simon Guggenheim Memorial Foundation. He is the author of seven books, including *Economics: Mathematical Politics or Science of Diminishing Returns?* (1992), which secured the Lakatos Award in the Philosophy of Science for 1993. His newest book is *Instrumental Biology, or, The Disunity of Science* (1994).

Larry S. Temkin is Associate Professor of Philosophy at Rice University. He received his B.A. from the University of Wisconsin in 1975, and his Ph.D. from Princeton in 1983. He also studied at Oxford University, and has been a Visiting Professor at the University of Pittsburgh. He specializes in ethics and social and political philosophy, and his essays have appeared in *Philosophy and Public Affairs* and *Philosophical Review*, as well as in anthologies published by Cambridge University Press and Yale University Press. His book *Inequality* (1993) presents a new way of understanding inequality that challenges standard assumptions and has far-reaching implications. His current research focuses on the nature of the good and of practical reasoning.

Allen Buchanan is Grainger Professor of Business Ethics and Professor of Philosophy and Medical Ethics at the University of Wisconsin, Madison. He has written numerous articles in ethics, epistemology, political philosophy, bioethics, and other areas of applied ethics, and is the author of *Marx and Justice: The Radical Critique of Liberalism* (1982), *Ethics, Efficiency, and the Market* (1985), *Deciding for Others: The Ethics of Surrogate Decision Making* (with Dan W. Brock, 1989), and *Secession: The Morality of Political Divorce from Fort Sumter to Lithuania and Quebec* (1991).

Allen W. Wood is Professor of Philosophy at Cornell University, where he has taught since 1968. He received his B.A. from Reed College and his M.A. and Ph.D. from Yale University, and has held visiting appointments at the University of Michigan and the University of California at San Diego. His interests center on moral and social philosophy and on German philosophy of the eighteenth and nineteenth centuries. His publications include *Kant's Moral Religion* (1970), *Kant's Rational Theology* (1978), *Karl Marx* (1981), and *Hegel's Ethical Thought* (1990).

Dan W. Brock is University Professor, Professor of Philosophy and Biomedical Ethics, and Director of the Center for Biomedical Ethics at Brown University, where he has taught since 1969. He earned his B.A. in economics from Cornell University and his Ph.D. in philosophy from Columbia University. He has published many papers in biomedical ethics, as well as in moral and political philosophy, and is the author of *Deciding for Others: The Ethics of Surrogate Decision Making* (with Allen Buchanan, 1989) and of *Life and Death: Philosophical Essays in Biomedical Ethics* (1993).

Elizabeth S. Anderson is Associate Professor and Arthur F. Thurnau Professor of Philosophy and Women's Studies at the University of Michigan, Ann Arbor. Her book *Value in Ethics and Economics* (1993) develops a pluralistic theory of value and explores the ethical limitations of markets through cases such as surrogate motherhood and cost-benefit analysis applied to environmental quality. She has written on equality and market socialism, democracy and social-choice theory, incommensurable goods, rational choice, and John Stuart Mill. She is presently conducting research in feminist epistemology.

Daniel M. Farrell is Professor of Philosophy and Chair of the Philosophy Department at Ohio State University. He has published widely in ethics, social and political philosophy, and the philosophy of law, including a series of recent papers on some of the moral and logical problems of deterrence in both domestic and international contexts. He is currently completing a book on these latter problems, in which he argues that deterrent threats and enforcements are justified (when in fact they are justified) not by their overall social utility but by their conformity to certain deontological principles for choosing among harms (or probabilities of harms) in various kinds of choice situations.

Thomas W. Pogge is Associate Professor of Philosophy at Columbia University. He studied sociology and philosophy at Hamburg University and Harvard University, and is currently teaching and writing mainly on Kant and moral and political philosophy, with a special emphasis on issues in global justice, human rights, and contractarianism. His most recent publications include *Realizing Rawls* (1989) and essays in the *Journal of Social Philosophy, Zeitschrift für Philosophische Forschung, Journal of Philosophy, Ethics,* and *Philosophy and Public Affairs*.

Michael Gorr is Professor of Philosophy at Illinois State University. He received his Ph.D. from Brown University in 1975, and is the author of *Coercion, Freedom, and Exploitation* (1989), as well as numerous articles in moral, political, and legal philosophy in journals such as *Philosophy and Public Affairs, Law and Philosophy,* and *Philosophical Quarterly*. He is currently working on a book on freedom of expression.

Baogang He is Lecturer in Political Science at the University of Tasmania. He received his Ph.D. from Australian National University, and is the author of more than a dozen English articles on political theory, Chinese politics, and Chinese political thought. He has worked on Chinese translations of a number of Western works, such as John Rawls's *A Theory of Justice,* and is presently working on the Chinese Transition toward Marketization and Democratization, a project funded by the Australian Research Council.

IMMANENT LIBERALISM: THE POLITICS OF MUTUAL CONSENT

By Roderick T. Long

I will not cease from Mental Fight,
Nor shall my Sword sleep in my hand:
Till we have built Jerusalem,
In England's green & pleasant Land.
—William Blake[1]

Part One of Marx's "On the Jewish Question" is a communitarian manifesto, one of the finest and subtlest ever penned.[2] But has it anything valuable to offer defenders of liberalism?[3]

I think it does; for in "On the Jewish Question" Marx points to a potential danger into which communitarians are liable to fall, and I shall argue that his discussion sheds light on an analogous peril for liberals. Specifically, Marx distinguishes between a genuine and a spurious form of communitarianism, and warns that a failure to recognize this distinction may lead communitarians to embrace liberal values in communitarian guise. Using Marx's analysis as a model, I hope to show that the same distinction may be found within the liberal tradition, posing a corresponding danger (communitarian values in liberal guise) into which contemporary liberalism has in large part already fallen.

I. Vicarious versus Immanent Communitarianism

Marx argues that the modern democratic state systematically spreads a communitarian illusion over an underlying liberal reality. Citizens of such states exercise the communitarian values of solidarity and fellowship

[1] William Blake, "Milton: A Poem in Two Books," in Mary Lynn Johnson and John E. Grant, eds., *Blake's Poetry and Designs* (New York: W. W. Norton, 1979), Preface, lines 13–16, p. 238.

[2] As opposed to Part Two, a cynically anti-Semitic diatribe unworthy of its author.

[3] I shall be using the terms "communitarian" and "liberal" fairly broadly, and some definitions are perhaps called for. I would define as communitarian those outlooks that place primary emphasis and value on the society of status, and as liberal those outlooks that place primary emphasis and value on the society of contract. (The terminology of status and contract will be elucidated further in Section II below.) I do not intend these as stipulative definitions, but rather as attempts to capture what strike me as the respective unifying ideals of the two broad intellectual traditions commonly identified as communitarianism and liberalism.

with other human beings—but only at the political level, through their ties to the state apparatus (in the form, e.g., of equal rights to the franchise). Such communal ties have no significance in people's actual, everyday lives, which remain competitive, individualistic, and atomized:

> The perfected political state is by its nature the species-life of man in opposition to his material life. All the presuppositions of this egoistic life continue to exist in civil society outside the sphere of the state, but as proper to civil society. When the political state has achieved its true completion, man leads a double life, a heavenly one and an earthly one, not only in thought and consciousness but in reality, in life. He has a life both in the political community, where he is valued as a communal being, and in civil society, where he is active as a private individual, treats other men as means, degrades himself to a means, and becomes the plaything of alien powers. . . . Man in the reality that is nearest to him, civil society, is a profane being. Here where he counts for himself and others as a real individual, he is an illusory phenomenon. In the state, on the other hand, where man counts as a species-being, he is an imaginary participant in an imaginary sovereignty, he is robbed of his real life and filled with an unreal universality.[4]

Under such a regime we are bound to one another only *indirectly*, through the machinery of the state. We enjoy fraternal union with our fellows *fictively*, by means of a kind of political play-acting that obscures the actual conditions of social life rather than reflecting those conditions. Like Ludwig Feuerbach's theists, we have projected our nature as social beings onto an external force rather than reclaiming it in our day-to-day existence.[5] We experience community—but only *vicariously*, through a political intermediary.

Such vicarious community is the result, Marx thinks, of the collapse of feudalism. The feudal system was a communitarian one, in the sense that people's political relationships to one another pervaded their lives and shaped the character of everyday experience; under such a system, no one could think of himself as a solitary individual with purely private interests. These political relationships, however, were not structured to promote the common advantage; instead, they served to reinforce and extend the power of the ruling elites. The rise of democracy might seem a welcome improvement, then. Unfortunately, by wedding political rela-

[4] Karl Marx, "On the Jewish Question," in David McLellan, ed., *Karl Marx: Selected Writings* (Oxford: Oxford University Press, 1977), pp. 45–46.

[5] Ludwig Feuerbach, *The Essence of Christianity* (1841). Marx's "On the Jewish Question" is evidently intended *inter alia* as an application to the idea of the state of Feuerbach's critique of the idea of God.

tionships to the common good, the democratic state thereby divests private life of the communitarian dimension it originally possessed:

> The old civil society had a directly political character. The elements of civil life, like, for example, property or the family or the type and manner of work, were, in the form of seigniorial right, estates, and corporations, raised to the level of elements of state life. They defined in this form the relationship of the single individual to the state as a whole, that is, his political relationship. . . . The political revolution overthrew this feudal power and turned state affairs into affairs of the people. . . . Particular professions and ranks sank to a merely individual importance. They were no longer the relationship of individuals to the state as a whole. Public affairs as such became the general affair of each individual and politics was a general occupation.
>
> But the perfection of the idealism of the state was at the same time the perfection of the materialism of civil society. . . . Political emancipation entailed the emancipation of civil society from politics, from even the appearance of a general content. Feudal society was dissolved into . . . egoistic man. This man, the member of civil society, is the basis, the presupposition, of the political state. . . . Man was therefore not freed from religion; he received freedom of religion. He was not freed from property; he received freedom of property. He was not freed from the egoism of trade; he received freedom to trade.[6]

In short, then, social relations under a democratic state are characterized at the level of political institutions by communitarian solidarity and equality, but at the level of actual life by liberal individualism and commercial interests. The citizens of the modern state have received "political" emancipation, emancipation on paper, in place of genuine "human" emancipation.

This is because communal fellowship at the political level is communal fellowship in name only:

> The state as state annuls private property . . . as soon as man declares in a political manner that private property is abolished, as soon as he abolishes the requirement of a property qualification for . . . participation at elections. . . . And yet the political annulment of private property has not only not abolished private property, it actually presupposes it. The state does away with difference in birth, class, education, and profession in its own manner when it declares birth, class, education, and profession to be unpolitical differences, when it summons every member of the people to an equal participation in

[6] Marx, "On the Jewish Question," pp. 55–56.

> popular sovereignty without taking the differences into consideration, when it treats all elements of the people's real life from the point of view of the state. Nevertheless the state still allows private property, education, and profession to have an effect in their own manner, that is as private property, as education, as profession, and make their particular natures felt.[7]

The democratic state does not *abolish* the impediments to communal life; instead, it *ignores* them (and thus allows these impediments to flourish). By so ignoring them, the democratic state is able to present a picture of human beings in their political capacity with all these impediments removed, creating the seductive illusion that a communitarian paradise has at last been achieved—while, in fact, society, having (as it were) kicked its communitarian elements upstairs, is more individualistic than ever.[8]

As an alternative to this fictive, vicarious communitarianism, Marx upholds the ideal of an *immanent* communitarianism—that is, one in which the communitarian ideals he cherishes are realized directly in people's everyday lives, rather than indirectly, and in an imaginary way, through the intermediary of the state:

> Political emancipation is the reduction of man, on the one hand to a member of civil society, an egoistic and independent individual, on the other hand to a citizen, a moral person.
>
> The actual individual man must take the abstract citizen back into himself and, as an individual man in his empirical life, in his individual work and individual relationships become a species-being; man must recognize his own forces as social forces, organize them, and thus no longer separate social forces from himself in the form of political forces. Only when this has been achieved will human emancipation be completed.[9]

Under Immanent Communitarianism, the social ties that constitute our essence are direct and real, and permeate our day-to-day existence and activity. Vicarious Communitarianism, on the other hand, by demanding that these ties be expressed at and through the political level, divests everyday life of communitarian significance, and thus turns out at bottom to be no more than a disguise for the liberalism it purports to oppose.

[7] *Ibid.*, p. 45.

[8] As an example of this, Marx refers to the architects of the French Revolution, who beneath their communitarian rhetoric were ultimately committed to a liberal conception of civil society.

[9] Marx, "On the Jewish Question," p. 57.

II. Status and Contract

Why should liberals care about any of this? After all, Marx's communitarian vision of liberal society as necessarily crass, legalistic, and selfish, a morass of atomism and anomie, is one that liberals reject. And I think they are correct in rejecting it (though to adjudicate this dispute between liberalism and communitarianism lies beyond my present purpose). So what relevance do Marx's warnings against Vicarious Communitarianism have for liberals?

The answer, I think, is that liberalism too can be either immanent or vicarious, according to whether its fundamental ideals are realized immanently in actual life or vicariously through the intermediary of the state; and it too can serve, in its vicarious form, as a mask for its opposite.

Different versions of liberalism represent different ways of implementing the fundamental idea of the *society of contract*. The terminology of *status* and *contract* was first introduced by the nineteenth-century English jurist Henry Maine:

> The movement of the progressive societies has been uniform in one respect. Through all its course it has been distinguished by the gradual dissolution of family dependency, and the growth of individual obligation in its place. The Individual is steadily substituted for the Family, as the unit of which civil laws take account. . . . Nor is it difficult to see what is the tie between man and man which replaces by degrees those forms of reciprocity in rights and duties which have their origin in the Family. It is Contract. Starting, as from one terminus of history, from a condition of society in which all the relations of Persons are summed up in the relations of Family, we seem to have steadily moved towards a phase of social order in which all these relations arise from the free agreement of Individuals. . . . The word Status may be usefully employed to construct a formula expressing the law of progress thus indicated, which, whatever be its value, seems to me to be sufficiently ascertained. All the forms of Status taken notice of in the Law of Persons were derived from, and to some extent are still coloured by, the powers and privileges anciently residing in the Family. If then we employ Status, agreeably with the usage of the best writers, to signify these personal conditions only, and avoid applying the term to such conditions as are the immediate or remote result of agreement, we may say that the movement of the progressive societies has hitherto been a movement *from Status to Contract*.[10]

[10] Henry Sumner Maine, *Ancient Law: Its Connection with the Early History of Society and Its Relation to Modern Ideas*, 10th ed. (London: John Morrow, 1906), pp. 172–74.

Contract relationships are relationships based on mutual agreement, and their attendant obligations derive their binding force from consent; status relationships are relationships into which one is simply born, and their attendant obligations derive their binding force from the nature of the social roles one finds oneself in.[11] A political community is described as a society of contract or a society of status according to whether the destinies of its individual members are determined primarily by their contract relationships or primarily by their status relationships.[12]

The paradigm case of a status relationship is the family; I have obligations to my parents in virtue of being their son, although I never voluntarily undertook such obligations. Under a regime of status, the political structure of society is modeled as far as possible on that of the family; this represents the position of contemporary communitarians:

> [W]e all approach our own circumstances as bearers of a particular social identity. I am someone's son or daughter, someone else's cousin or uncle; I am a citizen of this or that city, a member of this or that guild or profession; I belong to this clan, that tribe, this nation. Hence what is good for me has to be the good for one who inhabits these roles. As such, I inherit from the past of my family, my city, my tribe, my nation, a variety of debts, inheritances, rightful expectations and obligations. . . . For the story of my life is always embedded in the story of those communities from which I derive my identity. I am born with a past; and to try to cut myself off from that past, in the individualist mode, is to deform my present relationships.[13]

Under a regime of contract, on the other hand, society is viewed—to employ John Rawls's famous formulation—as a system of cooperation for mutual advantage among free and equal persons. It is in this sense that liberalism, as its etymology suggests, is an ideology of freedom:

> For by naturall birth, all men are equally and alike borne to like propriety, liberty and freedome. . . . Every man by nature being a King,

[11] In Plato's *Crito,* Socrates grounds political obligations on both status and contract relationships.

[12] The status/contract distinction bears some resemblance to Robert Nozick's distinction between patterned and entitlement conceptions of justice (Nozick, *Anarchy, State, and Utopia* [New York: Basic Books, 1974], pp. 150–74). The match is not perfect, however. The entitlement conception, as Nozick constructs it, is inconsistent with redistributive taxation; but a commitment to redistributive taxation is not necessarily at odds with the ideal of contract, *if* such redistribution is conceived as a necessary means of ensuring the genuinely *consensual* nature of socioeconomic interactions (e.g., by eliminating excessive differences in bargaining power).

[13] Alasdair MacIntyre, *After Virtue: A Study in Moral Theory,* 2d ed. (Notre Dame: University of Notre Dame Press, 1984), pp. 220–21.

> Priest and Prophet in his owne naturall circuite and compasse, whereof no second may partake, but by deputation, commission, and free consent from him, whose naturall right and freedome it is.[14]

A classic confrontation between these two views of society is Robert Filmer's *Patriarcha* versus John Locke's *Two Treatises of Government*; another is Edmund Burke's *Reflections on the Revolution in France* versus Thomas Paine's *Rights of Man*.

Strictly speaking, liberals do not generally have any objection to status relationships as such; they need not regard significant moral ties as originating from voluntarily chosen relationships alone. In this sense, liberals have nothing against communitarian values.[15] What liberals insist on is that people's lives not be coercively *controlled* by such relationships. This distinction is one that communitarian critics of liberal individualism often miss.

> [Let me state] the intrinsic natures of Toryism and Liberalism. . . . Dating back to an earlier period than their names, the two political parties at first stood respectively for two opposed forms of social organization, broadly distinguishable as . . . the régime of status [and] the régime of contract. . . . If, instead of using the word "cooperation" in a limited sense, we use it in its widest sense, as signifying the combined activities of citizens under whatever system of regulation; then these two are definable as the system of compulsory cooperation and the system of voluntary cooperation. The typical structure of the one we see in an army formed of conscripts, in which the units of their several grades have to fulfil commands under pain of death, and receive food and clothing and pay, arbitrarily apportioned; while the typical structure of the other we see in a body of producers or distributors, who severally agree to specified payments in return for specified services, and may at will, after due notice, leave the organization if they do not like it.[16]

[14] Richard Overton, *An Arrow against All Tyrants and Tyrany, Shot from the Prison of Newgate into the Prerogative Bowels of the Arbitrary House of Lords, and All Other Usurpers and Tyrants Whatsoever*, excerpted in G. E. Aylmer, ed., *The Levellers in the English Revolution* (Ithaca, NY: Cornell University Press, 1975), p. 69.

[15] For an argument that the liberal right to withhold consent to status relationships is actually a *prerequisite* for the right sort of communitarian values, see John Tomasi, "Individual Rights and Community Virtues," *Ethics*, vol. 101 (April 1991), pp. 521–36.

[16] Herbert Spencer, "The New Toryism," in Spencer, *The Man versus the State: With Six Essays on Government, Society, and Freedom* (Indianapolis: Liberty Fund, 1981), pp. 5–6; cf. Spencer, "From Freedom to Bondage," in *ibid.*, p. 498. For a fuller discussion, see Herbert Spencer, *The Principles of Sociology*, vol. 2 (New York: D. Appleton, 1884), pp. 244–48, 568–78, 603–21, 637–40, 648–61.

The rise of commercial society out of the ashes of feudalism is thus generally regarded as a triumph of contract over status.[17] But the proper evaluation of this transition is another matter. Liberals generally applaud it:

> In the Society of Contract man is born free, and comes into his inheritance with maturity. By this concept all rights belong to the individual. Society consists of individuals in voluntary association. The rights of any person are limited only by the equal rights of another person.
>
> In the Society of Status nobody has any rights. The individual is not recognized; a man is defined by his relation to the group, and is presumed to exist only by permission. The system of status is privilege and subjection. . . . [T]he Society of Status resists change. . . . In [feudal] society, the son was held to the father's calling, regardless of ability. . . . The Society of Status is obliged to restrict production to the energy level it can accommodate. It does so by collectivism. . . . Medieval farming gave a miserably low yield. . . . As the level of energy in Europe rose again . . . the overflow once more sought the outlet of trade.
>
> This is usually described as the emergence of the middle class. The term is grossly inaccurate. . . . What is now called the middle class was not and is not a class; it is a different form of society, a classless society, the free society, the Society of Contract. The merchants and independent craftsmen had none of the characteristics of class. . . . The traders necessarily formed a Society of Contract, and lived by contract law.[18]

For communitarians like Marx, on the other hand, the substitution of contract for status is socially disruptive, destructive, and ultimately demoralizing:

> The bourgeoisie, wherever it has got the upper hand, has put an end to all feudal, patriarchal, idyllic relations. It has pitilessly torn asunder the motley feudal ties that bound man to his 'natural superiors', and has left remaining no other nexus between man and man than naked self-interest, than callous 'cash payment'. . . . All fixed, fast-frozen relations, with their train of ancient and venerable prejudices

[17] In fact, matters are somewhat more complicated. Although laws seem to have become somewhat more contract-oriented in their *content*, the rise of the nation-state may have resulted in a legal system less contract-oriented in its *structure*. See Bruce L. Benson, *The Enterprise of Law: Justice without the State* (San Francisco: Pacific Research Institute for Public Policy, 1990); and Tom W. Bell, "Polycentric Law," *Humane Studies Review*, vol. 7, no. 1 (Winter 1991–92), pp. 1–10.

[18] Isabel Paterson, *The God of the Machine* (New Brunswick, NJ: Transaction Publishers, 1993), pp. 42–50.

> and opinions, are swept away, all new-formed ones become antiquated before they can ossify.[19]

One should not infer that Marx's attitude toward feudalism is on balance positive; while feudalism represents a society of status, it is a hierarchical, patriarchal one – not the egalitarian society of status that Marx himself advocates. Marx makes it clear that the collapse of feudalism represents only the substitution of one form of oppression for another. While Marx is careful not to romanticize feudalism, however, he does see in feudal social relations something important and valuable that is missing from modern liberal society.

Liberals customarily pride themselves on the fact that liberal regimes assign as much of human life as possible to the voluntary forces of *society*, rather than to the coercive powers of *government*.[20] Indeed, this is just what we should expect from an ideology that privileges contract over status. But Marx turns the liberal distinction between government and society on its head. While, as a long-run anarchist, he shares in the abstract the liberal preference for spontaneous social order over governmentally imposed order, Marx's complaint is that this preference produces catastrophic results once it is combined with a consignment of status to the governmental realm and contract to the social realm – for the inevitable consequence is then a privileging of contract ideals and a marginalization of status ideals:

> Thus none of the so-called [liberal] rights of man goes beyond egoistic man, man as he is in civil society, namely an individual withdrawn behind his private interests and whims and separated from the community. Far from the rights of man conceiving of man as a species-being, species-life itself . . . appears as a framework exterior to individuals, a limitation of their original self-sufficiency. The only bond that holds them together is natural necessity, need and private interest, the conservation of their property and egoistic person. . . . [C]itizenship, the political community, is degraded by the political emancipators to a mere means for the preservation of these so-called rights of man. . . . [T]he sphere in which man behaves as a communal being is degraded below the sphere in which man behaves as a partial being. . . .
>
> It is true that [liberalism's] revolutionary practice is in flagrant contradiction with its theory. . . . [In practice] the right of man to freedom ceases to be a right as soon as it enters into conflict with political

[19] Karl Marx and Friedrich Engels, *Communist Manifesto,* in McLellan, ed., *Karl Marx: Selected Writings,* pp. 223–24.

[20] For the *locus classicus,* see Thomas Paine, *Common Sense,* in Philip S. Foner, ed., *The Life and Major Writings of Thomas Paine* (Secaucus, NJ: Citadel Press, 1974), p. 4; and Paine, *The Rights of Man,* in *ibid.,* pp. 356–58.

> life, whereas, according to the theory, political life is only the guarantee of the rights of man, the rights of individual man, and so must be given up as soon as it contradicts its end, these rights of man. But the practice is only the exception and the theory is the rule. Even though one were to treat the revolutionary practice as the correct version of the relationship, the riddle still remains to be solved of why, in the minds of the political emancipators, the relationship is turned upside-down and the end appears as the means and the means as the end.[21]

Marx's solution is to reassert the claims of status over contract—not, of course, by giving government priority over society, but rather by reshaping society along status rather than contract lines. In short, he favors an Immanent Communitarianism, with status values realized directly at the level of society, and he warns communitarians against a Vicarious Communitarianism that, by attempting to realize status values only indirectly through the intermediary of the state, in effect turns the entire social realm over to the liberal ideal of contract.

III. Vicarious versus Immanent Liberalism

We can now see the corresponding dilemma for liberalism: Shall liberalism be immanent, realizing contract values directly at the level of society, or vicarious, realizing such values only indirectly and fictively through the intermediary of the state—thus running the analogous risk of turning the entire social realm over to the communitarian ideal of status?[22]

Posing this question casts the liberal social-contract tradition in a problematic light. At first glance, the social contract seems an obvious embodiment of the liberal ideal of the society of contract. The society of contract requires that human association be based on mutual consent; social-contract theory gives this requirement flesh by grounding political authority on the consent of the governed.

But on closer examination there is room for worry. Social-contract theory runs the risk of displacing consent from its immanent role at the level of society to a vicarious role at the level of the state. This opens the door to the Rousseau-Kant-Hegel paradigm of contractualism, which aims not at freedom *from* constraint, but rather at freedom *through* constraints expressive of the constrainee's true will. Thinkers in this paradigm see the function of consent as the *legitimation* of our chains, rather than their

[21] Marx, "On the Jewish Question," pp. 54–55.

[22] Herbert Spencer also sensed the problem: "Most of those who pass as Liberals, are Tories of a new type" ("The New Toryism," p. 5).

removal.[23] The danger to liberalism is that, in focusing on the role of consent *to* the political framework, liberals may lose sight of consent, or its absence, *within* that framework—bartering, in Benjamin Constant's terms, the liberty of the moderns for the liberty of the ancients.[24] This is fine from a communitarian perspective, of course, but surely undesirable from a liberal one.

Social-contract theory need not have such implications, of course. For Overton, Milton, and Locke, for example, the function of the social contract is to guard and preserve consensual relations in everyday social life, not to replace them. Contract values remain immanent, not vicarious. When consent to political authority takes center stage, however—as it does with Hobbes and Rousseau—and the state rather than society becomes the morally significant locus of contract relations, the result all too often is a de facto society of status resting on a de jure foundation of contract:

> If political rights are in question, if it is a case of choosing a legislator from their midst, oh, then, according to him, the people are full of a native wisdom; they are endowed with an admirable intuition; *their will is always right; the general will cannot be wrong*. The suffrage cannot be too universal. . . . Is there a man or a class that will dare to claim the right to act as a substitute for the people and to decide and to act for them? No, no, the people want to be *free*, and they shall be. They want to direct their own affairs, and they shall direct them.
>
> But once the legislator is elected and freed from his campaign promises, oh, then his language changes! The nation returns to passivity, to inertia, to nothingness, and the legislator takes on the character of omnipotence. His the invention, his the direction, his the impulsion, his the organization. Mankind has nothing to do but to let things be done to it; the hour of despotism has arrived.[25]

[23] See Jean-Jacques Rousseau, *The Social Contract, or Principles of Political Right*, in *The Social Contract and Discourses*, trans. G. D. H. Cole et al. (London: J. M. Dent and Sons, 1973), pp. 181, 191, 195–96 (emphasis added):

> Man is born free; and everywhere he is in chains. . . . How did this change come about? I do not know. *What can make it legitimate? That question I think I can answer*. . . . The problem is to find a form of association . . . in which each, while uniting himself with all, may still obey himself alone, and remain as free as before. . . . This is the fundamental problem of which the social contract provides the solution. . . . [W]hoever refuses to obey the general will shall be compelled to do so. . . . This means nothing less than that he will be *forced to be free*. . . . [W]hat man acquires in the civil state [is] moral liberty, which alone makes him truly master of himself; for the mere impulse of appetite is slavery, while *obedience to a law which we prescribe to ourselves is liberty*.

[24] Benjamin Constant, "The Liberty of the Ancients Compared to That of the Moderns," in Biancamaria Fontana, ed., *Benjamin Constant: Political Writings* (New York: Cambridge University Press, 1988).

[25] Frédéric Bastiat, *The Law*, in *Selected Essays on Political Economy*, trans. Seymour Cain (Irvington-on-Hudson: Foundation for Economic Education, 1975), pp. 86–87.

I do not wish to downplay the importance of consent to political authority. But any liberalism that treats such vicariously consensual relations as the primary determinant of a society's embodiment of liberal values preserves the setting only to lose the jewel. More faithful than such Vicarious Liberalism to the ideals of the society of contract is the Immanent Liberalism that focuses on establishing mutual consent not only at the level of government, but above all at the level of society.[26]

IV. Forms of Vicarious Consent

Contemporary liberalism, both in theory and in practice, places what should now strike us as a problematic emphasis on vicarious consent. One of the chief examples of this emphasis is the role assigned to the democratic electoral process as the chief vehicle of consent. Given the infrequency of elections, the minimal impact that any one voter is likely to have on electoral outcomes, the minimal input voters have in the selection of the options available on the ballot in the first place, and the inability of voters to determine what decisions their representatives will actually make, the connection between the voter's will and the actual result seems tenuous at best. When one adds to this the severe negative externalities that majority rule creates for minorities, it seems inadvisable for liberals to assign much weight to the legitimizing role of the franchise.[27]

Both capitalists and socialists are coming to recognize the limitations of democratic suffrage as a realization of the ideal of mutual consent. On the capitalist side:

> When a consumer buys a product on the market, he can compare alternative brands. . . . When you elect a politician, you buy nothing but promises. . . . You can compare 1968 Fords, Chryslers, and Volkswagens, but nobody will ever be able to compare the Nixon administration of 1968 with the Humphrey and Wallace administrations of the same year. . . . Not only does a consumer have better information

[26] This Immanent Liberalism may also be identified as *libertarianism*, so long as this term is understood in its broadest sense, encompassing both capitalist and socialist varieties. (Since the nineteenth century, liberals advocating a radical redistribution of power from the coercive state to voluntary associations of free individuals have frequently called their position libertarianism, regardless of whether their political sympathies were capitalist or socialist—or something in between. Today, for the most part, libertarian capitalists begrudge socialists, and libertarian socialists likewise begrudge capitalists, the title "libertarian"; yet there seems to me sufficient commonality of ideological concern and intellectual heritage between the two camps to justify using the term in a broad but univocal sense to cover them both.)

[27] Perhaps ironically, with regard to this issue it is Immanent Liberalism that endorses an end-state conception of justice. Vicarious Liberals often regard a political scheme as consensual if the process whereby it was chosen allowed input by the voters, whereas Immanent Liberals insist that the end state, regardless of how it was arrived at, must embody the ideal of mutual consent immanently.

> than a voter, it is of more use to him. If I investigate alternative brands of cars . . . decide which is best for me, and buy it, I get it. If I investigate alternative politicians and vote accordingly, I get what the majority votes for. . . . Imagine buying cars the way we buy governments. Ten thousand people would get together and agree to vote, each for the car he preferred. Whichever car won, each of the ten thousand would have to buy it. It would not pay any of us to make any serious effort to find out which car was best; whatever I decide, my car is being picked for me by the other members of the group. . . . That is how I must buy products on the political marketplace. I not only cannot compare the alternative products, it would not be worth my while to do so even if I could.[28]

On the socialist side:

> To attain self-management, we want institutions that allow people to initiate their own activities and to participate in all related decisions. . . . [T]he fundamental difficulty [with central planning] is that, even if the planners were all-wise and altruistic, there would still be no self-management. . . . Although it would be possible to elect the central planning board to accord with the fullest of known democratic principles, to conclude that this would resolve the problem is to miss the point. Self-management does not mean electing some person or agency to make our decisions for us. . . . Instead central planning embodies as a core characteristic an *authoritarian command relationship*, which, if it persists, can only eventually erode any self-management characteristics. . . . [T]here is a type of socialist planning other than the centrist variety. . . . It is a procedure in which units coordinate their activities by essentially governing themselves . . . with a dynamic that reinforces empathy between democratic councils.[29]

A periodic say in choosing one's governors, whatever its merits, is no substitute for a day-to-day say in running one's own life and one's interactions with others.

Liberalism's attachment to democracy is understandable. As we have seen, the core ideal of liberalism is the vision of society as a system of cooperation for mutual advantage among free and equal persons. The obvious political implementation of this ideal is self-government: the people running their own affairs. In other words, *demo-kratia*.

[28] David Friedman, *The Machinery of Freedom: Guide to a Radical Capitalism*, 2d ed. (La Salle: Open Court, 1989), pp. 131–32.

[29] Michael Albert and Robin Hahnel, *Unorthodox Marxism: An Essay on Capitalism, Socialism, and Revolution* (Boston: South End Press, 1978), pp. 255–73; cf. David L. Prychitko, "Marxism and Decentralized Socialism," *Critical Review*, vol. 2 (Fall 1988), pp. 127–48.

But *collective* self-government—i.e., majoritarian democracy—leads to the tyranny of the majority over the minority; and this conflicts with the liberal commitment to mutual consent. Immanent Liberalism's solution to this problem is to make self-government *individual* rather than collective; as far as possible, each individual is to govern himself or herself. Tyranny of the majority is checked by removing issues of central concern to people's personal lives from the sphere of political authority. All liberals adopt this Immanent Liberal approach to one degree or another; but in many cases this dimension is overshadowed by a different solution, a Vicarious Liberal one, that makes self-government vicarious rather than direct.

The "virtual" consent involved in electoral politics is supplemented by another form of vicarious consent: *tacit* consent. Residing within the territory of a state and accepting the benefits it offers is frequently offered as a sign that one consents to the state and its policies.[30] Even were this true, it would still make consent *indirect* in a way that no Immanent Liberal could find satisfying. In fact, however, such tacit consent is largely fictive: in a world whose entire territory is divided among a relatively small number of nation-states, none of them exactly a liberal paradise, and where relocation is costly in any case,[31] remaining in one's home state is an unreliable sign of satisfaction with that state's policies.[32] (Does the fact that I do not move away when my neighbor dumps garbage on my lawn constitute evidence that I consent to dumping?) And must not any benefits the citizen enjoys be weighed against the benefits of which the citizen is deprived by the state's policies? (Eating the meals one is given in prison is no sign of consent to imprisonment.) Moreover, to the extent that tacit consent does exist, such consent may be largely "man-

[30] The classic source of this argument is Plato's *Crito*. The view is also often ascribed to Locke; but the attribution is somewhat misleading. Locke insists (*Two Treatises of Government* [1690], ed. Peter Laslett [New York: Mentor, 1960], *Second Treatise*, ch. 8, sections 119–22) that nothing short of *express* consent can make anyone subject *in his or her own right* to the authority of the political community; as I read Locke, the only role he grants to *tacit* consent is as follows: The Lockean right to private property ensures that a property owner may set the terms on which others may use that property. In setting foot on another's property, then, one tacitly consents (not to abide by the property owner's will *simpliciter*, but) *either* to abide by the owner's will, *or* to leave the property. When the property owner has himself *expressly* subjected himself and his property to the authority of a political community, the visitor's tacit obligation to abide by the owner's will or depart is thereby extended to a like obligation to abide by the community's will or depart. (Property acquired by gift or sale is accompanied by something like a restrictive covenant to the same effect.) For Locke, submission through tacit consent is thus only a temporary, conditional, and derivative adjunct of submission through express consent.

[31] To the ordinary costs of relocation we may add the often prohibitive costs imposed by legal fiat, e.g., denial of exit (as in the former Soviet bloc countries) and denial of entry (as with immigration restrictions in the United States and other Western democracies).

[32] "By institutionalizing their monopolistic controls over all geographic areas on this planet, governments have transformed the known world into a vast prison system from which there is virtually no escape" (Carl Watner, *The Voluntaryist*, vol. 66 [February 1994], p. 6).

ufactured" through state control of public education and state-plus-corporate control of the mass media.

A still more vicarious and imaginary realization of contract values is the appeal to *hypothetical* consent—as, e.g., in Rawls's device of the "original position." Here the fictive character of the consent is frankly acknowledged; governmental coercion of citizens is justified by appeal not to the citizen's actual consent, but rather to the consent they *would* give in idealized circumstances—such hypothetical consent in turn having for its object, not the governmental coercion itself, but rather the abstract *principles* that are said to license the coercion.[33] It might seem as though the tie between citizens and what they are supposed to be consenting to could be no more attenuated; but in more recent modifications of his original theory Rawls has suggested that the hypothetical consent which does so much justificatory work is not after all that of the citizens themselves, but rather that of their (unchosen) *representatives*.[34] At this point the citizens have been denied even a *hypothetical* role in shaping their destinies! Surely we have here reached the pinnacle of Vicarious Liberalism.

It might be protested on Rawls's behalf that the device of the original position is meant to embody, not an *emergent* justification in terms of mutual *consent*, but rather a *teleological* justification in terms of mutual *advantage*.[35] The fact that citizens (or their representatives) would consent to Rawls's two principles of justice under idealized fair bargaining conditions would then serve merely as *evidence* that those principles do in fact track mutual advantage. But if in fact Rawls is merely after a teleological justification in terms of mutual advantage, then his rhetoric is seriously misleading. The whole attraction of his theory lies in its attempt to capture the "basic intuitive idea" of society, not just as a scheme for mutual advantage, but as a system of *cooperation* for mutual advantage among *free and equal* persons.

The public-goods argument is another example of the reliance on vicarious, fictive consent to justify governmental coercion. When some service is labeled a "public good," it is accordingly assumed that everyone wants it, and that their failure to contribute to its production is simply the result of a perverse Prisoner's Dilemma incentive structure that delivers results contrary to the participants' actual preferences. Seldom is any attempt made to show that those who are coerced into contributing really do pre-

[33] John Rawls, *A Theory of Justice* (Cambridge: Harvard University Press, 1971).

[34] John Rawls, "Justice as Fairness: Political Not Metaphysical," in *Philosophy and Public Affairs*, vol. 14, no. 3 (1985), pp. 223–51.

[35] A political system is *emergently* justified if it is justified because of the way in which it came about; by contrast, it is *teleologically* justified if it is justified because of its beneficial consequences. Emergent justifications are backward-looking; teleological justifications, forward-looking. For a more detailed discussion of these two types of justification, see David Schmidtz, "Justifying the State," *Ethics*, vol. 101 (October 1990), pp. 89–102.

fer the outcome, or that coercive provision represents anything more than the transformation of internal costs of provision into negative externalities.[36] Thus, the pacifist is assumed to consent to the "public good" of national defense, the Christian Scientist is assumed to consent to the "public good" of national health care, the person of unorthodox opinions is assumed to consent to the "public good" of a state-run education system that teaches orthodoxy, and the anarchist is assumed to consent to the "public good" of government itself.[37]

What all these forms of vicarious consent—indirect, implicit, imputed, or simply invented—have in common is that they are automatically taken to override the real-life *dissent* of actual people. This procedure is in accordance with Rousseau's formulation: "The citizen gives his consent to all the laws, including those which are passed in spite of his opposition, and even those which punish him when he dares to break any of them."[38] The citizen's situation is eerily analogous to that of the rape victim whose protests are dismissed on the grounds that "she really wanted it":

> [I]t has become commonplace among feminists to regard rape as the linchpin of a male protection racket in sexist societies. . . . When we are raped, we hear that we brought it on ourselves. . . . For we could have stayed home or gone out only with a guardian. . . . Belatedly, we find that a male guardian can often protect us from no one but himself, and we are at his mercy there. The protectorate tends not to recognize rape by guardians or by males to whom we have once been accessible. . . . No matter what the men do to them, it is not really rape, because *the rules give the women's status itself the value of consent*. . . .
>
> Another kind of rule gives female appearance, rather than status, the value of consent. Consider the rule that women who dress or move "provocatively" are "asking for it" [either in] the "sexy" way, where our clothes and manner accent femininity [or in] the "castrat-

[36] When the production of some good valued by A imposes uncompensated costs on B, we speak of a *negative externality*; on both ethical and efficiency grounds, economists generally favor *internalizing* such externalities, that is, requiring those who value the good (in this case, A) to bear the costs of its production. The coercive provision of "public goods" does precisely the opposite: it externalizes internalities—since members of the minority (B), who do not value the good, are forced to subsidize its production in order to benefit members of the majority (A), who do value it. Since members of the minority do not value the good, the costs are uncompensated; these costs include not only the forced contribution to the good's production, but in many cases the existence of the "good" itself. (Perhaps this could be justified on redistributionist grounds; but the public-goods argument is not generally put forward as a redistribution stratagem [imposing costs on B in order to benefit A], but rather as a scheme for *mutual* advantage.)

[37] Nor is any attempt generally made to show that *compulsory* contributions are necessary for the good's provision, despite the fact that there is not a single example of a so-called public good that has not been supplied solely by voluntary means at one time or another in history.

[38] Rousseau, *The Social Contract* (*supra* note 23), p. 277.

> ing bitch" way, where our clothes and manner manifest, rather, a refusal to make a feminine or "sexy" display of femaleness, and we consequently need to be "taught our place." . . . These rules confer the value, or part of the value, of consent upon a woman's status, appearance, behavior, or situation. . . .
>
> The most blatant rule, summing up the spirit of the institution of rape, is that when a woman says no she means yes. What must she say to mean no? . . . If both no and yes mean yes, neither means anything. The net result is that women are politically disabled from withholding consent to male sexual access. . . . It is sufficient [for consent] that the woman either is or is not wearing clothes that highlight her femaleness, that she is alone either with or without other men or women, that she says either yes or no, and so on. . . . [T]he rules of rape discredit her refusals.[39]

Just as the rules of a male-dominated society automatically impute sexual consent to women no matter what they say or do, thus making rape invisible, so analogously the rules of a Vicariously Liberal society automatically impute political consent to citizens no matter what they say or do, thus making oppression invisible:

> Perhaps it will be said that this consent is not a specific, but a general one, and that the citizen is understood to have assented to everything his representative may do when he voted for him. But suppose he did not vote for him, and on the contrary did all in his power to get elected someone holding opposite views—what then? The reply will probably be that, by taking part in such an election, he tacitly agreed to abide by the decision of the majority. And how if he did not vote at all? Why, then he cannot justly complain . . . seeing that he made no protest. . . . So, curiously enough, it seems that he gave his consent in whatever way he acted—whether he said yes, whether he said no, or whether he remained neuter! A rather awkward doctrine, this.[40]

[39] Claudia Card, "Rape as a Terrorist Institution," in R. G. Frey and Christopher W. Morris, eds., *Violence, Terrorism, and Justice* (Cambridge: Cambridge University Press, 1991), pp. 303–12.

[40] Herbert Spencer, *Social Statics: The Conditions Essential to Human Happiness Specified, and the First of Them Developed* (New York: Robert Schalkenbach Foundation, 1970), p. 190; cf. Lysander Spooner, *No Treason,* in George H. Smith, ed., *The Lysander Spooner Reader* (San Francisco: Fox and Wilkes, 1992), pp. 49–111; Sy Leon with Diane Hunter, *None of the Above: The Lesser of Two Evils . . . is Evil* (Santa Ana: Fabian Publishing, 1976); and R. S. Radford, ed., *The Power of Congress (As Congress Sees It)* (Orange: Pine Tree Press, 1976). Despite the similarity in logic between the Card passage and the Spencer passage, I have discovered that those who find the Card passage plausible tend to dismiss the Spencer passage, while those who find the Spencer passage plausible tend to dismiss the Card passage. This division strikes me as regrettable.

In both cases, the value of genuine and express consent has been marginalized in favor of a scheme of interpretation that views dissent through consent-colored spectacles (as it were), thus disallowing the possibility of a *no* that means *no*. The victims are merely "forced to be free."

V. Is Immanent Liberalism Naive?

I have said that for Immanent Liberalism the ideal of mutual consent is to be realized primarily at the level of society, rather than at the level of government. In this respect, however, Immanent Liberalism might be accused of missing Vicarious Liberalism's main point. In the social sphere as we actually know it, power differentials among interacting parties may vitiate the genuinely consensual nature of their relationship; and even interactions that are genuinely consensual may impose negative externalities on unconsenting third parties. Leaving everything to society may look on paper as though it maximizes the sway of mutual consent, but if such "consent" takes place within a sociopolitical framework that systematically advantages some and disadvantages others, it begins to look more like exploitation. In such cases, focusing attention on the sociopolitical framework itself seems less like a distraction from contract ideals than like a necessary means to securing those ideals. Doesn't this suggest that Vicarious Liberals simply have a more sensitive and sophisticated grasp of problems that Immanent Liberals are unwilling to face?

It is true, certainly, that power differentials and negative externalities of various sorts can undermine the consensual nature of social interactions; indeed, one of the principal functions of a legal framework is to correct for just such problems. This much is common doctrine between Immanent and Vicarious Liberals. The difference lies in the *way* that the framework is conceived as solving the problem. For the Immanent Liberal, the goal is still mutual consent at the everyday social level, and the role of the political framework is to foster this goal by neutralizing, as far as possible, the factors that impede such consent. For the Vicarious Liberal, on the other hand, consent to and through the political process largely *displaces* everyday social consent as the goal.

Consider, for example, the different approaches of Madison and Rousseau to the problem of majority faction. In good Immanent Liberal fashion, both thinkers recognize (in "Federalist No. 10" and *The Social Contract*, respectively) the inadequacy of majoritarian democracy as a realization of contract ideals:

> [M]easures are too often decided, not according to the rules of justice, but by the superior force of an interested and overbearing majority. . . . By a faction I understand a number of citizens, whether amounting to a majority or minority of the whole, who are united and actuated by some common impulse of passion, or of interest,

> adverse to the rights of other citizens, or to the permanent and aggregate interests of the community. . . . If a faction consists of less than a majority, relief is supplied by the republican principle, which enables the majority to defeat its sinister views by regular vote. . . . When a majority is included in a faction, the form of popular government, on the other hand, enables it to sacrifice to its ruling passion or interest both the public good and the rights of other citizens.[41]

> [W]hen intrigues arise, and partial associations are formed at the expense of the great association . . . it may then be said that there are no longer as many votes as there are men, but only as many as there are associations. . . . Lastly, when one of these associations is so great as to prevail over all the rest, the result is no longer a sum of small differences, but a single difference; in this case there is no longer a general will, and the opinion which prevails is purely particular. . . . [T]he vote of the majority always binds all the rest . . . [but only if] all the qualities of the general will still reside in the majority: when they cease to do so . . . liberty is no longer possible.[42]

Madison and Rousseau thus agree that, from the perspective of genuine liberalism, a majority pursuing its own ends at the expense of minorities is just one more special interest, no more entitled than an absolute monarch to speak for the people as a whole.[43]

Where Madison and Rousseau part company is in the character of their suggested solutions. Madison regards the elimination of the *causes* of faction as not only impossible but, more importantly, *undesirable*: the freedom to form one's own conception of the good, and to promote its realization through association with others of like mind, is of paramount importance, and the protection of this freedom is one of the chief aims of any legitimate government:

> There are . . . two methods of removing the causes of faction: the one, by destroying the liberty which is essential to its existence; the other, by giving to every citizen the same opinions, the same passions, and the same interests. . . . Liberty is to faction what air is to fire, an aliment without which it instantly expires. But it could not be a less folly to abolish liberty, which is essential to political life, because it nourishes faction than it would be to wish the annihilation of air, which is essential to animal life, because it imparts to fire its destructive agency. . . . As long as the reason of man continues fallible, different opinions will be formed. . . . The diversity in the fac-

41 James Madison, "Federalist No. 10," in Clinton Rossiter, ed., *The Federalist Papers* (New York: New American Library, 1961), pp. 77–80.

42 Rousseau, *The Social Contract*, pp. 203–4, 277–78.

43 Cf. Herbert Spencer, "The Great Political Superstition," in *The Man versus the State* (*supra* note 16), pp. 123–66.

> ulties of men . . . is not less an insuperable obstacle to a uniformity of interests. The protection of these faculties is the first object of government. . . . The regulation of these various and interfering interests forms the principal task of modern legislation. . . . And what are the different classes of legislators but advocates and parties to the causes which they determine? . . . It is in vain to say that enlightened statesmen will be able to adjust these clashing interests and render them all subservient to the public good. Enlightened statesmen will not always be at the helm. . . . The inference to which we are brought is that the *causes* of faction cannot be removed and that relief is only to be sought in the means of controlling its *effects*. . . . Either the existence of the same passion or interest in a majority at the same time must be prevented, or the majority, having such coexistent passion and interest, must be rendered, by their number and local situation, unable to concert and carry into effect schemes of oppression.[44]

Madison thus advocates a political framework whose incentive structure channels factional interests and neutralizes their effects, rather than attempting to suppress such interests. In short, Madison's solution is squarely in the Immanent Liberal tradition of designing the governmental level so as to preserve, rather than replace, mutual consent at the social level.[45]

Rousseau, on the other hand, attempts to control the *causes* of faction rather than their effects. Accordingly, he endorses all the strategies that Madison rejects.[46] Political parties and special-interest groups are forbidden outright; tremendous responsibility for eliminating social conflict is placed in the hands of "enlightened statesmen," in the form of the Legislator, who initially molds the souls of the citizens-to-be so as to make them accord with the general will, and of the Censors, who subsequently maintain the citizens' souls in the desired condition through state-imposed moral instruction, including an official and compulsory state religion.[47] In short, the Rousseauian polity eliminates faction by inculcating in its citizens "the same opinions, the same passions, and the same interests." Despite a strong Immanent Liberal streak, Rousseau in the end adopts a Vicarious Liberal strategy, curbing actual liberty in order to

[44] Madison, "Federalist No. 10," pp. 78–81.

[45] It might be argued that Madison's federalist solution has not in practice proven terribly successful in preventing special interests from capturing the political process; but my concern here is with the *kind* of solution that Madison offers, not with the merits of its specific details.

[46] Indeed, Madison's "Federalist No. 10" may well be intended in part as a reply to the arguments of Rousseau's *Social Contract*. For Madison's general attitude toward Rousseau, see "Universal Peace," in James Madison, *Letters and Other Writings of James Madison* (Philadelphia: Lippincott, 1865), vol. 4, pp. 470–72.

[47] On the abolition of factions, see Rousseau, *The Social Contract*, pp. 204, 278; on the Legislator, see *ibid.*, p. 214; on the Censors, see *ibid.*, p. 297; on the establishment of a state religion, see *ibid.*, pp. 303–8.

implement the general will, through which citizens enjoy their liberty vicariously.

The difference between Immanent and Vicarious Liberals, then, lies not in their attention or lack of attention to the political framework, but rather in the role they assign to that framework—as the *guarantor* and *enabler* of contract relations, or instead as the primary *embodiment* of those relations.[48] Nor is Immanent Liberalism *as such* committed to any particular view on the *extent* of government coercion needed to secure genuinely consensual interactions at the social level. Among the classic nineteenth-century proponents of Immanent Liberalism, for example, I would count not only Benjamin Tucker, who argued that socioeconomic inequities could be abolished by dismantling the entire state apparatus and replacing it with a system of "voluntary socialism" (perhaps better described as free-market anarchism)—but also John Stuart Mill, who over the years saw a need to assign an ever larger role to state regulation and redistribution in order to free the economically disadvantaged from intimidation by the wealthy.[49] The principal issue is not how prominent a role is assigned to the political framework, but whether that framework is made to serve the ideal of authentic voluntary cooperation, or instead to replace that ideal.

One reason that so many contemporary liberals are driven to embrace indirect or fictive versions of consent is, I suspect, an assumption that a social order based solely or primarily on genuine and express mutual consent is impossible in a pluralistic society, because it would require *unanimity* or something close to it. (Hence, e.g., Rawls settles instead for a *hypothetical* unanimity achieved by suppressing all the information on which a disagreement could be based.) But a concern with society-wide unanimity is relevant only to the extent that social order is seen as a product of *centralized* decision-making, rather than as emerging from networks of *local* mutual consent.[50]

[48] Does this mean that an absolute monarchy would be an acceptable political framework to Immanent Liberals, so long as the monarch enforced liberal rights? Some Immanent Liberals have indeed held that there is nothing *intrinsically* illiberal about absolute monarchy, and that its only drawback is the *pragmatic* difficulty of there being no guarantee that the monarch, or the monarch's successors, will continue to govern in a liberal fashion. I for one do not agree; it seems to me that, pragmatic considerations aside, there is also something *intrinsically* valuable, from a liberal perspective, in having a say in the laws to which one is subject. My point is simply that having such a say is *no substitute* for having a say in the day-to-day control of one's life; the value of the former derives rather from its being an *instance* of the latter.

[49] See Benjamin R. Tucker, *Instead of a Book, By a Man Too Busy to Write One: A Fragmentary Exposition of Philosophical Anarchism* (New York: Benjamin R. Tucker, 1893); similar views were defended by Francis Tandy, Lysander Spooner, and Gustave de Molinari. For Mill, see especially his *Principles of Political Economy* and *Chapters on Socialism*, in John M. Robeson, ed., *Collected Works of John Stuart Mill* (Toronto: University of Toronto Press, 1962–1991), vols. 2–3 and 5, respectively.

[50] Recall the fable of the king who proposed to command that the entire earth's surface be covered over with leather in order to protect his feet—until one of his subjects achieved the same effect by inventing shoes.

Many feminists are wary of the traditional liberal distinction between public and private spheres, and may be suspicious of Immanent Liberalism for similar reasons. But such suspicion would be unwarranted, I think. Feminist skepticism about the public/private or government/society divide stems largely from the fact that the private sphere, supposedly a sphere of freedom, has traditionally been one in which women are oppressed by men, and are moreover disabled from gaining legal relief by the government's hands-off attitude toward, e.g., domestic relations ("a *man's* home is *his* castle"). The feminist insistence that "the personal is the political" expresses a determination not to let relations of domination and subordination become invisible simply because they occur in the supposedly "noncoercive" sphere of society rather than in the "coercive" sphere of government.[51] Small wonder that feminists have not always found Paine's notion of an iron wall between government and society an attractive one, and that many feminists have made an uneasy peace with the patriarchal institution of the state (always a risky endeavor)[52] in order to enlist its coercive powers in the struggle against pervasive male privilege in the private sector.

Feminism and Immanent Liberalism need have no quarrel, however. On the contrary, the aspects of the public/private divide about which feminists have the greatest misgivings are precisely those that characterize *Vicarious* rather than Immanent Liberalism. Women have been among the primary victims of the imputation of vicarious consent—from the assertion, in earlier times, that women did not need the suffrage because they were "virtually represented" through their husbands, to the continuing reluctance even today to recognize rape in marriage, on the grounds (still asserted with alarming frequency) that by entering the marriage contract a wife tacitly licenses her husband's unconditional sexual access to her. The extent to which laws have relegated women to private-sphere exploitation by men is precisely the extent to which contract values have not been realized immanently in that sphere, while it is the patriarchal politics of status that have been the chief legitimizer of women's subjection. Legal authorization and reinforcement of male dominance may masquerade as deference to the autonomy of the private sphere, but in fact represents a governmental intrusion into that sphere on behalf of one group at the expense of another.

[51] See, e.g., Susan Moller Okin, *Justice, Gender, and the Family* (New York: Basic Books, 1989), pp. 124–33.

[52] The following proposition seems a fairly elementary one: To the extent that the state is a tool that serves to advance the interests of a wealthy white male elite, any increase in the power of government, whatever its intended result, can only tend to expand and entrench the power of the wealthy white male elite. Hence it is that laws passed to benefit oppressed groups often end up being used against them (as, e.g., when anti-pornography laws written with feminist intentions have been used—by male police and male judges—to censor feminist publications).

VI. Rawls as Communitarian

John Rawls is widely regarded, by admirers and detractors alike, as the chief standard-bearer of the cause of liberal individualism against the twin foes of utilitarianism and communitarianism. George Kateb even singles out *A Theory of Justice* as "the great statement of individualism in this century."[53]

Thanks in great part to Rawls's efforts, the battle against utilitarianism has largely been won. (There may be more skirmishes to come, but the tide has turned.) But Rawlsian arguments have proven rather less successful against communitarianism, which seems to respond only with renewed vigor. One reason for this difference in success, I suggest, is that Rawlsian theory, as a vicarious rather than immanent version of liberalism, grants too many of the communitarians' crucial assumptions (just as the bourgeois republican revolutionaries of Marx's example, by endorsing a vicarious rather than immanent version of communitarianism, granted too many of the liberals' crucial assumptions).

A number of critics have pointed out that Rawls's arguments for the difference principle appear to violate Rawls's own criterion of the separateness of persons and thus are implicitly communitarian.[54] While I am sympathetic to this criticism, my present concern is rather with the whole structure of Rawls's approach. Specifically, it seems to me that Rawls plays into the communitarians' hands by adopting the Vicarious Liberal strategy of displacing the ideal of mutual consent to the hypothetical founding of the liberal social order, rather than seeking to realize that ideal within the social order itself. Moreover, my concern is not with the Rawlsian theory in its own right, but rather with that theory as a symptom of the contemporary communitarianization of liberalism.

Communitarians like Michael Sandel fault Rawls's device of the original position for exemplifying a liberal delusion of "unencumbered selves," i.e., persons regarded as bare centers of agency rather than as constituted by a rich and vast network of particularized social ties. But Rawls's very use of this device shows how far Rawls *agrees* with the communitarian notion that human beings enjoy no *morally relevant* identity independent of their membership in a political community. In contrast to, e.g., Locke's contractors, the Rawlsian contractor brings no rights to the bargaining table; whatever rights she may have must come *out* of the contract. Rights are a product of political association, not its precondition.

[53] George Kateb, "Democratic Individuality and the Meaning of Rights," in Nancy L. Rosenblum, ed., *Liberalism and the Moral Life* (Cambridge: Harvard University Press, 1989), p. 184.

[54] Nozick, *Anarchy, State, and Utopia*, pp. 228–31; Michael J. Sandel, *Liberalism and the Limits of Justice* (Cambridge: Cambridge University Press, 1982), pp. 77–80; Jeffrey Paul and Fred D. Miller, Jr., "Communitarian and Liberal Theories of the Good," *Review of Metaphysics*, vol. 43, no. 4 (June 1990), pp. 803–30.

Ronald Dworkin has suggested that Rawlsian contractors enjoy at least one precontract right: "a right to equal concern and respect in the design and administration of the political institutions that govern them."[55] If this were indeed true, it would only serve to substantiate the extent of Rawls's concessions to communitarianism: even this one basic human right is only a right to a certain standing within a political community, not a right that could be claimed by one individual against another in personal interaction.

In fact, however, Rawls rejects even this one precontract right that Dworkin tries to offer him:

> This is an ingenious suggestion but I have not followed it. . . . I prefer not to think of justice as fairness as a right-based view. . . . I think of justice as fairness as working up into idealized conceptions certain fundamental intuitive ideas [that] reflect ideals implicit or latent in the public culture of a democratic society.[56]
>
> [J]ustice as fairness is framed to apply to what I have called the "basic structure" of a modern constitutional democracy. . . . Whether justice as fairness can be extended to a general political conception for different kinds of societies existing under different historical and social conditions, or whether it can be extended to a general moral conception, or a significant part thereof, are altogether separate questions. . . . [S]ince justice as fairness is a political conception of justice for a democratic society, it tries to draw solely upon basic intuitive ideas that are embedded in the political institutions of a constitutional democratic regime and the public traditions of their interpretation.[57]

Here the concession to communitarianism is still greater: Rawlsian justice is justified only for some societies and not others, and only to the extent that it reflects the defining cultural traditions of such societies.

It may seem unfair to saddle Rawls with the labels of Vicarious Liberal and crypto-communitarian. After all, the social order that Rawls ultimately derives from his theory is one in which contract ideals are to a great extent realized *immanently*, e.g., via the principle of equal liberty, as well as the requirement that socioeconomic positions be open to all.

It is undeniably true that the society that ends up getting justified by Rawlsian premises is in large part an Immanent Liberal one. To that extent the title of this section is an exaggeration. It is an exaggeration with a point, however; for it is not *because* the Rawlsian society exemplifies con-

[55] Ronald Dworkin, *Taking Rights Seriously* (Cambridge: Harvard University Press, 1977), p. 180.

[56] Rawls, "Justice as Fairness: Political Not Metaphysical," p. 236n.

[57] *Ibid.*, pp. 224–25.

tract ideals that it gets justified. Rather, it is justified because it is selected by hypothetical bargainers in Rawls's original position, and it is this position that is intended to exemplify contract ideals. If an authoritarian state and a rigid caste system had been favored by the hypothetical bargainers, then the mantle of legitimacy would have settled on those institutions instead. The fact that Rawlsian society in large part *really* and *immanently* embodies the liberal ideal of mutual consent plays no direct role in its justification; Rawls's attention is instead on the vicarious and fictive mutual consent embodied in the original position.[58] Like the communitarians, Rawls seems to attach more significance to the liberty of the ancients than to the liberty of the moderns; political participation—even the imaginary *shadow* of political participation—takes precedence over the living reality of day-to-day freedom.

Rawls might reply that such "day-to-day freedom" is vitiated by differences in bargaining power for which the original position corrects. Yet Rawls's favored mechanism for implementing such corrections—a powerful, discretionary state—always outweighs citizens in bargaining power. Likewise, in the real world, those with the most bargaining power are typically the corporate beneficiaries of government privilege, protection, and subsidy; bargaining differences in a genuine market context are tame by comparison. Rawls offers us little in the way of suggestions for avoiding the public-choice problems that notoriously accompany such asymmetries; it is primarily at the vicarious level of the original position, rather than at the immanent level of real life, that he is most concerned about eliminating unfair advantages in bargaining power.

Once again, my present concern is not the analysis of Rawlsian theory, but rather the analysis of liberalism. But I find it significant, and troublesome, that a theory that makes such fundamental concessions to communitarianism should be hailed by contemporary liberals as "the great statement of individualism in this century." It only shows how far the liberal mainstream has traveled down the road of Vicarious Liberalism, contenting itself with idealized consensual relations in an imaginary Kingdom of Ends, and abandoning any effort to realize that Kingdom "in England's green and pleasant land."[59]

[58] Needless to say, if the logic of the original position *had* in fact turned out to favor authoritarianism, Rawls would not have responded by embracing authoritarianism; in accordance with the procedure of reflective equilibrium, he would instead, I am sure, have rejected the device of the original position. My concern, then, is with the misleading structure of Rawls's argument: although *for Rawls himself* there may be a direct connection between liberal society and the ideal of mutual consent, *in Rawls's theory* the ideal of mutual consent is used, not to justify liberal society directly, but rather to justify the original position, which *in turn* is used to justify liberal society—yielding the implication, whatever Rawls's intentions, that the original position is justified by the ideal of mutual consent quite apart from whether or not it generates liberal results—in short, that the value of immanent consent is secondary, and subordinated to the value of vicarious consent.

[59] Blake, "Milton" (*supra* note 1), p. 238.

VII. Socialist versus Capitalist Liberalism?

Contemporary liberalism, both as a theoretical ideology and as a practical system of governance, has in recent memory had most of its energies devoted to a different conflict within liberalism, one that cuts across that between Immanent and Vicarious Liberalism. This is the conflict between socialist and capitalist versions of liberalism—or, more precisely, the conflict among various liberalisms defined in terms of their positions along the socialist/capitalist spectrum. This socialist/capitalist conflict is admittedly a significant one for liberalism; but although it has garnered more attention by far, I think it pales in importance beside the Immanent/Vicarious conflict. Socialists and capitalists in the Immanent Liberal camp arguably have far more in common with each other than with either socialists or capitalists in the Vicarious Liberal camp. To the extent that this is true, the current focus on socialist versus capitalist versions of liberalism is something of a distraction from the real issue.

When the socialist/capitalist distinction is combined with the Immanent/Vicarious distinction, the liberal landscape divides into four main camps, each a putative realization of the liberal ideal of society as a system of cooperation for mutual advantage among free and equal persons:

> *Vicarious Liberalism: socialist model (VL socialism, state socialism)*: Citizens are taken to consent to a framework in which decisions affecting their mutual advantage are made by a bureaucratic governmental elite.
>
> *Vicarious Liberalism: capitalist model (VL capitalism, state capitalism)*: Citizens are taken to consent to a framework in which decisions affecting their mutual advantage are made by a bureaucratic governmental elite together with a privileged corporate/managerial elite.
>
> *Immanent Liberalism: socialist model (IL socialism, libertarian socialism)*: Citizens themselves make decisions affecting their mutual advantage through participation in decentralized local cooperative associations.
>
> *Immanent Liberalism: capitalist model (IL capitalism, libertarian capitalism)*: Citizens themselves make decisions affecting their mutual advantage through mutually agreeable free exchanges on the unregulated market.

Strictly speaking, these are not separate camps so much as distinct tendencies which may be present in varying degrees or varying combinations in any particular liberal theory or liberal regime. For simplicity's sake, however, I shall continue to refer to them as camps; what I say about any one camp will apply to a mixture of tendencies just to the extent that the mixture embodies the outlook of that camp.

VL socialism and VL capitalism are recognizable as the prevailing ideologies of most existing socialist and capitalist regimes, respectively—though such ideologies are generally less bluntly worded, and prefer to employ rhetoric borrowed from their IL counterparts. As for those counterparts, among the proponents of IL socialism I would count such classic figures as Pierre-Joseph Proudhon, Pyotr Kropotkin, Oscar Wilde, and Emma Goldman, and such contemporary figures as E. F. Schumacher, Kirkpatrick Sale, and Noam Chomsky; among the proponents of IL capitalism I would count such classic figures as John Locke, Adam Smith, Herbert Spencer, and Lysander Spooner, and such contemporary figures (at least in some of their writings) as Friedrich A. Hayek, Robert Nozick, and Murray Rothbard. As this (very incomplete) list should make clear, neither the IL socialist nor the IL capitalist camp is characterized by overwhelming unanimity about much of anything.[60] What they do have in common is an attachment to the immanent realization of mutual consent, and a distaste for centralized control of any sort: the Jeffersonian slogan "Divide the counties into wards," the environmentalist slogan "Think globally, act locally," and the anarcho-capitalist slogan "Sell the streets!" all spring from the same decentralist root.

VL socialism and VL capitalism, for all their differences, also have a significant element in common: both exemplify "top-down" rather than "bottom-up" approaches. More specifically, each endorses a version of "trickle-down" economics. Under VL socialism, vast quantities of resources and power are transferred to the bureaucratic state, on the theory that some of these benefits will trickle down to the common people—while under VL capitalism, the bureaucratic state follows a "supply-side" policy of granting special privileges and protections to favored corporations, once again on the theory that some of these benefits will trickle down to the common people.[61] By contrast, IL socialism and IL capitalism both seek, albeit in rather different ways, to empower ordinary individuals in their everyday associations with one another.[62]

[60] Certainly the list shows at least that Immanent Liberalism per se is not committed to any particular view of the value of industrial growth or the legitimacy of the nation-state.

[61] From an Immanent Liberal perspective, the United States, despite a heavy dose of IL capitalist rhetoric, is a predominantly VL capitalist regime. Of the United States' two ruling parties, one represents a mostly VL capitalist vision, and the other a mix of VL capitalism and VL socialism. For example, the current debate over health care in this country may be seen as a struggle over the precise balance of power between, on the one hand, the state bureaucracy, and, on the other hand, the quasi-private beneficiaries of state privilege—e.g., the American Medical Association (with its state-granted power to control medical licensing) and the insurance industry (which has largely "captured" its regulators). That is, it is largely a debate *within* the Vicarious Liberal paradigm, rather than a challenge to that paradigm itself.

[62] It is an interesting question whether IL capitalist and IL socialist economic relations could coexist within the same political regime. Given the preference of both for a radically decentralized political order, I am inclined to think that in general the answer is yes; but of course this may not be true for some *particular* IL capitalist or IL socialist theories.

IL socialists and IL capitalists seem, for the most part, unaware of the affinities between their two camps. Each side tars the other with the brush of the other's VL analogue; that is, IL socialists generally dismiss IL capitalists as apologists for corporate privilege, while IL capitalists generally dismiss IL socialists as apologists for central planning. Yet each IL side accuses its own VL counterpart of what the other IL side accuses the first side of generally; that is, IL socialist critiques of VL socialism sound rather like typical capitalist denunciations of authoritarian state socialism, while IL capitalist critiques of VL capitalism sound rather like typical socialist denunciations of the capitalist ruling class. (For example, socialist historian Gabriel Kolko has expressed surprise, and some annoyance, at the popularity among free-market libertarians of his books[63] analyzing the influence of capitalist elites in turn-of-the-century America.) All this leads me to suspect that the main lines of opposition within liberalism have been misdrawn.

In response to capitalist criticisms, IL socialists vehemently insist that authoritarian socialism is not socialism at all, and that accordingly its evils should not be laid at the door of socialism per se:

> Since its origins, socialism has meant the liberation of working people from exploitation. . . . [T]he socialist ideal [is] to convert the means of production into the property of freely associated producers and thus the social property of people who have liberated themselves from exploitation by their master, as a fundamental step towards a broader realm of human freedom.
>
> The Leninist intelligentsia have a different agenda. . . . For the Leninist, the masses must be strictly disciplined, while the socialist will struggle to achieve a social order in which discipline [becomes] superfluous. . . . Libertarian socialism, furthermore, does not limit its aims to democratic control by producers over production, but seeks to abolish all forms of domination and hierarchy in every aspect of social and personal life. . . .
>
> The Leninist antagonism to the most essential features of socialism was evident from the very start. . . . Lenin and Trotsky, upon assuming power, immediately devoted themselves to destroying the liberatory potential of [Soviets and factory committees], establishing the rule of the Party. . . . Not only the masses, but even the Party must be subject to "vigilant control from above," so Trotsky held as he made the transition from revolutionary intellectual to State priest. Before seizing State power, the Bolshevik leadership adopted much of the rhetoric of people who were engaged in the revolutionary

[63] Gabriel Kolko, *Railroads and Regulation, 1877–1916* (Princeton: Princeton University Press, 1965); Kolko, *The Triumph of Conservatism: A Reinterpretation of American History, 1900–1916* (Chicago: Quadrangle Books, 1967).

> struggle from below, but their true commitments were quite different. This was evident before and became crystal clear as they assumed State power in October 1917. . . .
>
> Soon Lenin was to decree that the leadership must assume "dictatorial powers" over the workers, who must accept "*unquestioning submission* to a single will" and "in the interests of socialism," must "*unquestioningly obey the single will* of the leaders of the labour process." . . . Lenin and Trotsky proceeded with the militarization of labour . . . the transformation of the society into a labour army submitted to their single will. . . . At the same time, 'factionalism'—i.e., any modicum of free expression and organization—was destroyed "in the interests of socialism," as the term was redefined for their purposes. . . . [64]

Likewise, in response to socialist criticisms, IL capitalists vehemently insist that corporate capitalism is not capitalism at all, and that accordingly its evils should not be laid at the door of capitalism per se:

> The story of the emergence and growth of the corporation makes it clear that . . . it was, and still is, based on a *rejection* of traditional capitalism, not, as most Americans have been brought up to believe, on an embrace of traditional capitalism. . . . For the individualism, competition, and serendipity of traditional capitalism—the system of control Adam Smith described as the market's invisible hand—the corporation substituted . . . the visible hand of management [which] entailed . . . hierarchy and bureaucracy. . . . Power over the marketplace and preferment from the state figured prominently in the corporation's business strategies. . . . In the 1850s [railroads] began lobbying for federal land and cash subsidies. . . . [T]he industrial policy that resulted from their efforts transferred to dozens of railroads vast troves of land, cash, and other benefits. . . . The 1920s and 1930s were a high-water mark for the business lobby—and for the antimarket, cartelist policies it urged on an increasingly receptive nation. . . . In 1945 . . . the visible hand held unprecedented sway over the U.S. economy. The 100 largest industrial firms produced 70 percent of U.S. manufacturing output. . . . It was . . . a corporatist world of managed oligopoly radically unlike the competitive economy envisioned in the theories of Adam Smith—a world to which the corporation had aspired for almost a century. . . . [65]

[64] Noam Chomsky, "The Soviet Union versus Socialism," in Dimitrios I. Roussopoulos, ed., *The Radical Papers* (Montreal: Black Rose Books, 1987), pp. 49–51.

[65] Paul H. Weaver, *The Suicidal Corporation: How Big Business Fails America* (New York: Simon and Schuster, 1988), pp. 109–16, 198–99. Not all IL capitalists would agree with Weaver's suggestion that this VL capitalist plutocracy is now largely fading away; see, e.g., Mary Ruwart, *Healing Our World: The Other Piece of the Puzzle* (Kalamazoo, MI: SunStar Press, 1992).

Nevertheless, IL socialists typically view with skepticism or even derision the protestation, on the part of IL capitalists, that state capitalist regimes are not *truly* capitalist, just as IL capitalists typically view with skepticism or even derision the protestation, on the part of IL socialists, that state socialist regimes are not *truly* socialist. This is in large part because each VL camp has managed to co-opt the rhetoric of its IL counterpart. Hence, VL socialism cloaks itself in the language of IL socialism, while on the other side such terms as *deregulation*, *privatization*, and *laissez faire*—which originally reflected the IL capitalist agenda of subjecting monopolies both public and private to the discipline of market competition—have been appropriated by VL capitalists to defend governmental grants to private firms of protection, subsidy, and monopoly privilege without public accountability.[66] So-called socialist governments arrogantly hand down their autocratic five-year plans, all in the name of empowering the people; so-called capitalist governments grant to savings and loans free rein to play with deposits that taxpayers are compelled to insure, all in the name of deregulation.[67] Thus, each VL camp practices a two-pronged bait-and-switch strategy: those who find IL socialist rhetoric attractive are lured into joining the VL socialist cause; those who find IL capitalist rhetoric attractive are lured into joining the VL capitalist cause; those who are repelled by VL socialist reality are misled to VL capitalism as the antidote; those who are repelled by VL capitalist reality are misled to VL socialism as the antidote. The systematic result is that, first, it is made very difficult to find one's way into either of the IL camps, and second, for those who do find their way into one of the IL camps, it is made very difficult to recognize the other IL camp as a potential ally. Hence, the entire Immanent Liberal alternative to the perpetual struggle among Vicarious Liberals that characterizes mainstream politics is rendered effectively invisible.

[66] Among the most egregious examples of this co-opting process has been the appropriation of Adam Smith by proponents of VL capitalism. Smith was an avowed enemy of mercantilism, the VL capitalism of his day, harboring a profound distrust of businessmen and their tendency to seek special favors from government at the expense of the less privileged. Indeed, he devoted his masterwork, the oft-cited but seldom-actually-read *Wealth of Nations*, to a defense of consumers and laborers against the "mercantile interest." Yet during the 1980s it was common for members of the Republican administration to sport Adam Smith neckties while championing the top-down corporatist policies Smith detested (e.g., the savings and loan "deregulation" described in the text).

[67] It might be argued that deregulation was a step in the direction of Immanent Liberalism (capitalist model, at least) but did not go far enough, since it failed to abolish federal deposit insurance at the same time. But this objection makes the mistake of assuming that a particular act of deregulation has a fixed significance regardless of the context. Federal deposit insurance, by giving savings and loans a guaranteed claim on the taxpayers' money, in effect converted those savings and loans from purely private firms into autonomous arms of the state; hence, what would, without federal deposit insurance, have been a deregulation of private firms was instead, in the context of unrepealed federal deposit insurance, a "deregulation" of quasi-governmental agencies—a very different matter, and *not* a move in the direction of Immanent Liberalism. (And it is surely no coincidence that regulations were rescinded while federal deposit insurance was not.)

I have suggested that the opposition between Immanent and Vicarious Liberalism is deeper and more fundamental than the opposition between socialist and capitalist liberalism, and that a more productive political discourse might follow from reconceiving the political terrain in terms of the first rather than the second polarity. This does not mean that IL socialists and IL capitalists have nothing to disagree about—quite the contrary. But they also have much to learn from each other, and much to teach their VL counterparts. This, I maintain, is where more political dialogue should be focusing.

Vicarious Liberals may object that Immanent Liberalism has been marginalized in mainstream political discourse, not because it is invisible, but because it is simply impracticable: the ideal of mutual consent *cannot* be realized immanently in society to any significant extent, so we must settle for its vicarious realization instead. This might be true. Before such a verdict could be justified, however, one would have to take due account of the vast and growing literature, from both the libertarian socialist and libertarian capitalist camps, regarding the proper implementation of Immanent Liberalism.[68] This is a task on which, for the most part, mainstream liberalism has yet to venture.

It should by now be obvious that "Immanent Liberalism" is a label that covers a diverse range of approaches. There are significant disagreements, not only between the IL socialist and IL capitalist camps, but also within each camp. Immanent Liberals are united, not by a common answer, but by a common question: *How may the liberal ideal of mutual consent be realized as far as possible in everyday social life?* Let those of us who share the liberal vision pursue this question together, working to "build Jerusalem in England's green and pleasant land." For if we neglect this question, projecting human liberty onto the institutions of government, and contenting ourselves with a merely vicarious or imaginary realization of our ideal, we run the risk of turning the social world of living, breathing human beings over to the care of an illiberal (or only spuriously liberal) order of arbitrary power and imputed consent—whether of a predominantly state socialist or predominantly state capitalist variety.

Let us heed Marx's warning: "[W]hen man liberates himself politically, he liberates himself by means of a detour, through the means of something else. . . . The state is the intermediary between man and his freedom."[69]

Philosophy, The University of North Carolina at Chapel Hill

[68] Even to attempt an adequate bibliography here would require far too many pages. I will thus name just two recent efforts: on the IL socialist side, see Joshua Cohen and Joel Rogers, "Associations and Democracy," *Social Philosophy and Policy*, vol. 10, no. 2 (Summer 1993), pp. 282–312; on the IL capitalist side, see Don Lavoie, "Democracy, Markets, and the Legal Order: Notes on the Nature of Politics in a Radically Liberal Society," *ibid.*, pp. 103–20.

[69] Marx, "On the Jewish Question," pp. 44–45.

JUSTICE TO CHARITY

By Loren E. Lomasky

I. Introduction

Despite what one may be led to believe by breathless reports in the media, the acme of misery in America is not the woes, financial and otherwise, of Donald Trump and Michael Jackson. People lose their jobs, have their assets drained by reversals of fortune, suffer from illiteracy, malnutrition, lack of shelter, and other mishaps. The circumstances in which they find themselves are genuinely distressing. It would be an odd understanding indeed that failed to find these circumstances directly relevant to what morality asks of us. If morality is to count for anything, then surely it must take notice of exigent need. This is not merely the deliverance of a late twentieth-century Western moral consciousness massaged by the blessings of comparative affluence and graced with a newfound awareness of social justice. All traditional ethical codes of which I am aware, sacred and secular, demand that one take the distress of one's neighbor as bearing on one's own activities. "Am I my brother's keeper?" is the question; the well-nigh universal answer is "Yes." The disposition to be moved by and respond to distress is the virtue of *charity*.

It would, then, seem undeniable that among the moral duties that confront us are duties of charity. The proper recipients of such duties are those who are, either locally or globally, unfortunate[1] and for whom relief from distress is not countermanded by other moral considerations.[2] The proper bearers of the obligation are those who are situated so as to be able to respond to the misfortune and who would not be unduly burdened by doing so.[3] The precise contours will, of course, be determined

[1] By *global* misfortune I mean a set of circumstances that, taken together, render a person's life miserable on the whole. A *local* misfortune is one that disadvantages an individual at some particular time or with regard to some particular aspect of her doings while having little or no effect on the remainder of her affairs. So, for example, destitution is a global misfortune, while being hot, tired, eight months pregnant, and unable to find a seat on the bus is a local misfortune. What counts as appropriate charitable relief will be a function in part of whether the misfortune one aims to alleviate is global or local.

[2] E.g., it is not (under ordinary circumstances) an instance of charity to pass a hacksaw to a justly imprisoned felon.

[3] Sometimes we teach our children: "Be charitable to those less fortunate than yourself." This may pass muster as elementary moral pedagogy, but as a general prescription concerning when and toward whom to be charitable it is deficient for at least three reasons: (i) If you are *very fortunate*, then some of those less fortunate than yourself will be far removed from the domain of eligible charity recipients; multimillionaires are not obliged to bestow

by the circumstances in which the recipient and bearer of the duty find themselves. Much remains to be specified, but at least this much seems clear: unless morality recognizes strict duties of charity, it is insufficiently responsive to the plain fact that the woe of other persons *matters*.

In what follows I shall argue that this way of putting the matter is mistaken. One can maintain both that an adequate morality takes the misfortunes of other people to be a salient datum and that positing a duty of charity is a misconceived way to underscore that salience. That misconception is, however, deeply embedded in the strain of ethical thinking that has dominated the modern era, what I shall call the "jurisprudential paradigm." Briefly, if morality is modeled on law, such that its subject matter is taken to be individuals' rights and duties, then all moral concerns will be parsed in those terms. Morality will speak in a stentorian voice concerning what *must be done* and what *must not be done*; and with regard to that which is neither, it will adopt a discrete silence. The absence of command is *permission*, and how one chooses to behave within the zone of permissions is a matter of personal preference removed from the imperatives of morality-as-justice. If I am neither morally obligated nor forbidden to play golf, then it is simply not a matter of legitimate moral concern—not for me, not for anyone—whether or not I elect to golf. Similarly, if I am merely permitted but not obligated to relieve the distress of other persons, then whether I do so or not is beyond the purview of moral concern. Because the consequent will seem false to all but the doughtiest surviving Social Darwinists, the antecedent must be rejected. Ergo, duties of charity.

Note that the preceding argument presupposes what I have called the "jurisprudential paradigm" of morality. If, however, the language of morals is more capacious than a discourse of rights and duties, it remains an open question whether acknowledging the salience of other people's distress is best rendered by positing rights to receive charity and duties to provide it.[4] I shall, after disposing in Section II of a superficially appealing argument, contend in Sections III and IV that the jurisprudential par-

largesse on mere unimillionaires. (ii) If you are *very unfortunate*, then you are not generally obliged to assume further burdens in order to lighten the load of those even worse off than yourself. (iii) Because misfortunes are local as well as global, charity may call on you to respond to a (local) misfortune of someone who is (globally) more fortunate than yourself.

A complete taxonomy of the duty of charity would require additional qualifications and distinctions beyond those of this and the previous two notes. Because the aim of this essay is not to explicate but rather to cast doubt on the notion of a duty of charity, I abstain from such labors.

[4] Whether (i) each right has as its shadow a duty resting on some individual or set of individuals to satisfy that right, and (ii) all duties derive from the rights of some individual(s), are discussed in the philosophical literature under the rubric of the *correlativity of rights and duties*. Note that these are two logically independent theses; (i) may obtain even though (ii) does not. (The reverse is also logically possible, but I am unaware of its advocacy in the literature.) In Section IV, I examine the claim that duties of charity are *imperfect duties*, duties for which correlativity does not obtain.

adigm is impoverished. Rights and duties are the shell of morality, the hard and inflexible casing that safeguards the soft tissue of our vital practical concerns. Absent the protection provided by that tough exterior, we would be unable to give effect to that which matters to us as moral beings. However, the shell taken by itself is lifeless. Less metaphorically, I shall argue that morality should be understood as extending to the zone of permissions, and that this is where most questions of aid to the less well-off are located—most but not all: Section V investigates the case that can be made for welfare rights. It is acknowledged that, under a limited range of circumstances and to a limited extent, there may exist rights to receive aid and duties to provide it; but, for reasons adduced there and in Section VI, these are relatively minor adjuncts to the virtue of charity. Section VII offers brief concluding remarks.

II. Why There Can Be No Duties of Charity: A Bad Argument

Someone might try to short-circuit duties of charity in this way: To be charitable toward someone entails more than transferring needed goods. It additionally requires that one do so from the appropriate sort of motive. One must give, it is said, "from the heart." When the United Way volunteer comes round and extracts from the office curmudgeon a grudgingly tight-lipped, tight-fisted pledge, the curmudgeon gives to a charity but does not give charitably. Thus, if there is a duty to be charitable, it is at least in part a duty to act from appropriate feelings and attitudes. These, though, are not under our voluntary control. I can directly will to give ten dollars, but not to do so with an open and loving spirit. By an application of "ought implies can," it follows that there can be no general duties of charity.

There are two respects in which the argument is defective. First, and most obviously, it assumes that duties of charity are necessarily duties to be charitable. We can, however, distinguish between charitable *persons* and charitable *acts*. A charitable person is one who is disposed to be moved by the needs of others and who, in virtue of that disposition (and not some incentive external to it), regularly acts to relieve those needs. The virtue manifested is the biblical quality of *agapê/caritas*, the third term in the triad "faith, hope, and charity" (better: "love"). A charitable act, by way of contrast, intends the melioration of another person's misfortune but may or may not take that melioration to be intrinsically desirable.[5] So, for example, if the office curmudgeon makes his pledge

[5] Reference to intention is necessary because one who inadvertently or accidentally advantages another has not thereby performed a charitable act. If the remains of the pizza I toss into my garbage pail are subsequently scavenged by a hungry family, I have not performed the charitable act of feeding them, let alone acted charitably toward them. This is true, I believe, even if I am aware when I toss out the pizza that there is a very high likelihood that it will be discovered and eaten.

because not to do so would be to make himself an object of unfriendly gossip, he has nonetheless performed a charitable act. To borrow a locution from Aristotle, he has done what the charitable man would do, though he has not done it as the charitable man would do it. Even if it is not the duty of anyone to be charitable, one can have duties to perform charitable actions.[6]

Second, and more speculatively, it is questionable whether all "oughts" do imply "cans." If my entire fortune is nine dollars, that fact is a decisive counter to the claim that I ought to give ten dollars. It is less clear that my being of a cold and haughty temperament renders it false that I ought to give cheerfully. That I am unable through an act of will to feel charitable toward my fellows has less the character of an excuse than a moral indictment. There are not only certain things that I ought to do but also ways I ought to be. If I fall short of those ways, then I am, other things equal, morally deficient. The insertion of the *ceteris paribus* clause is to acknowledge that external happenstance can mitigate or eliminate one's responsibility for character defects. But the mere fact that I am not able to reform my character through a simple act of will is not itself an excusing condition.[7]

I may be culpable for the current deficient state of my character in virtue of antecedent voluntary actions that led to my current disability. If, for example, habitual self-indulgence has deadened me to the distress of others, then my absence of feeling is a condition for which I bear responsibility. Had I then chosen to act differently I would now be a different sort of person, one who is not only capable of performing charitable actions but also of being charitable. So construed, this is an instance of "ought implies could have done."[8] But even if no causal chain is traceable between past performances and current dispositions, it does not follow that the latter are a matter of moral indifference. It may be inappropriate for others to blame the individual whose actions are acceptable though his character is deficient, but it surely is appropriate for the agent himself to

[6] Arguing similarly, Kant declares: "[L]ove as an inclination cannot be commanded. But beneficence from duty, when no inclination impels it and even when it is opposed by a natural and unconquerable aversion, is practical love, not pathological [!] love; it resides in the will and not in the propensities of feeling, in principles of action and not in tender sympathy; and it alone can be commanded" (Immanuel Kant, *Foundations of the Metaphysics of Morals*, 400, trans. Lewis White Beck [Indianapolis: Bobbs-Merrill, 1959], p. 16).

[7] Sidgwick comments: "I agree that it cannot be a strict duty to feel an emotion so far as it is not directly within the power of the Will to produce it at any given time. Still . . . it seems to me that this emotional element is included in our common notion of Charity or Philanthropy, regarded as a Virtue: and I think it paradoxical to deny that it raises the mere beneficent disposition of the will to a higher degree of excellence, and renders its effect better" (Henry Sidgwick, *The Methods of Ethics*, 7th ed. [1907; reprint, New York: Dover, 1966], p. 239).

[8] Aristotle writes in *Nicomachean Ethics*, trans. Terence Irwin (Indianapolis: Hackett, 1985), 1114a20–23: "It was originally open to the person who is [now] unjust or intemperate not to acquire this character; hence he has it willingly, though once he has acquired it he can no longer get rid of it."

reflect, "I should be more open in my giving; I would be a better man if I were to do so." This is to offer a straightforwardly moral assessment, but it does not invoke any precondition of causal possibility.

The upshot is that one's inability to exercise direct control over one's feelings is no logical bar to the existence of duties of charity. One may, at a minimum, be morally obligated to perform charitable actions and, maximally, to be a charitable person.

III. An Alternative to Charity as Right or Duty

I noted in Section I that the jurisprudential paradigm presents a dilemma: either the misfortunes of others are not morally salient considerations or they generate duties to render aid. Why, though, should this understanding of morality be embraced?

With very few exceptions, modern moral theory has taken as its fundamental project the derivation of rationally acceptable means for the resolution of interpersonal conflicts. Individuals' interests collide; that is why morality is both possible and necessary. In the absence of some peaceable means through which differences can be brokered, the denouement is a perpetual state of war in which life is, Hobbes tells us, "solitary, poor, nasty, brutish, and short."[9] And so, from Hobbes onward, it is the quest for appropriate articles of peace to which philosophers have bent their efforts. An ethic of rights and duties is the inevitable product. If some item is contested between two parties, then a resolution of that conflict must of necessity indicate which of them has a right to that item and which a duty to withdraw. Just so long as rights and duties are acknowledged, the parties can live peaceably together. What more can be asked of a theory of ethics?

Considerably more, or so was the prevailing view of premodern moral philosophy. For the ancients, the primary practical question was not "What are my duties?" but "How may I live well?" Though answers differed in particulars, the common theme is that the good life is one informed by the *virtues*. A moral virtue is understood to be a settled disposition to feel and act in intrinsically good ways. "Why be virtuous?" is a question that admits only of the question-begging answer: "Because virtues are those good-in-themselves components of a life that is itself inherently good." Less easy to supply but more informative is a specification of which traits are virtues and how these may be inculcated, harmonized, and sustained. An examination of classical responses to these questions would be out of place here, but what is worth considering is the rationale underlying this conception of ethics.

[9] Thomas Hobbes, *Leviathan* [1651], ed. Michael Oakeshott (New York: Macmillan, 1962), Part 1, ch. 13.

Moral inquiry in the ancient world begins with the assumption that each of us has as a core interest the achievement of *eudaimonia*, a flourishing life. Thus, it is of considerable urgency for an individual that she identify and come to possess its components. Because we are social animals, it is undeniably the case that one such component of *eudaimonia* is a facility of avoiding conflicts with others and settling those conflicts more or less amicably when they do arise. Therefore, justice—the natural home of rights and duties—is among the virtues. The Greek world is in many ways distant from our own, but it was one in which there existed a well-developed conception of the importance of law as an arbiter of the affairs of contentious human beings. The Greeks' horror of the disorder that would ensue in the absence of law was at least as great as our own, and thus the conditions of justice receive considerable attention in their philosophical thought.

Nonetheless, Greek ethical inquiry extends considerably beyond the search for an interpersonal conflict-resolution device. There is more to the achievement of *eudaimonia* than scrupulously fulfilling one's duties to others and claiming from them one's rights. Indeed, of at least as much interest to these philosophers as *inter*personal conflict is conflict waged *intra*personally. They observed that individuals often prize in an ineffectual sort of way goods that their conduct routinely contravenes. One who recognizes that temperance is integral to living well may simultaneously choose to eat and drink more than he should; a man who realizes that he ought to confront a danger may instead flee from it. *Akrasia*, "weakness of will," is inimical to *eudaimonia* insofar as it thwarts pursuit of one's own good (and not, say, because it thwarts the "greatest happiness of the greatest number"). The primary problem is not right relations with others but rather the establishment and maintenance of an appropriate balance within oneself,[10] and this problem was typically depicted through a set piece in which different "parts of the soul" war with each other, "appetite" confronting "reason" with directive mastery of the self at stake.

That is not to maintain that other-regarding conduct is of merely peripheral or instrumental concern. Because the good life is a life lived among others, right relations with them is a constituent of living well. An individual without friends or with the wrong kind of friends, or with inappropriate affections toward them, is handicapped; and thus Aristotle devotes two books of the *Nicomachean Ethics* to an examination of the conditions of friendship. One who lives as a wolf among men thereby renders himself bestial, and thus a disposition to act justly toward one's compatriots is similarly prized as a constituent of *eudaimonia*. Note,

[10] It is the absence of such an internal balance that we overhear the Apostle lamenting in Romans 7:15 when he confesses: "That which I would I do not, while that which I would not I do."

though, that the value of duties and rights is not simply a given from which ethics commences, but instead flows from an appreciation of the personal value to an individual of leading as good a life as she can. Given this conception, it would be thoroughly misleading to say that one has a "duty to be virtuous." That would suggest that virtue is something onerous, the price of admission to civil society.[11] It would be better to say that the virtuous person is *privileged* with regard to enjoying the necessary preconditions for living a fully human life. Virtue is its own reward, not in some prissy, otherworldly sense, but insofar as it is manifested in a flourishing life in this world.

I shall not offer here an extended argument concerning the respects in which the ancient conception of ethics may be judged more satisfactory than that which infuses the modern, primarily liberal tradition, or, for that matter, those respects in which liberal thought importantly supplements its predecessor.[12] The purpose of the preceding excursus into the history of moral thinking is to remind ourselves that a framework of rights and duties is not the only structure within which we can find a place for the moral salience of the misfortunes of others. A humane individual who esteems living decently among others heeds their distress irrespective of an alleged duty to aid. He does so because he understands that he has a good, that they have a good, and that these are largely complementary rather than ingredients of a grim zero-sum game. The visage of the mean-spirited, miserly man is unlovely, and not only as viewed by others; those of us who have a tolerably adequate conception of what it is to live well would not wish to become such a person. The liability of misanthropy is not only that it showers negative externalities on others but that it precludes one from experiencing the range of goods that are enjoyed only through successful sociality.

Eudaimonia, therefore, incorporates "liberality" or "magnanimity." These virtues are not quite the same as charity; they incorporate a sense of *noblesse oblige*, the open-handedness a superior shows to an inferior. Charity, by way of contrast, is expressive of a relationship between individuals who, despite differences in fortune or rank, are seen as being in some fundamental sense equals.[13] The reflection "There but for the grace of God go I" exemplifies that disposition. This may be why classical Greece and Rome lacked a precise equivalent to the concept of *charity*; it

[11] The price-of-admission view is embraced with characteristic bluntness by Hobbes and, disclaimers and qualifications aside, is adopted by most of the tradition of modern moral philosophy.

[12] A more extended statement is offered in Loren Lomasky, *Persons, Rights, and the Moral Community* (New York: Oxford University Press, 1987), especially ch. 3, "Projects and the Nature of Ethics."

[13] The paradigmatic relation in which natural equals stand is, for classical philosophy, friendship, and Aristotle explicitly observes that, while friendship of a sort can obtain between persons who differ markedly in their stations and virtues, true friendship is feasible only between equals.

emerges within scriptural religion as a corollary of the doctrine that all men partake of a brotherhood within God's creation. From that viewpoint equality is basic, differences in position adventitious. Thus, the classification by the Church of charity as a *theological* virtue. But whatever the origins of the concept may have been, charity does not necessarily presuppose a theistic orientation. Other stances can offer a surrogate basis for the equality on which charity rests, e.g., Kant's insistence that persons, unlike things, are ends in themselves who equally are imbued with worth.[14] Nor is it the case that, in common usage, "charity" invariably attaches itself to a presupposition of equality: we speak nonmetaphorically about acting charitably toward children and even animals. Fine points of semantics aside, there is broad recognition within both the Greco-Roman and biblical traditions that openness to the needs of others is a virtue.

IV. Charity as an Imperfect Duty

Once the jurisprudential paradigm becomes dominant, it is not surprising that a corresponding shift in the conception of charity follows. Philosophers as distinct as Kant and J. S. Mill invoke the category of *imperfect duty* to maintain that charity is prescribed by morality yet is a matter for the free, uncompelled performance of individuals. A perfect duty is characterized as one in which the manner, object, and occasion of performance are precisely specified, while imperfect duties are "those in which, though the act is obligatory, the particular occasions of performing it are left to our choice, as in the case of charity or beneficence, which we are indeed bound to practice but not toward any definite person, nor at any prescribed time."[15] Thus, while it is a strict obligation of morality to be charitable (or: to perform charitable acts), the mode in which the obligation is discharged is to be chosen by the agent.

This attempt to combine duty and discretion is, for at least four reasons, awkward. First, there is no clean line that can be drawn between duties whose manner of performance is specifiable and those whose manner of performance is not. If Mark has borrowed five dollars from Martha, then it is a perfect duty (of justice) that he repay the sum; but, at his

[14] "In the realm of ends everything has either a *price* or a *dignity*. Whatever has a price can be replaced by something else as its equivalent; on the other hand, whatever is above all price, and therefore admits of no equivalent, has a dignity. . . . Thus morality and humanity, so far as it is capable of morality, alone have dignity" (Kant, *Foundations of the Metaphysics of Morals*, 434–35, p. 53). For Kant, humans are equal most fundamentally as beings who are capable of being motivated to moral action.

[15] John Stuart Mill, *Utilitarianism*, ed. Oskar Piest (Indianapolis: Bobbs-Merrill, 1957), p. 61. Mill goes on to remark: "In the more precise language of philosophic jurists, duties of perfect obligation are those duties in virtue of which a correlative *right* resides in some person or persons; duties of imperfect obligation are those moral obligations which do not give birth to any right."

option, he may repay by cash or check, a little earlier or later, with a smile on his face or a frown. The contractual arrangement between them may be specific with regard to any or all of these conditions, but that is to note that specificity is a matter of degree among perfect duties rather than a criterion distinguishing perfect from imperfect duties.

Second, to the extent that imperfect duties lack specificity, it becomes difficult or impossible to determine whether they have been fulfilled. Suppose that charity is indeed an imperfect duty; then it is unquestionably the case that someone who lives out her entire life without ever once coming to the aid of another has failed to discharge the duty. Suppose, however, that at age seventeen she had extended aid and then decided that she had had enough of that sort of thing, thereafter keeping her wallet tightly shut. (Or, alternatively, she lives an initial sixty years entirely unblemished by a single charitable act but resolves to perform a few once she is pensioned off.) Has the duty of charity been discharged? "No," one may respond, "that's too little of a good thing." But if that is too little, what, then, is enough? We might, to pick a number, hold that an individual is obligated to take advantage of no fewer than 25 percent of the opportunities for charitable action that come her way. Ignore the objection that any such ratio is thoroughly arbitrary and unmeasurable in practice; it suffices to note that the proposal seeks to eliminate the intolerable vagueness of imperfect duties by transforming them into perfect duties. A duty to be charitable 25 percent of the time is as determinate as a sharecropper's obligation to give 25 percent of his produce to the landlord. The attempt to transform imperfect duties into "real" duties is akin to the military tactic of saving the village by destroying it.

Third, it is not usually the case that any special regard or esteem is due to one when he fulfills his duties. If Mark pays Martha the five dollars he owes, perfunctory thanks would be an appropriate response. Should she fulsomely laud him for this act and praise him to others, Mark would have reason to feel miffed. Such extravagance in praise suggests that he is the sort of man who cannot be expected routinely to settle his trifling debts. If charity is a duty, then its performance is no occasion for special mention; one is simply doing what one is obliged to do anyhow. Charity, though, is meritorious. We not only approve but admire the charitable person.[16]

[16] It can be argued that charity becomes admirable only to the extent that it is supererogatory, above and beyond the call of duty. There is a baseline, the objection continues, below which charity is merely the fulfillment of duty and is to be approved no more than other dutiful acts. Charitable performances above the baseline are, however, meritorious.

There is, no doubt, some truth to the suggestion. We will not be inclined to esteem the person who only occasionally chooses to aid others. However, this reflection only marginally buttresses the imperfect-duty model. We lack the ability to ascertain where the hypothesized baseline lies; and if we could do so, we would then have to find some analytical category other than imperfect duty for charitable acts that fall above it. The attempt to assimilate charity within the jurisprudential understanding will have been de facto abandoned.

Fourth, and most serious, imperfect duties lack a proper beneficiary. They are not duties to anyone in particular, and thus if I fail to discharge an imperfect duty, there is no one who can justifiably complain that I have thereby wronged him. If I owe ten people one dollar each (a perfect duty), then should I fail to pay any one of them, that person has been dealt with unfairly. But if it is alleged that I have a duty (imperfect) to pay ten dollars to any one of ten people (my option which), a failure to comply is a moral wrong that wrongs no one. Had I given Anderson rather than Jones the entire sum, Jones would have had no complaint at getting nothing; but then my paying no one leaves Jones no worse off than he would have been had I discharged the duty. Symmetrical reasoning applies to each of the ten.[17] The conclusion is that these duties are imperfect in the colloquial sense, that they are *luft*-duties detached from the interests of assignable individuals. Lacking a point, their status within the overall moral economy is mysterious.

Note that charity understood as a virtue does not suffer from the liabilities itemized above. That there is no sharp line separating charitable from uncharitable individuals is not a theoretical defect; dispositional traits are naturally understood as being arrayed on a continuum rather than on/off. To be charitable is to be possessed of the appropriate beliefs and attitudes about how one ought to respond to the misfortunes of others, and to be disposed to express these through appropriate action. It would be an absurd mischaracterization to identify as charitable someone who only on rare occasions extends aid to another, or who, when he gives, does so grudgingly. It is similarly absurd to regard the charitable person simply as someone who is punctilious about the fulfillment of his duties. To be charitable is not merely to do what one (morally) must but to evince a commitment to pursue one's own good in a way that meshes with the good of others. That is why the charitable man is a proper object of esteem. Conversely, the complaint properly lodged against an individual deficient in charity is not that he has withheld items he is not at liberty to keep but rather that, by grasping too tightly onto that which is his, he thereby evinces disdain for the well-being of others. We do well to avoid forcing charity into the Procrustean bed of duty. It does not fit. The construction of ersatz imperfect duties multiplies rather than solves philosophical problems. Charity—and here is meant charity conceived as a

[17] It is tempting to retort: "*All* of them are wronged because what I owed to each was a 0.1 probability of receiving the entire amount." The objection misfires. Suppose that my strategy for discharging imperfect duties is always to give preference, if possible, to someone whose name begins with a vowel. Given the presence of Anderson, Jones had no chance of receiving my largesse, yet I have complied with my duty. "Jones can complain that the vowel selection-strategy itself constitutes unfair treatment of him." That is true only if what is owed Jones (and each of the other nine) is an equal chance of getting the money, as with a fairly conducted lottery. That is to say, however, that the duty owed is not an imperfect one at all, but rather a perfect duty to each that he enjoy an *ex ante* 0.1 probability of receiving the amount (coupled with the perfect duty *ex post* to pay the winner ten dollars).

social virtue—is a richer notion than can be paralleled by a legal model of rights and duties.

V. Charity and Welfare Rights

Although the concept of charity cannot be amalgamated without considerable loss into the jurisprudential paradigm, it does not thereby follow that there is no place whatsoever in the moral lexicon for rights to receive aid—welfare rights—and corresponding duties to provide it. Charity is a virtue we have reason to prize in ourselves and others irrespective of what we judge individuals' rights to be, but just as it is a misapplication of Ockham's razor to attempt to reduce all morally salient considerations to rights and duties, so is it mistaken to hold that a virtue ethics is complete unto itself. Our view of morality will be misshapen if we dispense with either.

The proper home of virtues is human *distinction*. To possess a particular virtue is to excel in the domain in which the virtue is operative. So understood, virtues include but extend beyond the realm of morality. The Greek term *aretê*, which we usually translate as "virtue," is more accurately rendered by "excellence." Thus, Aristotle can speak without any hint of paradox of the *aretê* of a shoemaker, a horse, or even a knife, and not simply the virtues of a human being as such.[18] Our use of the term "virtue" has largely become confined to morality (and, under the influence of Victorian sensibilities, specifically to sexual morality), but even contemporary usage allows us to say of Barry Bonds that he exemplifies to a high degree the virtues of a consummate baseball player insofar as he hits, fields, and runs with distinction.

When we attempt to improve ourselves or educate our children, we take as a model for emulation (I do not mean simply mimicry; creative flexibility is a component of excellence) the virtuous individual. That person is the incarnate standard of high-level achievement. To learn what it is accurately and coolly to appraise and confront dangers, we observe the courageous man and school ourselves to behave similarly; if we aim to develop skills in scientific or scholarly endeavors, we take our bearings from those who possess theoretical wisdom. No set of rules in a copybook can encapsulate what is required for mastery in an area of practical endeavor. That is not to say that rules are entirely without utility, but to note that how, when, and where one is to apply them is not something that can be learned by rote. A kind of apprenticeship is required, and that incorporates empathetic identification with those who have already

[18] Within the class of virtues that pertain to human beings as such, Aristotle recognizes two distinct subclasses, moral virtues and intellectual virtues. Just as the man who is temperate or magnanimous displays a characteristic human virtue, so too does the skilled solver of scientific problems.

achieved excellence, coupled with a regimen of habituation designed to make their traits one's own. To some extent this can be done vicariously; history and literature contribute at least as much to moral education as do tomes of moral philosophy.

Some virtues have wide-ranging application. Regardless of what ends we seek, we will do better if we act with steadfastness, temperance, and prudence. Others are more narrow in their scope, such as the specific virtues of the baseball player. Because of differences in scope, we have reason to prize some virtues above others: compassion counts for more than baseball-hitting skill.[19] Still, to the extent that we take some trait to be a virtue, we esteem the individuals who possess it—Barry Bonds as well as Mother Theresa. Were we to do what they do, we would be pleased if we could do it as they do it.

Rights and duties operate within a different sphere. Persons' rights impose what Robert Nozick calls "side constraints" on action.[20] They do not mandate ends to be achieved, but rather limit the means that may permissibly be employed to realize whatever ends one might have. It is in that sense that "Do not violate rights!" acts as a constraint on goal-directed action. Rights generate correlative duties. Depending on the right in question, these duties can be held "against the world" or against some specifiable individual. If Martha has a right to speak her mind freely, then everyone has a duty not to prevent her from doing so. If, by way of contrast, she has a right that Mark repay the five dollars he borrowed, then Mark (and no one else) has a duty to remit that amount.

While virtues aim at distinction, rights establish a moral minimum. The *least* that is permissible in one's conduct is to respect others' rights. I may—and should—do much more than merely avoid transgressing rights, but I *must not* do less. That is why no special appreciation is due to someone merely for compliance with duties. "You've gone a whole day without stealing so much as one thing from me; thanks a lot!" is either a joke or an insult.[21] We rarely invoke the category of rights when considering relationships that by their nature presuppose considerably more than minimal decency between the parties: proper conduct of friend with friend, lover with lover, or parent with child is not adequately expressed

[19] If an activity is judged to be unworthy in its own right, we will not admire mastery of it. Carlos the Jackal is notably more talented as an assassin than is John W. Hinckley, Jr., but we do not hold him up as a model for emulation. But one who thinks differently about the propriety of assassination—who is, say, engaged in the business of training junior hit men—may quite reasonably within that context assign *The Life and Times of Carlos* as required reading for his students.

[20] See Robert Nozick, *Anarchy, State, and Utopia* (New York: Basic Books, 1974), pp. 28–35.

[21] If circumstances render respect for rights exceptionally difficult or are such as would lead many people to give short shrift to rights, then gratitude becomes appropriate. We praise the person who makes an effort to return the cash-filled wallet found on the sidewalk because we recognize that most other finders would have pocketed the money. Here compliance with rights merges with moral excellence, and it becomes appropriate to import responses at home with the latter into the former.

in the language of rights and duties. When we do resort to that language it usually indicates that the relation has entered a pathological state. I do not mean to say that there are no rights and duties obtaining, say, between spouses, but rather that success in a marital relation entails far more than the minimal deference of respect for rights that is owed to a stranger.

Rights, then, are both maximally weighty and minimally demanding moral claims. The two aspects go together. I am obliged to respect the rights of individuals for whom I have no great sympathy, for whom I even have an active distaste. "Love your neighbor" may be a sustainable injunction when the neighbor is inherently lovable, but to love someone who is clearly odious demands a moral heroism that few of us possess. To *commend* heroism is one thing, to *insist* on it another, and a morality that aspires to be practical necessarily eschews the latter. (It is different for religions. There the telos is not harmonious relations among human beings, but an imitation of the divine perfection.) Grandiose manifestos of "basic human rights" undercut themselves by pitching the demands they would place on us at a level higher than that with which we can reasonably be asked to comply. They mistakenly conflate the language of virtue with the language of rights. Such conflation has become unfortunately frequent in recent years; it sometimes seems that no individual or group is able to formulate a moral agenda (for better working conditions; for kindness to animals; for courteous behavior toward those of a different race or those who are prone to unconventional sexual practices; for whatever) without an announcement proclaiming the discovery of a heretofore unknown "right" that is henceforth to be zealously maintained. This rights inflation is yet another unwelcome consequence of the hegemony of the jurisprudential paradigm.

Even if we set such extravagance aside, there is room for considerable controversy concerning just what rights there are, who has them, and why. As crucial as these questions are, it is beyond the capacity of this essay to develop a theoretical response.[22] I shall instead offer a few remarks to show why it is at least plausible to believe that an adequate accounting of rights and correlative duties will locate them somewhere within the territory that has been marked out by the tradition of classical liberalism. By "classical liberalism" I mean the view holding that the preponderance of basic rights[23] individuals possess are negative, man-

[22] I attempt to do so in *Persons, Rights, and the Moral Community*.

[23] The term "basic rights" is meant to pick out roughly the class of rights that have sometimes been denoted "moral rights" or "human rights." They are to be distinguished from (i) special rights, such as those established by a contract between two parties or that might obtain between individuals enjoying a special relationship such as parent and child; and (ii) rights created by particular enactments of a government or another collectivity capable of originating rights. I prefer the term "basic rights" because it is less question-begging than the alternatives: "moral rights" may suggest that special rights are something other than moral, while "human rights" implies that all and only human beings are the beneficiaries of rights claims while, for example, animals are not and incurably comatose people are.

dating forbearance on the part of others but not active provision of aid. "Libertarianism," as I understand the term, is the view maintaining that *all* basic rights are negative. Libertarian theories, therefore, constitute a subclass of classical liberalism but are not coextensive with it.

Why should we suppose that morality needs to recognize the existence of rights? After all, rights are awkward things, blocking the reformist agendas of those who are persuaded that they could cook some wonderful omelets if only they were permitted to break a few eggs in the process. The answer immediately suggesting itself is that rueful experience has taught us to be suspicious of the culinary credentials of these would-be chefs. Many of the greatest paroxysms of misery human beings have known, not least those that have marred the twentieth century, were brought about by reformer/revolutionaries confident in their ability to engineer Heaven on Earth. What they brought us instead were living hells. If we can maintain a rule of rights, we may be able to thwart their worst excesses.

Rights so understood are indeed plausible, but they are also superficial. They are no more than a concession to human fallibility. Were we better able dispassionately to judge the effect of our designs, so as to ensure that they actually are conducive to the greatest happiness of the greatest number, we could entirely dispense with the category of rights. Since our judgments are unreliable, especially when passions or interests are engaged, rights serve as handy "rules of thumb," generally reliable signposts by means of which we can more efficiently advance overall welfare. They are superficial because, as rules of thumb, they play second fiddle to general utility. We are to respect the rights of Jones (and Anderson, and Smith, and so on) only because we thereby do better with regard to overall welfare, not because of any special moral status enjoyed by Jones. Were we more gifted social engineers, we would be granted carte blanche to sacrifice any or all of Jones's interests whenever opportunities to enhance overall utility beckoned.

What is left out of the preceding paragraph's account is how things present themselves specifically to Jones. He might complain with no little justice against those proposing to sacrifice him to the great god Utility: "I understand that by quashing my interests you will be able to achieve benefits for others, benefits which, in terms of your impersonal standard of value, score greater than what I forfeit. But that's not good enough to satisfy me. What I have primary reason to value are those ends that are distinctively mine, those that I deeply care about. From the perspective of my *personal* standard of value, I lack sufficient reason to go along with your notions of what is socially optimal." That is to say, while annihilating Jones's interests may be justifiable according to the criteria of an abstract theory of social good, *it is not justifiable to Jones*. The result is easily generalized. Each other person has equivalent reason to object to a moral schema that would leave her own deepest concerns dispensable, that would render her a mere means to the achievement of high overall utility totals rather than an end in herself. Correspondingly, each has reason to value the secure enjoyment of moral space within which she is able to act on behalf of the conception of the good that is distinctively her own.

Rights emerge as the boundary markers of moral space. They establish a regime of mutual and reciprocal forbearance. Individuals who are rights-holders are not obliged to be the sacrificial victims or servants of ends distant from their own, but are instead acknowledged to possess a moral entitlement to devote themselves to projects that individually matter to them. Rights are responsive to the urgency from the perspective of an agent of carving out a life rendered coherent and meaningful in virtue of persistent attachment by him to his own directive ends. The rational acceptability of assuming the duties generated by the rights of others derives from recognizing that they too have reason to demand provision of moral space. Basic rights, then, can be characterized as "those moral constraints that impose minimal demands on the forbearance of others such that individuals can pursue projects amidst a world of similar beings, each with his own life to lead, and each owing the same measure of respect to others that they owe to him."[24]

As noted above, classical liberals have traditionally understood rights to be predominantly negative in character. One should not suppose that this is symptomatic of a moral myopia that blinkered an earlier, less "socially enlightened" age. Rather, it is a strict corollary of the logic of rights. If what people have reason to demand from others and to cede to them in return is moral space, then the primary moral right is to be let alone. One may do more than respect the liberty of others, but one must not do less. This is not, as critics of liberalism have often charged, arbitrarily to place liberty above all other values. Instead, it is to recognize that whatever it is that one may value, one needs liberty to pursue it, and one needs it from others in the form of their noninterference. Rather than enthroning one value above all others, liberalism decentralizes questions of value, leaving their resolution to the private initiatives of individuals. Freedom from interference is the freedom to direct one's affairs in accord with one's own judgments concerning what is to be cherished and what is to be to spurned.

A requirement of noninterference minimizes the involuntary implication of individuals in each other's designs. To require that I not violate your liberty to pursue the ends that matter to you is less invasive than to require me actively to further those ends. The former requirement represents the acknowledgment that pursuit of your ends is primarily your business and not, as utilitarianism would have it, a free-floating onus incumbent alike on all moral agents who are in a position to bring about the ends' advancement. This can, with some qualification, be understood

[24] Lomasky, *Persons, Rights, and the Moral Community*, p. 83.

as a judgment about relative costs: I shall likely regard as a lesser burden an obligation not to interfere with you than a requirement to render aid. For better or worse, though, that is not a universal truth. One encounters Pecksniffians and Puritans who find it intolerable to be precluded from foisting their conceptions of the good life on everyone, and when they are too numerous or too powerful the stability of a liberal order is imperiled.[25] That is why "liberal" denotes not only a political credo but also a temperament, and why an ethic of virtues must supplement an ethic of rights and duties.

But though the logic of rights indicates that they are primarily negative, it does not entirely rule out the existence of welfare rights. What each of us needs from all others is, first and foremost, noninterference, but for those who are unlucky this may not be enough. Whenever it is feasible for individuals to act on their own behalf to secure the goods they need to live decent lives, the responsibility to provide is theirs. There is, however, no assurance that liberty will universally guarantee to all persons the requisites for living as project pursuers. For one situated on the margin of exigency, adherence to an order of mutual noninterference can be extremely costly. If the choice confronting one is either to fall below a baseline of minimally satisfactory existence or to encroach on the moral space of others, one may lack sufficient reason to acknowledge a duty of noninterference. A moral hero will, we may believe, even then respect rights, but recall that what rights entail is minimal forbearance, not heroism.[26]

If a regime of rights is to be robust, it cannot demand of individuals more than they can reasonably be expected to provide. It cannot reasonably be demanded of a man that he forbear when to do so comes at the cost of all his prospects for living as a pursuer of personally valued ends. Thus, reciprocity dictates that individuals precariously perched on the edge of exigency can be obligated to respect the liberties of others only if they are simultaneously ensured a sufficiency of material goods.[27]

So conceived, welfare rights are not at odds with the program of classical liberalism. Instead, they render it justifiable at the margin. If all are entitled to a decent minimum below which they need not fall, the ben-

[25] An important recent investigation of the conditions of stability for a liberal order in which people profoundly differ with regard to their basic religious and ethical conceptions is John Rawls, *Political Liberalism* (New York: Columbia University Press, 1993). Although I believe that Rawls's account is hobbled by excess attachment to the jurisprudential paradigm, I cannot pursue that argument here.

[26] Hobbes, no enthusiast for heroes, observes: "When a man is destitute of food, or other thing necessary for his life, and cannot preserve himself any other way, but by some fact against the law; as if in a great famine he take food by force, or stealth, which he cannot obtain for money nor charity; or in defence of his life, snatch away another man's sword; he is totally excused . . ." (Hobbes, *Leviathan*, Part 2, ch. 27, p. 223).

[27] Two recent arguments to essentially the same conclusion are Allen Buchanan, "Justice and Charity," *Ethics*, vol. 97 (1987), pp. 558–75; and Jeremy Waldron, "Welfare and the Images of Charity," *Philosophical Quarterly*, vol. 36 (1986), pp. 463–82.

efits of an order of rights are withheld from no one. This conclusion is accepted by virtually all major classical-liberal theorists. Locke, for example, declares: "As justice gives every man a title to the product of his honest industry, and the fair acquisitions of his ancestors descended to him; so charity gives every man a title to so much out of another's plenty, as will keep him from extreme want, where he has no means to subsist otherwise."[28] Such contingent claims to provision by others do not undercut the primacy of negative rights. The latter are the norm; the former kick in only under exceptional conditions.[29]

I conclude that welfare rights (not properly referred to as "rights to charity") are, within strict limits, justifiable. It does not follow, of course, that these are to be identified with the grab-bag of benefactions typically put forth under the banner of "welfarism." All of the following qualify the legitimacy of welfare rights:

(1) That which individuals enjoy as a matter of right is a decent minimum. The formula is vague, but not infinitely expandable. As Locke notes, it is "extreme want" that demands melioration, not relative deprivation. Welfare rights are not a blank check that may be cashed in for whatever fosters a commodious existence.

(2) Again following Locke, it is only against "another's plenty" that individuals can press justifiable claims. Redistribution that impinges significantly on those obliged to provide is unwarranted.

(3) The claim against others to welfare goods is contingent. Those who are able to supply through their own efforts the requisites of a decent life are not to be granted a place at the public trough. Being forced to starve is tragic, but choosing to do so because one finds work unpleasant is culpable imprudence.

(4) Noninterference is the primary right, and much of the indigence we actually observe is the product of unwarranted interference. In a regime in which individuals enjoy full liberty to meet their own needs, it will not often be the case that they are unable to do so. No minimum-wage or occupational-licensure laws will restrict access to employment; zoning ordinances and housing codes will

[28] Locke, *First Treatise*, Book 1, ch. 4. Where Locke speaks of charitable relief, Hobbes explicitly turns to politically authorized welfare measures: "And whereas many men, by accident inevitable, become unable to maintain themselves by their labour; they ought not to be left to the charity of private persons; but to be provided for, as far forth as the necessities of nature require, by the laws of the commonwealth. For as it is uncharitableness in any man, to neglect the impotent; so it is in the sovereign of a commonwealth, to expose them to the hazard of such uncertain charity" (Hobbes, *Leviathan*, Part 2, ch. 30, p. 255). (I do not hereby mean to be seen as taking sides in the scholarly debate over whether Hobbes is or is not to be considered a proto-liberal.)

[29] I offer a more extended discussion of rights at the margin in "Rights without Stilts," *Harvard Journal of Law and Public Policy*, vol. 12 (Summer 1989), pp. 775–812.

not restrict access to housing; and opportunities to profit will not be ruled out of bounds by "victimless crime" statutes. Nor will an ethos of welfarism spawn an army of bureaucrats whose livelihood rests on the perpetuation of generational cycles of dependency within a welfare class.

(5) Welfare rights do not supplant private charity. Even though, in a strict sense, there is no duty to be charitable, many individuals voluntarily elect to respond to the misfortunes of others. To the extent that charitable provision is forthcoming, coercive redistribution is illegitimate.

Although rights to welfare are theoretically well-grounded, I am inclined to believe that the preceding stipulations, especially the fifth, render their interest largely theoretical in a different sense. A social order graced with individuals disposed to act compassionately toward their unfortunate fellows will be one in which persons only infrequently need resort to welfare rights—and one in which compassion is lacking will be unlikely to sustain a structure of rights at all.

VI. Wide and Narrow Philanthropy

The preceding argument has identified two respects in which charitable provision is superior to reliance on welfare rights. First, while rights are pitched only at the level of moral minima, charity as a virtue is situated within the realm of human distinction. Second, because there is a standing presumption against coercion, voluntary subscriptions are inherently preferable to mandated transfers. To these we can add a third: charity admits of discretion and imaginative application that is both improbable and inappropriate with regard to welfare rights.

Individuals can properly be taken to enjoy as a matter of right no more than the basic requisites for living as independent pursuers of ends that are their own. Mandatory transfers are, therefore, restricted to goods that are neutral among persons' possible projects. John Rawls calls these "primary goods," characterizing them as "things that every rational man is presumed to want," because "they normally have a use whatever a person's rational plan of life."[30] Not all primary goods are tangible; among the primary goods that have a prominent place in Rawls's theory are rights and liberties, powers and opportunities, and the social bases of self-respect. Whatever their importance in that context, however, intangible goods have limited applicability to questions of transfers and redistribution.[31] Money is the most fungible and thus the most project-neutral of

[30] John Rawls, *A Theory of Justice* (Cambridge, MA: Harvard University Press, 1971), p. 62.

[31] Affirmative action policies do raise such questions insofar as they aim at restructuring the network of social opportunities.

goods, and therefore justifiable redistributive measures will largely be confined to cash transfers. Of more dubious legitimacy are in-kind transfer programs. A case can be made for public provision of housing, food, and health services insofar as these are judged to be goods that people need irrespective of whatever else they want. That case will, however, rely to an uncomfortable extent on paternalistic rationales, and it is likely to conceal hidden agendas. (The construction industry will offer abundant support for public housing, agricultural interests for food stamps, and so on.) Although there may nonetheless be some legitimate role for in-kind provision, it is less by orders of magnitude than what is observed in the actual functioning of welfare states.

But while state-operated redistributive programs are required to maintain neutrality among competing ends, private philanthropy operates under no such constraint. Individuals who proffer aid are not simply responding in mechanical fashion to the misfortunes of others. Rather, they are giving effect to their own conceptions of how to live well among others. In this respect charitable provision is not unlike market transactions. When buyer meets seller in the market, each brings to the transaction her own subjective valuations; and the bargains into which they enter are predicated on the achievement of mutual satisfaction. Similarly, voluntary charitable giving centrally incorporates the preferences of donors as well as the needs of recipients. One chooses not only whether to give but also in what amount, to which beneficiaries, in what way, and for the sake of which ends. Private judgments concerning questions of value are thereby given fuller expression than could ever be achieved through mandatory, monolithic governmental programs.

This aspect of private charity is especially observable in morally contested domains. Planned Parenthood and right-to-life agencies compete for "clients" much as do Pepsi and Coca-Cola, and the competition is imbued with moral significance for their respective supporters. In the United States there exist thousands of foundations, large and small, dedicated to advancing particular conceptions of the good. To invoke the market metaphor again, these are key players in the marketplace of ideas. They purvey not only cash but values. Their giving intrinsically incorporates advocacy and thus enriches public discussion.

Much philanthropic activity is, of course, distant from controversial policy matters. To the best of my knowledge, there exist no consequential pro-cancer or anti-literacy factions.[32] Feeding the hungry, sheltering the homeless, clothing the naked, and healing the sick are consensus values. Still, even these charitable functions are morally rich. The choice of giving to one cause has an associated opportunity cost of alternative chari-

[32] Although these blights are spread in copious abundance by, respectively, tobacco companies and the public schools, in the spirit of this essay I shall charitably assume that furtherance of these evils is not their primary intention.

table giving (or noncharitable expenditure) forgone. A dollar donated to the Cancer Society is a dollar not given to literacy projects or to any of the myriad of other potential claimants on one's resources. Thus, to provide support even for uncontroversial causes is to make a morally significant choice in a way that writing out a check to pay one's taxes is not. That is not to make the preposterous claim that every donor does – or should – deliberate at length over each potential benefaction. Time and energy spent on deliberation also come attached to opportunity costs, and the individual who dithers endlessly before dropping a quarter into the street-corner Santa's kettle presents a ludicrous figure. Umbrella agencies such as United Way are a reasonable way to economize on scarce non-monetary resources. Still, even nondeliberated, uncontroversial acts of charity are manifestations of moral character. They are a means through which one identifies oneself with certain ends above others and expresses convictions about the sort of society in which one wishes to live and how to be a contributing member of it.

Even where ends are uncontroversial, the manner in which they are served can express a particular moral stance. Most American hospitals and private colleges were founded by religious denominations. In part, this can be explained as a service function to communicants who might otherwise have been underprovided along the relevant dimension, but it also incorporated judgments concerning what it is to live decently as a Catholic or Methodist or Jew. Institutional variety encouraged responsiveness to the diverse preferences of different clienteles. Even today, in the wake of considerable homogenization, attending Brigham Young University is noticeably different from pursuing studies at Notre Dame. Diversity would be yet greater if not for restrictive state regulation and direct service provision. The optimal extent of parochial diversity in these areas is disputable, and I do not claim that more is always better than less. Note, though, that even a determination on the part of an eleemosynary agency and its supporters to blend in rather than provide markedly distinctive services is itself a morally considerable decision.

Private charitable providers are at liberty to innovate and experiment to an extent that public bureaus are not. They do not await a legislative mandate to come into existence and are not hobbled by the terms of their enabling legislation or an encrusted civil service. Most important, they are not obligated to tender their services to all comers on an impartial basis. A public agency that withholds aid from some persons who meet formal eligibility criteria, or that provides significantly different services to different beneficiaries, thereby violates a core principle of political justice. States are required to be *neutral* among citizens, and the stipulation that they not advantage some persons or conceptions of the good above others sharply limits their discretionary authority. But that which constitutes impermissible discrimination on the part of a public agency can be entirely benign when exercised by private parties. The latter are not constrained to serve everyone alike, but may instead determine for themselves how their efforts can most effectively meet the interests of clients and supporters. If a private foundation finds that it has a comparative advantage in serving one subclass of potential beneficiaries, it is at liberty to specialize in what it does best. When old programs are seen to be of diminishing effectiveness, they can be supplanted by new ones. Experiments will be undertaken and new directions charted without fear of violating duties of neutrality.

Governmental programs are not altogether fossilized. Their administrators do not simply carry out a legislated algorithm. Programs can be modified in the light of experience, and occasionally—but only *very* occasionally—they are even allowed to die. The differences between private and public programs with regard to flexibility are matters of degree, but when these are sufficiently pronounced they amount to differences in kind. Public welfare mechanisms are simply incapable of generating knowledge to the extent that private philanthropic agencies routinely do. This is yet another reason why even the most scrupulous attention to welfare rights is incapable of substituting for the functions of private charity.

VII. Conclusion

The misfortunes of others *do* matter. Attention to this evident datum has fueled the claim that, just as we have duties not to interfere with others, so too do we have duties to provide charitable relief. The hegemony during the previous three centuries of the jurisprudential paradigm adds further impetus to this presumption and promotes the metastasis of conceptions of "social justice" that are fatal to the preservation of a realm of discretion in which individuals are able to pursue various ideals of moral excellence. But if morality is primarily a menu of rights and duties, then there is no other plausible way to recognize the salience of individuals' misfortunes than to acknowledge the legitimacy of the demands of social justice.

Against the social-justice conception I have argued that relieving distress is morally important because charity is a virtue. Individuals who are not *obligated* to aid others nonetheless *should* do so. One lives more satisfactorily among others if one is alive to their weal and woe. This is not to advance the bald claim that one should be charitable because it is in one's self-interest to be such. Rather, it is to say something substantive about how one should conceive the relation between one's own interests and the interests of others. Unless one takes the well-being of others to be complementary with one's own, charity has no application. The rich might "buy off" the poor through transfer payments, but these transactions would not amount to charity.

Welfare rights *are* a species of buying off, but that is not to impugn their moral legitimacy. The whole of rights, negative as well as positive, can be understood as an elaborate system of quids being exchanged for quos. A person has reason to forbear in her dealings with others as the price of their forbearance toward her. No antecedent affection or sympathy is presumed. What is true of rights and correlative duties, however, cannot be extrapolated to the remainder of morality.[33] The social virtues, of which charity is one, resist modeling as bloodless transactions among mutually disinterested individuals. Instead, they represent a willingness to conceive of others' fates as not entirely external to one's own. Rights and duties are morality's carapace, valuable because they protect individuals' ability to direct their affairs according to their own lights, to forge relations of intimacy and trust, and to aspire to distinction.

Charity is an excellence because it manifests care for what is worth caring about. That proposition does not presuppose some one monolithic standard of value. There are an indefinite number of ways in which one can effectively display charity because circumstances and individuals' conceptions of the good are themselves various. This multiplicity stands in contrast with the fixity that rights and duties must have if they are to be practical. Contingent rights to welfare are theoretically validated because there is a baseline below which individuals cannot be obliged to fall without thereby jeopardizing the foundations of moral reciprocity. Philanthropic activity sometimes addresses itself to lifting people above that baseline, but it also serves the interests of individuals, givers as well as receivers, along numerous other avenues. Charity's responsiveness to different varieties of the good renders it an especially apt virtue for a free society. As etymology suggests and experience confirms, liberality fits well with a liberal order. Should the ministrations of the welfare state drive out private philanthropy, we will be the poorer for it.

Philosophy, Bowling Green State University

[33] That is why David Gauthier's *Morals by Agreement* (Oxford: Clarendon Press, 1986) is, at the very least, mistitled.

EQUALITY, SUFFICIENCY, AND OPPORTUNITY IN THE JUST SOCIETY

BY ALEXANDER ROSENBERG

It seems to be almost a given of contemporary Anglo-American political philosophy that the just society is obligated to establish and ensure the equality of its members. Debate begins when we come to delineate the forms and limits of the equality society is obligated to underwrite.[1] In this essay I offer the subversive suggestion that equality is not something the just society should aim for. Instead I offer another objective, one which is to be preferred both because it is more attainable and because it is morally more defensible than equality, either as an ideal or as an operative principle. The demand for equality of treatment, of opportunity, or of outcome, is a distraction from morally more significant aims.

If a society is a moral agent obligated to provide some benefit or protection uniformly to its members, then there is something quite different from equality which it should aim to establish and preserve. Note the conditional form of the previous claim. The antecedent should be more controversial than it has been in contemporary moral and political philosophy. Can the state be a moral agent? One argument against this claim begins by noting that the state lacks the autonomy moral agents require. It is a creature of moral agents and is not an additional moral agent. Consequently, it has no responsibilities above and beyond the responsibilities of individual agents. It might have functions—for example, providing public goods—that no individual can fulfill. But these will not be its moral obligations, because it has none. If this is the case, the question of what the obligations of a just society are does not arise.

This essay proceeds on the assumption that the antecedent of this conditional is true: that society is a moral agent and that among its duties is an obligation to provide some benefit or protection to its members. I explore the consequences of the assumption without either endorsing or rejecting it. Even if the assumption is rejected, it may still be held, especially on contractarian grounds, that the interests of individual rational agents are served by assuring the provision of some benefits to all members of a society. And equality is the benefit most often identified as serving this interest and assuring the acquiescence of rational agents in a

[1] The *loci classici* of this debate are John Rawls, *A Theory of Justice* (Cambridge: Harvard University Press, 1971); and Robert Nozick, *Anarchy, State, and Utopia* (New York: Basic Books, 1974).

society that limits their freedoms. Thus, even if we reject the notion that societies have obligations to be just, the question of whether their functions include the provision of benefits to all members remains important.

Before proceeding, I need to secure concurrence in a constraint on the extent of moral obligation. It is a well-known principle in moral philosophy that "ought implies can"—if one is to be obliged to do something, then one must be able to do it. But it is the contrapositive of this principle which is of import here: "cannot implies need not." Unless deontic logic differs more completely from alethic logic than we know, this contrapositive must be valid if the original principle is. In the present connection, if (as I shall argue) equality is an unattainable goal, then it cannot be a morally obligatory one.

It might be argued that just because we cannot attain some end—for instance, complete equality—it does not follow that we need not *try* to attain it. Thus, even if complete equality is an unattainable ideal, it might nevertheless be obligatory to strive for it. For pursuing an unattainable goal may be the best way or the only way to achieve some other, attainable goal. Pursuing the unattainable goal of complete equality could be the best way of achieving the attainable goal of minimizing social unrest. But this cannot be an argument in favor of the obligation to attain complete equality. At most it is an argument for the obligation to strive for it. Besides, I shall argue, we should neither establish nor attempt to establish the sorts of equality egalitarian theorists might advocate.

But even if a commitment to equality is not morally obligatory because equality is unattainable, this does not mean that the just society is free of political and moral obligations to its members. Rather, it means that egalitarian political philosophers have misidentified what a society really is obliged to strive for in regard to treatment of its members. This, at any rate, will be the thesis to be explored below.

I. Equality of Outcome

Let us begin with the strongest conception of equality and see what is wrong with it. Then we can explore whether weaker forms avoid these difficulties or not.

By "thoroughgoing egalitarianism" I mean a theory which calls for equality of outcome in welfare benefits, goods, income, wealth, or advantages that people seek. Since different people like different things, what we should aim at is something more fundamental than equal baskets of commodities. Rather, it is traditionally supposed that equality of outcome requires equality of welfare. But there are well-known reasons why equality of welfare seems an inappropriate goal for egalitarians: differences among people's preferences may require us to lavish resources on some while stinting on others just in order to equalize welfare. We ought not equalize all individuals' levels of welfare if this means spending vast sums to satisfy someone with champagne tastes and small sums to please equally someone whose tastes run to Budweiser.

This problem has led some to argue that we ought to equalize for resources that humans employ to secure levels of welfare. These resources will include "natural" endowments—special talents and abilities—and social endowments, like inheritance and a stimulating home environment. In addition to advantageous resources, individuals are born with and also acquire disabilities that make it difficult to secure satisfactory levels of welfare. The obvious differences between people's natural and social advantages require expropriation and subsidization if we are even to approach equality in resources available to attain human goals.[2]

However, given individual differences in abilities and disabilities, it is impossible in the end to compensate or tax to attain real equality of welfare-outcome. How much should we give to a blind person to compensate for sightlessness? How much would you trade sight for? The phenomenally large court settlements of recent years are not just a tribute to the abilities of lawyers and a reflection of the deep pockets of insurance companies. They reflect the belief on the part of juries that things like sight are beyond price. There is no amount that will compensate for lost sight. The very large amounts some juries try to award are to them arbitrary numbers that reflect their inability to attach amounts to lost talents and acquired disabilities.

To raise a related question, how much should we tax someone with a talent but no interest in exercising it for his own material advantage? These are not rhetorical questions. They show that equality of welfare or equality of resources to achieve welfare is unattainable. What we cannot do, we are under no moral obligation to attempt to do. Moreover, making up for differences in talents and disabilities in order more nearly to approach equality of outcomes is just a disguised way of equalizing for welfare, since what counts as a marketable talent or an earnings-depressing disability is a function of the preferences of members of the society in which a talented or a disabled agent lives.[3]

Advocates of equalizing for differences in abilities and disabilities acknowledge the role of desert, ambition, and other morally relevant differences in generating some inequalities.[4] Suppose our egalitarian aim is to equalize for all outcomes except those which are earned or deserved, those for which the individual is responsible. In order to secure equal outcomes, it is clear that in addition to equalizing for naturally occurring dif-

[2] See, for instance, Ronald Dworkin, "What Is Equality? I, II," *Philosophy and Public Affairs*, vol. 4 (1981), pp. 185–246, 283–345.

[3] I argue for this view at length in "The Political Philosophy of Biological Endowments," *Social Philosophy and Policy*, vol. 5, no. 1 (Autumn 1987), pp. 1–31.

[4] For a full discussion of this qualification on outcome-egalitarianism, see George Sher, *Desert* (Princeton: Princeton University Press, 1987).

ferences[5] in abilities, we also have to equalize for humanly imposed differences in abilities which generate obstacles to equality: differences in the rewards associated with varying occupations and other institutional barriers, differences in the resources available to parents in the education of their children, differences in the willingness of parents to devote available resources to their children, etc.[6] Clearly, no individual has *earned* the advantages or disadvantages erected by these differences. They are all beyond his or her control.

Thus, outcome equality means that the just society will have to equalize for natural and social advantages and disadvantages in order to ensure the attainment of equal outcomes. Whenever, wherever, and for whatever cause we find outcomes to be unequal, the *causes* of these inequalities must be identified. And if these causes are undeserved, the just society will need to remove or compensate for them; for people should not be unequal as a result of the operation of forces over which they have no control.

But how could there be a *deserved* cause of differences in outcome? Only if there were some feature of an agent's character over which the agent has control, i.e., one that is not the result of social and natural causes. Agents have no control over traits which have their deterministic[7] sources in events that occurred prior to their birth, and therefore they are not responsible for these traits.[8] Accordingly, they do not deserve the benefits and costs which may accrue to such determined traits.

Only if there were differences in earned or deserved abilities and disabilities could the differences in welfare they produce be deserved. But radical egalitarians cannot accept the existence of such earned or deserved differences in character that make a difference in outcome. For, given radical outcome-egalitarianism, to be earned or deserved such traits would have to be within the control of the agent, and thus free from deterministic causes. If, following egalitarian strictures, we attempt to set natural and social differences at zero, but the result is nevertheless some differ-

[5] "Naturally occurring differences" are not hereditary or genetically determined differences. There are no such differences, for genetic factors always operate together with environmental factors in generating phenotypes. To the extent that environmental differences are small, differences in abilities may be traced to genetic factors. But these require environmental conditions in order to have effects, and their effects may disappear as changes in the environment obtain. For a fuller discussion, see Rosenberg, "The Political Philosophy of Biological Endowments"; and Elliot Sober, *Philosophy of Biology* (Boulder, CO: Westview, 1993), pp. 185–94.

[6] For an illuminating discussion of the problem of equalizing for parental investment in upbringing and education, see Neven Sesardic, "Egalitarianism and the Natural Lottery," *Public Affairs Quarterly*, vol. 7, no. 1 (1993), pp. 57–69.

[7] At and above the level of the biologically active macromolecule, phenomena remain close enough to deterministic to make the assumption of determinism a safe one for purposes of explaining the distribution of human traits.

[8] Here I adopt without further argument a view defended by Peter van Inwagen, *An Essay on Free Will* (Oxford: Oxford University Press, 1985), ch. 1.

ence of outcome in welfare among agents, there must be a cause. Presumably, it will be some difference in character, make-up, or personality among the agents. But these traits are no more under an agent's control than are his parents' income or inclinations. Thus, they are not deserved by the agent. They too must be the result of natural or human causes—in the agent's inheritance and environment, natural and social. If radical egalitarianism requires that we equalize for differences not under agents' control, it requires that we equalize for these differences in character. But in doing so, radical egalitarianism excludes desert, and has no room for the possibility that outcomes might be earned, that agents are autonomous and responsible for their own choices to a degree that makes any difference in the material quality of their lives.

Radical egalitarianism thus seems incompatible with a conception of moral agency and political arrangements that honor the autonomy of agents, that accord a special place to equality of rights over other equalities, and that reject paternalism. In a way, this is unsurprising, since outcome-egalitarianism is a natural result of utilitarian and other broadly "welfarist" reflections on the meaning of equality.

Egalitarians can hardly come to terms with merit and desert by giving up determinism, however. For determinism offers the only assurance that egalitarian interventions will have their intended result in equalizing human welfare. We cannot equalize levels of welfare directly, but only indirectly by influencing the causes of welfare; and this will only work if the causal determinants of welfare show the sort of regularity determinism demands.

Even if it could find some scope for personal desert, radical egalitarianism requires a degree of persistent interference in social and domestic relations that would make a workable society quite unattainable. Given the natural lottery which distributes differences in ability and disability, and the "social" lottery that distributes differences in initial endowments, family socialization, access to education, etc., inequality begins to grow from the first moment of an agent's existence. Radical egalitarianism of outcome will prohibit the transfer of any earned fungible benefit to any other agent who has not earned it. This prohibition will include spouses, children, friends, and anonymous recipients of charity. It will prohibit all unequal welfare-enhancing expenditures except those which exclusively enhance the welfare of the agent who earns the benefit.

How can such a prohibition against inequality-producing transfers be implemented, and what will its incentive effects be on agents who might earn sufficiently large rewards to enable them to make such transfers? Insuring undeserved-outcome equality will not just require 100 percent inheritance taxes; it will require severe restrictions on how any agent can spend any "earned" income differential, not just by yearly confiscation of unspent surpluses, but eventually by continuous exactions of fungible benefits that can make for unearned differences when transferred as gifts to others—to children, spouses, friends, etc. Individuals will only be allowed to spend earned or deserved fungible benefits on themselves. They will have no incentive to make investments whose returns exceed what they can spend on themselves, since no such returns can be made over as unearned gifts to anyone else. If there are such investments, they will have to be expropriated for distribution in compensation for differences in abilities.

As seems so often the case, the effect of egalitarianism, here too, is to shrink whatever pie it insists on dividing with scrupulous equality. If the overall welfare-reducing disincentive impact of radical outcome-egalitarianism is great enough to reduce the welfare of the least advantaged to a level below that of less radical egalitarian or nonegalitarian arrangements, then this sort of egalitarianism does not even recommend itself on welfarist criteria of adequacy.

In addition to preventing agents from employing their benefits to provide unearned fungible benefits to others, radical outcome-egalitarianism will have to prohibit or offset the differential effects of domestic upbringing and socialization on the earning-power and welfare-attaining powers of individuals. Since no one deserves the family, friends, or primary school he has, or the good or bad upbringing they provide, equality of undeserved outcomes in welfare will require interference with domestic arrangements, both to improve upbringing, and sometimes to worsen it, so that all end up with upbringings that equalize welfare.

No one has ever advocated the sort of outcome-egalitarianism whose strictures are here delineated. The trouble for egalitarianism of the sort writers have actually advocated is to find a principled way of excusing their egalitarianism from such a *reductio ad absurdum*. Doing so requires at least an account of the conditions under which differences in welfare or resources can be earned, and circumstances that make permissible the transfer of the smallest part of such benefits to others who have not earned them. I leave this account as an academic exercise for egalitarians, since the view suffers from other problems in any case.

II. Equality as a Distraction

If equality of welfare-outcome is not a reasonable responsibility of the just society, perhaps a weaker form of egalitarianism is supportable. Consider, for example, the doctrine that we ought to equalize for income or wealth. This is quite a different requirement from equalizing for welfare. After all, equal amounts of money income or endowment do not make for equal levels of happiness or satisfaction, and individuals equally endowed can make choices that, over the long term, result in wide differences in happiness, welfare, fulfillment, etc. These differences can be accepted by the income-egalitarian as earned, deserved differences which reflect the moral responsibility and autonomy of individual agents. It may even be permissible to dispose of income differentials in ways that advantage, to a limited degree, those who do not deserve these benefits, like children, spouses, friends, and recipients of charity.

Of course, equalizing for wealth or income still involves a massive and continuing interference in individual lives. At regular intervals we shall have to set all individuals equal in wealth or income. This at least is an undertaking we know how to accomplish in principle. Setting welfare-levels equal is something scientific theory tells us we cannot do, even if welfare egalitarianism requires it.

However, even the more modest egalitarianism of money is a serious distraction from important moral values the just society should at least permit, if not actually foster. This at any rate is a conclusion encouraged by an important essay of Harry Frankfurt's.[9] What is morally wrong about setting our sights on an equal distribution of wealth and income? Frankfurt writes:

> To the extent that people are preoccupied with equality for its own sake, their readiness to be satisfied with any particular level of income or wealth is guided not by their own interests and needs but just by the magnitude of the economic benefits that are at the disposal of others. In this way egalitarianism distracts people from measuring the requirements to which their individual natures and their personal circumstances give rise. It encourages them instead to insist on a level of economic support that is determined by a calculation in which the particular features of their own lives are irrelevant. How sizeable the economic assets of others are has nothing much to do, after all, with what sort of a person someone is. A concern for economic equality, construed as desirable in itself, tends to divert a person's attention away from endeavoring to discover—within his experience of himself and of his life—what he himself really cares about and what will actually satisfy him, although this is the most basic and decisive task upon which an intelligent selection of economic goals depends. Exaggerating the moral importance of economic equality is harmful, in other words, because it is alienating.[10]

According to Frankfurt, then, "the doctrine of equality contributes to the moral disorientation and shallowness of our time" not only because an individual's preoccupation with it drives out of consideration matters more important to the moral quality of his or her life, but because philosophers defending it as morally valuable for all, in and of itself, are diverted from considerations of greater moral importance. Frankfurt's point is that

[9] Harry Frankfurt, "Equality as a Moral Ideal," in Frankfurt, *The Importance of What We Care About* (Cambridge: Cambridge University Press, 1988), pp. 134–58.

[10] *Ibid.*, pp. 135–36.

imposing a test for distributions like the envy test—wealth and income are fairly distributed when no rational agent wishes to trade his or her endowment or income for another's[11]—makes jealousy into an important moral measuring rod. Surely the just society should not enshrine a doctrine that contributes to "moral disorientation and shallowness."

It is no easy matter to expound in any detail what really is important to people, what they do care about and should care about; and it is beyond the scope of any one essay even to gesture in the direction of answers to these questions. In thinking about this matter there are apparent distinctions to bear in mind between what people really care about, what they perhaps mistakenly think they really care about, and what they ought to care about. If what people care about is different from what people ought to care about, problems of paternalism and the legislation of morality emerge. Does the just society make people care about what they do not want to care about? If what people really care about is no different from what they merely think they care about, then what we really care about may turn out to be a subjective matter, varying from individual to individual, and from time to time, and providing no real alternative to what Frankfurt calls "alienation."

It would be implausible to argue that equality in wealth and income is a necessary condition for each agent's attaining what he really does in fact care about. This implausible suggestion gives way to the slightly more plausible claim that equality is necessary for each agent's attaining what he *morally ought* to care about. To such a suggestion there is a nice *tu quoque* response inspired by a point that Frankfurt makes in another connection:

> [M]any egalitarians (including many academic proponents of the doctrine) are not truly concerned whether they are as well off economically as other people are. They believe that they themselves have roughly enough money for what is important to them, and therefore they are not terribly preoccupied with the fact that some people are considerably richer than they. Indeed, many egalitarians would consider it rather shabby or even reprehensible to care, with respect to their own lives, about economic comparisons of that sort. And, not withstanding the implications of the doctrines to which they urge adherence, they would be appalled if their children grew up with such preoccupations.[12]

Only a few university professors can be accused of really believing that great increases in their income or wealth would enable them more fully to attain what they really do care about for themselves as persons.

It might also be argued that as close an approximation as possible to

[11] See Hal Varian, *Intermediate Microeconomics* (New York: Norton, 1987), p. 538.

[12] Frankfurt, "Equality as a Moral Ideal," p. 148.

economic equality is required in order to minimize differences of political power. For differences in political power could be exercised in ways that prevent many, most, or some individuals from identifying and attaining what they really do or ought to care about. Certainly very great discrepancies in wealth, when combined with certain sorts of political organizations, may enable individuals to have improper control over the lives of others; but it is pretty clear that, at best, equality in wealth and income is only one of many ways available to prevent these sorts of outcomes from materializing.

III. Equality of Opportunity

Perhaps Frankfurt's arguments are reason enough to reduce the egalitarian's aim from equality of outcome—whether defined in terms of welfare or money—to equality of opportunity. Even if the arguments against the moral standing of egalitarianism leave its proponents unimpressed, most of the rest of us find equality of opportunity a much more defensible normative goal. And many will identify the existence of equality of opportunity as a responsibility of the just society. As I shall argue, however, many of the problems that daunt the stronger versions of egalitarianism so far canvassed remain serious when we endorse opportunity as the thing to be equalized.

Equality of opportunity seems at least formally to allow for inequality of outcome, and thus leaves room for individual responsibility, for desert in the distribution of benefits. Not only does it leave room for autonomy, but many philosophers hold that it is required by autonomy, and by the inalienable rights of individuals which reflect this autonomy. They hold that equality of opportunity can be derived from and justified by these rights. But what if both practically and theoretically, equality of opportunity as an end must collapse into equality of outcome as a means?

Equality of opportunity seems to mean that each person faces the same balance of obstacles to the attainment of goals or benefits that every other agent faces. Opportunities are equal when all individuals have the same initial chance of attaining any benefit, so that whether they attain it or not is up to them, and their efforts. As with equality of welfare, there is a serious measurement problem here. How do we tell whether obstacles and opportunities have in fact been equalized? In recent decades, federal, state, and municipal governments in the United States have measured equality of opportunity by examining aggregate *outcomes*, and they do so statistically. Inequality of outcome is used as an indicator of inequality of opportunity. When a defined class of individuals is proportionately underrepresented in the class of agents who secure some benefit, there is a prima facie case of inequality of opportunity. The class becomes a "protected" one, and the legal burden of proof is on the shoulders of those who hold that opportunities have been equalized.

As noted in Section I, and as emphasized by the disabled and physically challenged, real equality of opportunity requires equalization for social or humanly constructed barriers and for naturally generated ones as well. Thus, if aggregate indicators of outcome, or individual complaints, provide grounds to suppose that opportunities are not equal, government needs to set about removing obstacles for some, and providing obstacles for others, compensating for obstacles it cannot remove, and handicapping (in the manner of a horse race) those individuals with neither natural nor socially constructed obstacles. Equalizing opportunity does not simply mean removing obstacles, whether human or natural. It means weighing and balancing sets of different obstacles that face individuals and determining whether they are equal. It requires us to burden some with extra obstacles if we cannot remove the obstacles from others; it requires us to withdraw advantages when they are unequally distributed, or to add burdens if these advantages cannot be withdrawn. Just as the U.S. Department of Labor's Employment Service adds points to the examination results of veterans, it might have to subtract points from the examination results of the more well-prepared among test-takers. Instead of norming a civil service test to a level which assures equality of outcome in pass-rates among various groups, one sets the passing grades according to whatever standard assures equality of outcome for groups about which society is concerned.[13]

Handicapping—positively and negatively—is a difficult task which we cannot discharge given our present understanding of individuals and their social and natural dispositions. Minimally, we would need a complete list of obstacles and advantages that make for inequality of opportunity, if we wished to secure equality of opportunity. Since we are unlikely to secure such a systematic list, there seems no alternative to relying on aggregate measures of outcome as the indicators of equality of opportunity.

In fact, given a large and heterogeneous society, the establishment of aggregate measures of outcome to determine equality of opportunity is inevitable, and the abolition of such measures is impossible to hope for. And the problem is not just that in the absence of enough reliable social science we cannot tell whether opportunities are equal except by casting an eye to outcomes. Even if we had reliable social theory, individuals would have strong incentives to claim that inequality of aggregate outcome *shows* that we have not equalized for obstacles. Individuals who earned below-average outcomes would have an incentive to claim that the cause was unequal opportunities, especially if they also constituted an identifiable class, like an ethnic or racial minority, or a set of individuals

[13] This practice of "race norming" was actually implemented in grading the General Aptitude Test Battery administered by the U.S. Department of Labor's Employment Service before its prohibition by the Civil Rights Act of 1991.

sharing a common trait like left-handedness or red hair. The numbers of these individuals will be so large in any modern society that individual investigation of their claims will be impossible. Moreover, those who claim to represent the interests of these minorities, in the distribution of resources society employs to approach equality of opportunity, have an incentive not to accept anything less than statistical equality of outcome as a guarantee of equality of individual opportunity. Their constituencies may lose entitlements, and they will lose their positions, if outcomes cease to count in the measurement of opportunities. It is a political fact of life that equality of aggregate outcome will remain the only test for equality of opportunity a significant fraction of our society will accept. It is also a scientific fact of life that equality of aggregate outcome is the only operational measure of equality of opportunity we are ever likely to have or to be able actually to apply. Equality of opportunity requires statistical equality of outcome as its test. Political philosophy must reconcile itself to this limitation.

In the real world, equality of opportunity requires that the same proportion of every significant group in our society be represented among the recipients of every significant benefit available in our society. But employing equality of aggregate outcome as a measure of equality of opportunity is daunted by another problem. For this measure provides at most only an assurance that society is proceeding in accordance with a principle of distribution of benefits by merit, and distribution of benefits by merit is only part of equality of opportunity.

Most benefits, especially those associated with education, occupation, and recreation, are scarce goods, and unless desert or merit is required for each of them, even proportional representation in outcomes will be no assurance of equality of opportunity. Given scarcity, even if there are no differences among individuals in initial desert or merit, some individuals will have been deprived of an equal opportunity to attain some benefits, even when all significant groups are proportionately represented in receipt of all benefits. For example, consider the benefit of securing a seat on the U.S. Supreme Court. Even though the proportion of Italian Americans on the Court exactly mirrors their proportion in the population, it may still be true that some Italian Americans—indeed, ones with legal minds and experience that exceed those of the Court's sole Italian American member, Justice Antonin Scalia—have been deprived of an equal opportunity to find their way to the Court. Unless there are initial differences in desert or merit, scarcity must preclude equal outcomes, and so suggest the failure of equal opportunity. But for there to be initial differences in desert seems impossible—how could entrants into society have earned or deserved differences before life began?—and initial differences in merit (i.e., ability) are supposed to be compensated for in order to assure equality of opportunity. Under conditions of scarcity, equality of opportunity will require not just equality of aggregate outcome with respect to each type of benefit in the society, but equality of aggregate outcome with respect to all benefits. Otherwise, those who are shut out of a benefit will complain of inequality of opportunity, and those who secure it will be the beneficiaries of moral luck.[14] But the aim of equality of opportunity is to equalize (to the extent possible) for moral luck, for undeserved advantages. If an arrangement allows for such undeserved advantages, it cannot be one that honors real equality of opportunity.

To avoid this outcome, every benefit will have to be fungible in money, and all individuals will have to be taxed or subsidized to bring them to equality. In other words, real equality of opportunity is going to require, in the end, equality of outcome in wealth and/or income. But this is the very end which Frankfurt suggested would distract us from what is morally important.

It is important to emphasize that a commitment to equality of opportunity is something quite different from a commitment to a meritocracy in which each individual's benefits are the result only of natural or fairly acquired social advantages. Equality of opportunity must mean more than equality of opportunity between all those with the same talents, resources, handicaps, and disabilities. This is not equality of opportunity for all—it is equality of opportunity for all those in the same condition to compete; it is fairness in the establishment of and assessment of qualifications for positions to which benefits accrue.

In the end, scarcity in the benefits available in our society, and ignorance about the causes of differences in ability and disability, coupled with a real commitment to equality of opportunity, jointly lead to a distribution of benefits among agents in shares which are as equal as they can be in money value, and otherwise simply reflect random chance. For if a benefit is too scarce to be provided to all who deserve or merit it equally, then the only fair distribution is a lottery *with compensation for the losers*. Otherwise, an undeserved inequality is generated. The most direct way to avoid undeserved inequalities is to strive for equality in wealth and income.

But doing this, Frankfurt tells us, is a distraction from morally more serious matters. Furthermore, if what I have said above is right about equality of opportunity requiring us, willy-nilly, to equalize for outcomes, then equalizing for opportunities requires a society to ignore morally more serious matters just as much as equalizing for outcomes. Now, Frankfurt has a positive alternative to equalizing for outcomes—one we should consider, whether we are egalitarians about outcomes or about opportunities. For it turns out to have advantages over equality that Frankfurt himself fails to recognize.

[14] I use "moral luck" in Thomas Nagel's sense of the term; see Nagel, "Moral Luck," in his *Mortal Questions* (Oxford: Oxford University Press, 1979), p. 26. See also Barbara Goodwin, *Justice by Lottery* (Chicago: University of Chicago Press, 1992).

IV. The Doctrine of Sufficiency

Instead of a doctrine of economic equality, Frankfurt urges an alternative which does not distract us from what is really important for attaining what we care about. He calls it the doctrine of sufficiency: "With respect to the distribution of economic assets, what is important from the point of view of morality is not that everyone should have *the same* but that everyone should have *enough*. If everyone had enough, it would be of no moral consequence whether some had more than others. . . . [W]hat is morally important with respect to money is for everyone to have enough . . ."—where enough presumably means enough to attain "the requirements to which their individual natures and their personal circumstances give rise," that is, enough for a person to "discover—within his experience of himself and of his life—what he himself really cares about and what will actually satisfy him."[15]

Frankfurt advances this principle in spite of his belief that it is much harder to establish sufficiency than equality: "Calculating the size of an equal share is plainly much easier than determining how much a person needs in order to have enough."[16] It is in principle easy to take the whole wealth of the nation and divide by the population, or to determine the per-capita gross national product and pass it around at the end of each year. However, it may be more difficult to determine what amount of money will buy a level of support sufficient for worthy purposes.

But Frankfurt is wrong. Operationalizing sufficiency is probably far easier than establishing equal shares. To begin with, establishing equal shares faces all the problems of establishing total wealth or income. The rich have the incentive and the resources to hide wealth, and everyone else has an incentive to exaggerate his poverty. Then there is the problem of redistribution, and the prospect that those charged to effect the redistribution will enrich themselves. More philosophically serious is the objection that, on the one hand, equalizing for money income will not equalize for welfare or utility, and, on the other hand, equalizing for utility is impossible since welfare, satisfaction, and other such factors are not interpersonally comparable. Similarly, equalizing for money income will not equalize for differences in abilities and disabilities, and thus will not achieve anything like the egalitarian's aim.

These problems do not face those who advocate the distribution of wealth or income in ways that ensure to each person the minimum competence to attain what he really cares about, or ought to care about. There is, of course, the philosophical and personal problem facing each individual of determining what he really does or ought to care about, and it should not be presumed that these goals will be very similar among dif-

[15] Frankfurt, "Equality as a Moral Ideal," pp. 134–36.
[16] *Ibid.*, p. 137.

ferent agents, beyond some baseline requirements for a meaningful life. But there should be enough commonality among creatures of roughly the same kind for exaggerated claims about what is required for sufficiency to be rejected. And at least to the extent that the decisions about what really is important can be decentralized to individuals, there will be little scope for paternalism and uniformity in the uses to which resources are put.

Like egalitarianism, the doctrine of sufficiency can be expected to demand considerable redistribution of wealth and significant subsidization of individuals, particularly in a society like ours, characterized by vast wealth and large numbers of individuals without sufficient resources to attain anything a moral agent should care about. But unlike egalitarianism, the doctrine of sufficiency may leave considerable differences in income and wealth once everyone has enough. In this respect, sufficiency is probably easier to implement as a social policy, since the rich will have less reason to oppose and obstruct its attainment. Moreover, the doctrine of sufficiency at least leaves it open to empirical investigation – to social and behavioral science – to help us improve our estimates of what is broadly sufficient at least for many types of individuals, and to determine even more accurately what is enough for some individuals whose needs may be of special concern. To the extent that there are individual differences between what people do and should care about having or being, information about these interests can fine-tune distributions which will be morally acceptable even if unequal. There is no problem of interpersonal-utility or subjective-welfare comparisons for the doctrine of sufficiency. In this respect, Frankfurt is wrong to concede that equality – whether of utility, welfare, income, or wealth – is an easier standard to apply and implement.

Notice that a sufficiency of wealth or income to attain what an individual cares about is *ipso facto* an important kind of equality of opportunity without equality of outcome. If each person has just enough to attain his real interests, then each has an equal opportunity to attain them. Of course, if some individuals have more than enough, and the rest have only enough to discover what is important to them, and to secure it, then we do not have equality of resources, but we may still have equality of opportunity – at least the opportunity to secure what is most important to a person. And this seems to be the sort of equality on which we can set store. Indeed, some may identify it as the sense in which any representative democratic government is committed to equality of opportunity. On their view, equality of opportunity is equality of sufficiency.

Establishing sufficiency of opportunity to secure what each of us really cares about, and what each of us should care about, is no easy task. It raises philosophical problems both about what is valuable to all human agents, and about how and why different and incompatible things can be prized by different equally rational, responsible, autonomous, and thoughtful agents. It raises issues of the enforcement of morality. Once we have identified to our or to most people's satisfaction what it is we *should* all care about, and what it is individuals with different attributes should care about in addition, we are faced with a crucial question: Can we force those who decline to care about what they ought to care about to accept what we deem is sufficient for them? Some of the problems of equalizing for welfare may face the doctrine of sufficiency. For example, we do not wish to equalize welfare for champagne tastes versus Budweiser preferences, but what if tastes have an important role in determining what people do or should care about? If they do, and if they differ widely enough across persons, then providing each person enough to determine, and attain, what is important to him may result in the same unjustifiable pattern of distribution that attempting to equalize for welfare does in a world of divergent tastes. Sufficiency had better not be a matter largely of taste and preference.

Avoiding these problems for the doctrine of sufficiency raises other problems of moral certainty and paternalism that merely cutting up the pie equally does not raise. Of course, it may turn out that there are great differences between what people should care about, but that these differences do not warrant large differences in the resources each individual requires to attain what he should care about. In this happy circumstance, the problems of being certain of what each different individual should really care about and the paternalistic possibilities of imposing cares on them do not arise for those in charge of distribution and redistribution.

The doctrine of sufficiency has important political attractions that doctrines of equality lack. It is easier to implement, more likely to secure acceptance by self-interested parties, and as noted above, easier to monitor once in place. In a society like ours in the U.S., one way of assuring sufficiency is to increase our economic output—to increase the size of the pie. If we can increase the total wealth and income of the society, then even the smallest slice of the pie can be increased in ways that require no redistribution away from larger slices. If we can make the smallest slices sufficiently large to enable whoever must settle for them to attain what they really care about, we need deprive no one else of what he might think he needs to attain his ends. Increasing the wealth of the whole society, and of each of its members, encourages generosity, makes redistribution easier, reduces the temptation to cutthroat competition for social benefits, and makes it easier to accept the success of others. Of course, it may turn out that limits to growth make redistribution and expropriation essential to attaining sufficiency for every member of the society. Beyond a certain level of income and wealth for all, however, continued interference of the sort required to ensure equality of wealth and/or income will not be necessary. Thus, those with more may not have the motive to resist the doctrine of sufficiency that they have to reject equality.

On the other hand, agents with an incentive to secure more than an equal share of unearned benefits will have less opportunity to do so. For it will be easier to tell whether the benefits they seek are more than sufficient to move toward a goal they declare and society accepts as one they really care about. By contrast, it is difficult to tell whether people's welfare is really being equalized. The doctrine of equality puts no premium on increasing the total wealth and income of the society. It only mandates a division of wealth, without providing any motivation to increase it. Indeed, given the preference structure of many people, egalitarianism probably provides incentives whose unintended consequences are to reduce wealth. For it provides individuals with incentives to hide their resources, and to demand more unearned benefits than they require. Both of these tendencies have well-known and negative impacts on a society's ability to maximize its productive output. By contrast, the doctrine of sufficiency has no such consequences. It requires that society take steps to increase social wealth and income, no matter what the level of income is, until we reach a point at which everyone has enough to achieve what he really cares about. And after that level has been reached, it provides no disincentive to additional accumulation by individuals.

Perhaps the doctrine of sufficiency may also enable us to find a way to resolve a trilemma that political philosophy and social policy have increasingly recognized: In most democratic societies the majority will firmly reject the distribution of positions without respect to merit, and the minority will join the majority in rejecting interference with family autonomy in order to provide the education, skills, and attitudes required to secure desirable places in a meritocracy. And yet, empirical research suggests that only such interference with the family's authority over children in their most formative years will provide these prerequisites for meritocratic success. Egalitarians have sometimes recognized this problem, and have—as in China—chosen to deal with it by interfering in family autonomy.

James Fishkin has expressed the problem in terms of our commitment to three irreconcilable principles: equality of opportunity, the distribution of benefits on the basis of merit, and the autonomy of the family.[17] Fishkin states the three principles as follows:

> *Merit:* There should be widespread procedural fairness in the evaluation of qualifications for positions.
>
> *Equality of Life Chances:* The prospects of children for eventual positions in the society should not vary in any systematic and significant manner with their arbitrary native characteristics.

[17] James Fishkin, *Justice, Equal Opportunity, and the Family* (New Haven: Yale University Press, 1983).

> *The Autonomy of the Family:* Consensual relations within a given family governing the development of its children should not be coercively interfered with except to ensure for the children the essential prerequisites for adult participation in society.[18]

The trilemma is easy to see. If "prospects" are really to be equalized, differences in merit must be ignored, unless there are no differences in merit. The only way to eliminate differences in merit is to eliminate differences in the endowments—natural and social—which families provide to their children—that is, to violate the autonomy of the family. If the family's autonomy is to be protected, then differences in merit will emerge, and life chances will be unequal, or alternatively, merit will be ignored in setting life chances equal. And so on. Can we escape from the trilemma? If not, which principle should we abridge?

Abridging the autonomy of the family is just not a practical suggestion. Even where societies have come close to trying it, as in China, the result has been failure and grave harm. Ignoring merit not only is productively inefficient, and thus harms everyone, but leads to serious unrest. On the other hand, as I have argued, equalizing life chances is not a principle we ought to sustain. Or at least, since we cannot do so, we need not do so. Really equalizing "prospects" either means giving everyone of equal ability a chance at scarce goods, in which case it is a disguised version of the principle of merit, or it requires us to close off the scope in people's lives for autonomy, responsibility, and desert. For the only way to really equalize "prospects," given differences over which we have no control, is to equalize for outcomes—unless, of course, equalizing life prospects means something like providing enough to each person to determine what he really cares about and to attain it. If we are to substitute for Fishkin's principle of equal life chances a commitment to sufficiency, then of course the philosophical trilemma disappears. Once we assure to each individual a competence sufficient to attain what the individual ought to care about, we may leave it to the autonomous family to assure that its dependents are raised to employ these resources to their intended aim. And if the family fails to provide adequately for its dependents, the just society has no further responsibility. Those who reject this conclusion must reject the principle of the autonomy of the family. For the apparent alternative of aiming to achieve substantial equality of opportunity or outcome is unattainable and thus not obligatory.

V. Conclusion

The doctrine of sufficiency is by no means an unarguable or obvious improvement over any of the various forms of egalitarianism as a thesis

[18] James Fishkin, "Liberty versus Equal Opportunity," *Social Philosophy and Policy*, vol. 5, no. 1 (Autumn 1987), pp. 38–39.

about the obligations (if any) of a just society. For instance, even if operationalizing sufficiency seems a less daunting undertaking than providing a metric to measure for equality, it is still no easy matter. But sufficiency is clearly worth a good deal of further investigation, particularly if, as I have argued, even sorts of equality which are widely endorsed are unattainable. Sufficiency seems to have obvious advantages over any form of egalitarianism which requires redistribution, and which therefore confers incentives on individuals to misrepresent their endowments and their preferences. Sufficiency does not obviously offend other firm principles that do conflict with all but the most anodyne political egalitarianism. And it is free from the moral defects that seem to attend egalitarianism.

Philosophy, University of California, Riverside

JUSTICE AND EQUALITY: SOME QUESTIONS ABOUT SCOPE

By Larry S. Temkin

I. Introduction

Can a society be just if it ignores the plight of other societies? Does it matter whether those societies are contemporaries? Moral "purists" are likely to assume that the answer to these questions must be "no." Relying on familiar claims about impartiality or universalizability, the purist is likely to assert that the dictates of justice have no bounds, that they extend with equal strength across space and time. On this view, if, for example, justice requires us to maximize the expectations of the worst-off group in our society, it also requires us to maximize the expectations of the worst-off group in any society, at any time, so far as it is in our power to do so. Is such a position plausible? Is it more plausible than alternative positions? I am unsure about the answers to these questions, but both the questions, and the answers, are important. Clearly, the nature and extent of a just society's obligations will vary markedly depending on the scope of the correct principles of justice.

Unfortunately, the topic of justice is as large as it is important. Indeed, there are probably at least as many views about the nature and foundations of justice, as there are about the nature and foundations of morality. Therefore, to help limit my topic, and make my task more manageable, I shall focus my discussion on that aspect of justice which is concerned with how people fare relative to others. Specifically, I shall focus on equality, which I believe is one important aspect, or component, of the larger notion of justice.[1] My aim is to articulate several positions one might hold regarding equality's scope, and to present considerations and implications relevant to those positions. As we will see, one's views about equality's scope will be intimately related to one's other views about justice and morality in ways that have interesting and significant implications.[2]

[1] The view that equality is a part of justice is discussed in my book *Inequality* (New York: Oxford University Press, 1993); see, for example, p. 13. I shall not directly defend the view here, since the issue is mainly terminological, and does not affect the substance of my remarks.

[2] In *Inequality*, I discuss a number of issues that might be deemed relevant to inequality's scope. These include whether inequality is individualistic or holistic; the respects in which inequality is complex; whether inequality matters more in poor societies or rich societies; whether population size affects inequality; whether the proper units of egalitarian concern should be complete lives, corresponding segments of people's lives, or simultaneous seg-

Two preliminary comments: First, this essay does not attempt to settle the issues it raises. Rather, it tries to illuminate the importance and complexity of a set of issues that has too often been ignored. Second, although this essay focuses on equality, it should still be of interest to nonegalitarians, as many of the considerations presented here will also be relevant in assessing the scope of other aspects or principles of justice.

The remainder of the essay is divided into seven sections. Section II presents several possible views about equality's scope. Section III discusses the implications for equality's scope of different views about natural justice, including those of John Rawls and Robert Nozick. Section IV details the implications for intergenerational inequality of David Gauthier's contractarian approach. Section V indicates how the plausibility of certain features of common-sense morality may be relevant to the plausibility of different views regarding equality's scope. Section VI addresses Richard Epstein's argument regarding the conflict between *intra*generational and *inter*generational equity. Section VII discusses some practical implications regarding the moral desirability of transfers between the young and the old, as well as theoretical implications regarding the topics of transitivity and temporal neutrality. Finally, Section VIII summarizes and concludes the essay.

II. Different Possible Views about Equality's Scope

Does inequality matter equally between all people at all times? More particularly, if A is worse off than B through no fault of her own, does the extent to which the inequality between them is objectionable depend on whether they are contemporaries and/or members of the same society?

Many answers to this question are possible. Let us briefly consider a few of these answers. At one end of the spectrum, an egalitarian might maintain that the inequality between A and B only matters if they are contemporaries in the same society. At the other end of the spectrum, one might hold that the extent to which the inequality between A and B matters is completely independent of whether they are living at the same time or in the same society. It will be useful to give these positions mnemonic (though, alas, rather inelegant) names. We might say that on the first position, the value of equality is both Relativized to Time and Relativized to a Society; hence, let us call such a position *RTRS* egalitarianism. Correspondingly, we might say that on the second position the value of

ments of people's lives; and whether inequality is only bad when it makes someone worse off than she would otherwise be. The issues of scope discussed in this essay—whether inequality matters between people living in different societies or at different times—are largely distinct from these other issues. Correspondingly, most of the considerations presented here are different from, though compatible with, the considerations presented in *Inequality*.

equality is both Neutral across Time and Neutral across Societies; hence, let us call such a position *NTNS* egalitarianism.

One might hold that the inequality between A and B only matters if A and B are contemporaries, but that the extent to which it matters is completely independent of whether they are members of the same society. Let us call such a position *RTNS* egalitarianism, since the value of equality would be Relativized to Time, but Neutral across Societies. Conversely, one might hold that the inequality between A and B only matters if A and B are members of the same society, but that the extent to which it matters is independent of whether they are contemporaries. Let us call such a position *NTRS* egalitarianism, since the value of equality would be Neutral across Time, but Relativized to a Society.

Naturally, an egalitarian might hold any number of variations of, or compromises between, the foregoing positions. For example, one might simply hold that in comparing situations regarding inequality, weight needs to be given to each of the above positions (or at least to more than one). Alternatively, one might hold that different positions are more or less plausible regarding different kinds of inequality; for example, for certain kinds of natural inequalities, NTNS may seem plausible while RTRS may not, while the reverse may hold for certain kinds of social inequalities.

Other positions would hold that the extent to which A and B's inequality matters will be a matter of degree, rather than all or nothing, for one or both of the temporal and societal dimensions. Thus, an egalitarian might hold that inequality between A and B only matters if they are members of the same society, but matters to a greater or lesser degree depending on whether they are contemporaries, or depending on the extent to which they are separated in time. On such a view, inequality between an American and a Tanzanian would not matter, while inequality between two Americans would, with the inequality mattering most if the Americans were contemporaries, and increasingly less as there were more years between them. Alternatively, an egalitarian might hold that inequality between A and B only matters if they are contemporaries, but matters to a greater or lesser degree depending on the extent of the societal relations between them. On such a view, inequality between a twentieth-century American and a twenty-second-century American would not matter, while, assuming A were an American, the inequality between A and B would presumably matter less and less depending on whether B was, respectively, an American, a Briton, a Frenchman, a Chilean, or a New Guinea aborigine.[3] Naturally, a third alternative would be to regard inequality as a matter of degree along both dimensions. On such a view,

[3] Note that this view need not give any privileged position to any particular society or form of life. *Ceteris paribus*, the inequality between A and B would count just as much if both were Chilean as if both were American. The point is simply that the extent to which the inequality between people is bad would depend on the nature and extent of the societal relations between them.

the extent to which A and B's inequality matters would vary in accordance with the closeness of both their temporal and societal relations.

Each of the positions presented might be modified to reflect different attitudes toward time. Thus, for example, an egalitarian might be concerned about present inequalities, future inequalities, and inequalities between present and future generations, yet not be concerned, or be concerned to a lesser degree, about past inequalities, or inequalities between past generations and present or future ones. Such a "bias" toward the present and future is a common feature of many judgments made in moral and rational discourse, and might be incorporated into the egalitarian's position in a number of ways.[4]

I have sketched various answers that might be given to the question of whether inequality matters equally between all people at all times. I do not claim that each of the suggested answers is plausible, much less that each is equally plausible. Nor do I claim that the sketched answers are complete—no doubt there are many ways of modifying or filling them out—or that they are the only ones that might be given. Nevertheless, I hope to have given some sense of the wide range of possible answers to the question asked, and I am confident that no single answer would be accepted by all, or even most, egalitarians. Indeed, I suspect that not only will different answers seem plausible to different people, but that in many cases different answers will seem plausible, though perhaps to a greater or lesser degree, to the *same* people.

To give a greater idea of the complexity of the question at issue, let me discuss just a few of the important topics that may be relevant to it.

III. Equality's Scope and Questions about Natural Justice

One question philosophers differ about is the status of natural justice. Some believe there are only *social* injustices, no natural, or cosmic, ones. They believe that for there to be an *injustice*, there must be an agent, or perpetrator, of the injustice. On this view, claims about natural injustice are best understood as a vestige of theism. Others believe that there can be natural as well as social injustices. Sometimes the difference between these positions is mainly terminological, but the positions can be unpacked in various ways, so that in some cases there can be substantive differences both between, and within, the different positions.

For example, some believe it is a natural injustice that some are born blind while others are born sighted. In saying this, they are making a claim both about the kind of situation it is, and the sort of reasons it provides for acting. They recognize that even in cases where there is no per-

[4] An extremely interesting discussion of our attitudes and biases about time appears in Derek Parfit, *Reasons and Persons* (Oxford: Oxford University Press, 1984), Part 2; see esp. ch. 8.

petrator of an injustice, the situation can be such that if someone *had* deliberately brought it about she would have been perpetrating an injustice. In such cases they think considerations of justice give us reason to improve the situation *if we can*, though the fact that the situation is unjust does not depend on our being able to rectify it. On such a view, we can be responsible for improving or removing injustices that we are not responsible for creating. Moreover, the considerations of natural justice transcend societal bounds. Thus, on such a view, the natural injustice associated with blindness grounds a justice-based reason to benefit the blind in other societies as well as our own.

Someone like Rawls would deny the notion of natural injustice. For Rawls, the fact that some are born blind and others sighted is an "outcome of natural *chance*," an "*accident* . . . of natural endowment," a matter of "natural *fortune*"; it is *not* a matter of *injustice*.[5] Still, Rawls would agree that if the blind were among the worst off in our society, then it would be unjust for us to fail to improve their situation if it were in our power to do so.[6] Hence, the difference between Rawls's position and the preceding one is partly terminological, insofar as Rawls would deny that there could be an *injustice* where there is no perpetrator of the injustice, yet would agree that we could be criticized on grounds of justice for failing to improve a situation that we were not responsible for creating. Notice, however, that the difference between Rawls's position and the preceding one is not *only* terminological. On Rawls's theory, we can criticize a society's principles and institutions on grounds of justice for failing to maximize the expectations of the worst-off group *in that society*, but not for failing to maximize (or even improve) the expectations of the worst-off group in some *other* society. Thus, on a Rawlsian view, justice does not require us to benefit the blind in other societies, even if it requires us to benefit the blind in our own society (because they are among the worst off), and even if the blind in other societies are worse off than the blind in our society.[7]

It is perhaps worth emphasizing that here, and throughout this essay, my interest is in the substantive normative questions, not the terminolog-

[5] The quotations are from pages 12, 15, and 18, respectively, of John Rawls, *A Theory of Justice* (Cambridge: Harvard University Press, 1971), emphases added.

[6] Rawls writes: "The natural distribution is neither just nor unjust; nor is it unjust that persons are born into society at some particular position. These are simply natural facts. What is just and unjust is the way that institutions deal with these facts" (*A Theory of Justice*, p. 102).

[7] Strictly speaking, this is misleading. Although the theory Rawls presents in *A Theory of Justice* would not itself require us to aid the blind in other societies, Rawls acknowledges that his theory is not intended to capture the *whole* of our notion of justice. Thus, it is, I think, *compatible* with Rawls's position, that the full and complete theory of justice would support the sort of claim advocated by the position described in the previous paragraph. Still, for this essay's purposes the interesting point to note is how Rawls has provided a model for thinking about justice which would make a society responsible for both naturally and socially produced conditions within that society, without entailing a similar responsibility for naturally or socially produced conditions in other societies.

ical ones. Granting that for one to have a natural incapacity is a matter of chance, accident, or fortune, it is a terminological question whether we should also call a natural incapacity a natural *injustice*. The important normative question, however, is not what we *call* natural incapacities, but the nature of our obligations, if any, toward those with natural incapacities. People whose linguistic sensibilities differ regarding the notion of natural injustice, might nevertheless agree regarding their substantive moral views. Likewise, people whose linguistic sensibilities agree regarding the notion of natural injustice, might nevertheless differ regarding their substantive moral views.

Some go well beyond Rawls in their substantive opposition to the notion of natural injustice. For example, someone like Nozick might acknowledge that those born blind have been unlucky, that their misfortune is regrettable, and that it would be nice, good, or perhaps even desirable for us to act on their behalf, but Nozick would deny that we act wrongly or unjustly if we fail to do so.[8] On such a view, justice only requires us to rectify those misfortunes for which we are, in some relatively narrow and straightforward sense, directly and socially responsible.[9] So-called "victims of the natural lottery" may warrant our sympathy, and there are a variety of reasons we may have for helping them, but they have no claim on us regarding *justice*; and this is so whether or not they are members of our society.

Now I believe that there is an intimate connection between the notions of justice and equality. Indeed, as I have already indicated, I believe that the notion of equality is properly regarded as one aspect or element of the wider notion of justice. More particularly, I believe that at the core of the egalitarian's concern is the view that—at least in some cases—it is unfair or unjust for some to be worse off than others through no fault of their own.[10] If this is right, then while to some extent one's wider views about justice will be determined or influenced by one's views about equality,

[8] See Robert Nozick, *Anarchy, State, and Utopia* (New York: Basic Books, 1974). Nozick, of course, is not an egalitarian. Neither, for that matter, is Rawls (see pp. 8, 31–33, and 245–48 of my *Inequality* for reasons supporting this claim). It is still worth considering their positions, however—not merely because they have been so influential, but because one might share their views regarding natural justice and still believe equality is one ideal, among others, that should be given some weight. The point of my remarks is to illustrate how certain views regarding equality's scope may seem more or less plausible depending on one's views regarding natural justice (and vice versa).

[9] It is not easy to spell out the criteria we would use to identify the misfortunes for which we are, in the relevant sense, responsible. But I take it the issue is not merely one of unavoidability or *some* social role in the causal nexus. That is, on the view in question, I take it there might be cases where we are not required to ameliorate the effects of some "natural" misfortune, even if that misfortune was socially preventable. For example, even if society could develop and distribute a vaccine which would prevent natural blindness, there might be no *requirement* regarding *justice* that it either do so or improve the lot of those born blind.

[10] Unfortunately, as I note in *Inequality*, "it is one matter to note that egalitarians have such a view, and quite another to unpack what it involves" (p. 13). Some of the complexities involved in the egalitarian's view were discussed in my article "Inequality," *Philosophy and Public Affairs*, vol. 15, no. 2 (Spring 1986), pp. 99–121, as well as in my book *Inequality*.

the reverse will also hold. Correspondingly, one's views about inequality's scope—that is, about the cases where inequality is objectionable—may certainly be influenced, if not strictly determined, by one's other views regarding justice, including, of course, one's views about natural justice.

Consider that most people believe it is a matter of luck, a cosmic accident of Fate, as it were, that any particular individual is born in a particular place and at a particular time. Colloquially, this might be expressed in any number of ways, for example, that "LT is lucky to have been born in the twentieth century rather than during the Dark Ages," or that "LT is lucky to have been born in the United States, rather than Chad," or, more specifically, that "LT is lucky to have been born a Northern white in the 1950s rather than a Southern black in the 1830s." Such thoughts needn't be grounded in the view that LT might *in fact* have been born in a (substantially) different time and place; they might, for example, be grounded in the recognition that it is a matter of (extraordinary) luck that any *particular* person—say, LT—is born at all. But, of course, the circumstances—including the time and place—of one's birth can play a large role in the quality of one's life. Correspondingly, insofar as such circumstances appear to be a matter of luck (of natural good or bad fortune), inequalities resulting from such circumstances may or may not seem objectionable, depending on one's views about natural justice.

Those who share a Nozickian view about natural justice may not only be unconcerned about "natural" inequalities within societies—say, between the blind and the sighted—they may be unconcerned about the "natural" inequalities between rich and poor countries, or between present generations and past or future ones. For such people, who (unlike Nozick himself, perhaps) may still care about social inequalities,[11] a version of RTRS egalitarianism may seem plausible, but a position like NTNS egalitarianism may not. On the other hand, those who share a Rawlsian view about natural justice may be concerned about "natural" inequalities within societies, but not between societies. They may be attracted to some version of NTRS egalitarianism. And, of course, those who believe that there are natural injustices, and that there is reason to alleviate these wherever and whenever they occur, may well find themselves most attracted to some version of NTNS egalitarianism.[12]

[11] In my experience, there are many who are principally concerned with social, rather than natural, inequalities. For example, they will strongly object to institutions that discriminate against the handicapped, but will not feel an obligation to remedy natural handicaps. Or they will find vast inequalities between athletes and ditch diggers unjust, and strongly objectionable, in a way that they do not regard similarly large inequalities between the healthy and the congenitally ill. (Of course, some hold the reverse view, objecting to some natural inequalities, but not to so-called "market" produced inequalities, like those between athletes and ditch diggers.)

[12] Some worry that NTNS egalitarianism has the counterintuitive implication that it is better not to want one's descendants to be better off than one's own generation, all other

Let me stress that I am not claiming any *necessary* connection, or one-to-one correlation, between one's views about natural justice and one's views about the proper scope of equality. There are various views one might take about natural justice,[13] and each of these is compatible with a number of different views regarding equality's scope. The issues in question are not wholly independent, however. Questions about natural justice and equality's proper scope cannot be settled in isolation, since many complexities and factors relevant to the former will also be relevant to the latter, and vice versa.

IV. Equality's Scope on Gauthier's Contractarian Approach

Another position with implications regarding equality's scope is the kind presented by David Gauthier in *Morals by Agreement*.[14] Gauthier has presented a kind of contractarian or social-convention theory. Roughly, on his view, morality in general, and justice in particular, are composed of the impartial constraints it would be rational for mutually unconcerned agents to accept on the maximization of their individual utilities so that they may reap the benefits of cooperation. As Gauthier acknowledges, on his view "animals, the unborn, the congenitally handicapped and defective, fall beyond the pale of a morality tied to mutuality. The disposition to comply with moral constraints . . . may be rationally defended only within the scope of expected benefit."[15] The question is whether rela-

moral factors considered. But this does not follow. First, there is nothing wrong with *wanting* an outcome that might not be best from an impersonal perspective. For example, I might want to win the lottery, even if I knew a better outcome would result if it were won by a needy family, or a deserving charity. Second, and more importantly, as indicated above, I believe the egalitarian's core belief is that it is unfair or unjust for some to be worse off than others *through no fault of their own*. It is *undeserved* or *nonvoluntary* inequalities that are morally objectionable. Thus, if we *want* our children or descendants to fare better than us, and voluntarily take steps to bring this about, there need be no objection to the resulting inequality, even on NTNS egalitarianism. For more discussion of the "no fault" clause, see Section 1.2 of my *Inequality*.

[13] The ones suggested above are merely illustrative. No doubt there are many ways the views presented could (or might need to) be revised or filled out, as well as other views that might be advocated.

[14] David Gauthier, *Morals by Agreement* (Oxford: Oxford University Press, 1986). Note that, like Nozick and Rawls, Gauthier is not an egalitarian. Indeed, on page 270 of his book Gauthier explicitly acknowledges that "[e]quality is not a fundamental concern of our theory." Still, Gauthier has offered an important and influential theory. Moreover, I think one might be attracted to the *sort* of contractarian position Gauthier has offered, and still (want to?) be an egalitarian. Correspondingly, it is worth considering the connections, if any, between a theory like Gauthier's and inequality's scope.

[15] Gauthier, *Morals by Agreement*, p. 268. Note that, for Gauthier, morality is tied to *mutuality* in the sense that "moral constraints aris[e] . . . from what are . . . conditions of mutual advantage" (p. 268) among mutually unconcerned agents. Roughly, among purely self-interested agents, there will be certain moral constraints it will be to each of their advantages to adopt, so as to best promote their individual goals. That is, it is to their mutual advantage, as rational mutually unconcerned (self-interested) agents, to accept certain moral constraints.

tions between different generations—including but not limited to relations of inequality—also lie beyond the scope of Gauthier's theory, since "co-operation is possible only among contemporaries who actually interact."[16]

Gauthier believes his theory can accommodate the intuitive view that relations between non-overlapping generations are subject to the constraints of morality and justice. His argument for this is worth quoting in some detail. He writes:

> The generations of humankind do not march on and off the stage of life in a body. . . . Each person interacts with others both older and younger than himself. . . . Mutually beneficial co-operation directly involves persons of different but overlapping generations, but this creates indirect co-operative links extending throughout history. Each person, in considering the terms on which he is to co-operate with those in an earlier generation than himself, must keep in mind his need to establish similar terms with those of a later generation, who in turn must keep in mind their need to co-operate with members of a yet later generation, and so on. Thus, although each individual might be prepared to agree with his contemporaries that they should exhaust the world's resources without thought for those yet to be born, the need to continue any agreement as time passes, to extend it to those who are born as it ceases for those who die, ensures that, among rational persons, the terms must remain constant, so that exhaustion of the world's resources does not present itself as an option. No matter when one lives, one should expect the same relative benefits from interaction with one's fellows as were enjoyed by one's predecessors and as will be enjoyed in turn by one's successors. (p. 299)

Later, Gauthier concludes his discussion regarding intergenerational relations as follows:

> Our theory, equalizing relative rather than absolute benefits, requires progress without ignoring the claims of present persons. Viewing society as a bargain in which the terms remain constant over time,

[16] *Ibid.*, p. 298. Playing the devil's advocate, Gauthier adds the following:

> Although an individual can do much to benefit or harm his descendants, only those whose lives overlap with his can benefit or harm him in return. . . . [Hence, i]n maximizing his utility without regard for future generations whose lives will not overlap with his own, he runs no risk of obtaining a sub-optimal outcome. Any constraint he might accept would result in a simple transfer of utilities from himself to future persons; it could not lead to mutual benefits. . . . So an individual does his descendants no injustice in not concerning himself with them. If the world is not left a fit place for their habitation, much less their well-being, this merely characterizes the circumstances in which they find themselves; their rights are not affected.

> so that each generation offers its successor the same agreement that it accepted from its predecessor, we are able to give a clear account of justice between generations. (p. 305)

Unfortunately, I am less sure than Gauthier about the clarity (not to mention plausibility) of his account. Hence, before considering the implications of his position for intergenerational inequalities, let us consider how one might interpret it. To do this, it will be useful to begin with an example. For simplicity, the example assumes a fixed amount of natural resources available to the world's people. It also assumes generations of equal size, and a direct and constant correlation between quality of life and resources consumed. These simplifying assumptions ignore many of the most important factors that are in fact relevant to questions about intergenerational division of resources—such as the renewability or discovery of resources, variable generational sizes, changes in individual and social welfare functions, and scientific and technological advances that might significantly alter the usefulness and availability of natural resources. But although, in the real world, such factors are crucially important for determining a just and rational rate of savings, they introduce a host of complications that can be avoided for our present purposes. The aim of my example is to illuminate Gauthier's theory, so as to consider its theoretical implications regarding inequality's scope. My simplifying assumptions enable me to do this in a relatively clear and straightforward way, a way that is not prejudicial to Gauthier's theory. My example does not reveal how we or other generations should in fact answer the difficult questions concerning resource consumption.[17]

Suppose, for the sake of argument, that we divide the world's population into four generations: 1, 2, 3, and 4, including all those whose ages are, respectively, over 75, 50 to 75, 25 to 50, and under 25. For simplicity, suppose further that the world's resources are in the control of generations 1, 2, and 3. Together, the mutually unconcerned members of the different generations agree that they would benefit from cooperation; to secure the desired cooperation, generations 1 through 3 agree to share the world's resources not only with each other, but with generation 4. More particularly, it is agreed that the world's resources will be divided equally among all the existing generations.[18] Twenty-five years later, generation 1

[17] For a fascinating, though hardly neutral, account of the conflict regarding resource consumption between "doomsters"—like the ecologist Paul Ehrlich—and "boomsters"—like the economist Julian Simon—see John Tierney, "Betting the Planet," *New York Times Magazine*, December 2, 1990.

[18] Recall that Gauthier explicitly acknowledges that "each individual might be prepared to agree with his contemporaries that they should exhaust the world's resources without thought for those yet to be born" (p. 299). For Gauthier, everything is up for grabs, in the sense that it is only rational for me to constrain my behavior when it is "within the scope of expected benefit" (p. 268). That is, I and my contemporaries have reason to negotiate consumption of the world's resources, as long as it is in our mutual interests to do so.

has passed away, having consumed one fourth of the world's resources. By then, generation 5 has come on the scene. Naturally, generation 5 is unwilling to cooperate with generations 2 through 4, unless its members, too, receive a fair share of the world's resources. Recognizing the reasonableness of their demands, generations 2 through 4 extend to generation 5 the same terms that were originally agreed upon and extended to them, to wit, all of the world's existing resources will be divided equally among all the existing generations. Twenty-five years later, generation 2 has passed away, having consumed three sixteenths of the world's original resources—one sixteenth less than that consumed by generation 1. By then, generation 6 has come on the scene. To secure their cooperation the terms of the agreement are extended to them, and so on.

Does the foregoing exemplify a just agreement between generations on Gauthier's account? First, there is a sense in which the terms of the agreement "remain constant over time, so that each generation offers its successor the same agreement that it accepted from its predecessor." Second, there is also a sense in which "no matter when one lives, one . . . [can] expect the same relative benefits from interaction with one's fellows as were enjoyed by one's predecessors and as will be enjoyed in turn by one's successors." More specifically, the foregoing agreement equalizes relative, though not absolute, benefits in the sense that it ensures that, for each generation, the benefits of cooperation with overlapping generations are an equal share—in the example, one fourth—of all the resources available to later generations at the time of passing of the preceding generation. To be sure, there is a literal sense in which, contra Gauthier, the agreement appears to regard "exhaustion of the world's resources" as an option; however, in the spirit of Gauthier's remarks, the way in which the agreement would continually be extended "to those who are born as it ceases for those who die" ensures that the option is never realized. In sum, in many respects the foregoing example would appear to meet Gauthier's criteria for a just agreement between generations.

I suspect that few would regard the suggested agreement as just. Calculation reveals that by the time generation 4 has passed from the scene they will have consumed less than half (42 percent) of the resources consumed by generation 1, while by the time generation 10 has passed from the scene, 250 years later, they will have consumed less than one thirteenth (8 percent) of the resources consumed by the first generation. Surely, many would object to the claim that, other things equal, a just agreement would permit one generation to consume 25 percent of the world's available resources, twice that of an overlapping[19] generation, and thirteen times that of a non-overlapping generation only 250 years in the future.

[19] A and B are *overlapping* generations if there is a time when at least some members of both A and B are alive.

Gauthier might be among the objectors. He might argue that despite misleading appearances to the contrary, the foregoing example does *not* accurately reflect his position. Specifically, it fails to take account of a crucial step in his argument, namely, that "each person, in considering the terms on which he is to cooperate with those in an earlier generation than himself, must keep in mind his need to establish similar terms with those of a later generation, who in turn must keep in mind their need to cooperate with members of a yet later generation, and so on." The idea is that, as rational bargainers, the members of generations 2, 3, and 4 will recognize their future need to reach an agreement with generations 5, 6, and 7; hence, they will be unwilling to bargain with generation 1 as if the world's resources and the fruits of cooperation only need to be divided four ways. Nor would it be rational for them to bargain as if the world's resources only need to be divided seven ways, since they know that, as rational bargainers, the members of generations 5, 6, and 7 will be taking account of *their* future need to reach an agreement with generations 8, 9, and 10, when they bargain with generations 2, 3, and 4—and that that later agreement will, in turn, be influenced by the future need of generations 8, 9, and 10 to reach an agreement with generations 11, 12, and 13, and so on. The upshot of all this is that there will be a leveling pressure extending backwards from future generations to the present. Indeed, if one assumed that among mutually unconcerned rational individuals there would be no incentive to grant a greater share of the world's resources to an immediately preceding or succeeding generation, then the pressure would be to reach an agreement according each generation an *equal* share of the world's resources. Hence, if there were going to be *n* generations, each would receive one *n*th of the world's resources.

Does Gauthier's view, then, have the surprising result of actually supporting equality of resources between generations? No. For Gauthier, it is rational for one generation to share the resources over which it has control only insofar as the benefits of cooperation thereby induced outweigh the attendant loss in the use of such resources. In the example presented earlier, it will no doubt be in the interests of generation 1 to share its resources with generations 2 and 3, who have resources of their own to throw into the communal pot. It may even be in their interests, as the example supposes, for generation 1 to share its resources with generation 4. This may serve the dual role of both directly securing the cooperation of generation 4, and helping to secure the cooperation of generations 2 and 3, who stand to gain more from the ongoing cooperation of generation 4 than generation 1 itself does. Nevertheless, it is hardly likely to be in the interests of generation 1 to secure the cooperation of generations 2, 3, and 4 if doing so would require them to forsake the vast majority of the resources over which they have control. Yet this is precisely what might be called for if the terms of agreement called for anything like an equal sharing of resources among all generations.

Suppose, for example, that generation 1 controlled one third of the world's resources, and that there was reason to believe that human history would continue another twenty-five hundred years (that is, one hundred more generations). Surely the members of generation 1 would be better off in terms of the quality of their lives if they were to reach *no* agreement with generations 2, 3, and 4, than they would be if they were to agree to share their resources equally with the hundred generations yet to come. In the former case the members of generation 1 could consume a full third of the world's resources, in the latter only one one-hundredth. This would amount to forsaking almost 97 percent of the resources over which they have control, so as to secure the cooperation of generations 2, 3, and 4. It is hard to believe such a trade-off would be worth it (in self-interested terms)—especially if one bears in mind that the members of generation 1 could still benefit from cooperation with *each other*—which might mean being able to cooperate with approximately one quarter of the world's population.

It appears, then, that for Gauthier the pressures to reach an agreement equalizing resources over future generations will be strongly counteracted, indeed overridden, by the disincentive of any generation to share resources over which it has control beyond the point at which there is a payoff in doing so (in terms of the benefits of cooperation with other generations). Thus, on Gauthier's account, one would expect agreements between generations to countenance the use and consumption of resources in accordance with what would maximize the expected benefits of cooperation between generations while at the same time being in proportion to the amount of control each generation has over those resources.

The preceding considerations suggest the following. On a view like Gauthier's, the extent to which intergenerational inequalities matter will depend on the exact nature of the agreement initially formed between overlapping generations and extended forward from generation to generation. A detailed account of the former must therefore await a detailed account of the latter. Still, the general features of an account of intergenerational inequalities seem apparent. First, it seems unlikely that equality will never matter: at least between overlapping generations, certain inequalities will be objectionable. Second, it is very unlikely that equality's value will be neutral between generations; that is, the extent to which inequality between two generations matters will depend, in part, on their temporal proximity. Specifically, the agreement between generations is likely to be such that inequalities which might be highly objectionable between temporally "close" generations, might not matter at all, or would matter much less, between temporally "distant" generations. Indeed, I suspect the drop-off rate will be fairly steep. Thus, even if there is always *some* disvalue to certain inequalities between two generations, inequality which would be highly objectionable if the generations were overlapping might be much less so if they were even a few generations apart.

I have been arguing that on a view like Gauthier's the value of equality will be a matter of degree, at least along the temporal dimension. In doing this, I have focused—as Gauthier himself largely does—on the relations between present and future generations. Let me next observe that my conclusion may need to be revised for cases involving past generations.

In reading Gauthier, it is easy to suppose that the principles and concerns of justice must remain constant over time, since the terms of the bargain giving rise to those principles and concerns are themselves to "remain constant over time, so that each generation offers its successor the same agreement that it accepted from its predecessor." From this it may also seem to follow that the principles and concerns of justice will be symmetrical with respect to how the past and the future stand to the present. Such a view fits well with Gauthier's observation that "each person interacts with others both older and younger than himself, and enters thereby into a continuous thread of interaction extending from the most remote human past to the farthest future of our kind . . . creat[ing] indirect co-operative links extending throughout history" (p. 299).

Nevertheless, as I interpret Gauthier and the logic of his argument, his view is an essentially forward-looking one. It expresses what I referred to earlier as a "bias" toward the present and future. For Gauthier, the reason contemporaries cannot simply agree to consume the world's resources without regard for future generations is that they recognize that there will be a "need to continue any agreement as time passes." Note, however, that the passage of time (or at least our understanding of it) is asymmetrical.[20] As time passes, the future "moves" into the present, and the present into the past. The past does not "move" into the present, nor does the present "move" into the future. Hence, the *reason* contemporaries have for concerning themselves with future generations will not apply regarding past generations.

The foregoing may seem obscure, depending on an elusive, if not illusive, metaphysical premise; but the central point is not particularly mysterious. From the standpoint of mutually unconcerned rational individuals, there would appear to be no need to cooperate with, and hence no reason to be concerned about, members of an earlier generation which is *past*. Our reasons (and indeed our ability) to cooperate with earlier generations end when those generations die off. There are, of course, various affections and emotions we may have which would lead us to *want* to consider the interests of past generations—that is, we may not, in fact, be mutually

[20] Unfortunately, I must leave aside the many issues associated with the interesting and deep question of how best to understand the phenomenon of time's passage. Those whose metaphysical views challenge the "standard" view about time's passage—who think, perhaps, that time's passage is an illusion—may want to revise or reject the following argument.

unconcerned rational individuals. Similarly, there are various ways our agreements with past individuals may have limited our options, or otherwise bound our actions, such that we cannot help but act in the interests of past generations. The key point, however, is that for Gauthier we do not have reason to concern ourselves with those who were once alive, but are now dead, the way we do for those who are not alive now, but will be later.

Though not alive now, future generations will one day be in a position to cooperate, and hence bargain, with other intermediate generations. The terms of such bargains will ultimately affect the terms of the bargain that the present generation is able to reach with the succeeding generation. Hence, it is against the interests of one generation to ignore the interests and bargaining position of future generations in considering the terms on which it is to cooperate with an earlier generation. However, unlike future generations, past generations will not be in a position to cooperate, and hence bargain, with intermediate generations. To be sure, they once were in such a position; but they no longer are, nor will they ever be again. Whatever they may have had to offer other generations to secure their cooperation has already been offered. Whatever they had to give to the communal pot has already been given. In a sense, past generations are like "animals, the unborn, the congenitally handicapped and defective, [which] fall beyond the pale of a morality tied to mutuality" (p. 268). Since they are *past* generations, there is nothing they can (or will be able to) do either for us or for intermediate generations, and hence there is nothing with which they have to bargain. From this it follows that for Gauthier there is no moral reason to concern oneself with the interests of past generations, since, as noted earlier, on his view "the disposition to comply with moral constraints . . . may be rationally defended only within the scope of expected benefit."[21]

I think Gauthier himself recognizes and accepts the position for which I have been arguing. Recall his observation regarding "the need to continue any agreement as time passes, to extend it to those who are born *as it ceases for those who die*" (p. 299, emphasis added). I take it that if the agreement from which the constraints of morality and justice are derived ceases, so do the constraints.

If my interpretation of Gauthier's view is correct, the principles and concerns of justice will be asymmetrical in their treatment of different generations. Specifically, the scope of those principles will be limited to present and future generations; past generations will fall beyond their

[21] Gauthier, *Morals by Agreement*, p. 268. Put crudely, one might say that the difference between future and past generations is like the difference between someone who will come into a great deal of money in later years, and someone who once had a lot of money but is now bankrupt and will remain so. A self-interested merchant (like the present generation?) has reason to interest the former in his wares, and to try to strike a deal with him, but not the latter.

pale. Thus, on a view like Gauthier's, inequality between two generations will not matter if one of those generations is a past generation. Moreover, this is so even if the inequality could be reduced or removed. (Note that it is always possible to reduce inequality between a past generation and a present or future generation by improving or worsening the situation of the present or future generation. In addition, it *may* be possible to reduce inequality between a past generation and another generation by improving or worsening the situation of the *past* generation, *if* one accepts a preference-satisfaction theory according to which someone could be made better or worse off even after they are dead by the satisfaction or frustration of certain of their future-directed or temporally neutral preferences.) Regarding inequalities between present or future generations, our earlier conclusion stands. On a view like Gauthier's, at least some such inequalities will be objectionable, though the extent to which this is so will be a matter of degree depending on the temporal proximity of the generations in question.[22]

[22] I have been pointing out some of the implications of a view like Gauthier's for equality's scope. I have not been assessing the plausibility of such a view. However, let me observe the following. As noted above, Gauthier has a way of responding to the charge that on his view present generations could exhaust the world's resources without regard to future generations. But his position depends, I think, on the premise that there *will* be future generations whose interests need to be considered. It seems to me that on Gauthier's view present overlapping generations *could* agree to divide up the world's resources between, say, the next eight generations, as long as they took steps to ensure that there would not *be* a ninth generation. Perhaps they might be able to set some kind of ecological or genetic timebomb which would accomplish their end.

One might respond by arguing that such a move would be blocked by the interests the eighth generation would have in having a ninth generation with whom to cooperate, but I doubt such a response will work. First, it seems to me that for Gauthier members of the present overlapping generations only need to worry about the interests of the eighth generation insofar as those interests may ultimately affect the bargains available to present generations through their effect on the bargaining of intermediate generations. But as rational agents the members of each generation must play the hand they are dealt. They must bargain based on the options available to them. If having a ninth generation is not an option for the eighth generation, it is unclear that this would, or even could, have an overridingly adverse affect on the agreements available to the present overlapping generations. Second, as mutually unconcerned individuals, members of the eighth generation might actually be better off with an agreement extending to them the right to consume one eighth of the world's resources but depriving them of the opportunity of cooperating with future generations, than they would be under an agreement giving them an opportunity to cooperate with future generations, but at the cost of their having to share the world's resources with many generations to come. Third, for the reasons described by Parfit in *Reasons and Persons*, ch. 16, pp. 351–80, it may be that from the standpoint of mutually unconcerned individuals, members of the eighth generation would wholeheartedly *approve* of the agreement in question, because *they* would not be alive if an alternative agreement had been adopted involving the continuance of the human race beyond eight generations. *Others* would constitute the eighth generation on an alternative agreement, not *they*. Thus, it might be that every person who would ever live would approve of the agreement that would end the human race after eight generations and divide up the world's resources between them.

As I interpret Gauthier's view, there would be nothing morally objectionable about such an agreement. I find such a position untenable, and think it indicates an important area where Gauthier's view needs to be revised or supplemented, if not rejected.

V. Equality's Scope and Features of Common-Sense Morality

I have explored in some detail possible connections between certain general views about justice and morality and certain particular views about equality's scope. As the reader has no doubt surmised, many other positions or factors might also be relevant to our topic. Due to time and space limitations, let me just mention, and comment on, a few of these.

There is little question that common sense permits, and perhaps even requires, differential treatment of "identifiable" people from "statistical" people. An entire nation, or even an entire world, can get caught up in efforts to prevent the imminent death of some sailors lost at sea or a little girl trapped underground (not to mention some whales trapped by an ice floe) while remaining largely, if not wholly, unmoved by the knowledge that a greater number of statistically predictable lives could be saved if the same resources were spent on improving a dangerous intersection, reducing toxic emissions, or making a vaccine more widely available. Dramatic rescues obviously capture our imagination in a way that mundane safety precautions do not; for many, they seem to represent what is most good and noble about the human spirit. To many, it seems proper, fitting, even *right* that resources are spent on dramatic rescues to save certain *identifiable* lives even though they might be spent more *effectively*—in terms of the number of *statistical* lives saved—in other ways.[23]

Similarly, common sense seems to frequently permit, perhaps even require, differential treatment between "actual" people and "possible" people.[24] For example, common-sense morality seems to permit parents to take certain risks and make certain choices that might have adverse effects on their future possible children which it would not permit them to do (or at least not as readily permit them to do) if their children were already alive. It seems, for instance, that on common-sense morality it is less objectionable for me to move to a war-torn country for the sake of

[23] I do not mean to suggest that the *only* factor influencing people's judgments about such cases is the factor of "identifiable" versus "statistical" lives. As suggested, I think there is something especially appealing about the dramatic nature of the high-cost rescue missions. Thus, I think many would approve of dramatic rescues of identifiable people even when the money could be used in perfectly ordinary ways to save the lives of other *identifiable* people, say, John, Mary, and Tim in the burn ward at St. Mary's Hospital. The issue of "identifiable" lives versus "statistical" lives is *one* factor that seems to play a role in people's thinking about certain cases; it need not be the only one, or even the most important.

[24] It is not uncommon for discussions to blur together, or perhaps even treat as synonymous, the issues of "identifiable" versus "statistical" lives and "actual" versus "possible" lives; and there are, I think, important connections and similarities between them. But they are not the same issue. A possible person may be identifiable. For instance, with in vitro fertilization, we may know the particular sperm and ovum from which a possible person will develop, and her parents may have already given *her* a name! By the same token, statistical lives are frequently actual lives. The ten statistical people who will die this year if we do not alter a certain intersection may all be living, breathing, *actual* people, we just do not yet know who they are. The fact that we cannot identify them in advance of their deaths does not make them merely possible people (though their deaths, of course, are merely possible until they occur).

some cause—fully expecting the conditions in the country to persist for the foreseeable future and also fully expecting to have and raise a family there—than it would be for me to move to the war-torn country on the same grounds *with* my children. Analogously, it seems that on common-sense morality it would be less objectionable for me to work at a job imposing some risk of radiation damage on my possible future children than it would be for me to bring radioactive material into my home, exposing my actual children to the same level of risk of radiation damage. Similarly, although common-sense morality clearly condemns the wanton disregard of future generations which is all too frequently exhibited in both the public and the private spheres, it appears to permit members of the present generation to impose costs, burdens, and risks on future generations which it would condemn (or at least more seriously criticize) were they imposed on other members of the present generation—for example, large budget deficits, unfunded social-security obligations, burial of nuclear waste, depletion of natural resources, long-term environmental threats, and failure to adequately maintain the infrastructure or make capital improvements for the future.

Another well-known feature of common-sense morality is that it permits, and often requires, preferential treatment of family and friends. More generally, common-sense morality holds that the extent of one person's obligations toward another is partly determined by such factors as the nature, degree, and "closeness" of the relations between them, as well as their social and institutional roles.

The foregoing observations are commonplace. They also raise, as the reader is no doubt aware, a host of deep, important, and complex issues which lie at the core of the nature of morality, and with which much of contemporary moral philosophy has been concerned. Is common-sense morality simply mistaken in the judgments it makes? Does it generally yield the "right" answer, but for wrong or misleading reasons? What sort of principles, if any, would support the intuitive judgments common-sense morality makes? What sort of picture of morality would support, condemn, or best explain the apparent dictates of common sense? Should we accept an agent-neutral or consequentialist morality, an agent-relative or deontological morality, or some other morality entirely? Or is there something importantly right about a number of moral views which support and condemn, in varying degrees, the various judgments of common sense?

I raise these questions not to answer them, nor to rehash much of the contemporary debate in moral philosophy. I raise them because I think the complex and difficult issues relevant to answering them will also be relevant, though not necessarily in any obvious, straightforward, or determinate way, to the issue of inequality's scope (and vice versa).

Suppose we think, in the end, that common sense is right in granting special weight to special relationships. Our reasons for thinking this *might* support a view like RTRS egalitarianism, or, more likely, a view making the value of inequality a matter of degree both within society and between societies, as well as, perhaps, across time. Perhaps we should be more concerned about inequalities involving those with whom we have special relations. Perhaps membership in the same society is but one special relation to consider, and a relation which may or may not be a particularly important one, at that.

Similarly, suppose we think, in the end, that common sense is right in putting more emphasis on actual people than possible people. Our reasons for thinking this may support the value of equality being relativized to time, or perhaps being a matter of degree across time.

Analogously, if we think common sense is right to be more concerned about "identifiable" people than "statistical" people, this may be relevant regarding which inequalities we should be most concerned to alleviate along both the societal and temporal dimensions. It may, for instance, help explain the appeal of (without necessarily justifying) a view like RTRS egalitarianism. After all, some programs for reducing inequality—e.g., certain food programs—would target "identifiable" people for aid; other programs—e.g., certain educational programs—would aid a number of "statistical" people; and in general, for both practical and theoretical reasons, programs of the first sort are more likely to be available and effective within a society at a given time than between societies or across time.

Naturally, if we think common sense is wrong in some or all of the respects we have been discussing, our reasons for thinking this may also be relevant to our views regarding inequality's scope. Thus, for example, if one believes that, *ceteris paribus,* there is no reason to treat "identifiable" lives differently from "statistical" lives, or actual lives differently from possible lives, or mom differently from a stranger, I suspect one's (agent-neutral) reasons for believing this would also support a view like NTNS egalitarianism.[25]

Finally, let me note a further factor related to some of the foregoing remarks. Specifically, let me suggest that reflection on the nature of society itself, together with certain views about why social inequalities should be particularly objectionable, may be relevant to inequality's scope.

It is a platitude to note that early societies shared a multitude of bonds and special relationships. Membership in such societies frequently involved a common history, language, religion, race, commerce, culture, politics, and so on. In early tribal societies it may also have involved bonds of extended kinship, along with a shared set of communal hopes, goals, and aspirations. Given certain features of common-sense morality noted above, it readily follows that members of early societies might have

[25] Unless, of course, they ruled out egalitarianism completely, which *some* such reasons may do, but certainly not all.

had a number of special duties and obligations toward one another, including, perhaps, special obligations to reduce or remove inequalities within their society. More particularly, one can see how, given certain features of common-sense morality, the nature of early societies might have given rise to the common-sense view, still strongly and widely held, that inequality matters within societies but not between societies, or at least that the former matters much more than the latter.

But the bonds and special relationships that united members of early societies have considerably loosened in modern societies. It is not necessarily that they no longer hold, but that they often hold to a lesser degree. Moreover, even where they retain their original force, they frequently span across societies, connecting certain members of different societies rather than all of the members of one society. It is, of course, a commonplace to observe that modern societies are more heterogeneous than their earlier counterparts. However, it is important to bear in mind what it means for a society to include many who do not share a common history, language, religion, race, commerce, culture, politics, and so on. For example, many Chinese, Mexican, and Polish Americans may share significant cultural bonds with members of their native lands that they lack with each other, or with other Americans. Similarly, American Catholics, Jews, and Muslims may share significant religious bonds with members of their faith in other lands, bonds that they lack with other Americans; and American bankers, oilmen, and manufacturers may have significant commercial bonds with their counterparts elsewhere that they lack with many of their own countrymen.

The point of the foregoing is not to minimize the powerful effects of assimilation. Americans share many bonds, and no doubt most have more in common with most other Americans than with most non-Americans. Still, most Americans will share significant bonds and special relationships with certain non-Americans, and often those bonds will be stronger and more important than those they share with some Americans.

The preceding suggests the following. On certain tenets of common-sense morality, inequality may be more or less objectionable depending on the nature of the bonds and relationships between whom the inequality obtains. Thus, it is important to recognize that the bonds and special relationships obtaining among the members of a society no longer hold in the same way as they once did. Correspondingly, the view that inequality only matters, or matters much more, within societies, but not between them, is no longer as plausible as it once was. To be sure, in general inequality may matter more within societies than between them, and in general inequality may matter more between some societies than others depending on how closely related the societies are; but differences here would be a matter of degree, and there may be no hard and fast rules of dominance or priority. Depending on the exact nature of the relevant bonds and relationships, inequality between certain members of different societies may matter more than comparable inequality between certain members of the same society. Similarly, inequality between certain members of "largely unrelated" societies might matter more than comparable inequality between certain members of "closely related" societies. In sum, certain reasons why people may have thought inequality matters more within societies than between societies may, given the nature of modern societies, support inequality's value being a matter of degree both within societies and between societies, as well as, perhaps, across time.

VI. Epstein's View and the Conflict between Intragenerational and Intergenerational Equity

I have considered a number of factors that may be relevant to whether inequality matters equally between all people and all times. In this section, I would like to take up an interesting claim Richard Epstein makes in his essay "Justice across the Generations."[26] Specifically, let me comment on Section II of Epstein's essay, "The Family and the Future."

In his introduction, Epstein contends that:

> (1) Taxation and regulatory policies that are designed to secure equality of wealth in the next generation do so at the cost of reducing the levels of capital accumulation, so that intragenerational equity (if compelling at all) is at odds with intergenerational equity. (p. 86)

The argument for (1) is supposed to be contained in Section II, but what Epstein actually argues for in Section II is the following "moral":

> (2) [W]here the freedom of the present generation to make unfettered dispositions is crimped, the alterations in its consumption patterns will reduce the total stock of wealth available in the future. . . . The effort to redistribute wealth within the second generation reduces the amount of wealth passed on to that generation. We cannot have it both ways. (p. 91)

Now (2) is an interesting claim. It may even be plausible, for many of the reasons Epstein presents. Still, while (2) supports the first clause of (1), it does not necessarily support the second ("so that") clause. More generally, and more importantly for my purposes, from an egalitarian perspective (2) is largely (though not wholly) beside the point.

[26] Richard Epstein, "Justice across the Generations," in *Justice between Age Groups and Generations*, Philosophy, Politics, and Society, 6th series, ed. Peter Laslett and James Fishkin (New Haven: Yale University Press, 1992), pp. 84–106.

Suppose we grant Epstein's conclusion, that greater equality in the future can only come at the cost of a reduction in "the total stock of wealth available in the future." Such a conclusion would be important, but hardly startling. Similar conclusions are frequently argued for regarding the present: for example, that one could only create equality within our society by significantly reducing the quality of life of those who are best off, in ways that would have a deleterious effect on the total amounts of both wealth and utility in our society. Among other things, such conclusions remind one that utility and equality are separate ideals and, more particularly, that utilitarian considerations may (and often do) conflict with egalitarian ones; but such conclusions do *not* show which, if either, of the ideals is more important, much less that one of the ideals must be entirely rejected in favor of the other. Thus, even if Epstein is right that "the effort to redistribute wealth within the second generation reduces the amount of wealth passed on to that generation," and hence right to believe that there are reasons – e.g., utilitarian ones – to oppose such redistribution, there may *also* be reasons to favor such redistribution – e.g., egalitarian ones. Naturally, whether one should ultimately oppose or favor such redistribution *all things considered* will depend on the actual extent of the gains and losses with respect to the relevant (conflicting) ideals, as well as the comparative importance of those ideals. But nothing Epstein says in Section II is telling, or even particularly illuminating, about such issues.

One can see, then, that from an egalitarian perspective, (2) – which is what, I claim, Epstein *actually* argues for in Section II – is largely beside the point. On the other hand, egalitarians should be concerned about (1), at least if "equity" in the second clause is understood to include considerations of equality. More specifically, insofar as one is an egalitarian, one should be interested in the claim that:

(3) *Intra*generational equality is at odds with *inter*generational equality.

Two points regarding (3): First, even if intragenerational equality *were* at odds with intergenerational equality, it might still be the case that one should give *some* weight to *both* concerns. Second, it is by no means clear that intragenerational equality *is* at odds with intergenerational equality. Let me expand on the second point.

It is generally assumed that for most of the past two hundred years advances in civilization have offset declines, such that on average the overall quality of life of succeeding generations has been higher than that of preceding ones. Many believe that trend is likely to continue, due, among other things, to ongoing discoveries and developments in science, technology, and resources. But then note the following: First, even if Epstein is right that "[t]axation and regulatory policies that are designed to secure equality of wealth in the next generation do so at the cost of reducing the levels of capital accumulation," so that "[t]he effort to redistribute wealth within the second generation reduces the amount of wealth passed on to that generation," it may still be true that the second generation will be wealthier than the first, as a result of the discovery and creation of new sources of wealth. In other words, the fact that less wealth is passed on to the second generation as a result of pursuing egalitarian policies only ensures that the second generation will be less wealthy than *they* otherwise would be; it does *not* ensure that they will be less wealthy than the *first* generation. This *might* be the case, depending on the exact nature and extent of the egalitarian policies pursued, but it needn't be. Second, even if in fact the second generation ends up being less *wealthy* than the first, members of the second generation may still be *better off* than members of the first, and this may be so not only because there may be many social and psychological benefits from living in a more equal society, but because scientific and technological advances may enable them to use their limited resources much more efficiently than members of the first generation. Thus, even if the second generation is less wealthy than the first, their lesser resources may serve them in better stead in terms of enabling them to maintain a higher quality of life.

The preceding suggests two ways in which the effect of adopting a policy to promote equality in the second generation might be to leave the members of the second generation worse off than they would otherwise have been, but *not* worse off than the members of the first generation. In such cases, *intra*generational equality need not be at odds with *inter*generational equality. To the contrary, from an egalitarian perspective, the laudable goal of reducing inequality within the second generation might be achieved in conjunction with the laudable goal of reducing inequality between the second generation and the first.[27]

[27] In Epstein's defense, let us acknowledge that discussions about future generations often take place in a context where the dominant concern is that present generations will consume *so much* of the world's resources as to leave future generations with lives that are (a) low in quality, (b) so miserable as to be not worth living, or (c) (much) worse off than ours. In such a context, an argument establishing that efforts to promote equality within future generations will inevitably lead to those generations being even worse off (both in absolute terms and relative to the present generation) must seriously worry egalitarians and nonegalitarians alike. More particularly, it appears that in such contexts claim (3) would hold, as the *intra*generational equality of the future generations would be at odds with the *inter*generational equality between those generations and the present one. However, the context in question is not the only relevant one for discussions about future generations, and the concern stated above, though legitimate, is partly misplaced and partly misleading. For example, many would agree, at the outset, that we ought not to leave future generations *worse* off than past or present ones; their question would be whether—given likely advances in science and technology—we have an obligation to leave future generations *better* off than past or present ones, and if so, to what extent. Such a starting-point is markedly different from the one noted above, and, as we have seen, it has rather different implications for a claim like (3).

In Epstein's introduction he writes: "[T]he debate on equity between the generations focuses too much on duty, and too little on practice and incentive" (p. 85). His contention is that "the issue here is not that of intentions, or of obligations. It is that of the connection between means and ends. A classical liberal regime of limited government, focused regulation, low taxation, personal liberty, and private property *does better by* future generations than an alternative regime that consciously enlists large government to restrain liberty and limit the present use of property for the benefit of future generations" (p. 85, emphasis added). If it works, the argument of Section II supports Epstein's contention, *insofar as* "does better by" is understood in terms of total wealth. But, of course, there are many ways that governments may "do better by" future generations other than in terms of total wealth. They may, for example, do better by future generations in terms of justice or equality. Will "a classical liberal regime of limited government, focused regulation, low taxation, personal liberty, and private property [do] better by future generations than an alternative regime" *all things considered*? This is an open question which Epstein's argument of Section II does not even address, let alone answer.

I have contended that the actual conclusion Epstein argues for in Section II of his essay is different from the one he claims he will argue for in his essay's introduction, is not particularly startling, and, from an egalitarian perspective, is largely beside the point. Still, Epstein draws attention to an important set of questions the egalitarian must address. As Epstein has recognized, policies which reduce inequality *within* one generation may or may not reduce inequality *between* that generation and a past or future one. More generally, policies which reduce inequality *within* one society may or may not reduce inequality either *within* or *between* other past, present, or future societies.

Any form of government, social, or political policy which is advocated because it has favorable egalitarian implications in one setting must be thoroughly assessed in terms of any other egalitarian implications it may have. This is one lesson Epstein's essay suggests with which I concur. Since, then, there are many different ways policies might affect inequality for better or worse, egalitarians will ultimately have to assess policies in terms of the relative importance of *each* way eventually deemed significant. Among other things, this will involve addressing the many issues raised by the present essay.

VII. Implications

This essay raises a host of practical and theoretical implications. Some of these have already been noted, while many others are relatively clear and require little or no elaboration. However, in this section, let me briefly discuss three topics for which this essay's considerations are relevant. The first concerns the pressing practical problem of inequality between overlapping generations, specifically, between the young and the elderly. The second and third concern the theoretical topics of transitivity and temporal neutrality. Unfortunately, this is not the place to give these topics the full attention they deserve. Still, I can, at least, point out certain connections between my earlier claims and these extremely important topics.

As our population ages we face enormous pressures on many fronts, including, but by no means limited to, health care, social security, insurance, taxation, housing, and employment. These pressures portend major changes in the fabric of society, spanning social, political, cultural, economic, and personal levels. This raises a host of pressing moral questions concerning the desirability of transfers between the young and the old. Many of this essay's considerations are relevant to this issue. Let me note just one respect in which this is so.

In Section III, I observed that people hold different views regarding the significance of natural injustice. Correspondingly, I observed that people may hold different views regarding the significance of natural inequality. Thus, for example, one might hold that, *ceteris paribus*, natural inequality is *just* as objectionable as social inequality; that natural and social inequalities are both objectionable, but that, *ceteris paribus*, the latter are worse than the former; or that only social inequalities are morally objectionable (natural inequalities may be unfortunate, but justice does not require that they be reduced or removed). Clearly, which of these views is accepted will make a great difference to the desirability of transfers between the young and the old. After all, even if one grants that there is significant social inequality between the young and the elderly—i.e., that however unintentionally or nonmaliciously, society systematically discriminates against the elderly—surely many of the most conspicuous and substantial respects in which the elderly are worse off than the young are due to natural rather than social causes.

Consider a typical litany of factors commonly associated with old age: losses in hearing, eyesight, memory, health, and loved ones. Such factors play a considerable role in the widely held view that in general the elderly are worse off than the young.[28] Yet even if we, as a society, can take steps to delay or alleviate the effects of such factors, most would contend that they are a natural part of the aging process for which no one, least of all society, is to blame. It appears, then, that a large part of the inequality between the elderly and the young is natural rather than social. Thus, the extent to which transfers from the young to the old are desirable will depend, in large part, on the extent to which natural inequali-

[28] One is reminded of the old joke that growing old isn't so bad when one considers the alternative. The alternative, of course, is understood to be death, as many believe—to put the point crudely—that it is better to be old than dead, but better to be young than old.

ties are objectionable.[29] By the same token, if one believes, as many do, that we cannot ignore the elderly's plight insofar as it "merely" results from natural causes, then this may support the substantive—if not terminological—claim that one must be concerned with "natural injustice" as well as social injustice.

Let me next turn to the topic of transitivity. Elsewhere I have argued that contrary to the predominant view of philosophers, economists, psychologists, and others, "all-things-considered better than" may not be a transitive relation.[30] This will be so, I argued, if the moral factors or ideals that determine our all-things-considered judgments vary in their relevance and significance depending on the situations being compared. That is, if the factors that determine how A and B compare differ in their relevance and significance from those that determine how B and C compare, or how A and C compare, then it may well be the case that *all things considered* A is better than B, and B is better than C, yet A is *not* better than C. Now in supporting and assessing the significance of this claim, I argued that a number of important and widely held moral factors would yield the intransitivity of "all-things-considered better than," including certain plausible versions of the person-affecting principle,[31] utilitarianism, maximin, and egalitarianism. Let me add, here, that several of the positions considered previously might also support the conclusion in question.

Consider the view that the value of equality between generations depends on the temporal proximity of the generations in question, such that a given amount of inequality between overlapping or "close" generations matters more than the same amount of inequality between generations that are (temporally) "distant." Such a view is likely to lead to intransitive all-things-considered judgments, if, as I believe, equality is but one of several moral ideals that play a genuinely significant role in our all-things-considered judgments.[32]

Suppose, for simplicity, that one believes there are three factors relevant to comparing any two situations all things considered—utility, equality, and perfection. Let A, B, and C be three situations such that the

[29] Other interesting and important considerations relevant to the desirability of transfers between young and old are discussed in chapter eight of my *Inequality*.

[30] Larry S. Temkin, "Intransitivity and the Mere Addition Paradox," *Philosophy and Public Affairs*, vol. 16, no. 2 (Spring 1987), pp. 138–87.

[31] This is the principle according to which, roughly, one outcome is better (or worse) than another, only if it affects people for the better (or worse).

[32] As will be clear from the ensuing discussion, in saying that a moral factor plays a "genuinely significant" role in our all-things-considered judgments, I am saying that it does more than merely "break ties" yielded by other moral factors or ideals. Thus, to believe that several ideals are each genuinely significant is to believe, among other things, that (at least in some cases) "slight" losses with respect to some ideals could be outweighed by "sufficiently high" gains with respect to other ideals. For example, if equality, utility, and perfection are each genuinely significant, then there may be some cases where one situation is (slightly) better than another with respect to two of the ideals, yet worse all things considered, because it is "sufficiently" worse with respect to the third ideal.

following relations hold. A is worse than B regarding utility and perfection, but A is better than B regarding equality, and the extent to which this is so is *just* enough to make it the case that, all things considered, A is (slightly) better than B. B is worse than C regarding utility and perfection, but B is better than C regarding equality, and the extent to which this is so is *just* enough to make it the case that, all things considered, B is (slightly) better than C. It follows that if "all-things-considered better than" were a transitive relation, then A would have to be better than C, since, all things considered, A is better than B, and B is better than C. Yet A may not be better than C on the above view that the value of equality between generations depends on the temporal proximity of the generations in question. After all, while A and B may be temporally close enough that the extent to which A is better than B regarding equality outweighs the extent to which A is worse than B regarding utility and perfection, and while B and C may be temporally close enough that the extent to which B is better than C regarding equality outweighs the extent to which B is worse than C regarding utility and perfection, it may well be that A and C are *not* temporally close enough that the extent to which A is better than C regarding equality outweighs the extent to which A is worse than C regarding utility and perfection. One can see, then, that on the view in question "all-things-considered better than" may not be a transitive relation, since in terms of each of the factors that are relevant and significant for making each comparison, it could be the case that A is better than B, and B is better than C, but A is not better than C.[33]

Considerations analogous to the preceding ones will apply, *mutatis mutandis,* to any view where the value of equality will be a matter of degree depending on the particular relations of the individuals or societies being compared. That is, assuming equality is but one genuinely significant ideal among others, "all-things-considered better than" is likely to be an intransitive relation wherever the extent to which a given amount of inequality matters depends on the particular relations of those between whom the inequality obtains. Thus, for example, if one thinks that the extent to which inequality matters depends on the "closeness" or special relationships of the individuals or societies being compared, then, for reasons of the sort given above, it might be that, all things considered, A is better than B, and B is better than C, yet A is not better than C. After all, there may be a "closeness" or set of special relations obtaining between A and B, and between B and C, which is lacking between A and C, and, on the view in question, the presence or absence of the relevant "closeness" or special relations will play a relevant and significant role in, first, directly determining how situations fare regarding inequality, and, then, indirectly determining how situations compare all things considered.

[33] There are various ways one might try to respond to this kind of argument, other than simply rejecting the view that temporal proximity can be morally relevant along the lines suggested. Unfortunately, I cannot pursue the matter here, though I believe it raises many important issues. See my "Intransitivity."

Other positions discussed in this essay may also generate intransitivities. But let me not defend this claim here. Instead, let me end this section by commenting on the topic of temporal neutrality.

Earlier I observed that many people have a "bias" toward the present and future. Such a bias may express itself in several ways. For an egalitarian, it may involve either rejecting or "discounting" the value of equality within past generations, or between past generations and other generations (be they past, present, or future). Though rarely recognized or explicitly acknowledged, I suspect many egalitarians would incline toward such a view. Surely, one might think, it is not morally objectionable that most of those in our society are much better off than the vast majority of those who lived in previous centuries, at least not to the same extent that it is objectionable that some members of our society are much better off than others, or that our society will be much better off than future ones unless we carefully conserve resources.

It may seem implausible for an egalitarian to give (much) weight to the comparative status of past generations, just as it may seem implausible for a preference utilitarian to give (much) weight to the preferences and desires—however central, strong, and future-directed they may have been—of those long since dead. Still, incorporating a bias toward the present and future into one's moral ideals has straightforward implications that must first be recognized, and then accepted or rejected depending on their plausibility. For example, for any two situations A and B, there may be no fact of the matter as to which is better, all things considered, from a temporally neutral perspective. Perhaps the most one can say is how A and B compare, all things considered, from particular temporal perspectives. Thus, it might be the case that, at T1, A is worse than B all things considered; at T2, A is better than B all things considered; and at T3, either might be better than, equal to, or worse than the other. This might be so if, at T1, A and B are both present or future states—so that egalitarian considerations are important and equally relevant in assessing both—if, at T2, A is past while B is still present or future—so that egalitarian considerations are important and relevant in assessing B, but less important or irrelevant in assessing A—and if, at T3, A and B are both past—so that egalitarian considerations are either not relevant for assessing A and B or are relevant but less important.

Rejecting temporal neutrality is bound to give rise to intertemporal conflicts or dilemmas.[34] These may be either *inter*personal or *intra*personal in nature. That is, looking toward the future from the standpoint of T1,

[34] Intertemporal dilemmas have been discussed by many writers. Two of the most influential works addressing this topic are Thomas Nagel's *The Possibility of Altruism* (Oxford: Clarendon Press, 1970), and Parfit's *Reasons and Persons*. See also Jon Elster's important *Ulysses and the Sirens* (Cambridge: Cambridge University Press, 1979), and Thomas Schelling's fascinating "Ethics, Law, and the Exercise of Self-Command," in *Liberty, Equality, and Law: Selected Tanner Lectures on Moral Philosophy*, ed. Sterling M. McMurrin (Salt Lake City: University of Utah Press; and Cambridge: Cambridge University Press, 1987), pp. 163–99.

we may have good reason to adopt policy P, and to hope that the aims of P are fully realized, while recognizing that if moral ideals are temporally biased, there may be good reason, from the standpoint of T2, for either ourselves or future generations to try to undermine P and to be glad if its aims have not been achieved. The possibility of our occupying both T1 and T2 may give rise to prudential as well as moral conflicts, and possible dissociation of our present and future selves. The possibility of different generations occupying T1 and T2 may give rise to moral conflicts, and possible dissociation of projects and goals as between generations.

Conflicts of the above sort may seem particularly troubling to consequentialists, but they pose a problem for anyone who gives at least some consideration to which act, of those available, would have the best consequences. It might be that P would have the best consequences from the perspective of all times up to some future time T1, that Q would have the best consequences from the perspective of all times from T1 to T2, and that R would have the best consequences from the perspective of all times after T2. If one must act at some point in time prior to T1, does that settle the issue in favor of P? Should one consider a fourth act, S, that might not have the best consequences from the perspective of *any* particular point in time, but which would represent a compromise between the other perspectives? Should one try to guess as to the probable end (and perhaps beginning) of human history, so as to be able to give proportionate weight to the different "best" outcomes in accordance with their probable duration? These are but a few of the many questions needing to be addressed by those whose moral ideals are temporally biased. It is far from clear what the answers to these questions should be, much less whether they will ultimately be more plausible than the unpalatable implications of strict temporal neutrality.

VIII. Summary and Conclusion

In this essay, I have considered various questions regarding equality's scope. Let me summarize my results. In Section II, I noted several possible views as to whether inequality matters equally between all people at all times. Specifically, I suggested that one might hold any of the following positions: RTRS egalitarianism, where the value of equality is both Relativized to Time and Relativized to a Society; NTNS egalitarianism, where the value of equality is both Neutral across Time and Neutral across Societies; RTNS egalitarianism, where the value of equality is Relativized to Time but Neutral across Societies; and NTRS egalitarianism, where the value of equality is Neutral across Time but Relativized to a Society. As characterized, the positions were all or nothing. Inequality between A and B either mattered to a certain extent or it did not, depending on—or, as the case might be, independently of—whether A and B were contemporaries or members of the same society. I next observed that one might hold variations of, or compromises between, the suggested positions. I pointed out that one might view different positions as more or less plausible for different kinds of equality, that one might think the extent to which a given amount of inequality matters will be a matter of degree along the temporal or societal dimensions, or that one might modify the suggested positions to reflect different attitudes toward time, for example, a "bias" toward the present or future.

In Section III, I considered several positions which might influence, as well as be influenced by, one's egalitarian position. I began by arguing that different views about natural justice will be more or less compatible with different views about equality's scope. Specifically, I suggested that on different views about natural justice (some version of) NTNS, NTRS, or RTRS egalitarianism may seem plausible. Roughly, the views about natural justice were, respectively, the view that there *are* natural injustices—e.g., that some are born blind while others are not—and that there are reasons of justice to alleviate these wherever and whenever they occur; the (Rawlsian) view that while there are no natural *injustices* there are reasons of justice to be concerned about natural misfortunes *within* societies insofar as these adversely affect the lot of the worst off; and the (Nozickian) view that there are no natural injustices and no reasons of justice to be concerned about natural misfortunes either within or between societies. I did not claim any necessary connection between one's views about natural justice and one's views about equality's scope, but claimed that many complexities and factors relevant to the former would also be relevant to the latter, and vice versa.

In Section IV, I considered Gauthier's contractarian theory. Though Gauthier himself is not an egalitarian, I believe there is room, on his theory, to regard certain inequalities as objectionable. However, I argued that on a view like Gauthier's the value of equality will not be neutral across time. Specifically, I argued that inequality between generations will not matter at all, if one of the generations is past, while inequality between present or future generations will matter to a greater or lesser extent depending on the temporal proximity of the generations in question. Moreover, I claimed that there would likely be a fairly steep discount rate regarding inequality, so that a given amount of inequality between people just a few generations apart would be significantly less objectionable than the same amount of inequality between contemporaries.

In Section V, I noted that one's views regarding inequality's scope may depend, in part, on one's reasons for accepting or rejecting the commonsense views that, *ceteris paribus*, we should be more concerned about those with whom we have special relations than with others, or about "identifiable" lives than "statistical" lives, or about actual people than possible people. Specifically, I pointed out that reasons for granting special weight to special relations may support a view like RTRS egalitarianism or, more likely, a view where the value of equality is a matter of degree depending on the relevant "closeness" of the people being compared. Similarly, reasons for thinking we should be more concerned about actual than possible people may support the value of equality being relativized to time, or being a matter of degree across time, while reasons for being more concerned about "identifiable" rather than "statistical" people may be relevant regarding which inequalities we should be most concerned to alleviate and may, for example, help explain the appeal of a view like RTRS egalitarianism. On the other hand, reasons for rejecting the common-sense view of the issues in question might well support a view like NTNS egalitarianism. I concluded Section V by observing that certain reasons why people may have thought inequality matters more within societies than between societies—reasons having to do with the nature and multitude of bonds and special relationships obtaining in early societies—may in fact, given the character of modern societies, support inequality's value being a matter of degree both within and between societies, as well as across time.

In Section VI, I discussed Richard Epstein's contention that "intragenerational equity . . . is at odds with intergenerational equity." I began by claiming that what Epstein actually argues for is the conclusion that "[t]he effort to redistribute wealth within the second generation reduces the amount of wealth passed on to that generation." Though important, this conclusion is hardly startling. It merely reminds us that equality and utility are separate ideals, and that sometimes one must make trade-offs between them. I next considered the more intriguing claim that intragenerational equality is at odds with intergenerational equality. I began by noting that if intragenerational equality *were* at odds with intergenerational equality, perhaps one should give weight to both concerns. I then offered reasons to believe that, for cases of the sort Epstein considers, intragenerational equality is probably not at odds with intergenerational equality. Specifically, I argued that given some plausible empirical assumptions, reducing inequality within the next generation might be achieved in conjunction with reducing inequality between the next generation and the present one. Still, I acknowledged that, in general, policies reducing inequality *within* one society may or may not reduce inequality either *within* or *between* other past, present, or future societies. Correspondingly, policies that are advocated because they have favorable egalitarian implications in one setting must be thoroughly assessed in terms of any other egalitarian implications they may have.

In Section VII, I discussed three topics: the desirability of transfers between the young and the old, transitivity, and temporal neutrality. I noted that much of the inequality between the young and the old is due to natural causes. Hence, our views concerning the undesirability of inequality between the young and the old will be intimately connected with our views regarding natural injustice, in particular, with whether we believe natural inequalities are morally objectionable. I then showed how the view that the value of equality between generations depends on the temporal proximity of the generations in question is likely to generate intransitivity in our all-things-considered judgments. More generally, I argued that intransitivity is likely to result from any view where the value of equality will be a matter of degree depending on the particular relations of the individuals or societies being compared. In essence, this is because there may be a "closeness" or set of special relations obtaining between A and B, and between B and C, which is lacking between A and C, so that the value of equality is greater in comparing A with B, and B with C, than it is in comparing A with C. After all, there is no reason to expect transitivity in comparing outcomes, if different factors are relevant for comparing those outcomes or, similarly, if a factor's significance varies with the outcomes being considered. I then discussed the view that inequalities within past generations, or between past generations and other generations, do not matter, or matter less than other inequalities. I suggested that many egalitarians would probably incline toward this view, but noted that it raises a number of questions. I showed that on this view there may be no fact of the matter as to which of two situations is better all things considered from a temporally neutral perspective. I also pointed out that this view is bound to give rise to intertemporal conflicts, and that these might be either *intra*personal or *inter*personal in nature. Specifically, I noted that, for individuals, this view would give rise to both prudential and moral conflicts, and possible dissociation of our present and future selves. Similarly, for different generations, this view would give rise to special moral conflicts, and possible dissociation of projects and goals as between generations.

In this essay, we have seen that various questions need to be addressed regarding inequality's scope, and that very different answers can be given to these questions. Although I, myself, incline toward a position like NTNS egalitarianism, the essay purposely does not try to choose among these answers. Instead, it offers considerations and implications relevant for understanding and assessing the positions in question.[35] We have seen that the issues concerning inequality's scope cannot be settled in isolation from a wide range of separate, yet related, issues which are themselves deep, difficult, and very complex. Since there is substantial disagreement regarding the latter issues, we should expect similar substantial disagreement regarding the former ones. On the other hand, firm convictions regarding inequality's scope might illuminate some of the

[35] For further considerations relevant to assessing these positions, see my discussions of deontological, impersonal, impartial teleological, and person-affecting egalitarianisms in *Inequality*. Note 15 on pages 253–54 reflects some key considerations that push me toward NTNS egalitarianism, notwithstanding deep reservations I have about such a position.

other, related issues, and shared convictions about inequality's scope might lead to a reassessment and convergence of some of our other, related views.

One may find various views plausible regarding inequality's scope, and instead of choosing between them, may think that several should be accommodated. One may believe that such an approach is necessary to accurately capture and reflect the complex nature of morality, in general, and equality, in particular. On such a view much work would still remain. One might try to show that the different positions only conflict at the surface level, and are not fundamentally incompatible. Assuming one could satisfy oneself that this was so, one would want to consider how much weight to attach to the different positions vis-à-vis each other in cases where their judgments conflict. Moreover, in doing this, one would want to consider whether different positions may be plausible to a greater or lesser extent in different cases.

On the practical side, it is difficult to exaggerate the importance of the kinds of considerations this essay discusses. Consider the following questions. How should we allocate resources within our society between the naturally disadvantaged and the socially disadvantaged? How should we allocate resources between the poor in our society and those in other societies? Suppose we could reduce inequality within our society but, for practical and political reasons, only by increasing inequality between our society and other societies, or between the present generation and past or future generations—under what circumstances, if any, should we do so? These are concrete, practical questions which our society faces in one form or another on a daily basis. How our society answers such questions has significant and far-reaching implications regarding the social and political programs we pursue. And, of course, how such questions *should* be answered will both depend in part on inequality's scope, and partly determine the moral permissibility of the programs we adopt.

It would be easiest if we could ignore other societies—but it is not clear that a just society can do so. Nor is it clear that the dictates of justice extend with equal strength across space and time. What is clear is that determining the scope of the correct principles of justice is important, as well as difficult. Indeed, although this essay focuses on equality, I hope to have said enough to establish that any satisfactory account of justice's scope will have profound practical and theoretical implications.

Philosophy, Rice University

EQUAL OPPORTUNITY AND GENETIC INTERVENTION*

BY ALLEN BUCHANAN

I. INTRODUCTION

What does the prospect of being able to alter a human being's "natural assets" by genetic engineering imply for our understanding of the requirements of justice, and of equal opportunity in particular? Although their proponents are reluctant to admit it, some of the most prominent contemporary theories of justice yield a quite radical conclusion: If safe and effective intervention in the genetic "natural lottery" becomes feasible, there will be at least a strong prima facie case for doing so in the name of equality of opportunity (or of some other egalitarian principle of justice, such as the principle that persons are entitled to equal concern and respect), if this is the most effective way to meet the demands of justice.

The most obvious instance of such a theory is that of John Rawls. His view is that equal opportunity requires that individuals be compensated for the fact that they have *lower life-prospects* as a result of the influence of not only social but also natural contingencies, because these factors are "arbitrary from a moral point of view."[1] Being born into a family that values education or born with a natural talent for developing complex cognitive skills is "morally arbitrary," Rawls thinks, because in both cases it is an *undeserved* natural asset or resource that gives rise to special advantages, to higher life-prospects. The fundamental idea here is that simply to allow such undeserved differences to lead to lower life-prospects for those who had bad luck in the social or natural lotteries is somehow unjust, because it is incompatible with a proper recognition of the basic moral equality of persons.

According to Rawls, the proper response is first to implement a principle requiring that persons of equal talent and motivation have equal prospects of attaining social offices and positions. But this, he thinks, is not sufficient. In addition, in order to compensate those who will still suffer disadvantages in the distribution of natural assets, social and economic inequalities must be so "arranged" as to maximize the life-prospects of the worst off. Since talent and even motivation are presumably in part genet-

* I am indebted to David Benatar and Dan Brock for their astute comments on an earlier draft of this essay.

[1] John Rawls, *A Theory of Justice* (Cambridge, MA: Harvard University Press, 1971), p. 72.

ically based (and hence result from "morally arbitrary" natural contingencies), merely ensuring that those with the same talent and motivation have the same prospects of attaining offices and positions will not be enough. What is required is that social primary goods be redistributed in such a way as to compensate for the unequal distribution of natural primary goods.[2]

[2] In this essay I will be concerned mainly with Rawls's views on equal opportunity and natural inequalities as expressed in *A Theory of Justice*. One reason for doing this is that my aim is to explore a type of position, namely resource egalitarianism, which, while held by others in addition to Rawls (such as G. A. Cohen and Ronald Dworkin), seems to rely upon Rawls's discussion of these matters in *A Theory of Justice*. Resource egalitarians tend to take as relatively uncontroversial the very Rawlsian views I intend to subject to critical examination in this essay. In particular, resource egalitarians in the so-called "Equality of What?" literature (with the possible exception of Amartya Sen) appear to take it as a given that justice requires some sort of compensation for those whose life-prospects are lower as a result of undeserved lesser shares of social or natural resources. (See, e.g., Ronald Dworkin, "What is Equality? Part 1: Equality of Welfare," *Philosophy and Public Affairs*, vol. 10, no. 3 [Summer 1981]; Ronald Dworkin, "What is Equality? Part 2: Equality of Resources," *Philosophy and Public Affairs*, vol. 10, no. 4 [Fall 1981]; John Roemer, "Equality of Talent," *Economics and Philosophy*, vol. 1, no. 2 [October 1985]; G. A. Cohen, "On the Currency of Egalitarian Justice," *Ethics*, vol. 99 [July 1989]; Norman Daniels, "Equality of What: Welfare, Resources, or Capabilities," *Philosophy and Phenomenological Research*, vol. L Supplement [Fall 1990]; and Richard Arneson, "A Defense of Equal Opportunity for Welfare," *Philosophical Studies*, vol. 62 [1991].) It is this claim about a fundamental connection between natural inequalities and the requirements of justice, what I have called the Resource Redress Principle, which seems to play a prominent role in at least some of Rawls's arguments for the Difference Principle and for the Principle of Fair Equality of Opportunity in *A Theory of Justice*.

In Rawls's later work *Political Liberalism* (New York: Columbia University Press, 1993), there may be less reliance on the Resource Redress Principle as a relatively free-standing principle that is to be supported by appeal to "moral intuitions" or "considered judgments." Instead, *Political Liberalism* can be interpreted as basing the Principle of Fair Equality of Opportunity and the Difference Principle (as well as Rawls's First Principle of Justice) ultimately upon the complex idea (or ideal) of what free and equal persons who regard themselves as such would agree to as fair terms of social cooperation. Although I will attempt no systematic critique of the later Rawlsian position here, I will remark that attempting to base everything ultimately on the idea or ideal in question seems to place Rawls on the horns of a dilemma. Either he must admit that the concept of what free and equal persons who regard themselves as such (and seek fair terms of social cooperation) would agree to is too vague to yield anything as determinate and controversial as his principles; or he must lean heavily on what I have elsewhere called his Traditionist mode of justification, attempting to ground his principles in the ideals of freedom and equality (and of fair cooperation) that he claims are distinctive of "our" political culture, that of modern (post 1776) political liberalism. The difficulty with the latter response is that it is dubious indeed to assume, as Rawls does, that there is a clearly dominant political culture in actual modern liberal-democratic societies that endorses his principles or in whose commitments his principles can be grounded. And, remarkably, Rawls does nothing to substantiate his claim that the materials for developing a consensus on his principles are actually present in the political consciousness or major documents and institutions of, say, American society.

If I understand it properly, the Traditionist mode of justification has a substantial empirical component insofar as it requires establishing that the principles of justice that are to be justified are based on ideals that are actually present in a given political culture or tradition. A political culture or tradition is embodied in the political consciousness of a group of people and in the major political institutions of that society, and is expressed in the major documents (such as the constitution) of the society. Yet any attempt to connect the actual features of American (or other modern liberal-democratic) political consciousness and of our society's major documents or institutions with Rawls's interpretation of the ideal of a free

Several other prominent theorists, who differ from Rawls and each other in a number of respects, share with him the assumption that justice requires distributing (and redistributing) social resources in order to compensate for inequalities in natural resources, that is, the genetic assets with which individuals are born.[3] These theorists see the chief task for achieving a just society to be that of devising a resource-allocation mechanism to achieve an overall equal distribution of resources by compensating for inequalities in the distribution of natural resources by special redistributions of social resources.[4]

There are a number of bold if not extravagant assumptions at work in this approach. First of all, to talk of compensating for a lack of natural resources by special allocations of social resources is to assume that natural and social resources can be compared and aggregated. This is not the assumption I wish to question, however. Instead, I want to focus on the fundamental moral assumption that gets this whole approach going in the first place, namely:

> Equality of opportunity (or, more simply, the fundamental equality of persons) requires that individuals be compensated for having lower life-prospects as a result of their (less fortunate and undeserved) natural *or* social endowments.

For reasons that will become apparent as we proceed, I shall call this assumption the "Resource Redress Principle."

Notice that the Resource Redress Principle appears to be a *second-best principle*. It seems to rest on a more basic principle to the effect that, at least from the standpoint of the most basic principles of justice, the ideal situation is one in which all resources, natural and social, are distributed equally, at least so far as they are undeserved. Let us call this the Resource Equality Principle:

---

and equal person is conspicuously absent from Rawls's work. For example, he does not examine the U.S. Constitution and attempt to show that it expresses an ideal of free and equal persons that is determinate enough to ground a construction of the original position capable of yielding his principles.

[3] It seems that all of the theorists who offer a "resourcist" answer to the question "Equality of What?" fall into this category. In other words, to the extent that one is committed to the thesis that defines resourcist versions of egalitarian theories of justice—namely, that justice requires an equal distribution of resources—it seems that "resources" here must be understood broadly enough to include natural resources (genetic endowments) as well as social resources. Included in this class of theorists are Ronald Dworkin and G. A. Cohen. John Roemer regards himself as a resource theorist but apparently restricts the resources to be distributed equally to a type of social resource, alienable productive assets. (See Dworkin, "What Is Equality? Part 2"; Cohen, "On the Currency of Egalitarian Justice"; and Roemer, "Equality of Talent.")

Whether there is a principled way an egalitarian resource theorist can restrict resources to social as opposed to natural resources is quite unclear. Dworkin, at least, is quite explicit that the term "resources" is to include natural assets as well as social ones.

[4] Roemer, "Equality of Talent," p. 154.

> All resources, natural and social, ought to be distributed equally (at least so far as they are undeserved).

So long as we assume that we cannot intervene directly in the distribution of natural assets so as to achieve an equal distribution of them, the proper response to such natural "inequities" is to compensate for them by redistributing social resources. Thus, in the face of the unfeasibility of redistributing natural assets, we retreat from the first-best Resource Equality Principle to the second-best Resource Redress Principle.

However, given the prospect of genetic engineering, the assumption that redistributing natural assets is unfeasible is no longer plausible. We are now left wondering why theorists such as Rawls, G. A. Cohen, and Ronald Dworkin have not considered the possibility of responding directly to genetic "inequities." If equal opportunity (or a more fundamental principle of the equality of persons) requires us to redress or compensate for inequalities influenced by genetic differences, why not simply avoid them by eliminating the genetic differences in the first place?[5]

How we answer this question will depend upon how literally the Resource Equality Principle is to be interpreted. There are two relevant interpretations. One takes equality in an *aggregative* sense, the other in a *distributive* sense. According to the former, the Resource Equality Principle requires only that each person's *overall* bundle of resources be equal to every other person's overall bundle. Understood in this way, the Resource Equality Principle can be satisfied even if there are inequalities among some of the resources composing the overall bundle, so long as the totals are equal. In particular, on the aggregative interpretation of the Resource Equality Principle, two persons could have equal resources even if one had inferior genetic endowments, so long as her share of social resources compensated for this deficiency in such a way as to yield an overall resource bundle equal to the other person's overall resource bundle. In contrast, the distributive interpretation would require that resources be equal among all persons at least for every major category of resources, including natural and social resources as major categories. Thus, according to the distributive interpretation of the Resource Equality Principle, natural resources (genetic endowments) are to be equal, unless there is no way to render them equal, in which case we retreat to the Resource Redress Principle, which allows us to compensate for uncorrectable natural inequalities by redistributing social resources.

[5] On p. 100 of *A Theory of Justice,* Rawls appears to equate the principle of equal opportunity with what he calls the principle of redress, and to say that equal opportunity thus understood is required by the principle of equal respect for persons:

> This [the principle of redress] is the principle that undeserved inequalities call for redress; and since inequalities of birth and natural endowment are undeserved, these inequalities are to be somehow compensated for. Thus the principle holds that in order to treat all persons equally, to provide genuine equality of opportunity, society must give more attention to those with fewer native assets and those born into the less favorable social positions.

For our purposes, the chief difference between the two interpretations of the Resource Equality Principle is this: the distributive interpretation *requires* genetic equality, where it is possible to achieve it; the aggregative interpretation allows us to forgo efforts to achieve genetic equality *if* overall resource equality can be achieved by compensating for inequalities in natural endowments by redistributing social resources, but also *permits* efforts to achieve genetic equality.

Those who are disturbed by the prospect that justice, and in particular equal opportunity, might require massive genetic intervention may therefore find the aggregative interpretation of the Resource Equality Principle more congenial. However, it is worth emphasizing that although the aggregative interpretation does not by itself require genetic intervention to equalize resources, it does *permit* it. On the aggregative interpretation, the Resource Equality Principle simply says that overall resources are to be equal. It neither requires equalization of natural endowments nor rules it out as impermissible. However, if it turned out that in certain circumstances the *only* way to achieve overall resource equality were to intervene genetically, then the Resource Equality Principle would require this. And presumably, if genetic intervention were the *most efficient* way to achieve overall resource equality, then the Resource Equality Principle (again on the aggregative interpretation) would also require it, barring some powerful countervailing moral consideration. In sum, opting for the aggregative as opposed to the distributive interpretation of the Resource Equality Principle does not eliminate the possibility that this principle would allow genetic intervention. Indeed, it does not even rule out the possibility that the principle would require it under certain circumstances.[6]

At this point it might be well to address a note of skepticism about the

[6] As compared with the distributive interpretation, the aggregative version of the Resource Equality Principle also has a serious drawback. It requires very strong (cardinal) comparability among all types of resources, including natural and social. To compare different individuals' bundles of total resources of all types, presumably requires knowing what contribution each item in the bundle makes toward an individual's well-being.

However, at this point the aggregative version of the Resource Equality Principle threatens to undermine the whole rationale for a *resourcist* as opposed to a welfarist approach to matters of justice. That rationale consists of two elements. On the one hand, those advocating a resourcist approach (and rejecting welfarist approaches) typically deny the possibility of making such strong welfare comparisons. On the other hand, some resourcists, including Rawls and Ronald Dworkin, contend that due respect for the autonomy of persons makes it impermissible to impose any public standard of comparability (which the aggregative version of the Resource Equality Principle would require), because doing so would violate the right of each person to determine his or her own good. The appeal of a resourcist approach to questions of justice is supposed to consist chiefly in the fact that it avoids both the problem of devising a strong metric for comparing welfare across persons and the violation of respect for individual autonomy that would occur if there were an attempt to impose any such measure as a public standard of justice. Thus, while it is true that opting for the aggregative rather than the distributive interpretation of the Resource Equality Principle avoids the implication that resource equality *requires* genetic intervention in the "natural lottery" in all circumstances, it does so at the cost of adopting a version of the Resource Equality Principle that threatens to undermine the whole resourcist approach.

real-world consequences of the fact that a particular moral theory would permit or under certain circumstances require genetic intervention to equalize resources. Given that our society (or at least the most politically powerful segment of it) tolerates if not encourages quite substantial social and economic inequalities, how serious a risk is there that those who influence public policy would ever contemplate genetic intervention in the name of equal opportunity or justice?

Neither I, nor anyone else, so far as I can tell, is able to predict reliably whether there will ever be a serious effort to justify genetic intervention by appeal to equal opportunity or justice. However, there is some evidence that the probability of this occurring is not negligible. After all, there is, unfortunately, the recurrent tendency, at times rather pronounced in American history in the last hundred years, to fix upon rather facile biological-determinist explanations of deep social ills, and to propose morally dubious or even despicable social programs in the name of high moral principles. From the early eugenic notion that poverty and sexual immorality are the result of "defective germ plasm," to the more recent attempt to explain certain forms of socially deviant behavior as the phenotypical expression of a "criminal gene" (the so-called super-male or XYY genotype), significant segments of the public, as well as some public officials and some leaders of the scientific community, have leaped to biological-determinist conclusions in a disturbingly wide range of cases, and shown a facility for rationalizing repressive programs on moral grounds.[7]

As the technical possibilities for direct and dramatic genetic manipulation rapidly increase, the temptation to try to solve major social problems by genetic intervention—conclusively and in one generation—will no doubt increase. Moreover, if the history of biological determinism is any guide to its future manifestations, proposals for such genetic "quick fixes" or "magic bullets" will surely be publicly justified by their proponents by appeal to moral principles. For these reasons, it is by no means fanciful to consider the implications of ethical theory for genetic intervention.

Accordingly, in the remainder of this essay I will examine two arguments that purport to support the Resource Redress Principle and the Resource Equality Principle. The first is a very basic argument that takes as its first premise the so-called "Formal Principle of Justice," according to which equals are to be treated equally (and unequals unequally). The second focuses on the notion of equal opportunity, arguing that a proper understanding of it requires adherence to the Resource Equality Principle or, at the very least, the Resource Redress Principle. In the end I will conclude that neither of these two arguments is sound. The second of the

[7] For excellent analyses of various aspects of the American eugenics movements in international comparative perspective, see *The Well-Born Science*, ed. Mark Adams (Oxford: Oxford University Press, 1990); especially illuminating is Adams's introductory essay. See also Daniel Kevles, *In the Name of Eugenics* (New York: Alfred A. Knopf, 1985).

two, the argument from equal opportunity, will be dealt with in considerable detail, mainly because of the importance of distinguishing it from quite distinct arguments appealing to different notions of equal opportunity that do have some implications for genetic intervention.

II. The Argument from the Formal Principle of Justice

I will begin by focusing upon Rawls, because I believe his work is the *locus classicus* of the ideas to be explored.[8] (Indeed, it seems as though others, including Dworkin and Cohen, who subscribe to the Resource Redress Principle tend to take Rawls's view as an unquestioned point of departure.) At least so far as they can be gleaned from Rawls's discussions in *A Theory of Justice*, the two arguments to be subjected to critical scrutiny in this essay have this in common: both appeal to the idea that justice requires redressing or compensating undeserved (and hence "morally arbitrary") inequalities in life-prospects.

On one interpretation, at least, the first argument, the argument from the Formal Principle of Justice, simply *assumes*, apparently on the basis of an appeal to widely and confidently held considered moral judgments, that any inequalities in life-prospects due (at least in part) to "undeserved" differences in natural or social endowments are "morally arbitrary" in the particular sense relevant to the Formal Principle itself: undeserved differences in natural or social endowments are *not* the sorts of inequalities that may serve as bases for *unequal treatment* of persons as such. As a first approximation, the argument from the Formal Principle of Justice is as follows:

(1) Equals are to be treated equally (and unequals unequally) (The Formal Principle of Justice).
(2) All persons, as such (that is, as persons), are equal (The Principle of the Equal Worth of Persons).
(3) To allow some persons to have lower life-prospects than others, as a result of differences in natural or social resources that are undeserved, would be to treat persons, as such, unequally. Therefore,
(4) (So far as it is possible to do so,) social and natural resources are to be distributed equally, so far as they are undeserved (The Resource Equality Principle).

The weakness of this argument lies not in the Formal Principle of Justice, nor in the Principle of the Equal Worth of Persons, but in the third premise. The Formal Principle of Justice, taken in its bare abstractness, is unexceptionable. In order to apply it, however, it is necessary to specify

[8] See Rawls, *A Theory of Justice*, pp. 63–80.

what counts as a *relevant* equality, since any two (or more) persons, simply because they are different individuals, will be unequal in *some* respects. Those who appeal to the Principle of Formal Justice to try to justify the Principle of Resource Equality focus upon personhood itself as the relevant equality, since they are attempting to base a principle requiring the equal distribution of resources ultimately on the notion of *the fundamental equality of persons*.

Now it is true that respect for the fundamental equality of persons requires treating persons equally whenever one is in a situation in which one can be said to be treating them in one way or another. But of course, what counts as treating them equally will vary with the context. For example, if the context is that of considering job applicants, then treating them equally usually will mean being objective in the application of whatever the relevant criteria for job qualifications happen to be. In another context, treating persons equally may mean paying everyone the basic respect of listening to their grievances or concerns, or of taking everyone's interests, or certain of their interests, into account.

It is quite a jump, however, from these relatively uncontroversial statements to the thesis that treating persons as such equally requires eliminating or compensating for all differences in people's resources, social or natural, so far as these are undeserved. In one obvious sense, in simply allowing these differences to persist by not intervening in the natural lottery, one is not *treating* people at all, either equally or unequally.

If the so-called natural lottery were in fact a lottery run by society (or by the state, assumed to be the agent of society), then it would make straightforward sense to talk about the use of this lottery as a way of treating people. However, the "natural lottery" is not a lottery at all, or at least not one run by society or by any other human agent or agency. As it stands, then, the argument from the Formal Principle of Justice is unsound. The third premise is false, or at least dubious and in need of convincing support.

For the argument to have a chance of working, it must be revised to include the following premise:

(2′) If a process is technically within our collective control, such that we can intervene to change its effects, then in *allowing* that process to affect people in certain ways (i.e., in *not preventing* it from affecting them in those ways), we are thereby treating people in those ways (The Extended Responsibility Principle).

Also needed is another premise:

(2″) We can intervene to redress or compensate for differences in natural or social endowments that are undeserved.

Premises (2′) and (2″)—along with (1) and (2)—do yield (3), and the conclusion (4), the Resource Equality Principle, does follow.

For the sake of this essay, I will simply accept premise (2″) as given, without exercising a healthy skepticism about the probable limits of genetic intervention. Instead, I shall concentrate on an obvious but nonetheless serious difficulty with premise (2′). It says, in effect, that anything that *can* be brought within our control is *already*, morally speaking, *an exercise of our agency*, at least in the sense that it is something for which we are morally responsible. Not preventing persons from being affected unequally, where they do not deserve the factors that lead to these inequalities, is said to be *treating those persons* with less than equal respect, and is in that sense morally identical to voluntary acts that violate the fundamental respect owed to all persons as such. Instead of the familiar "ought implies can," we have a principle of "can implies ought," or rather: "If we can prevent X from occurring, but do not prevent X from occurring, then we are responsible for X."

Unless something like this is accepted, it is hard to see how one can bridge the gap between the Formal Principle of Justice and the Principle of the Equal Worth of Persons in such a way as to derive the desired conclusion, namely, the Principle of Resource Equality. However, as a general principle, (2′) is not only not self-evident, but implausible. A commitment to (2′) would expand the domain of moral responsibility to tyrannical dimensions. To attribute to a person's moral account everything that he or she does not prevent but could prevent seems incompatible with recognizing and respecting the fact that we each have one life to live, that we are each separate persons who are entitled to give our own projects a certain preference, and who accordingly require a substantial moral space within which to pursue our own conceptions of the good.

To appreciate just how demanding the Extended Responsibility Principle is, it is necessary to distinguish it clearly from a much more reasonable principle of moral responsibility, the Harm Prevention Principle.

> HPP: If one is able to prevent a *harm* to an innocent person, knows one can do so, and can do so without excessive costs, but allows the harm to occur, then one is responsible for the harm befalling that person (barring any countervailing moral obligation that precludes one from acting so as to prevent the harm).

HPP implies that we can, under certain circumstances, be morally responsible (blameworthy) for harms that we do not literally cause. It emphasizes the importance for moral responsibility of *the ability to control* potentially harmful outcomes, rather than limiting responsibility to cases in which an individual causes a harmful outcome. For example, HPP implies that I am morally responsible for the death of an innocent hit-and-run victim who lies bleeding on the roadside, who will die if I do not act, and whom I could save without excessive costs (merely by calling an ambulance), at least so far as no moral duty forbids my doing so.

It is not my aim here to argue in favor of HPP (or for some further qualified formulation of it), though I believe some such principle is in fact defensible. Instead, my purpose in articulating HPP is to avoid the error of confusing it with (2′) and thereby failing to appreciate how dubious (2′) really is. The latter principle, the Extended Responsibility Principle, is a much broader principle of moral responsibility than HPP, the Harm Prevention Principle. HPP only ascribes moral responsibility for *harms* that we can prevent (and then only subject to important qualifications). The Extended Responsibility Principle goes much farther, by ascribing responsibility to us for *all* outcomes that we could prevent, whether they constitute harms or not. Such a principle of responsibility places a very great burden on us all—indeed, one might say, an indefinitely large burden.

Of course, it is possible to render the Extended Responsibility Principle *equivalent* to the Harm Prevention Principle when applied to cases of lower life-prospects due to bad luck in the genetic lottery. We could achieve this equivalence by simply *stipulating* that just by having life-prospects lower than others', as a result of one's genetic endowment, one is *thereby harmed*.

However, to indulge in this stipulation would be to beg the question, either by assuming a very unpersuasive conception of harm or by assuming the truth of the very principle to be established, namely the Resource Equality Principle. For it would make sense to say that simply having lower life-prospects than others due to my genetic endowment is a harm *only* if it were granted that equality of life-prospects is the normative baseline, as it were, such that any shortfall from equality *constitutes* a harm. But that assumption, so far as I can tell, is not only undefended by those who advocate the Resource Principles (Resource Equality or Resource Redress), but indefensible as well. At any rate, some argument in support of it is needed; and the argument in question could not, on pain of a vitiating circularity, rely on a premise to the effect that lower life-prospects due to genetic luck constitute a harm because everyone is entitled to equal resources or to equal life-prospects.

Merely having lower life-prospects would perhaps be a harm (or a harm in the sense of a wrong, a violation of a right) *if* it were assumed that justice or equal opportunity requires equality of life-prospects. However, that assumption, as I also observed earlier, begs the question in favor of the resource-egalitarian view. Thus, in the absence of an argument to show that equal opportunity or some other principle of justice requires equal life-prospects, or an argument to show that having lower life-prospects is itself a harm, recasting the argument from the Formal Principle of Justice by utilizing the principle that one is as responsible for omissions (failures to prevent) as for commissions appears to fail.

Now one might make the mistake of assuming that having lower life-prospects constituted a harm if one erroneously assumed that when we talk of "bad luck" in the genetic lottery in this context, we mean such rotten luck that a person's prospects are so low as to constitute a *deprivation*. It is one thing to say that being born blind or paralyzed is a harm; quite another to say that being born with a somewhat lower compliment of talents than someone else is a harm (no matter how small the difference in talents is). The former case of bad luck in the genetic lottery could, without any hyperbole, be called a deprivation; the latter could not. Later, in examining the second main argument for the Resource Principles, I will attempt to show that that argument too is unpersuasive, once we distinguish carefully between our responsibility to prevent deprivations and our alleged responsibility to prevent any inequalities whatsoever.

One last attempt to rescue the argument from the Formal Principle of Justice (to the Resource Redress Principle) may be worth considering. Suppose the claim is not that any lower life-prospect is itself a harm (or deprivation), but instead that a situation in which some persons, through no fault of their own, have lower life-prospects than others is *suboptimal* – less good than it would be if none had lower prospects because of undeserved natural differences. I am not even sure that this claim is correct, but suppose for a moment that it is. Its truth would still not be sufficient to show that treating persons equally as persons requires avoiding such a "suboptimal" situation, *unless* another premise were added:

> To not prevent a suboptimal state of affairs (when one could do so) is to fail to treat persons as persons equally.

Or, perhaps the same basic idea might be put a bit less ponderously, and with more emphasis on the idea that it is outcomes that are suboptimal *for persons* that are of concern, as follows:

> (i) We ought to prevent persons' lives from being less good than they would otherwise be, and
> (ii) to fail to do so when we can is to treat them as less than equal, as persons, at least if others enjoy the benefits in question and there is no justification for this inequality on grounds of desert.

The difficulty with this proposition is that both components of it are quite questionable and in need of argumentative support.

With regard to (i), it is one thing to say that one ought to try to prevent undeserved deprivations or to prevent harms, quite another to say that one ought to prevent any condition in which persons' lives are less good than they could be, no matter how good in fact they are. (It might be more plausible to say that if one *did* prevent such "suboptimal" outcomes it would be a good, or a commendable thing, but "ought" here seems dubious.)

Further, even if (i) were granted, there is no obvious link between the obligation or moral imperative it states and the notion of treating persons (as persons) equally that is indicated in (ii). For remember, the whole point is supposed to be that, as a matter of justice, persons are to be treated equally, so far as they are persons. Yet there seems to be a lack of connection here between the idea that one ought to avoid suboptimal outcomes for persons and the idea that if one failed to do so, one would somehow violate a principle of justice that persons as such are not to be treated unequally or indeed treated unjustly in any other way. To put the same point differently, it does not seem that a person could justifiably charge that he had been treated as less than an equal, qua person, and thereby *wronged*, simply because others could have prevented his having lower life-prospects as a result of less-fortunate natural endowments but did not do so, regardless of how good his life-prospects were.

Of course, we might imagine a society in which persons' self-understandings were ingrained with a thoroughgoing egalitarianism according to which preventable lower prospects *would* be seen as a lack of equal regard—as a failure to treat persons equally, as persons, as a matter of justice. However, the question before us is whether we should adopt such a point of view. My suggestion is that, at least for many of us, this is not in fact our point of view, and that so far no good reasons have been given to persuade us to adopt it.

My tentative conclusion, then, is that attempts to base the Resource Equality Principle on the Formal Principle of Justice do not work. Accordingly, I propose to examine now the second argument to support the Resource Principles, without dogmatically assuming that no other argument might be given in favor of them.[9]

[9] Some of Rawls's later writings suggest a different argument in favor of the Resource Equality Principle, one which does not rely (at least not explicitly) upon the Formal Principle of Justice. The central idea of this line of argument is that free and equal persons, who regard themselves as such, and as members of a society of such persons understood as a cooperative venture for mutual advantage, would not simply accept a situation in which they had lower life-prospects due to undeserved differences in natural or social resources. See, for example, Rawls, *Political Liberalism*, pp. 15–34.

Perhaps Rawls's point can be expressed this way: In a situation in which undeserved differences in natural or social resources led to some having lower life-prospects, those with lower life-prospects, so far as they viewed themselves as free and equal persons in a cooperative venture for mutual benefit, would *take* themselves to be treated as less than equals by their fellows. That is to say, *from* the perspective of persons conceived as Rawls conceives them for purposes of a liberal theory of justice, allowing undeserved differences in natural or social resources *would count* as unequal treatment of equals, thus violating the Formal Principle of Justice. In other words, if the members of society allowed such factors to result in lower life-prospects for some persons, then those persons, so far as they conceived of themselves as free and equal and so far as they conceived of society as a cooperative venture for mutual advantage among free and equal persons, would take this state of affairs to

III. The Argument from Equal Opportunity

If, as I have suggested, arguments from the Formal Principle of Justice are to no avail, then a more promising approach for those who endorse the Resource Principles might be to try to ground them in a moral principle or concept that already enjoys wider support—the concept of equal opportunity. Of course, for this strategy to work, the concept of equal opportunity with which the argument begins must be one that is not only recognizable as a concept of equal opportunity but also one which enjoys wide acceptance. The most obvious way to achieve this would be to appeal to the actual history of the development of the concept of equal opportunity, beginning at an early stage in its development, and showing that the underlying principle that drives its expansion leads ultimately to the desired destination: the Resource Principles. On one interpretation of his discussion of equal opportunity in *A Theory of Justice*, this is precisely what Rawls attempts to do. For convenient reference, let us call this the Expansive Instability Argument.[10]

As Rawls states the Expansive Instability Argument, the moderate, relatively uncontroversial notion of equal opportunity with which he begins is that of Careers Open to Talents. This conception is then shown to be *unstable*: once we acknowledge that equal opportunity requires the elimination of legal barriers to opportunity and once we see the principle upon which the requirement of the elimination of legal barriers rests, we must ultimately—on pain of inconsistency—admit that justice requires redressing or compensating *all* inequalities in life-prospects due to "morally arbitrary factors," whether the latter be natural or social. Rawls's strategy is to begin with this very limited conception of equal opportunity and show how the principle which underlies it, when properly understood, leads to a succession of *more expansive* conceptions of equal opportunity, and ultimately to the conclusion that a proper and consistent

be a public *expression* of a collective judgment that they were not in fact moral equals to those with higher life-prospects.

The problem with this argument for the Resource Equality Principle is that the crucial statement about the beliefs of individuals who view themselves as free and equal cooperators for mutual advantage with others seems to beg the question. As a descriptive, empirical generalization about the way people, or most people in a society like ours, in fact see themselves, it remains wholly unsupported by anything Rawls says. Moreover, in a pluralistic society such as ours in which there are significant differences of judgment about what recognition of the fundamental equality of persons requires (not to mention about whether justice requires intervening in or compensating for bad luck in the natural lottery), it is unlikely that the needed empirical support would be forthcoming. On the other hand, if the statement is taken as a normative one that is somehow implicit in the normative concept of a free and equal person, then it seems equally dubious. (There may be disputes, of course, over which is the correct normative concept of a person.) Precisely what is at issue is whether a proper recognition of the equality of persons as free beings requires implementation of something like the Resource Equality Principle.

[10] See Rawls, *A Theory of Justice*, pp. 72–73.

appreciation of equal opportunity requires the acceptance of his Second Principle of Justice.

The underlying principle—the one which is supposed to ground the initial, very limited conception of opportunity (Careers Open to Talents), but pull us inevitably beyond it to the more expansive conceptions—is simply what I have called the Resource Redress Principle. Upon reflection we are bound to admit, Rawls thinks, that it is not the legal character of obstacles to social positions and offices that makes them unacceptable, but that they are instances of something much more general: undeserved (and hence "morally arbitrary") inequalities in the distribution of primary goods (resources) resulting in lower life-prospects for some.

In other words, according to the Expansive Instability Argument, it is allegiance to the Resource Equality Principle that underlies our commitment to careers being open to talents, and once we recognize this, we see that we must, in all consistency, go beyond Careers Open to Talents to more expansive conceptions of equal opportunity. As we shall see, by using the eighteenth-century phrase "careers open to talents," Rawls strongly suggests that a historical view of the development of the concept will help illuminate the principle that underlies its development.

There are two reasons to believe that the most promising interpretation of the Expansive Instability Argument anchors it in the actual history of the development of the concept of equal opportunity. The first is that doing so increases the chances that the basic strategy of the argument—that of beginning with what is widely accepted and relatively uncontroversial and moving toward a conclusion that is, at the outset, highly controversial—will actually be implemented. By showing how the "inner logic" of the concept led us in the past to accept one expansion of the notion of equal opportunity, Rawls may smooth the way for a new expansion. If we accept the initial expansion and see that it was required by a certain principle we accept, then we should accept the next expansion that same principle requires.

The second reason for appealing to the historical development of the concept is distinct but related: In his later works Rawls has increasingly relied upon what I have elsewhere labeled a Traditionist mode of justification.[11] He now sees his task as that of showing how his principles of justice are rooted in certain ideals that are embedded in the political culture and institutional traditions of modern liberal-democratic society. Therefore, focusing on the historical origins and actual development of the concept of equal opportunity in the political doctrines, major legal documents, and political institutions of that sort of society is not only appropriate, but necessary if this mode of justification is to be employed.

[11] Allen Buchanan, *Secession: The Morality of Political Divorce from Fort Sumter to Lithuania and Quebec* (Boulder: Westview Press, 1991), pp. 82–83.

It is the Expansive Instability Argument that I shall show to be unsound. Four important conclusions will emerge from the analysis. First, there *is* a historically rooted concept of equal opportunity that has undergone a process of expansion; but it does *not* require intervening in the natural lottery in order to reduce natural inequalities, nor does it require compensating for all undeserved natural inequalities by redistributing social resources. Second, equal opportunity, under certain conditions, may require constraints on the uses of technologies for genetic enhancement. Third, given a somewhat controversial extension of the concept of equal opportunity—yet one far less extreme than that employed in the two Resource Principles—justice may, under certain conditions, require genetic interventions, not to avoid natural inequalities, but to prevent *deprivations*. Fourth, at least in its most familiar and uncontroversial applications, equal opportunity is not a *primary* principle of justice; rather, it is a *remedial* principle, one that comes into play as a response to violations of other, more basic principles of justice. And none of these more basic principles includes anything so extreme as the two Resource Principles.

IV. The Concept of Equal Opportunity: Its Historical Development

In criticizing the Expansive Instability Argument, my strategy will be to provide a characterization of the principles that underlie the successively more expansive conceptions of equal opportunity without relying upon anything so extreme as the Resource Principles. In doing so, I will show that Rawls simply begs the question in favor of the Resource Redress Principle by invoking it gratuitously to explain the first stage of the development of the concept of equal opportunity and then arguing that consistency requires that we accept its more radical implications.

We can begin where Rawls does, with a sketch of the development of the concept of equality of opportunity. Rawls first notes what we would now regard as a rather conservative and uncontroversial conception of equal opportunity: the requirement that careers be open to talents. One of the slogans of the French Revolution and of liberalism's struggle against hereditary privilege, this is simply the idea that there should be no *legal* barriers to preclude *qualified* persons from seeking and obtaining valued social positions and offices.

In the historical setting in which it was first voiced, this principle of equal opportunity had a dual thrust. First, it could be seen simply as the demand that a preexisting *meritocratic principle* be consistently applied—that the best-qualified candidates, regardless of their class background, be awarded positions in fair competition. Second, the slogan "careers open to talents" was a rejection of the presumption that the hereditary aristocracy was in fact an aristocracy, that noble lineage conferred superior qualifications for office. Understood in this way, the slogan only required a consistent application of a preexisting commitment to a meritocratic principle, but was revolutionary nonetheless because it rejected a theory of natural superiority that created a presumption of superior merit in a certain class of individuals.

This interpretation of the concept of equality of opportunity as Careers Open to Talents is compatible with the recognition that there may have been, at the same time, a shift in the way merit was understood, or, more precisely, a change in the conception of the bases of merit. As the idea took hold that the social good was best secured through increases in productivity spurred by the motive of private gain, a different conception of the qualifications needed for various social positions developed along with it. Thus, the "talents" required for various positions were those needed to enhance national wealth, and the earlier aristocratic (and largely military) virtues became less relevant. Nevertheless, even if the standard of merit was being transformed by the same socioeconomic forces that produced the challenge to aristocratic privilege, the fact remains that the moral appeal of equal opportunity as Careers Open to Talents is easily explained simply by recourse to the idea that, at least in certain areas of social life, justice requires a consistent application of the meritocratic principle. That principle states that, at least for positions where ability to perform the tasks that define the role is the proper criterion for filling the position, individuals should be allowed to compete fairly, simply on the basis of their qualifications, without any legal barriers to doing so.

There is no need whatsoever to invoke any grand principle about the role of social (or natural) contingencies as such in shaping individuals' life-prospects. It is entirely gratuitous to assume, as Rawls apparently does, that the commitment to equal opportunity as Careers Open to Talents rests on the conviction that justice requires redressing or compensating for differences in life-prospects due to morally arbitrary social contingencies. All that is needed is an appeal to what is obvious: the idea that, in areas of life in which the meritocratic principle is appropriate, it is to be applied consistently.

Similarly, a second stage in the evolution of the concept of equal opportunity can also be explained without recourse to anything so extreme as the Resource Principles. Rawls is right in saying that once we see that there should be no legal barriers to qualified persons competing for valued social positions and offices, we must, in all consistency, be concerned about less formal barriers. The same moral concern which led us to embrace the conception of equal opportunity as Careers Open to Talents requires that we attempt to eliminate barriers to opportunity posed by racial, gender, or ethnic prejudice, even if these manifest themselves in extralegal ways, through the operation of less formal social practices and individual acts of discrimination. Let us call this second conception of equal opportunity, which does seem to be a natural and indeed inevitable expansion of Careers Open to Talents, equal opportunity as Comprehensive Nondiscrimination.

Again, notice how far this expansion of the concept of equality of opportunity (beyond the narrow confines of Careers Open to Talents to that of Comprehensive Nondiscrimination) is from the radical notion that justice requires redressing or compensating for any and every lowering of life-prospects due to any morally arbitrary social or natural contingency.

This second conception of equality of opportunity is indeed an expansion of the first conception: it recognizes that qualified persons may be precluded from positions and offices not only by laws that literally bar them from competing, but also by pervasive social practices that embody deeply ingrained racial, ethnic, or gender prejudices. Especially when it is applied to cases of racial discrimination in filling positions, this second conception of equality of opportunity also invokes, perhaps more explicitly than the conception of Careers Open to Talents, a principle of the equality of persons. When a qualified African American is excluded from being seriously considered for an apprenticeship in a union, he has a double grievance: not only has he been treated unfairly because his qualifications were disregarded, but also he has been insulted and demeaned so far as his equal status as a person is concerned. Racial discrimination in hiring of this sort, whether it achieves exclusion by laws (as in apartheid South Africa or the Jim Crow South) or by informal racist practices, violates two principles of justice: the meritocratic principle and the principle of equal respect for persons. The principle forbidding racial discrimination, then, is simply one application, focused on the case of race, of a more basic principle of equal respect for persons that provided part of the impetus for rejecting the presumption that the hereditary nobility were natural superiors. Nothing more need be said to explain the moral appeal of this second conception of equal opportunity, and nothing more need be added to explain how it developed out of the earlier concept of Careers Open to Talents. The second conception simply applies the meritocratic principle more consistently, by recognizing that qualified persons can be excluded from meritocratic competition by informal as well as legal barriers, and also rejects the idea of a class of natural superiors as the latter is applied to the case of race, gender, or ethnicity.

The only concept of respect for the fundamental equality of persons at work here, however, is a purely negative one: persons are not to be victimized by discrimination, legal or otherwise. No notion that all "morally arbitrary" social (or natural) inequalities are a matter of concern from the standpoint of justice is present or needed.

It is essential to emphasize that what Rawls identifies as the successor to the concept of equal opportunity as Careers Open to Talents is something quite different from what I have described as the first natural expansion of the concept: Comprehensive Nondiscrimination. In the following passage he states that the principle underlying Careers Open to Talents requires us next to embrace what he calls Liberal Equality.

> [Where the requirement of careers open to talents is satisfied there is formal equality] . . . in that all have at least the same legal rights of access to all advantaged social positions. But since there is no effort to preserve an equality, or similarity, of social conditions, except insofar as this is necessary to preserve the requisite background institutions, the initial distribution of assets for any period of time is strongly influenced by natural and social contingencies. . . . Intuitively, the most obvious injustice of the system of natural liberty [in which careers are open to talents] is that it permits distributive shares to be improperly influenced by these factors so arbitrary from a moral point of view.[12]

What is needed, Rawls then concludes, is an expansion of the concept of equal opportunity from Careers Open to Talents to what he calls Fair Equality of Opportunity. The idea is that "positions are to be not only open in a formal sense, but that all should have a fair chance to attain them."[13] By a "fair chance" Rawls means something quite specific: "[T]hose who are at the same level of talent and ability, and have the same willingness to use them, should have the same [i.e., equal] prospects of success. . . ."[14]

At the very least, something of a leap has occurred here. As indicated earlier, the most obvious candidate for a successor to the concept of equal opportunity as Careers Open to Talents is the concept of equal opportunity as Comprehensive Nondiscrimination. The latter simply extends the notion of impermissible barriers to opportunity from legal discrimination to extralegal, informal discrimination. And in fact, not only in this country, but in other countries as well, at least in the West, when legal systems and social practices have extended the notion of equal opportunity beyond Careers Open to Talents, they have done so by recognizing that informal modes of discrimination, such as racist or sexist hiring practices, are unjust restrictions on opportunity and must be eliminated where possible.

It is surprising, given the strategy of the Expansive Instability Argument as I have characterized it, that Rawls simply passes over this stage in the development of the concept of equal opportunity. It is even more surprising that he moves instead to the much more radical notion that equal opportunity requires that those with equal talent and motivation

[12] Rawls, *A Theory of Justice*, p. 72.
[13] *Ibid.*, p. 73.
[14] *Ibid.*

have equal chances of attaining valued positions. It would be very difficult—in fact, I think, impossible—to find evidence of the wide acceptance of this concept of equal opportunity among individuals in modern liberal societies. At any rate, Rawls fails to provide any such evidence. It would also be difficult to show that such a concept is somehow embodied in the political doctrines or legal institutions of such societies. Again, Rawls offers nothing to indicate that it is.

More importantly, if my analysis of the principles that underlie Careers Open to Talents and its successor, Comprehensive Nondiscrimination, is even approximately accurate, Rawls's concept of Fair Equality of Opportunity has no apparent logical or conceptual connection with either. It certainly cannot be seen as an expansion of the concepts of Careers Open to Talents or Comprehensive Nondiscrimination if, as I have argued, these concepts rely upon the consistent application of the meritocratic principle and a negative concept of the equality of persons that only rejects the spurious natural inegalitarianism of views that hold aristocrats or whites or women, etc., to be natural superiors.

The concept of equal opportunity as Comprehensive Nondiscrimination, then, is a much better candidate for a successor to Careers Open to Talents than is Rawls's concept of Fair Equality of Opportunity; and the principles that underlie the former two concepts, and that account for the expansion of the first into the second, do *not* require the adoption of Fair Equality of Opportunity.

Although Rawls does not mention it, there is a third stage in the historical development of the concept of equal opportunity, at least in our (U.S.) society, that is somewhat more controversial. This conception of equal opportunity is sometimes labeled Strong Affirmative Action. It differs from the second (Comprehensive Nondiscrimination) and from the first (Careers Open to Talents), requiring that in some cases equal opportunity mandates departures from the strict meritocratic principle. A policy requiring that African Americans, Hispanics, Native Americans, or women be given preference in hiring for faculty positions even when there are *better*-qualified male or nonminority candidates would fall under this third conception.

It is not my aim here to defend or to attack this third conception of equal opportunity. Instead, I only wish to show that *if* this conception is justifiable, its justification does *not* commit us to anything resembling the Resource Principles. To my knowledge, the best, indeed the only, plausible justification for Strong Affirmative Action, is the idea that under certain historical circumstances a strict adherence to the meritocratic principle would simply perpetuate the negative effects of past injustices toward members of certain groups. For example, since blatantly racist legal and social practices in the past (if not in some cases in the present) have led to African Americans' having, on average, lower educational attainments than whites, requiring them to meet the same educational qualifications as other candidates will perpetuate the tendency for African Americans to not attain higher-paying, more rewarding jobs. In order to compensate for the continuing disadvantages of lower educational attainment—disadvantages due to violations of meritocratic and nondiscrimination principles of justice—it may be necessary to depart from the meritocratic principle. In its most powerful version, this argument includes the idea that by thus departing from the meritocratic principle we will give unjustly disadvantaged persons the opportunity to develop their qualifications, to become better qualified through more challenging work than they would otherwise be able to obtain.

Whether or not this justification for Strong Affirmative Action is compelling is disputable. What is clear is that nothing in this justification relies on or entails the thesis that *every* lowering of life-prospects due to *any* "morally arbitrary" social contingency requires redress or compensation. Instead, the third conception of equal opportunity, Strong Affirmative Action, focuses only on one kind of social contingency—that which is the result of, and tends to perpetuate, the negative effects of injustices.

To summarize: Rawls's Expansive Instability Argument contends that once we acknowledge the more limited conceptions of equal opportunity, beginning with Careers Open to Talents, we are led, as a matter of consistency, to the idea that not only "morally arbitrary" social contingencies but also natural contingencies require redress or compensation, so far as they lead to some having lower life-prospects. As we have seen, however, the earlier stages in the development of the concept of equal opportunity lead to the Resource Redress Principle *only* if one erroneously reads into them the idea that equal opportunity requires redressing or compensating for any lowering of life-prospects due to social contingencies. The slide from redressing or compensating for social contingencies to redressing or compensating for natural contingencies occurs only if one begins with the assumption that equal opportunity requires that all "morally arbitrary" social contingencies be redressed or compensated. But nothing in the development of the concept of equal opportunity so much as hints at anything so radical as this latter assumption.

In each of the three stages of the development of the concept of equal opportunity—from Careers Open to Talents, to Comprehensive Nondiscrimination, to Strong Affirmative Action—"social contingencies" are a focus of concern. However, what makes them so is not that they are "morally arbitrary" (in the sense of being things individuals cannot be said to deserve). Rather, it is the fact that these "social contingencies" that act as barriers to opportunity are *injustices* or (in the case of the third conception) that they help perpetuate the negative impact of injustices. And what counts as an injustice in all of these cases is characterized by appeal to relatively uncontroversial principles of justice *other* than the principle of equality of opportunity itself: namely, the meritocratic principle and a fundamental prohibition against racial, ethnic, or gender discrimination, in the case of the first two conceptions, and a principle of rectificatory justice in the case of the third. (What is controversial about Strong Affirmative Action is not the idea that we should try to eliminate the effects of past injustices, but rather the assumption that this obligation overrides the meritocratic principle.)

As I indicated earlier, my assumption is that if there is an argument from the concept of equal opportunity to the Resource Principles, then it is Rawls's Expansive Instability Argument. That argument has proven to be not only unsound, but irretrievably so. The problem with that argument is not that it lacks an easily supplied premise or that it grounds only an approximation of the conclusion it seeks to establish. On the contrary, nothing in the history of the development of the concept of equal opportunity seems to provide material that could be used to reach Rawls's radical conclusion.

Consequently, in the absence of some other argument to support them, the Resource Principles seem dubious indeed. Neither of these principles is self-evident, and, as we have seen, we cannot hope to justify either of them by showing that it is needed to explain our more widely and confidently held considered judgments about what equality of opportunity requires. Nor, given my own revised account of Rawls's appeal to the historical development of the concept of equal opportunity, does it appear that the Resource Principles are good candidates for what I have referred to as Rawls's Traditionist mode of justification for principles of justice. If my sketch of the development of the concept of equal opportunity is even roughly correct, Rawls will have to do much more to show that the Resource Principles are somehow latent in "our" political traditions or culture.

In the next section, I will consider some of the consequences of accepting the more basic (first-best) Resource Equality Principle. Once these are appreciated, the principle will be seen not only to be unsupported, but quite dubious on its face.

V. Resource Equality and the Disappearance of Persons

Perhaps the first thing to notice is that none of those who subscribe to the Resource Redress Principle have advocated the redistribution of natural assets (genes or complexes of genes). Instead, they have only called for the redistribution of social assets to compensate for some having lesser natural assets than others. However, to my knowledge none of them have given a clear argument to show why, contrary to appearances, allegiance to the Resource Redress Principle, and to the Resource Equality Principle upon which it rests, does *not* create a presumption in favor of redistributing genes in the name of justice, once the technology for doing so is at hand.

It might be replied that Rawls, at least, has an answer: Intervening in the genetic lottery is forbidden by the lexically prior principle of equal liberty. The latter principle includes a right to the freedom and integrity of the person that such intervention would violate.

The inadequacy of this reply becomes apparent once one realizes how radical the notion of intervening in the genetic lottery to equalize natural resources really is. We should not assume that this would merely be a matter of *redistributing* genes among antecedently existing persons (something like the analog of redistributing organs among a group of individuals). Instead, it seems likely that true genetic equality (if we can even make sense of that idea) would best be approximated by engineering individuals from scratch. If this is the case, then it is not at all clear that the right to freedom and integrity of the person of those who were thus engineered would be violated, since those individuals *would not exist prior to the intervention*.

Of course, Rawls might argue that it would not be the freedom or integrity of the person of the recipients of redistribution, but of their parents (or, rather, of those who would not be permitted to be parents of their "natural offspring") that would be violated. The difficulty is that once the possibility of profound genetic intervention is acknowledged and the presumption in favor of engaging in it to equalize natural assets is in place, it is hard to see why, on Rawls's own account, the right of parents to engage in genetic roulette should take absolute priority over the right of persons to be spared the (alleged) inequity of having lower life-prospects as a result of their inferior native endowments. For remember, according to Rawls, to allow this inequity is somehow to fail to honor the fundamental moral equality of persons and thus to do them a profound injustice.

For resource theorists who do not endorse a lexically prior principle of liberty that could provide a possible restraint on the commitment to achieving an equal distribution of all resources, natural and social, the problem is more severe. They seem to be committed to a view of distributive justice that, in effect, shatters what one would have thought was a framework assumption of any theory of distributive justice: namely, that we can distinguish between (1) persons, as the subjects among whom assets are to be distributed, and (2) the assets that are to be distributed among them.

In their defense it might be said that if the egalitarian resource theorists are willing to make a highly problematic metaphysical move, this framework assumption is salvageable. The trick would be to distinguish between those features of a person that are person-constituting, that are elements of his or her identity as a subject of justice, and those nonessential characteristics that are resources, and thus subject to the principle that resources are to be distributed equally or that inequalities in resources are to be eliminated.

Unfortunately, even if some principled way of distinguishing these two sorts of properties of the individual could be devised, it is not at all clear that this would solve the problem. Unless an additional argument were given to show that a person has a *right* to his or her identity-constituting properties, the mere fact that radical genetic manipulation might violate the conditions of identity would seem to carry no conclusive *moral* weight against it. For if the fundamental commitment is to ensuring that, so far as this is possible, persons have equal resources, then why should it bother one that in order to achieve the desired equality one must act so as to determine which persons, having which characteristics, will exist?

It is important to understand that an appeal to the idea that all valid moral principles are "person-affecting" principles provides no bar against the presumption in favor of achieving equality of resources by radical genetic manipulation, that is, by intervention on gametes or embryos. On any reasonable interpretation of the idea that moral principles must be "person-affecting," the scope of moral principles cannot be limited to actual persons—otherwise there would be no moral constraints on any of our behavior that we know will affect future generations. In other words, the thrust of the injunction that all moral principles must be "person-affecting" is simply that, so far as there are any valid moral principles that constrain our behavior that affects future persons, those principles ultimately must be based upon regard for the well-being and freedom of those persons who will come to exist, rather than upon some impersonal standard or value such as maximizing the total of utility per se or creating a better world, where what makes the world better is something other than the benefits for persons who exist in it. The principle that radical genetic intervention is to be employed, where necessary, to achieve equal resources is not, therefore, incompatible with the requirement that moral principles be person-affecting, on a reasonable interpretation of the latter requirement. Thus, appeal to the idea that valid moral principles are person-affecting cannot itself rule out radical genetic manipulation for the sake of achieving resource equality.

VI. A Fourth Concept of Equal Opportunity: The Absence of Undeserved Deprivation

Earlier I argued for a more conservative interpretation of the stages of development of the concept of equal opportunity. There I appealed, in effect, to what are sometimes called our "moral intuitions" (or considered moral judgments) as well as to the actual development of political doctrines concerning equal opportunity and of the legal institutions embodying them, at least in those Western countries that have institutionalized conceptions of equal opportunity. I argued that in the various cases falling under the three concepts of equal opportunity previously discussed, our intuitions, as well as the development of the institutional embodiment of these concepts, can be explained by less radical moral principles than the Resource Principles. (The three concepts of equal opportunity were Careers Open to Talents, Comprehensive Nondiscrimination, and Strong Affirmative Action.)

Perhaps, however, there are some widely and confidently held considered judgments about equal opportunity that have not yet been examined. Perhaps accounting for *them* will drive us in a more radical direction, toward the Resource Principles—and into the arms of the genetic engineers.

What I have in mind is the following sort of case. Suppose that a child is born blind or with some other major disability. Do we not believe that some special treatment is required, as a matter of justice? In the clearest case, assume that a relatively simple (though not costless) operation will restore the child's sight, that neither the child nor her family can afford it, and that no private philanthropic organization steps forward to pay for the operation. Unless there are public resources available for the child, she will go through life with a profound disability. Alternately, consider a case in which sight cannot be restored, but a special allocation of resources can enable the child to learn braille, to live independently (perhaps with the help of a guide dog, a specially equipped apartment, etc.). Again, suppose that private resources are not forthcoming. Some might say not only that a special allocation of the needed resources is required as a matter of justice, but also that the relevant principle of justice is that of equal opportunity.

It should be clear that none of the three conceptions of equal opportunity sketched earlier can encompass such cases. It need not be the case that the blind individual is being excluded, either legally (contrary to the concept of Careers Open to Talent) or by informal barriers of prejudice (contrary to the concept of Comprehensive Nondiscrimination), from competing successfully for positions for which she is qualified. Nor need the obstacle be the lingering effects of former discriminatory practices (to which the concept of Strong Affirmative Action is addressed).

Instead, her blindness—in the absence of special resources—may simply prevent her from being qualified for many if not all desirable positions. So we cannot make a case for allocating special resources to her or to anyone with a major natural disability on the ground that the meritocratic principle is not being applied consistently in her case or on the ground that she is being excluded as a result of prejudice which demeans and devalues her by classifying her as an inferior individual (as in the case of racist, ethnic, or gender discrimination). Nor will these sorts of cases fit under the third (Strong Affirmative Action) conception of equal opportunity: she lacks the qualifications for various positions, not because she is the victim of past injustices, but because she is naturally blind.

Some, of course, might argue that this is not a matter of equal opportunity because it is not a matter of *justice* at all, but rather of charity.[15] My strategy will not be to try to settle the issue of how we are to distinguish the domain of justice from that of charity. Instead, I will simply argue that the most plausible interpretation of these sorts of cases as falling under the notion of equal opportunity does not require anything so extreme and far-reaching as either of the Resource Principles.

I would like to suggest that what bothers us about the situation of severely disabled persons, and what leads us toward a commitment to improving their opportunities through special allocations, is not the conviction that every lowering of life-prospects due to misfortune in the natural lottery requires social redress or compensation. Instead, what is at work here, what fully accounts for our intuitions, is a much more modest principle, namely that, other things being equal, no person should be barred from the chance to have a minimally decent life as a result of undeserved natural (or social) deficits. In other words, the relevant concern here is with *deprivation*, not with inequality as such.[16]

To believe that concern for equal opportunity requires doing something to compensate for this severe disability, we need not believe that there is something inequitable about every case in which an individual's life-prospects are lower than they would be if he had the natural assets which those with superior natural assets have. All that is necessary is that we believe that we have an obligation, perhaps a very limited one, to prevent an undeserved natural *deficit* or *disability* from resulting in a *deprivation*, a lack of some important constituent of a minimally decent or adequate human life.[17]

No doubt many will find the notion of deprivation, dependent as it is on the notion of a minimally decent or adequate life, to be unsatisfyingly vague. It is vague. However, when properly contextualized by reference

[15] For a discussion of the difficulty of drawing a coherent line between justice and charity, see Allen Buchanan, "Justice and Charity," *Ethics*, vol. 97, no. 3 (1987), pp. 558–75.

[16] Those familiar with the extremely illuminating work of Amartya Sen will no doubt find familiar this notion of deprivation and of justice requiring a distribution of resources to prevent deprivation rather than to achieve equality as such. (See, e.g., Amartya Sen, "Equality of What?" in Sterling M. McMurrin, ed., *Liberty, Equality, and Law* [Salt Lake City: University of Utah Press, 1987]; and Sen, *Commodities and Capabilities* [New York: Elsevier Science Publishing Co., 1985].) To my way of thinking, though in some respects Sen's approach seems to be in the resourcist camp, he succeeds in avoiding the mistakes I attribute in this essay to other resourcists such as Cohen, Dworkin, and Rawls.

[17] It is important to add the qualifier "other things being equal" here. For one thing, a serious effort to bring the most severely disabled up to the level of a "decent" life would be prohibitively expensive—would entail an unacceptable restriction on the opportunities of the better off. What I have in mind is what is sometimes referred to in bioethics circles as the "medical black holes problem." Given an indefinitely expanding technology, efforts to bring every severely disabled person up even to some rather modest level of functioning could absorb vast amounts of resources. My own view is that justice does not require this sort of sacrifice.

to the specific forms of human flourishing available in particular societies and by reference to the constraints which the resource base available in particular societies places on reasonable redistribution, it is not vacuous. (For most people in modern, industrial societies, for example, having a chance at a decent life requires the ability to read and access to certain basic health care, at least during childhood, among other things.) In spite of its inherent vagueness, I find the idea that justice requires a response to deprivation much more reasonable than the sweeping thesis that justice requires redressing or compensating for any lowering of life-prospects due to having a lesser share of natural assets.[18]

VII. The Remedial, Derivative Nature of Equal Opportunity

Our analysis of the principles that account for the development of the concept of equal opportunity yields an important conclusion about the role of equal opportunity in a theory of justice. That analysis revealed three distinct conceptions of equal opportunity: (1) Careers Open to Talents, requiring the removal of legal barriers to advancement by qualified individuals; (2) Comprehensive Nondiscrimination, requiring removal

[18] A resource egalitarian might make one last attempt to persuade me otherwise. Suppose that we know that unless something is done to prevent it, a child will be born, not with a deprivation, but with somewhat lower life-prospects due to some genetic condition. Are we not morally obliged to prevent this from occurring, if we could do so without excessive costs and without violating any important moral principles (such as that requiring respect for the rights of prospective parents, etc.)?

It is hard to know what to make of this example, even if one shares the intuition of those who advance it—namely, that we should intervene. Part of the problem, of course, is the vague inclusiveness of the qualifying phrase "without excessive costs and without violating any important moral principles." But even apart from that, there is another problem with such an appeal to intuitions. Even if one admits that it would be *a good thing*, morally speaking, to undertake the intervention (subject to the qualifying phrase), and even if one goes further to say that we *ought* to undertake it, we are still quite some distance from the desired conclusion, namely, that equal opportunity or some other principle of *justice* (such as equal respect for persons as such) requires us to do so.

For one thing, it does not seem to be the case that justice demands that we bring about everything that is morally good or everything that would be an improvement for some person. For another, we usually think of what is a matter of justice as being that which a person is entitled to *as a matter of right*, such that if she is not provided with it, she may correctly charge that she has been *wronged*. However, from the fact (if it be such) that in some sense it would be better (even better from a moral point of view) if persons did not have lower life-prospects due to undeserved natural differences, or that it would be a good thing if we prevented this, it does not follow that by not intervening to bring about this better state of affairs we wrong those with lower life-prospects. Moreover, I think it is fair to say that many of us simply do not share the resource egalitarian's intuition that if we (society? the state?) do not intervene in such a case, then the individual in question can reasonably say that she has been wronged, that some right of hers has been violated.

If, on the other hand, the point of this appeal to intuitions is not that to not intervene is to wrong the person, but rather simply that it would be a good thing to intervene and that, other things being equal, we ought to bring about good things, then one can hardly quarrel with it. Considerably more will be needed, however, to show that not intervening is incompatible with a proper recognition of the fundamental equality of persons, with equal opportunity, or with some other principle of justice.

not only of legal barriers but also of informal barriers of racial, gender, or ethnic prejudice; and (3) Strong Affirmative Action, requiring special preference for candidates who may be less than optimally qualified, in order to combat the lingering effects of discrimination. In each of these three conceptions, equal opportunity was seen to be a derivative principle, to be explained entirely by reference to other, more basic principles of justice. In (1) and (2), the relevant principles were the meritocratic principle and a principle of nondiscrimination against persons (on the basis of race, ethnicity, gender, etc.); in (3), the relevant principle was a principle of rectificatory justice requiring special efforts to negate the harmful effects of past injustices.

When one characterizes the moral significance of any instances falling under any of these three conceptions, the phrase "equal opportunity" is eliminable without loss. In that respect, at least with regard to (1), (2), and (3), equal opportunity is at best a *derivative* (or secondary) principle of justice, and one that is remedial in the sense that it requires a response to violations of other, more basic principles. Contrary to what Rawls and others have assumed, it is not even the *sort* of principle that could be basic in a theory of justice.

It will be recalled, however, that we also considered another area in which some might think a conception of equal opportunity applies: cases where we believe that special allocations of resources are required to prevent persons from suffering deprivation, due to misfortune in the distribution of natural endowments. Here two questions arise. First, is this properly described as a matter of equal opportunity? Second, if it is, is the notion of equal opportunity here playing a merely secondary (and in principle eliminable) role, as in the other cases of equal opportunity analyzed above, or is this a case where equal opportunity is a basic principle of justice?

I see nothing that forces us to describe the fourth situation (providing special resources to the naturally severely disabled) as a case of equal opportunity. It may be more natural, in fact, to describe it as a case in which what best explains our intuition that some special allocation of resources is called for is a principle of basic welfare (or basic welfare rights), rather than of opportunity. Such a principle would state, roughly, that every person has a right to the resources necessary for a minimally decent life.[19]

[19] If it is to be plausible, such a principle would have to be qualified by a clause to the effect that supplying a person with resources necessary for a minimally decent life does not involve excessive costs. Given the apparently indefinitely expanding horizon of medical technology, enormous amounts of resources could be expended in making marginal improvements in the lot of the most severely disabled individuals (the "medical black holes problem" I mentioned in note 17). A proper recognition that persons have only one life to lead and that they should be allowed to give special preference to their own projects and to those with whom they are closely affiliated surely places significant limits on what each of us owes to others as a matter of general obligations of justice.

Suppose, however, that one were to insist that the principle underlying our intuitions in such cases is in fact a principle requiring that every person have *an opportunity* to lead a minimally decent life, and that it is this principle that underlies the notion that we should prevent deprivations, where the latter are thought of as harmful conditions or deficits so serious as to pose obstacles to achieving a minimally decent life. This way of understanding our response to the case of naturally severely disabled persons apparently would see the response as resting on a principle of equal opportunity, though only in this attenuated sense: it would require a kind of minimal egalitarianism with regard to opportunity – everyone is to have an opportunity for a minimally decent life. This principle of equal opportunity, however, is presumably to be understood as a basic, rather than a derivative, principle of justice. It does not appear to rest upon other principles of justice such as the meritocratic principle, a principle of nondiscrimination, or a principle of rectification.

If this is the correct characterization of the principle that underlies our intuitions in the fourth type of case, then the conception of equal opportunity at work in it is quite distinct from, and indeed sharply discontinuous with, that implicit in the three stages of the development of the concept of equal opportunity sketched above. As I have noted, there is a clear continuity among the first three stages – the same principles, of merit and nondiscrimination, are appealed to in all three (although in the case of Strong Affirmative Action the principle of rectification is said to override the current application of the meritocratic principle whose past violation calls for rectification).

In contrast, none of these principles is appealed to in the case of special allocations for the naturally severely disabled, if we describe this as an instance falling under the principle that every person is to have an opportunity to lead a minimally decent life. This suggests either that it is misleading to characterize all four types of cases as matters of equal opportunity or that there are two quite distinct concepts of equal opportunity at work: a remedial, secondary, and eliminable conception in the first three, and a quite distinct, primary conception in the fourth. If this is correct, then there is no univocal answer to the question of whether equal opportunity is a basic or a derivative principle in the theory of justice. Some principles of equal opportunity (the first three) are derivative, and at least one other (the fourth) is basic.

VIII. The Role of Equal Opportunity in the Uses of Genetic Intervention: Preventing Genetically Based Deprivations and Placing Constraints on Genetic Enhancement

So far I have argued that the Resource Redress and Resource Equality Principles are not supported either by the Formal Principle of Justice or by a principle of equal opportunity (whether the latter is understood as a remedial principle of justice based on the meritocratic principle and a negative principle of respect for persons as nondiscrimination, or as a primary principle of justice requiring that we prevent undeserved deprivations). Thus, unless some *other* justification for it succeeds, the Resource Equality Principle provides no reason to undertake redistributions of genes in the name of equal opportunity, and the Resource Redress Principle, understood as a second-best principle, lacks support because the first-best principle upon which it is supposed to rest is itself groundless. I now wish to suggest, however, that there are two *other* roles that a plausible conception of equal opportunity can play in determining the moral uses of genetic intervention technology.

The first role is that of placing *constraints* on the uses of genetic enhancement technology, under conditions in which differences in access to this technology would be likely to exacerbate other, independently characterizable injustices. The second is that of imposing obligations to use genetic interventions to prevent genetic harms that would constitute deprivations. I will now consider each of these roles briefly, in turn.

Suppose that it becomes possible to identify, synthesize, and implant in embryos complexes of genes that will greatly increase the probability of an individual possessing certain desirable characteristics to a significantly higher degree than the average person in a given population. Such characteristics might include superior memory, ability to concentrate for long periods of time, and general resistance to disease and to psychiatric maladies (such as depression). If access to this technology were solely dependent on ability to pay, then its use might exacerbate and perpetuate disadvantages that certain groups (such as African Americans, Native Americans, and Hispanics) suffer as the result of past injustices of discrimination.

For example, employers would be more likely to select a person for a desirable career track involving much investment in the individual's training over a long period of time if that candidate could produce a "genetic enhancement certificate" credibly stating that his resistance to disease and to psychiatric maladies was much greater than average, his memory was superior, etc. If members of certain disadvantaged minorities were unable to afford this extra credential, they would face yet one more barrier to attaining desirable positions. (Of course, if health insurance continues to be employer-based, as it currently is in the U.S., and if employers are required to offer health insurance to their employees, then employers would have an added incentive to hire those who had benefited from genetic enhancement of their resistance to disease and to shun those who lacked it.)

It is important to see that this effect might occur even if the actual results of genetic enhancement were in fact markedly less significant than was generally supposed. One can easily imagine situations in which job candidates who could produce "genetic enhancement certificates" would have an advantage in competition for positions, even if the benefits of the genetic interventions in question were less pronounced than advertisements portrayed them as being. (Similarly, today, possession of a college diploma serves as a *necessary* qualification for entering competition for most white-collar jobs, even though in many cases the educational experience the individual received in college is of dubious relevance to the actual skills needed for the job, and even though individuals who are excluded because they lack a diploma are in many cases better qualified.)

What are the implications of such a scenario for equality of opportunity? The answer, of course, depends upon which conception of equal opportunity is assumed. *If* equal opportunity requires Strong Affirmative Action, then this principle of justice might, under certain circumstances, require public subsidies for genetic enhancement for groups that have suffered from past discrimination in order to avoid the perpetuation of their injustice-based disadvantages. Or, if providing access to enhancement technology for *everyone* proved too expensive, equal opportunity might conceivably require that *no one* is to have access to certain extremely significant enhancements if this could be demonstrated to perpetuate the effects of past discrimination.

A second, and in some respects more radical role for equal opportunity (yet one still much more conservative than that envisioned by the Resource Equality Principle) would be to require genetic intervention to avoid safely and easily correctable genetically based deprivations that would not respond to treatment after birth. As I observed earlier, whether efforts to avoid deprivations properly fall under the heading of equal opportunity is far from obvious. Supposing that they do, however, there is obviously a strong prima facie case for intervening with gene surgery on the embryo (or perhaps even the gamete) to prevent blindness, if there is a case for allocating special resources to correct or compensate for blindness after the child is born. At least in cases in which postnatal remedies are not available, genetic intervention to prevent deprivations has a great deal of moral plausibility.

The most obvious countervailing consideration, of course, would be respect for the privacy and autonomy of the prospective parents. Complex and daunting issues arise here, not just concerning the permissibility of requiring genetic surgery against the will of one or both of the prospective parents, but also regarding the impact on individual and familial privacy and on confidentiality in the physician-patient relationship that would result from any serious effort to screen embryos or gametes for deprivation-producing defects. My purpose here, however, is not to settle—or even systematically to delineate—these problems. Instead, I only wish to note that there is a strong prima facie case for using genetic interventions to prevent deprivations, while at the same time distinguishing *this* justification for intervening in the "natural lottery" from appeals to the Resource Principles advocated by Rawls and other radical egalitarian resource theorists of justice.

Business Ethics, Philosophy, and Medical Ethics,
University of Wisconsin–Madison

EXPLOITATION*

By Allen W. Wood

It is commonly thought that exploitation is unjust; some think it is part of the very meaning of the word 'exploitation' that it is unjust. Those who think this will suppose that the just society has to be one in which people do not exploit one another, at least on a large scale. I will argue that exploitation is not unjust by definition, and that a society (such as our own) might be fundamentally just while nevertheless being pervasively exploitative. I do think that exploitation is nearly always a bad thing, and will try to identify the moral belief which makes most of us think it is. But I will argue that its badness does not always consist in its being unjust.

I. Is Exploitation a Moral Concept?

Worries about exploitation. The concept of exploitation has probably been most closely associated with the Marxian charge that wage labor is exploitative, but recently it has also figured in controversies about whether surrogacy contracts are exploitative of the birth mother.[1] In most of these uses, the concept of exploitation is left unanalyzed, and this has sometimes provoked the suspicion that we may need a more precise, technical conception of exploitation if claims using it are to be properly evaluated. Alan Wertheimer, for example, has noted with regret that there is no canonical (non-Marxist) account of exploitation, suggesting

* I am grateful for written comments on earlier drafts of this essay by G. A. Cohen, David Lyons, Julie Maybee, and Alan Wertheimer, and for oral comments and discussion by Elizabeth Anderson, Neera Kapur Badhwar, Dan Brock, Daniel Farrell, Michael Gorr, Terence Irwin, Loren Lomasky, Roderick Long, Fred Miller, Ellen Frankel Paul, Thomas Pogge, Larry Temkin, and Steve Wall.

[1] The claim that surrogacy contracts are exploitative can be found in: Peter Singer and Deane Wells, *The Reproductive Revolution* (New York: Oxford University Press, 1984), p. 125; Mary Warnock, *A Question of Life: The Warnock Report on Human Fertilisation and Embryology* (Oxford: Blackwell, 1985), p. 46; Heidi Malm, "Paid Surrogacy: Arguments and Responses," *Public Affairs Quarterly*, vol. 3 (1989), p. 61; Martha Field, *Surrogate Motherhood* (Cambridge, MA: Harvard University Press, 1989), p. 25; George J. Annas, "Fairy Tales Surrogate Mothers Tell," in Larry Gostin, ed., *Surrogate Motherhood* (Bloomington: Indiana University Press, 1990), p. 43; Rosemarie Tong, "Overdue Death," in *ibid.*, p. 45; Alexander Capron and Margaret Radin, "Choosing Family Law over Contract Law as a Paradigm for Surrogate Motherhood," in *ibid.*, p. 62; Elizabeth S. Anderson, "Is Women's Labor a Commodity?" *Philosophy and Public Affairs*, vol. 19 (1990), p. 84; and Debra Satz, "Markets in Women's Reproductive Labor," *Philosophy and Public Affairs*, vol. 21 (1992), pp. 123–24. Thoughtful replies to these claims have been made by Richard J. Arneson, "Commodification and Commercial Surrogacy," *Philosophy and Public Affairs*, vol. 21 (1992), pp. 132–64; and Alan Wertheimer, "Two Questions about Surrogacy and Exploitation," *Philosophy and Public Affairs*, vol. 21 (1992), pp. 211–39.

that this fact casts doubt on the claim that surrogacy involves any objectionable form of exploitation.[2] Yet Marxists themselves, when they have set about providing such a technical analysis, have sometimes been led to raise questions about whether 'exploitation' (in their technical and allegedly "Marxian" sense) really identifies anything which should be of interest to social critics.[3] This is apt to render all charges of exploitation suspect, and make us wonder whether the notion itself may be too diffuse to be taken seriously.

In my view, however, social critics who have used the notion of exploitation naively, without explicating it, have generally been less guilty of obfuscation than the philosophers and economists who have been worried about providing more reflective accounts. In particular, I think most of these accounts have proceeded on assumptions which already distort the concept and tend to undermine its critical use. Accordingly, my aim will be to clarify the concept not by providing a technical analysis but by exploring what I think people mean when they object to behavior or social arrangements as exploitative, and identifying the moral convictions which give such objections their force.

Moral and nonmoral concepts. Most philosophers who reflect on the concept of exploitation tend to follow the practice of dictionaries, distinguishing a "nonmoral" sense of 'exploitation' from a "moral" sense, and taking the latter sense to involve the idea of making use of someone or something unjustly or unethically.[4] Since they suppose that it is only the latter, "pejorative" meaning of the term which interests social critics, they provide what I will call a "moralized" account of exploitation. That is, they suppose that the term 'exploitation' (in the "pejorative" sense) already has wrongfulness or moral badness built into its very meaning. 'Murder', for example, is taken to be a moral concept in this sense when it is taken to mean "wrongful homicide." On such a moralized account of the concept of murder, to justify the claim that a homicide is an act of murder one must show it to be wrongful. Further, if I claimed that a certain homicide was an act of murder, but insisted nevertheless that it was not wrongful, I would be taken to be misusing the term, or at least using it with some new and nonstandard meaning. By contrast, terms like 'homicide' or 'abortion' are not normally taken to be moral terms in that to call an act by these names leaves open the question of whether it is wrong or justifiable.

Of course, it is true that some people believe, for example, that all acts of abortion, simply as such, are wrong; but they do not take this to be

[2] Wertheimer, "Two Questions," p. 212.

[3] For instance, see John Roemer, "Should Marxists Be Interested in Exploitation?" in Roemer, ed., *Analytical Marxism* (Cambridge: Cambridge University Press, 1986), pp. 260–82.

[4] Under the verb 'exploit', *Webster's* (1966) distinguishes "to turn a natural resource to economic account: to utilize" from "to make use of meanly or unjustly for one's own advantage or profit"; *American Heritage* (1985) distinguishes "to employ to the greatest possible advantage" from "to make use of selfishly or unethically."

part of the very *meaning* of the word 'abortion'. They do not think that those who defend abortion are misusing the word or using it in a different sense, but take them instead to be expressing opposed moral convictions using the very same term in the very same sense. Analogously, if someone proposed a nonmoralized account of exploitation, that would not necessarily preclude saying that all acts of exploitation, simply as such, are morally wrong. Hence it would not preclude using the term pejoratively, as the term 'abortion' may be used pejoratively by someone who thinks abortion is always wrong. It would merely deny that the moral wrongness was built into the very meaning of the term 'exploitation'.

Innocent and noninnocent exploitation. There clearly do seem to be cases of exploitation which we regard as innocent or even admirable. Nobody thinks it is wrong or unethical for a chess player to exploit her opponent's inattention in order to win the game. We may even compliment a lawyer for exploiting the weaknesses in her adversary's case in order to win a just verdict, or congratulate a resourceful person for exploiting her opportunities to the full. Realizing this, philosophers think that in such cases 'exploit' is being used in a neutral, innocent, or positive sense, quite distinct from the pejorative sense which interests us in cases of "wrongful exploitation."[5]

But why should we suppose that 'exploitation' has a special *meaning* when applied to cases of injustice or wrongdoing? Terms like 'appropriation', 'transaction', 'seizure', or 'agreement' apply sometimes to acts which are wrongful and sometimes to acts which are not, but we do not suppose that the word 'transaction' has a different meaning in the case of wrongful or unethical transactions from the one it has in the case of rightful and proper transactions. If instances of exploitation are thought to be more often or more typically wrongful than instances of appropriation or transaction, perhaps that might be explained by the nature of exploitation as such, as it appears in both just and unjust cases, or by our substantive moral convictions about the kind of thing an act of exploitation itself is.

Michael Gorr writes that "[i]t is difficult even to conceive of a case in which we would describe someone's behavior as the *justified* exploitation of another person."[6] That is right, but it does not follow that 'exploitation' is a moral term or that we must provide a moralized account of it. The "difficulty in conceiving" here is not a difficulty in understanding what someone might *mean* in holding that the exploitation of a person is morally justified. Rather, it is that we cannot imagine ourselves *agreeing* with a moral belief on this subject which is so deeply opposed to the one we hold.

[5] See Joel Feinberg, *Harmless Wrongdoing* (New York: Oxford University Press, 1988), p. 178; Wertheimer, "Two Questions," p. 212.

[6] Michael J. Gorr, *Coercion, Freedom, and Exploitation* (New York: Peter Lang, 1989), p. 147.

Exploitation defended. In Plato's *Gorgias,* Callicles maintains that by nature some people are stronger than others, hence better and superior, and that it is only natural justice that the superior should use their strength to rule over the inferior and "to remove by force what belongs to the inferior."[7] Callicles does not directly use any word which should be translated as 'exploit', but it seems quite a fair rendering of his view to say that he regards it as only natural justice that the strong should *exploit* the weak. Callicles clearly wants to argue that exploitation is right and just in those very cases where most of us take it to be wrong and unjust.

Or consider the similar views of Friedrich Nietzsche, which *are* sometimes explicitly couched in terms of exploitation. Nietzsche says that the economic life of modern society "represents a maximum in the exploitation (*Ausbeutung*) of humanity." Yet Nietzsche does not call for the abolition of this exploitation, as he knows the decadent moralists will do. Instead, he insists that it would be best for the exploitation even to be heightened, if only it could be given a new meaning through the emergence of a higher type of human being, who "stands upon and lives off" the masses. If the exploiters were strong, spiritual *Übermenschen*—rather than the philistine capitalists who presently exploit the masses—then as far as Nietzsche is concerned, the exploitation of humanity would be entirely welcome.[8]

The difference between Callicles or Nietzsche and ourselves is not plausibly regarded as a merely semantic difference, as though we are using 'exploit' in a "pejorative" sense and they are using it in some neutral or nonpejorative sense. On the contrary, they are taking a stand in direct opposition to conventional moral opinions about exploitation, and this is something they can do only if they assert that exploitation is good or just while using the word in the same sense as we do when we more conventionally hold that it is bad or wrong. It may be correct to say that Nietzsche is using the word 'exploitation' in order to shock us, but it is incorrect to say that he is using it in a different (nonstandard or nonpejorative) *sense* in order to shock us. On the contrary, what really shocks us about Callicles or Nietzsche is their *moral opinions*. Nietzsche heightens the shock by not mincing words or employing euphemisms, but asserting directly that he approves of something we regard as objectionable and referring to this thing using the very same word we would use in objecting to it. If Nietzsche used that word, but in a different and less pejorative sense, that would diminish rather than enhance the shock value. If,

[7] Plato, *Gorgias*, trans. Terence Irwin (Oxford: Clarendon Press, 1979), 488b5.

[8] "Morally speaking, [modern society] represents a maximum in the exploitation of humanity; but it presupposes those on whose account this exploitation has meaning. . . . My concept, my metaphor for this type is, as one knows, the word *Übermensch*" (Friedrich Nietzsche, *Werke* [Leipzig: Naumann, 1901], vol. 15, p. 421; see Nietzsche, *The Will to Power*, ed. Walter Kaufmann [New York: Random House, 1967], section 866, pp. 463–64).

however, the word we use already had wrongness or badness built into its meaning, then in saying that the maximum exploitation of humanity by a superior race would be a good thing, Nietzsche would be contradicting only himself and not conventional moral opinion.

Wrong because exploitative. Another problem with moralized accounts of exploitation is that they make it more difficult to understand many arguments in which the concept of exploitation is used. Some people argue that commodified surrogacy is wrongful or bad *because* it is exploitative. In such an argument it is natural to take the premise that surrogacy involves exploitation as claiming that surrogacy has some property such that, in light of certain moral principles, the fact that surrogacy has that property is, under the given circumstances, a ground for regarding surrogacy as wrongful or bad. But following a moralized account of exploitation, if I say that a practice is exploitative (using the word, of course, in the "pejorative" sense), then my statement already *means* that the practice is wrongful or bad, and thus that before using the term (in that sense) I should already have shown that surrogacy is wrongful or bad. In that case, I cannot be justified in asserting the premise of my argument until I have already independently established its conclusion. If that is so, however, then the whole argument form which says that a practice is wrongful *because* it is exploitative looks merely rhetorical, if not downright confused. At most, such a statement could be understood as *categorizing* the wrongfulness of the act (where this wrongfulness has already been admitted), or as rhetorically emphasizing this wrongfulness to someone who already believes the act is wrong but is suspected of giving this belief insufficient deliberative weight. The statement cannot be understood as providing a substantive argument for considering the act wrongful, which might convince someone not antecedently persuaded of its wrongfulness – just as saying that an act is "wrong because it is murder" (where 'murder' is understood to mean 'wrongful homicide') cannot provide anyone with a new reason for thinking the act is wrong, but can at most serve to categorize the wrong (as a case of 'murder', i.e., 'wrongful *homicide*') or rhetorically drive home its wrongfulness through the use of the vivid term of condemnation (whose appropriateness would be accepted only by someone already persuaded that the act is wrong).

Analogously, a moralized account of exploitation will not permit us to understand the inference "wrongful because exploitative" as providing a genuine argument for considering some practice wrongful by invoking a contentful moral belief to the effect that exploitativeness is a substantively wrong-making feature of acts. For on a moralized account, "exploitation is wrong," like "murder is wrong," would be morally vacuous, true merely in virtue of the meaning of 'exploitation'. If 'murder' means 'wrongful homicide', then no one who did not already accept the judgment that a particular homicide is wrongful could have any reason to accept the judgment that it is a case of murder. Likewise, whatever substantive moral beliefs lie behind the claim that the practice in question is wrong must have established this conclusion before we could be justified in saying that this practice is exploitative.

No wonder, then, that those who want to provide more precise or technical accounts of exploitation, beginning from the standpoint that these must be moralized accounts, should have begun to doubt whether there is any moral interest at all in social criticisms which employ the concept of exploitation. But here the fault does not lie with the social critics; it is the philosophers, with their attempts at analytical clarity, who are guilty of introducing conceptual confusion.

Suppose for a moment that there is substantive disagreement over the question of whether certain kinds of exploitation are good or bad, just or unjust. In that case, moralized accounts of the concept of exploitation will have the effect of disguising substantive moral commitments, and thereby enabling people less honest than Callicles and Nietzsche to conceal the extent to which they share similar views. Thus, a Callicles who accepted a moralized account of exploitation may (and not only may, but must) say that since it is (in his opinion) always naturally just for the strong to take by force whatever they want from the weak, the strong are not in the least guilty of *exploiting* the weak (not, at any rate, in any "pejorative" sense of the term).

It is no good merely to say here that we may still challenge Callicles' controversial claims about what is naturally just. For this observation completely misses the main point, which is that the contemptibly mealy-mouthed reformulation of his position forced on poor Callicles by the moralized account would entirely divest his strong character of that robust moral candor which Plato portrays as its one redeeming virtue. It also totally overlooks the additional point that whether or not an instance of exploitation is held to be wrongful or unjust, it may still be important, for both moral and nonmoral reasons, to recognize it as a case of *exploitation*. But that merely returns us to the main question: What is exploitation?

II. What Exploitation Is

Exploitation as use. The fundamental synonym for the verb 'exploit' is 'use'. The exploiter must be a person or group of people, a human or human-like subject, with the capacity for setting ends and using means; the object of exploitation is one such means. This object can be virtually anything that can be used: nonhuman things, such as natural resources, and even abstractions, such as occasions and opportunities.

Not every use counts as exploitation, however. A hiker in the woods who takes a drink from a stream is not exploiting it, though a miller who builds a mill on it is. The difference, I suggest, is that the exploitation of a resource is a use implying its availability to the exploiter in a plannable and manipulable way, especially some degree of control over the resource. We do exploit unpredictable opportunities or fortunate circumstances, but in those cases the opportunity or circumstance fits into some preexisting plan of the exploiter's, and the exploiter must do something, involving a degree of planning and manipulation, to *take advantage* of the fortunate circumstance, bringing it into the exploiter's control or within the purview of the exploiter's plans or machinations. When some unpredictable event suddenly drops success into my lap, I make use of the good luck, but I do not exploit it.

Exploiting things about people: advantage-exploitation and benefit-exploitation. There are many things about human beings that can be exploited: their talents, traits, habits, capacities, activities, desires, and circumstances. We exploit people's strengths and their weaknesses, but usually not in quite the same sense. We exploit some attribute of the person from which we derive benefit or use to achieve our end. Let us call this "benefit-exploitation" or, for short, "b-exploitation." It is in a different sense that we exploit someone's weakness or vulnerability, which gives us a hold or advantage over the person and puts at our disposal the attribute which we b-exploit. I shall call our exploitative relation to this weakness or vulnerability "advantage-exploitation" or "a-exploitation." The charming spy enchants a governmental official, playing on the victim's need for affection in order to obtain a state secret. Here the spy a-exploits the victim's need for affection (regarded as a vulnerability) and b-exploits the victim's official position or access to state secrets (regarded as an attribute from which the spy may reap some benefit).

As their names are meant to imply, a-exploitation and b-exploitation constitute a complementary pair, and a-exploitation is the foundation of b-exploitation.[9] Without b-exploitation there would be no *use* of the object of exploitation, while without a-exploitation there would be no control or manipulation of the object of exploitation, which is the element distinguishing exploitation (of nonhuman as well as human objects) from simple use. People and their abilities, activities, and so on may be nonexploitatively at our disposal, as through generosity or a mutual exchange of services where neither side is taking advantage of the other. The use of another through generosity or exchange may also be exploitative, but only when there is some element of vulnerability (a-exploitation) in the situation, such as when the exchange of benefits results from one person's having some decisive bargaining advantage over the other, or when the generosity is viewed as a weakness to be played upon. For this reason, we may also look upon a-exploitation as that which makes b-exploitation

[9] John Kleinig describes various cases of exploitation, then writes that they all "involve one party's playing on some character trait of the other for the purpose of securing some advantage" (Kleinig, "The Ethics of Consent," *Canadian Journal of Philosophy*, vol. 11 [1981]). In my terms the "playing on" is a-exploitation, while the "securing some advantage" is b-exploitation.

possible. The vulnerability exploited in a-exploitation is what puts at our disposal the benefit exploited in b-exploitation.

Human vulnerability. We might wish to clarify the notion of *vulnerability* here. But I am skeptical about the extent to which such clarification is achievable through any devices used by such technicians as philosophers, economists, or decision theorists. (Perhaps one reason these people are perplexed by exploitation is that their technical resources are as yet not up to handling it.) It has been suggested to me that you are made vulnerable to me in the required sense by something that enables me to control you, or that you are made vulnerable to me in a transaction by anything that makes us unequal with respect to the transaction (with my enjoying the superiority in that respect).[10] Suppose, however, that I am a cringing servant and you are my master. If I regularly pilfer from you, a-exploiting your naive trustfulness so as to b-exploit your wealth, I have not gained any control over you, nor have I acquired any superiority over you; if it may be said that I have become unequal to (superior to) you *with respect to that transaction* (that is, the pilfering), I am not sure that describing it in this way is any clearer than simply speaking of you as being vulnerable to my pilfering.

Clearly needs and desires can sometimes constitute vulnerabilities. An addict's need or desire for drugs, for example, is clearly a vulnerability which pushers may a-exploit. The emotional needs of lovers obviously make them vulnerable to those they love, and hence create opportunities for a-exploitation by the latter. Many human needs and desires can be viewed as vulnerabilities, and accordingly many dealings between human beings can be put in an exploitative light. As we become more sensitive to this unattractive side of human social life generally, we may very well begin to perceive a great deal more exploitation in it than we thought there was. I think that such a change in sensitivity might very well be a positive result of becoming clearer about what exploitation is and about its importance in human life.

Sensitivity and perceptiveness, however, are attributes of common sense. The changes in perception and sensitivity I am recommending are to be driven by common sense and not by inflexible philosophical conceptions or dogmas. Surely it would be implausible to the point of absurdity if someone were to suggest that *any* need or desire constitutes a vulnerability. To suppose this would be to make exploitation virtually ubiquitous in human social life and as much a factor in quite a number of innocent human relations as it is in many very nasty ones. If the account I am proposing is right, then those who have an interest in denying or disguising exploitation will also have an interest in making us insensitive

[10] These suggestions were made to me in conversation by Elizabeth Anderson and Dan Brock, respectively. But the formulations are my own, based on my memory of informal exchanges, and they may not do justice to what these individuals had in mind.

to the difference between human interactions which play on genuine vulnerabilities and those which do not. We should therefore be suspicious of those who question whether such a distinction can be drawn.

The need for love may make us vulnerable, but a healthy personality is one that loves, and chooses its objects of love, in such a way that it will not be easily victimized or exploited. Thus, although greater sensitivity may make us aware of much more exploitation in love relationships than we thought was there, nothing in the concept of exploitation I am proposing makes it reasonable to suggest that all love relationships are inherently exploitative. Likewise, if someone claimed that *every* market exchange is exploitative simply on the ground that in such exchanges people use the needs of others to achieve their ends, then I think that claim would have exactly as much plausibility as the claim that every need or desire motivating market behavior is a vulnerability open to exploitation (the plausibility of both claims would, in my opinion, be very small).[11]

On the other hand, if one party to an exchange has a significantly stronger bargaining position than the other (as capitalists have in relation to workers, or prospective adoptive couples typically have in relation to the women they hire to be surrogate mothers), then that difference constitutes a clear case of vulnerability on the part of the weaker party; the weaker party is therefore a-exploited whenever the difference is used by the stronger party to obtain more favorable terms in the bargain. To the extent that market exchanges really do systematically involve this sort of differential advantage, they certainly may be considered systematically exploitative.

The notion of vulnerability needs clarification in other ways too. Joel Feinberg thinks there are three-person cases in which A exploits B but A receives a benefit not from B but from another person, C.[12] For example,

[11] Michael Gorr reminds me of a passage in Marx's early notebooks where it is said that under the system of private property each person regards the other's needs only as sources of dependence and power, with the result that "mutual pillaging" is the basic social relationship between people (see Allen W. Wood, ed., *Marx: Selections* [New York: Macmillan, 1988], pp. 37–38). Though Marx does not use the term 'exploitation' here, I think it would be quite accurate to say that it was Marx's intent in these passages to put all market exchanges in an exploitative light. But the claim that all market exchanges are necessarily exploitative, if taken literally, seems to me simply wrong (and not something the mature Marx ever said or would have been inclined to say). However, there are a couple of points the young Marx is making in this passage that seem to me very insightful and on target. Marx is portraying the standpoint of the political economists, who (then as today) do tend to represent people's interest in one another as exclusively *exploitative* in a fairly straightforward sense, since they interpret the needs and desires of others as merely so many opportunities for me to satisfy my utility function. Marx wants to contrast production under such a system with a society in which we might "produce things as human beings," looking upon the needs of the other instead as opportunities to affirm our human potentialities and our commonality with other human beings, which is surely a more attractive picture of what human life might be like than what we see portrayed either in the theories of the economists or in the actual capitalist social order they intend to depict.

[12] Feinberg, *Harmless Wrongdoing*, pp. 184–92.

a tabloid may exploit the unhappy situation of a celebrity, while neither helping nor harming the celebrity, but receiving a benefit from the public which pays to read about the celebrity. By 'vulnerability', however, we do not necessarily mean vulnerability to being *harmed*, but only vulnerability to being *used*. The celebrity's misfortune or misconduct, which led to the unhappy situation, is clearly what makes the celebrity's life vulnerable to use by the tabloids; hence (in my terminology), the celebrity's situation is an object of a-exploitation, even if we suppose that the celebrity is neither helped nor harmed by the publicity. On the other hand, the sensational or heartrending character of the celebrity's situation (as the feature which sells papers) is an object of b-exploitation. In this case the exploitation may also be seen as directed at the public: its prurient or sentimental tastes (regarded as a weakness) can be seen as the object of a-exploitation.

I do not mean to say that in any case of exploitation there must always be a neat pair of distinguishable objects of a- and b-exploitation. The point of pairing a-exploitation and b-exploitation is merely that where human beings and their attributes are the objects, exploitation usually involves some element of vulnerability on the part of what is exploited, and also some use of the attribute benefiting some project of the exploiter.[13] But there are exceptions. We sometimes exploit not only the qualities of others, but also our own qualities. This appears to be a case of b-exploitation, but it does not correspond to any a-exploitation, unless of someone else's vulnerability. We can exploit our own talents, however, without a-exploiting anything. Exploiting our own talents can be like exploiting natural resources, where the place of vulnerability is supplied by our having control over what we b-exploit or deploying it as part of some plan of ours. Sometimes there also seems to be a-exploitation without any clear object of b-exploitation distinct from the object of a-exploitation: the chess player a-exploits her opponent's lapse of attention, but there is nothing else of the opponent's besides this inattention which she needs to use (or b-exploit) in order to win the game. There can also be b-exploitation of *other* people's talents or capacities without a-exploitation, as when a manager exploits the base-stealing ability of his leadoff man in order to grab a quick first-inning lead. Here there is no vulnerability on the part of the leadoff man which is a-exploited by the manager, but there may be a control over the leadoff man (who will steal second when the manager gives the sign), and there is certainly the use of the leadoff man's ability as part of the manager's plan for victory.

[13] This can be illustrated by the example of the tabloid mentioned above. The tabloid a-exploits the public's tastes, and these tastes do enable the tabloid to reap benefits. But various things suggest themselves as the means it uses: for example, these tastes themselves, or the public's purchasing power, or the market system through which the papers are sold; and none of these is readily identifiable as a distinct object of b-exploitation neatly correlated with the tabloid's a-exploitation of the public's tastes.

Exploiting people themselves. We may well wonder what it means to exploit a *person,* as opposed to exploiting the person's capacities or activities or weaknesses. Generally speaking, what we are talking about here is b-exploitation, but as before, b-exploitation presupposes a-exploitation. In order for a person to be exploited, he or she has to be vulnerable to the exploiter, and it is this advantage over the exploited person that the exploiter plays upon in order to make use of the exploitee. But in which cases where I b-exploit your talents, capacities, activities, and so forth am I also exploiting *you*?

Pretty clearly not in every case. When Dusty Baker exploits Darren Lewis's speed, he does not thereby exploit Darren Lewis himself. If in the course of a casual conversation I ask you for a couple of small favors, slyly insinuating that if you refuse I may divulge some nasty secrets about your sexual or financial indiscretions, then I am a-exploiting your indiscretions and b-exploiting your ability to do the favors, but I do not seem to be exploiting *you yourself*. On the other hand, if I begin to use the same information to blackmail you out of considerable sums of money, then we might very well say that I am exploiting *you*; but this could depend on how regular and how large the payments turned out to be.

It seems to me there is no sharp dividing line here. We say that a *person* is exploited whenever we think the b-exploitation encompasses a sufficiently wide range of what the person does or is; and if I am sufficiently sensitive about the humiliation involved in having my weakness a-exploited, we may say that I "feel exploited" or "don't like being used" (thereby implying that it is *me*, and not merely something about me, that is being b-exploited). The exploitation of a person's labor—when this means the person's chief life-activity—clearly counts as exploitation of the person. When it is said that surrogacy exploits the mother, however, the idea is not *only* that surrogacy exploits her labor (whether in the birthing sense or in the more general working sense); the point is rather that it exploits her ability to carry and give birth to a child, which is taken to be such an intimate part of what she is that it could not be exploited without also exploiting *her*. Or it may be that having this ability put at someone else's disposal through her vulnerability is felt to be sufficiently humiliating to her that she is justified in regarding *herself* as exploited.[14]

[14] On the other hand, I think it would be hyperbole to say of an exploitation film, which exploits the public's bad taste or morbid curiosity, that it also exploits *the public*. Pornography is sometimes alleged to exploit *women*—not just the women who pose for pornographic pictures, but all women (see, e.g., Andrea Dworkin, *Intercourse* [New York: Free Press, 1987], and Catharine MacKinnon, *Only Words* [Cambridge, MA: Harvard University Press, 1993]). The idea appears to be that pornography encourages a one-sided image of all women as sexual playthings, as objects of domination and humiliation, and this is seen as creating for all women a wide range of vulnerabilities which make possible various forms of a-exploitation with women as their victims. The claim that pornography exploits all women strikes me as hyperbole; but if the issue of whether a person is exploited turns on "how much of the person" is included in the exploitation, then we might expect that there will be a tendency to hyperbole on the part of those whose aim is to persuade us of the seriousness of a given kind of exploitation.

To sum up: When people, or something about them, are its objects, exploitation consists in the exploiter's using something about the person for the exploiter's ends by playing on some weakness or vulnerability in that person. This is the basic idea behind all exploitation involving human objects. It applies equally to cases where exploitation is commonly considered unfair, wrongful, or unethical and to cases where it is not. There is no semantic distinction between "pejorative" and "nonpejorative" *senses* of 'exploitation', any more than the words 'seizure' and 'payment' mean something different when the seizure is wrongful or the payment involves a breach of ethics. What there may be is a distinction between some cases in which exploitation is (or is taken to be) morally innocent, and other cases in which, on the basis of substantive moral principles, exploitation is taken to be morally objectionable and in which the use of the term 'exploitation' calls attention to precisely those features of the situation in virtue of which it is found to be objectionable.

III. What Is Wrong with Exploitation

Not the distribution of benefits and harms. Many people seem to think that exploitation (at least in the "pejorative" sense) has to be unfair or unjust, and that the injustice consists in a redistribution of harms and benefits, with benefits flowing from the exploited to the exploiter. This is suggested by Marx's depiction of capitalist exploitation as the appropriation by capital of the worker's surplus labor, and it is quite explicitly involved in some Marxist accounts of exploitation, such as John Roemer's idea that being an exploiter consists in being able to command more labor embodied in goods than you have performed, or Jeffrey Reiman's insistence that exploitation involves unpaid labor.[15] In the same vein, Feinberg says that

[15] Roemer, "Should Marxists Be Interested in Exploitation?" p. 260; Jeffrey Reiman, "Exploitation, Force, and the Moral Assessment of Capitalism: Thoughts on Roemer and Cohen," *Philosophy and Public Affairs*, vol. 16 (1987), pp. 3–41. I call these "Marxist" accounts only because that is the way their authors advertise them. There is no reason to ascribe any of them to Marx himself, since he has no technical concept of exploitation. Marx's economic theory does have a technical concept of the "rate of exploitation" (s/v, the ratio of surplus value to variable capital). But Marx gives it this name only because he already believes, on perfectly reasonable grounds that do not depend on his theory of value or any other technical notions, that capitalism involves the exploitation of wage labor; s/v is merely a technical device for *measuring* this exploitation. Marx need not think that every conceivable instance in which these technical concepts might be employed would be an instance of exploitation, only that the economic relations to which they apply in actual capitalism are in fact exploitative economic relations. Thus, it is beside the point that Roemer can construct examples of 'exploitation' in his technical "Marxist" sense which do not intuitively strike us as unjust. For instance, Karl has fewer assets than Adam, but because Karl prefers low work and low consumption, he loans some of his assets to Adam, who prefers more work and more consumption, and who pays Karl "interest" on what he borrows. Here Adam is "exploited"—in the technical "Marxist" sense—by Karl, even though Adam has greater initial assets and becomes progressively richer over time than Karl is (Roemer, "Should Marxists Be Interested in Exploitation?" pp. 272–74). But as Roemer presents it this is not really an example of exploitation at all (except in the technical "Marxist" sense he has defined), because neither Karl nor Adam is depicted as being in any way vulnerable to the other; they

it is the element of "wrongfulness" which "distinguishes [exploitation] from non-exploitative utilization," and that "[one] element in exploitation is some redistribution of benefits and harms." According to Alan Wertheimer, "[w]e typically say that A wrongfully exploits B when A takes unfair advantage of B. A must benefit from the transaction. . . . In addition, A exploits B only when the transaction is harmful or unfair to B."[16]

The drift of these remarks, however, seems to me in an important sense exactly wrong. Moreover, some of the writers on this topic appear to be aware of this. Gorr is struck by the fact that an exploitative offer typically expands the offeree's freedom of choice and that accepting it will normally net the offeree an increase in utility.[17]

Nor involuntariness, since exploitation is often voluntary. Feinberg too, in apparent contrast to the drift of the remarks just quoted, realizes that exploitation may benefit the exploited, and may occur "with the exploitee's fully voluntary consent"; exploitation may also be mutual, with each party acting in turn as exploiter and exploited, both benefiting from the arrangement.[18] Wertheimer, showing that he knows better as well, even realizes that exploited parties typically benefit *more* from an exploitative arrangement than exploiters do, and rightly points out that this should not surprise us. "It is precisely because the exploitee stands to gain so much from the transaction (relative to the exploiter) that his bargaining position is comparatively weak."[19] This also explains why exploitation should often be voluntary on the part of the exploitee, since it is only to be expected that you will voluntarily consent to an arrangement by which you benefit.

Marx's view of capitalist exploitation is not undermined, but on the contrary, confirmed by these observations. Back when the American press still thought it necessary to combat Marxist ideas, journalists simultaneously exercised their wit and proved their loyalty by noting satirically how eager unemployed workers are to subject themselves to (what Marxists regard as) "exploitation." More earnest defenders of the capitalist system have often represented capitalists as the benefactors of those they employ, and infer from this that it must be mistaken (indeed, a sign of cruel ingratitude) for wage laborers to think of their bosses as exploiters. But the mirth is misplaced and the inference invalid. Since being benefited and being exploited are often merely two sides of the same coin,

---

simply have different preferences and find a mutually satisfactory arrangement for satisfying them. Such examples, needless to say, bear no resemblance to the extraction of unpaid labor from workers by capital under real-life capitalism, where the weakness of the worker's bargaining position and its systematic exploitation by capital is *the* fundamental structural feature defining the entire economy.

[16] Feinberg, *Harmless Wrongdoing*, pp. 199, 192; Wertheimer, "Two Questions," p. 213.

[17] Gorr, *Coercion, Freedom, and Exploitation*, p. 162.

[18] Feinberg, *Harmless Wrongdoing*, pp. 176, 191, 195–96; Wertheimer, "Two Questions," pp. 213, 222–23.

[19] Wertheimer, "Two Questions," p. 223.

and people may often be in dire need of the benefits in question, they can often be eager to be exploited.

The point is that it goes along with being vulnerable, or in a weak bargaining position, that you should have a lot to gain from being taken advantage of, and a lot to lose if you cannot find someone able and willing to take advantage of your vulnerability. Someone who is propertyless and starving has a lot to gain by striking a deal with an employer who is willing to offer bare subsistence in exchange for long, hard labor under dangerous conditions—and a lot to lose (namely, life itself) if no such exploitative bargain is in the offing. We can make the same point with a less controversial example. A gambler who owes a large amount of money to ruthless and violent characters will be in desperate need of the loan shark who offers the needed funds at a usurious rate of interest; such a person will be more than willing under these conditions to consent to virtually any terms of payment.

Not coercion either. Perhaps it will be said that people in such desperate straits are *forced* or *coerced* into making such deals. Certainly it is often said by Marxists that exploited workers are forced or coerced. This is often true in the sense that the exploited have no acceptable alternative to the arrangement under which they are exploited. But it does not follow that the exploiters themselves are coercing the exploited. (This is true only if the exploiters themselves are the ones who put the exploited in their vulnerable situation; Marx portrays things in this light when he represents the capitalist class as a whole as dispossessing the working class as a whole.)

Yet even if an exploitee has other *acceptable* alternatives to a given exploitative arrangement, and thus is not *forced* to accept the arrangement even in that sense, these alternatives may be either equally exploitative or far less desirable. For example, suppose that going on public assistance is an alternative to taking employment under exploitative conditions, but when the welfare system is administered by people with a rugged individualist mentality, it may turn out—and quite intentionally—that the poor should always choose to be exploited, when they are lucky enough to find an exploiter, rather than to live in misery and humiliation on the dole, even if by doing so they would escape being exploited. For this reason, it seems to me quite mistaken of Reiman to make it part of his concept of exploitation that an exploited class must be *forced* to yield up unpaid labor.[20]

Certainly not "free-floating" evils. Exploitation, then, is not necessarily harmful to the interests of the exploited; on the contrary, it will typically benefit them to be exploited. Nor is it always correct to say that the

[20] Reiman, "Exploitation, Force, and the Moral Assessment of Capitalism," p. 3. Coercion is also made a requirement for exploitation in other interpretations of Marxist claims; see, e.g., Richard Arneson, "What's Wrong with Exploitation?" *Ethics*, vol. 91 (1981), pp. 202–27.

exploited are forced or coerced into accepting an exploitative arrangement. So what is bad about exploitation? Those who operate with a moralized account of exploitation must hold that even where exploitation is beneficial to the exploited and fully voluntary on their part, there must be something bad about it or the term could not be used at all (at least in the "pejorative" sense). Feinberg's view of such cases is that they must involve some wrong or badness other than harm to or involuntariness on the part of the exploited: either a harm to someone else, or some "free-floating" evil. Where he cannot find any harm or evil of either sort, Feinberg thinks that one person's use of another via the latter's vulnerability is "not exploitative at all," or at any rate not "blamable exploitation." Feinberg is admirably sensitive to the wide range of evils which (in his view) can turn the harmless (or even voluntary and beneficial) use of a person or features of a person into exploitation, and also to the variety of controversial cases (commercial fortune-telling, ticket scalping, various kinds of wrongful gain, threat, extortion, and blackmail) in which we can wonder whether exploitation should be legally prohibited, or whether it is wrong though it should not be illegal, or whether it is completely justified and hence (in his view) not a case of exploitation "in the pejorative sense."[21]

Obligations to help others? Not quite. I should now explain why I find this entire approach wrongheaded. In order to do so, I need to begin being more explicit about why I think most of us are disposed to see exploitation in general as something bad. Most of us believe that when people are weak or vulnerable, others should not use their weakness or seek to benefit from it, but instead should seek to help them and rescue them from their bad situation. This is closely related to our reason for objecting to exploitation, but I do not think Gorr is correct in saying that exploitation occurs only when there is some *moral obligation* to help which the exploiter is failing to fulfill.[22]

This is clearly not so in cases where exploitation is not morally objectionable (a fact which is only concealed from Gorr by his adoption of a moralized account of exploitation). Even where exploitation is morally objectionable, it need not involve the violation of an "obligation to help." If I am a private detective hired by your wife to spy on you, I owe you no "obligation to help" making it incumbent on me not to tell her about your cheating—on the contrary, I owe her the obligation to inform on you. But I clearly do exploit you in a morally objectionable manner if I blackmail you by threatening to tell her.

The real reason. I suggest that the moral belief that makes exploitation objectionable is the following: Proper respect for others is violated when we treat their vulnerabilities as opportunities to advance our own inter-

[21] See Feinberg, *Harmless Wrongdoing*, pp. 184, 191; see also *ibid.*, ch. 32, in which Feinberg tries to resolve many controversial issues surrounding wrongful gain.

[22] Gorr, *Coercion, Freedom, and Exploitation*, pp. 163–65.

ests or projects. It is degrading to have your weaknesses taken advantage of, and dishonorable to use the weaknesses of others for your ends. This moral belief, I submit, is widely shared, and it is why the term 'exploitation' seems to us to refer to something bad, unfair, or unethical. This has nothing to do with the meaning of the word itself, but reflects a positive moral conviction which most of us hold.

Even when exploitation is both beneficial and voluntary on the part of the exploitee, it still involves the exploiter's a-exploitation of the exploitee's vulnerability, on the basis of which the exploiter furthers (through b-exploitation) some end of the exploiter's own. If we hold the moral belief I have just mentioned, then we must see something bad about this.[23] We think that in a wide range of cases it is degrading to human beings that they should be so treated, even if the exploitative arrangement is voluntary on both sides and no matter what the resulting distribution of benefits and harms.[24]

Confirmation of this account. One point in favor of this diagnosis is that those who reject this moral belief are precisely the people who see nothing bad about exploitation. Callicles and Nietzsche, for instance, see the world as divided by nature into the strong and the weak, and think that it is both natural and right that the world should contain these two types, and that the vulnerabilities of the weak should be taken advantage of by the strong. (Indeed, both think that this is what these vulnerabilities are naturally there *for*.) If my account is correct, then we should expect people with such views to approve of exploitation, as in fact they do.

Another point in favor of this account is that in cases where we do not regard exploitation as morally objectionable, there is normally some reason for thinking that our use of another's vulnerability will not be degrad-

[23] Compare John Kleinig's view that the exploitation of another's weakness is wrong even when it does not violate another's right, does not wrong the other, and does not treat the other unfairly (Kleinig, "The Ethics of Consent").

[24] Do these objections to exploitation rest on Kant's principle that we must not treat others merely as means, but always at the same time as ends in themselves? Both Kant and the moral belief I have ascribed to us permit us sometimes to use others as means. Kant permits this when we treat them at the same time as ends, and the belief I ascribe to us permits it when our use does not involve taking advantage of another's vulnerability. But Kant's principle is sometimes interpreted in such a way that it is a sufficient condition for treating another as an end that the other consent (or even *be able* to consent) to this treatment. For example: "If we treat other agents as mere means, . . . it is not merely that we act in ways to which they *do not* consent; we act on maxims to which they *could not* consent" (Onora O'Neill, *Constructions of Reason* [Cambridge: Cambridge University Press, 1989], p. 138). If this is a correct interpretation of Kant's principle, then it is much weaker than the belief I am ascribing to most of us. For on this belief we find exploitation objectionable even when people can and do consent to it. On the other hand, perhaps treating others as ends in themselves demands far more than that they be able to consent, or even than that they actually consent, to the way we treat them. Perhaps in order to treat others as ends in themselves we must also refrain, at least in a great many situations, from making use of their vulnerabilities for our ends, whether they consent to it or not. In that case, Kant's principle might turn out to be equivalent to the belief I am ascribing to most of us, which accounts for our moral objection to exploitation.

ing to that other, or to the extent that it is, that the degradation is deserved or at any rate morally acceptable. Some instances of exploitation (exploiting the weaknesses of one's opponent in a game) can be regarded as innocent. One would not enter into the game with good sportsmanship if one did not expect (or even want) one's opponent to use one's weaknesses wherever possible, and competitive play remains morally innocent only as long as this sort of exploitation does not take a form which degrades the competitors.[25] Sometimes (e.g., the lawyer exploiting weaknesses in her opponent's case) we think people's vulnerabilities *ought* to be taken advantage of (for the sake of a just outcome).

Some disputed cases. Even in cases which are not innocent in these ways, we may think that exploitation is good (or morally acceptable, or at least satisfying on the whole), as when a person receives poetic justice through the a-exploitation of some morally bad quality—especially, as Feinberg points out, when the exploitee is "hoist with his own petard"—that is, a-exploited on the basis of a quality associated with a propensity to be an exploiter. Probably because he is disposed to a moralized conception of exploitation, Feinberg thinks it is even unclear whether, for example, the character Doyle Lonnegan (played by Robert Shaw in the movie *The Sting*) is exploited at all.[26] (Lonnegan, a powerful, wealthy, and utterly villainous mobster, is taken for half a million dollars by a gang of grifters, one of whom was killed on his orders early in the film.) However, I think nothing could be more obvious than that the elaborate con game portrayed in the film was an example of exploitation in exactly the same sense in which the term would apply if the same grifters had perpetrated one of their scams on a perfectly innocent victim.[27]

Another kind of case mentioned by Feinberg is that in which someone "cashes in" on the weaknesses of others precisely by helping them—as

[25] The difference between innocent and noninnocent exploitation is quite comparable, I think, to Richard Miller's distinction between innocent and noninnocent competition between people (see Miller, "From Responsibility to Justice," unpublished manuscript). Exploitation, as playing on others' weaknesses, is a typically competitive type of behavior; thus, generally speaking, it will be innocent only where human competition is innocent. I take Miller to agree with my view that noninnocent competition, which is pervasive in many social forms, including our own, constitutes the essence of some of the largest and worst social evils.

[26] Feinberg, *Harmless Wrongdoing,* pp. 203, 207.

[27] It seems to me a misinterpretation of the film, moreover, for Feinberg to suggest that what the grifters do to Lonnegan is supposed to be morally acceptable, all things considered. For the movie is not supposed to leave us righteously rejoicing in the triumph of virtue; on the contrary, we smile *wickedly* along with the story's low-life heroes, who—liars and con-men though they are—have at least the honesty not to seek any moral justification for their crooked schemes. If we take satisfaction in Lonnegan's being exploited, this is simply because the evil of that exploitation is more than offset by the fact that this character receives a particularly delicious kind of poetic justice: for the scam brings low a powerful man who has lived by exploiting others, and the very weaknesses in Lonnegan which the grifters a-exploit—his greed, arrogance, vengefulness, cruelty—are precisely the vicious qualities which have made him an especially odious exploiter.

a business does when it supplies householders with protective devices during a crime wave, or as doctors do when they treat patients. Because Feinberg holds that exploitation requires that there be some sort of wrongness, unfairness, or unethical conduct on the part of the exploiter, he thinks that we cannot speak of exploitation at all in these cases unless those who help charge unfair prices for their services or gain disproportionately in comparison to those they help.[28] I disagree. Those who help people in a position of weakness typically exploit them as well, and they do so whether they make just profits, unjust profits, or even no profits at all, as long as they also use the vulnerability of the recipients to further some end of their own other than the helping itself. This they typically do, even if the end is an entirely innocent and noble one, such as developing or exercising their own moral virtues. No doubt in such a case we are disclined to dwell on the exploitative aspect of the situation, not least because the helpers' further end may be in itself perfectly legitimate or even laudable, and because they are, after all, providing help to those who need it.

It is essential to keep in mind here, however, that when people are vulnerable and in need of help, it is not only the *helping* itself which they need. If one accepts the moral belief I have ascribed to most of us, then they are also beings with dignity, with whom not all is well as long as they lack the conditions under which a human being can be respected. Those who fulfill all their "obligations to help," or even display supererogatory virtue in helping, may (just by helping, and thereby exhibiting the terrible vulnerability of those they help) bring mercilessly to light the absence of these conditions.

Helping those in need therefore often has a profound moral ambivalence about it, making *solidarity* with them a far more vital achievement than any positive contribution to their welfare. (This is a point which radicals have generally gotten right, while liberals have often gotten it wrong.) For this reason, it seems to me extremely important for would-be benefactors of the weak and vulnerable to be fully (and even painfully) aware of the inevitably exploitative side of their beneficence. This is needed both to preserve the dignity of those they help and to protect the helpers themselves from a certain blind arrogance which sometimes afflicts those who have been fortunate enough to parlay the doing of good into a successful career or life-defining activity.[29]

[28] Feinberg, *Harmless Wrongdoing*, pp. 184, 193–94.

[29] Such examples also occasion the observation that, contrary to many dictionaries, there is nothing necessarily *selfish* about exploitation. It is true that those who use the weakness of others for their own ends typically do so for selfish ends, but there is nothing requiring that the ends be selfish. Imagine a nation struggling to free itself from the dominion of a foreign power which has set up a puppet government. A patriot learns that a collaborationist official is hiding some scandalous secret, and blackmails the official to cooperate in a resistance plot to overthrow the puppet government. Here the patriot clearly exploits the offi-

IV. Exploitation and Justice

Can exploitation be just? It is often thought that exploitation is bad because the exploiter takes *unfair* advantage of the exploitee. But if I am right about the source of our objection to exploitation, then we have reason to consider exploitation bad even when it involves no unfairness or injustice. For if the badness of exploitation lies in the fact that it is base and dishonorable of the exploiter, and insulting and degrading to the exploited, for the former to make use of the latter's vulnerability, then this badness seems to be present even where the exploitation involves no unfairness, injustice, or violation of rights. This means that even if issues about exploitation are chiefly issues of distribution (the distribution of power), they still cannot be reduced to issues about distributive *justice*. In other words, a just distribution of power may still be highly objectionable if it leads to just, but still highly objectionable, forms of exploitation.

But in what cases should exploitation be considered unjust or a violation of rights? If we use Mill's admirably clarifying and theoretically neutral definition of justice or right—that a person's right is a valid claim on society to be protected in the possession of something[30]—then it follows that exploitation is unjust or violates a person's right if and only if the exploited person has a valid claim on society's protection against the exploitation.

If the account of exploitation described above is correct, there is also a distinction to be drawn between two ways in which society might go about protecting people against exploitation. Either society could make it more difficult for the powerful to use their power to exploit the vulnerable, or it could redistribute power so that people are less vulnerable to use by others, and hence less susceptible to exploitation. Let us call the first way of protecting people "interference"[31] and the second way "redistribution." Exploitation is unjust, then, whenever the weakness exploited is one which society should either prevent others from taking advantage of (by means of interference) or else prevent from occurring altogether (by means of redistribution).

Prima facie it might be reasonable to expect society to protect people from forms of exploitation which degrade them or violate their human-

---

cial: he a-exploits his vulnerability to blackmail and b-exploits his governmental position. The patriot's ends are not in the least selfish, however; the patriot may reap no personal gain from the overthrow of the puppet government, and we may even imagine that he knows all along that he will have to sacrifice his life in the course of carrying out the revolutionary plot.

[30] John Stuart Mill, *Utilitarianism*, ed. George Sher (Indianapolis: Hackett, 1979), p. 52.

[31] "Interference" includes the prohibition of acts through which exploiters might make use of their power, but perhaps it more often involves the refusal of the state to recognize and support exploitative arrangements; consider, for example, the law's refusal to support the collection of interest on loans at usurious rates, or the proposal that surrogate motherhood be permitted but that surrogacy contracts be legally unenforceable against the birth mother.

ity, or which involve exploiters using their advantage in order to gain a very good mode of life for themselves while the exploited are condemned to a very bad or impoverished kind of life. Before we accept even such principles as these, however, we need to know what society is capable of accomplishing along these lines, and what costs it would incur in trying. These are large questions, but perhaps I can usefully make a couple of observations about how the approach I have been taking might impact on the issues of wage labor and surrogacy.

Capitalist exploitation. Regarding the first issue, people have usually thought that the controversial question is whether wage labor is exploitative. But if what I have said about the concept of exploitation is accepted, then it should be obvious—not a matter worthy of any dispute at all—that Marx was right: capital virtually always exploits wage labor. At least this is self-evident if it is granted that those who own the means of production enjoy a decisive bargaining advantage over those who own little besides their capacity to labor, and that this fundamental vulnerability on the part of labor decisively influences the terms of wage contracts. Collective bargaining and governmental regulation of the labor market can sometimes strengthen the bargaining position of workers (though the role of the state has more often been to weaken it), but the fundamental bargaining advantage of capital over labor is an ineradicable structural feature of the modern capitalist (or so-called "free market") economy. More generally, it is obvious that markets are bound to involve exploitative transactions whenever there are significant inequalities in the holdings of those who trade with one another, and whenever these inequalities significantly affect the terms of the transactions.[32]

It is another question whether capital's pervasive exploitation of labor is just or unjust. Using his own highly reductive account of justice (according to which the justice of a transaction is no defense of it), Marx thought that capitalist exploitation was generally just.[33] Those more favorably disposed toward capitalism argue for the same conclusion on various grounds: that it would be a violation of people's natural property rights either to interfere with capitalist transactions or to redistribute wealth in such a way as to forestall exploitation; or that the attempt to prevent capitalist exploitation either by interference or redistribution will necessarily involve excessive costs in individual liberty or the economic

[32] In this way, I wholeheartedly agree with John Roemer that the basic issue involved in capitalist exploitation is one of the initial distribution of assets (Roemer, "Should Marxists Be Interested in Exploitation?" pp. 262–63, 274, 281–82). I fault Roemer only for employing a technical definition of 'exploitation' which makes exploitation a matter entirely independent of initial distribution. For that obscures the fact that this has always been the main issue about capitalist exploitation.

[33] This is an exegetical thesis I have explained and defended in many places and over a long period of time. See M. Cohen, T. Nagel, and T. Scanlon, eds., *Marx, Justice, and History* (Princeton: Princeton University Press, 1980), pp. 3–41, 106–34; and Allen Wood, *Karl Marx* (London: Routledge, 1981), ch. 9.

productivity of society. I will not comment on such arguments here, except to characterize, a bit later, the sort of position they support.

Surrogacy and exploitation. On the issue of surrogacy, it seems to me once again self-evident that it involves exploitation of the birth mother whenever she is in a position of significant economic disadvantage compared to the adopting parents. This is a simple consequence of the fact, just noted, that exploitation is endemic to all market transactions whose terms are significantly affected by the fact that the participants are in unequal bargaining positions. Some argue that surrogacy is exploitative because it involves the commodification of childbearing. I agree with this, but I do not agree with the reason often given for it, that there is something special about childbearing that ought to exempt it from commodification. For even if this is true it would not show why there is anything *exploitative* about commodifying what should not be commodified. The commodification of childbearing is apt to be exploitative simply because in a market to which people bring unequal assets, the commodification of *anything* is apt to be exploitative.

Once again, it is a separate question whether surrogacy contracts are unjust or violate anyone's rights. When the issue is posed entirely in terms of the enforceability of such contracts, it is assumed that interference (in the form of rendering the contracts unenforceable) is society's only means of preventing exploitation. This may be because, for various reasons, redistribution is not seen as a viable way of avoiding exploitation. The economic vulnerability typical of surrogate mothers is not generally regarded as avoidable within a modern market economy, and the psychological vulnerabilities involved here do not seem preventable by any means within society's power. But there is always a dilemma when we must consider interference alone as a remedy for exploitation. As we have noted, an exploitative arrangement may benefit both parties, and is even likely to benefit the exploitee more than it benefits the exploiter. By interfering with exploitative arrangements, we may prevent one person from taking advantage of another's weakness, but we thereby also risk consigning the vulnerable person to an even worse fate than being exploited. If we decide that interference is too cruel to those in a position of weakness, we may decide that the exploitation, however bad it may be in various respects, violates no one's rights and has to be considered just. Radical remedies for exploitation, where they exist, are therefore always redistributive.

Can exploitation be abolished? People are encumbered with weaknesses or vulnerabilities of many kinds—physical, psychological, emotional, economic, political. They are also mutually dependent and competitively motivated, so that they have strong incentives to exploit the weaknesses of others. Exploitation is therefore a pervasive fact of the social life of human beings, and yet (for those who share the moral belief I have ascribed to most of us) it is also a profound evil which tends to infect nearly all their relationships with one another. Those who see the extent of exploitation cannot realistically hope that it will ever be wholly abolished, yet they ought to hope (as Marx did) that the largest and most systematic forms of it can someday be abolished.

Radical remedies for exploitation are always redistributive. They involve transfers of power (political, economic, institutional, emotional) from the strong to the weak. But powerful individuals and groups seldom abandon their advantages willingly, and by the nature of the case they have great resources with which to protect their position. Therefore, redistributive remedies to exploitation are inevitably difficult, costly, and potentially explosive in their social effects, and they always face prospects of success which are uncertain at best. This entails that there will always be strong arguments in favor of saying that society either cannot or should not be expected to do what is necessary to protect people against exploitation. Following the Millian analysis of rights and justice, this directly entails that there will be strong arguments for saying that exploitation is just.[34]

In other words, there will inevitably be strong arguments for a position not too far from that of Callicles and Nietzsche. Such a position need not hold, with them, that exploitation itself is just or a good thing, but it will hold that exploitation is something we must learn to live with. For the present, I am not concerned to dispute this position. Nor am I concerned for the moment to deny, what many of its supporters also believe, that capitalism is the freest, most just, and most productive economic order the world has ever known, that it is the social order which best accords with what we know of human nature, that no one has found a better or more workable system, or that every attempt to refound society on a radically less exploitative basis has not only been unsuccessful but had an utterly disastrous outcome.

Instead, I wish only to insist that people who think this way should recognize a simple truth which is entirely consistent with everything just conceded: that since under capitalism there are vast differences in economic power and ample opportunity in the market system for the strong to use these differences to their advantage, capitalism is also a highly exploitative social order, perhaps the most exploitative the world has ever known.

[34] Some might prefer to speak here of injustices whose rectification is prohibitively costly. That would require a modification of the Millian analysis of rights and justice which we have been using. From this analysis it follows that if it would be prohibitively costly for society to protect me in the possession of X, then society should not protect me in the possession of X, and so I do not have a right to X, and my being deprived of X is no injustice. Perhaps this is a basis for objecting to Mill's analysis of rights, but it does not seem to me a serious objection in practice. For it seems to me not to make a great deal of difference in practice whether we say of wage laborers or surrogate mothers that they have no right to be protected from exploitation, or that they have such a right but it is prohibitively costly for society to enforce it.

If you agree with Callicles and Nietzsche that this is all quite as it should be, then this admission need not disturb you. But if you agree with the moral belief I have ascribed to most of us—that it is an affront to people's human dignity to have their weaknesses used, and shameful to use the weaknesses of others—then you should find yourself in a troubling position. You should be ready to acknowledge that despite capitalism's long list of alleged virtues, we have strong grounds not to show any great loyalty to it. You should be willing to admit that even if we have yet to find a social system better than capitalism, we nevertheless have good and sufficient reasons to keep on looking for one, and reason too to put some of the cherished advantages of capitalism at risk in trying to achieve a better form of society. Finally, if the analysis of exploitation presented earlier in this essay is accurate, then you must also face the fact that you cannot honestly escape your ambivalent feelings about the society in which you live by the shallow ruse of arguing that since capitalism is just and 'exploitation' (in the "pejorative" sense) is by definition wrongful or unjust, capitalism cannot be exploitative.

Philosophy, Cornell University

JUSTICE AND THE ADA: DOES PRIORITIZING AND RATIONING HEALTH CARE DISCRIMINATE AGAINST THE DISABLED?

By Dan W. Brock

I. Introduction: Health-Care Rationing in Oregon

It is sometimes said that a society should be judged ethically by how it treats its least-fortunate or worst-off members.[1] In one interpretation this is not a point about justice, but instead about moral virtues such as compassion and charity. In our response to the least fortunate among us, we display, or show that we lack, fundamental moral virtues of fellow feeling and concern for others in need. In a different interpretation, however, this point is about justice and a just society—the justice of a society is shown especially in how it treats its least-fortunate members.

A general focus on the least fortunate or worst off masks considerable complexity and controversy in how that group should be defined. One natural way to define it is by referring to some global measure of well-being or quality of life, applied at a point in time or over some period of time. But most plausible theories of justice apply different principles to the distribution of different benefits and burdens—for example, votes, punishment, income, and health care. Even with a specific good such as health care, which will be my concern in this essay, there are alternative accounts of who are the worst off. One natural definition of the worst off with regard to health care is those without health insurance or other means of access to needed care. In a more fundamental sense, the worst off with regard to health care are those with the greatest health-care needs. Health-care needs are not some single thing like money which can be readily quantified on a single scale, such as dollars. Instead, health-care needs are diverse; most people have numerous health-care needs, often at a particular point in time, much less over a lifetime. Different health-care needs have different degrees of importance, measured, at least on the first cut, in terms of the degree of expected harm that will come to a person if a particular health-care need goes unsatisfied. The notion of harm from lack of health care also masks complexity in the benefits health care provides to people and the different kinds of harm that lack of needed health care can produce. One of the most important ben-

[1] John Rawls, *A Theory of Justice* (Cambridge, MA: Harvard University Press, 1971); Allen Buchanan, "Justice and Charity," *Ethics*, vol. 97, no. 3 (1987), pp. 558–75.

efits of health care, however, a benefit which is especially important from the perspective of justice, is its role in maintaining function, either by preventing disability or restoring function after disability.

The relevance of function to justice is familiar and obvious—maintaining function helps maintain people's opportunities, and some requirement of equality of opportunity is common to otherwise different theories of justice. In the most fully developed theory of justice in health care, Norman Daniels has argued that health care's importance from the standpoint of justice is its role in protecting or restoring fair equality of opportunity.[2] In very general terms, health care treats disease, understood broadly as a physical or mental condition which results in a reduction or limitation in normal human function. Through this lens of function and opportunity, it is natural to understand the worst off to be, or at least to include, persons with disabilities or handicaps, which are typically defined as chronic limitations in significant areas of normal human function. An important aspect of social justice is then how a society treats its disabled or handicapped members, and in particular how it meets their health-care needs.

The specific issue of what the handicapped or disabled are owed in access to health care has in fact recently been joined in one specific debate about health-care reform—the reform plan just recently put into effect in the state of Oregon, which aims initially to restructure the Oregon Medicaid program.[3] Since I will address the issue of justice and the handicapped in the context of the debate over the Oregon reform plan, a brief account of that plan is needed.[4] The Oregon reform plan is intended to respond to the two central issues of health-care reform generally in the United States—controlling the growth of health-care costs and extending access to health care to all citizens. In public policy debates about how to achieve these goals, it has been increasingly recognized that we cannot provide all beneficial care to everyone, without regard to how great the costs and how small the benefits of particular services. (This is not to say, however, that supporters of health-care reform plans will readily and publicly acknowledge that their plans will limit or ration health care.) It is not economically rational to ignore the opportunity costs of providing low-benefit/high-cost health care when there are higher-benefit uses to which resources devoted to that care could be put. It is also unjust to expend resources in health care without regard to the costs of the benefits

[2] Norman Daniels, *Just Health Care* (Cambridge: Cambridge University Press, 1985). Daniels follows Rawls in understanding fair equality of opportunity as requiring equal opportunities for persons with similar talents and abilities.

[3] Medicaid is a joint federal/state government program in the United States to provide health care to the poor.

[4] I draw on Michael J. Garland, "Justice, Politics, and Community: Expanding Access and Rationing Health Services in Oregon," *Law, Medicine, and Health Care*, vol. 20 (1992), p. 70.

produced when the result is overutilization of health care and an inability to meet fully other public responsibilities required by justice, such as the education of children.

Typical measures in the past to limit the growth of costs in the Medicaid program, the principal public program to extend access to health care to the poor in the United States, have included tightening eligibility requirements to the point where now well over one half of the people living below the federal poverty level nationwide are ineligible for Medicaid on income grounds. Those still covered by Medicaid are eligible, at least in theory, for a relatively generous package of benefits, although it often remains difficult in practice to secure services because of the program's very low levels of reimbursement to health-care providers. In 1989, the state of Oregon proposed to make a more rational and fair use of limited resources devoted to health care for the poor by bringing everyone in the state living below the federal poverty level into its Medicaid program; the income eligibility level for Medicaid in Oregon was then approximately 60 percent of the federal poverty level. To make this extension of benefits possible within resource constraints, Oregon's program would also explicitly limit the services that would be covered and reimbursed by Medicaid. Instead of "rationing people" in or out of the program, Oregon proposed to bring in all citizens living below the poverty level and to "ration services" by providing the same health-care services to all participants.

The Oregon Basic Health Services Act of 1989 established the Oregon Health Services Commission (OHSC), charged with prioritizing all forms of health-care services. To do this, OHSC initially set out to rank treatments provided to patients in specific conditions, so-called treatment/condition pairs, essentially by a cost-benefit analysis; this would enable Oregon to use any given level of appropriation for the Medicaid program from the state legislature to secure the highest level of overall benefits from limited resources. The OHSC's initial effort ranked over sixteen hundred services and contained some widely publicized and apparently anomalous results; for example, capping teeth with exposed pulp was ranked just above appendectomies for acute appendicitis and surgery for ectopic pregnancy, despite the life-threatening nature of these latter two conditions. Different analyses of these counterintuitive results have been offered, but the central difficulty was that people's intuitive rankings of the relative importance of different health-care services is a one-to-one ranking (e.g., one appendectomy versus one tooth capped), and in a one-to-one ranking an appendectomy is clearly far more important than capping a tooth.[5] A cost-benefit ranking, on the other hand, takes account

[5] David Hadorn, "Setting Health Care Priorities in Oregon: Cost-Effectiveness Meets the Rule of Rescue," *Journal of the American Medical Association*, vol. 265 (1991), pp. 2218–25; David Eddy, "Oregon's Methods: Did Cost-Effectiveness Analysis Fail?" *Journal of the American Medical Association*, vol. 266 (1991), pp. 2135–41.

of the vastly higher cost of the appendectomy; since it is possible to do about 150 tooth cappings for the cost of one appendectomy, the aggregate benefit of the tooth cappings was determined to exceed the benefit of one appendectomy.

Faced with these results, the OHSC changed its methodology and developed seventeen categories which were prioritized principally by the degree of benefit the category of care provided to a patient. Some of the categories were kinds of outcomes of care provided to patients in specific conditions (e.g., "acute, fatal conditions for which treatment prevents death"; "chronic conditions which are fatal and for which treatment improves life span and quality of life"). Other categories were types of care (e.g., "maternity care, including disorders of the newborn"; "prevention care for children"). All treatment/condition pairs were placed within one of the categories, and then those within each category were ranked. Costs of different treatments were now used principally to break ties between treatment/condition pairs that were judged to provide roughly equal benefits. Thus, Oregon largely abandoned a cost-benefit analysis and prioritization of different services in favor of a relative-benefit analysis and prioritization.

To perform this prioritization required two distinct steps. First, an expected outcome for a patient had to be associated with each treatment/condition pair; this was an empirical determination which would ideally rest on outcome studies and data, although the OHSC found that the necessary data often either did not exist or were extremely limited. Second, a relative value had to be assigned to the different expected outcomes; this was an evaluative determination, and was done largely on the basis of telephone surveys of a random selection of Oregon citizens. Adapting the Quality of Well-Being Scale (QWB) developed by Robert Kaplan and John Anderson, citizens were asked how much particular impairments of health or quality of life—described in terms of "physical or emotional symptoms and of different degrees of impairment in mobility, physical activity, and social activity"—would reduce quality of life (the citizens polled did not themselves have the impairments they were asked about).[6] This enabled the OHSC to assign a relative value to different outcome states of treatments, and then to calculate the net benefit for each of 709 treatment/condition pairs. The OHSC then made further "by hand" adjustments of the resultant ranking where its members believed the ranking reflected mistakes from inadequate data about outcomes, or from other sources. It was this ranking of treatment/condition pairs, based on their expected benefits and reflecting the valuations of outcomes obtained from Oregon citizens in the telephone poll, that Oregon used in applying to the Health Care Financing Administration

[6] Robert Kaplan and John Anderson, "A General Health Policy Model: Update and Applications," *Health Services Research*, vol. 23 (1988), pp. 203–35.

(HCFA), the federal agency that administers the Medicaid program, for waivers of certain federal Medicaid requirements—waivers that were necessary for Oregon to put its new program into effect.

I take the Oregon prioritization to be a paradigmatic attempt to make more rational use of health-care resources in the face of explicit acknowledgment of resource scarcity. The QWB scale is one among a number of measures that have been developed by health-policy analysts for making comparative assessments of the benefits of different health-care services and programs; another is quality-adjusted life years (QALYs), a measure of the number of years of life extension, adjusted for differences in the quality of life of those years, provided by different health-care services or programs.[7] While the various measures differ in detail, my concern here is with the central feature they all share—recognition that the relative benefits of health-care services can be assessed in terms of their effects in extending patients' lives and improving or protecting the quality of their lives or their well-being. These measures also make explicit at the policy level an often implicit notion of "medical need"—a notion that physicians use at the clinical level when they make rough assessments of the relative importance of patients' needs for health-care services based on the degree of gain in length and quality of life that specific services are expected to provide. Thus, both at the level of health policy and at the level of clinical medicine, when health-care services must be prioritized, it is typically assumed that the prioritization should be in terms of their relative benefits to patients (I set aside, for now, the relevance of costs).

Virtually all prominent proposals for national health-care reform in the United States seek to rein in the growth of health-care costs without explicit rationing of care, which is considered by most political analysts to be so controversial that it must be avoided, in name if not in fact. Unlike these national reform plans, the Oregon plan is the most explicit, and certainly the most widely publicized, program in the United States to openly prioritize and ration health-care services; as a result, from the time when it was initially proposed, the Oregon plan has drawn much attention and criticism.[8] Probably the most common criticism has been that the plan is a case of "us" rationing "them"—that is, of middle- and upper-class Oregonians placing limits on the health-care services available to the poor, limits the middle and upper classes do not and likely would not accept for themselves. This is a serious criticism, although its force has been mitigated to a degree by the intent of the plan's proponents ultimately to bring nearly all Oregonians under the same benefit package and limits in the future. This issue did not figure into the Bush administra-

[7] See Dan W. Brock, "Quality of Life Measures in Health Care and Medical Ethics," in *The Quality of Life*, ed. A. Sen and M. Nussbaum (Oxford: Oxford University Press, 1993).

[8] Norman Daniels, "Is the Oregon Rationing Plan Fair?" *Journal of the American Medical Association*, vol. 265 (1991), pp. 2232–35.

tion's response to Oregon's waiver request, however, and it will not be my concern here.

Instead, then Secretary of Health and Human Services Louis Sullivan surprised most who were following the fate of the Oregon plan by denying the waiver request in 1992 on the ground that the plan was in violation of the Americans with Disabilities Act (ADA) because it would unjustly and illegally discriminate against disabled and handicapped persons.[9] The ADA went into effect as federal law in 1990 to "establish a clear and comprehensive prohibition of discrimination on the basis of disability."[10] The act includes separate titles prohibiting discrimination on the basis of disability in employment, public services, transportation, and public accommodations. Since it prohibits discrimination on the basis of disability in both public and private services and programs, in health care "it applies to programs provided by the government, benefits provided by employers, and services provided by physicians."[11] The precise legal implications for the Oregon plan (as well as for other forms of health-care prioritizing and rationing) of the ADA and other legislation protecting disabled persons are both complex and controversial, and I shall not explore them here. My concern will be with the moral issues, although I shall take as a starting-point the legal issue as it was posed by Secretary Sullivan.

Secretary Sullivan's denial of Oregon's waiver request employed language and analysis that had been prepared by the National Legal Center for the Medically Dependent and Disabled, at the request of Representative Christopher Smith (R, NJ).[12] Some observers saw the secretary's denial in political terms, leaving until after the 1992 presidential election the potentially volatile political issue of approving a plan that had been widely labeled as unjust rationing for the poor; these observers saw the appeal to violation of the ADA as largely a smoke screen for the administration's real political motives. Whatever the motives of the Bush administration and Secretary Sullivan, I shall argue that there are serious (and surprisingly complex and controversial) issues of moral and political philosophy, and specifically of justice, underlying this challenge to Oregon's priority setting and to health-care rationing more generally. What is at stake are the broad issues with which I began this essay, issues regard-

[9] Unpublished letter from Secretary of Health and Human Services Louis W. Sullivan to Governor Barbara Roberts of Oregon, August 3, 1992.

[10] Public Law 101–336, July 26, 1990, 104 Stat. 327, 42 USC 12101–12213, 47 USC 225 and 611.

[11] David Orentlicher, "Rationing and the Americans with Disabilities Act," *Journal of the American Medical Association*, vol. 271 (1994), pp. 308–14. Orentlicher provides a comprehensive legal analysis of the likely application of the ADA (and other legislation protecting the disabled) to a variety of forms of health-care rationing.

[12] Unpublished letter from Thomas J. Marzen and Daniel Avila, National Legal Center for the Medically Dependent and Disabled, Inc., to Representative Christopher H. Smith, U.S. House of Representatives, December 5, 1991.

ing what treatment disabled persons are due on grounds of justice, and more specifically, how they should be treated in the prioritization of claims on scarce resources in public programs. I shall identify three more-general problems of justice that are part of the specific issue of justice to the disabled: first, the conflict between maximizing benefits and ensuring fair chances; second, the problem of compensation for handicaps; third, what I call the perspective problem—whether we should use the perspective of a nondisabled person or a disabled person in evaluating the quality of life of disabled persons for purposes of resource allocation.

Before proceeding, I need to note that in response to the initial waiver denial, Oregon revised its methodology, and in turn its ranking, in order to remove the apparent conflicts with the ADA noted by Secretary Sullivan. In an attempt to avoid explicitly ranking benefits—that is, outcomes—by gains in length and quality of life, the new methodology assessed outcomes on the "probability (percent of the time) that within five years the average person with a particular condition receiving a specified treatment would (1) die, (2) have significant residual effects (symptoms) because of or in spite of treatment or (3) become asymptomatic."[13] Since the Clinton administration in 1993 granted the waivers that Oregon sought, it presumably decided either that the conflict with the ADA had been removed or that it would let the plan go forward subject to possible subsequent legal challenges. However the legal question may ultimately be resolved, my concern will be with the methodology and ranking Oregon initially submitted to the Department of Health and Human Services, a ranking which prioritized services on the basis of their relative effects on length and quality of life. It is this methodology which allows us to pose most sharply the question of whether a relative-benefit, or cost-benefit, prioritization and rationing of health-care services wrongly discriminates against persons with disabilities.

II. Prioritization by Benefits of Treatment: Maximizing Benefits versus Ensuring Fair Chances

Consider the problem of prioritizing life-sustaining treatment for nondisabled and disabled persons. The analysis of the National Legal Center for the Medically Dependent and Disabled imagined the following scenario:

> A person is injured and two alternative treatments are recommended. Both treatments cost the same and are equal in every other respect—except that after Treatment A the person will live, but after Treatment B the patient not only will live but also will regain the use of his legs as a result. The State only has enough money to fund one

[13] *New York Times*, March 20, 1993, p. 8.

> treatment and it chooses to fund Treatment B because it provides the greatest improvement in the person's function for the same amount of money.[14]

The National Legal Center granted that this would not be discrimination based on disability, but it then posed a different scenario, again assuming that the state has only enough money to fund one treatment:

> Patient A and Patient B are both injured in an accident. Treatment A is recommended for Patient A, while Treatment B is recommended for Patient B. However, Treatment A will sustain Patient A's life but will not restore the abilities A lost after the accident (such as an ability to walk), while Treatment B will sustain B's life *and* restore his ability to walk. If the basis for funding B but not A is a quality-of-life judgment that being able to walk is of greater benefit than not being able to walk, for example, then a decision to deny treatment for A would be discrimination based on A's resulting level of disability. In effect, B's life would be considered more valuable than A's life because B will regain an additional function while A would not. Under the second scenario, a distinction between two effective treatments would be based not on treatment effectiveness, because both treatments would sustain life, but on an inappropriate assessment of the underlying quality-of-life each patient will have after treatment. This scenario describes the Oregon Plan.[15]

The Center's point may be even more forceful if we imagine Patient A to have had his disability before the accident, because then there should be no reason for supposing in the Center's second scenario that Treatment A is less effective than Treatment B because it fails to restore full function. In the Center's first scenario, there is a choice of treatments by a single individual, and thus no issues of distributive justice are raised. In the Center's second scenario, the question concerns prioritizing treatments for different individuals, and thus issues of distributive justice are raised.

David Hadorn has responded that this case has no practical significance:

> Speaking as an emergency physician with 10 years of experience, it is inconceivable that patients injured in an accident would be left untreated and allowed to die because of predicted residual disabilities. To suggest otherwise merely raises a red herring. . . .[16]

[14] Marzen and Avila, unpublished letter.

[15] *Ibid.*

[16] David C. Hadorn, "The Problem of Discrimination in Health Care Priority Setting," *Journal of the American Medical Association*, vol. 268 (1992), pp. 1454–59.

Hadorn is no doubt correct about the actual practice followed in emergency rooms, but the difficulty the scenario raises is not so easily dismissed. There is a deeper and more far-reaching ethical issue at stake whose theoretical and practical import is brought out most clearly and starkly in the case of organ transplantation, where the scarcity is not economic (for example, the new Oregon Medicaid program pays for transplantation) but scarcity of organs. Patients with failure of one or another major organ outrun the supply of such organs for transplantation, with the result that each year in the U.S. several thousand patients die while on waiting lists for transplantation. How should we decide who gets these scarce lifesaving resources?

In an essay published some years ago, I argued that the selection of recipients typically raises a conflict between two competing moral considerations.[17] On the one hand, we want to use scarce resources to do the most good, that is, to secure the best outcomes by maximizing the benefits they produce as measured, for example, by quality-adjusted life years (QALYs). In order to maximize benefits in transplantation, a variety of factors that help predict the success of a graft (e.g., tissue matching, organ size, etc.) and that affect the amount of the expected benefit from a successful graft (e.g., life expectancy with the transplant) are often used to select recipients. But we know, of course, that when benefits are distributed to different individuals, it is ethically controversial whether it is just or fair to all individuals affected by the distribution always simply to maximize total benefits without regard to their distribution to particular individuals. Utilitarians, and consequentialists more generally, will argue that maximizing overall benefits is not unjust, but utilitarianism's implications for distributive justice are one of its most controversial features.

The other moral consideration conflicting with maximizing benefits in organ transplantation is fairness. It could be argued that if the pool of donated organs is a public resource of the society on which particular individuals in need of transplants typically do not have differential moral claims, then each person in need should have a fair, which in this context may mean equal, chance of being selected to receive the scarce resource. In the case of organs, one way to give all in need an equal chance of getting a transplant is to use a lottery system to select recipients from among all those who are in need and who meet some minimal standard for expected success of the transplant; other practical systems, such as "first come, first served," may approximate the equal-chances requirement. The equal-chances account is supported by the fact that although there may be differences in the expected benefits from giving the organ

[17] Dan Brock, "Ethical Issues in Recipient Selection for Organ Transplantation," in *Organ Substitution Technology: Ethical, Legal, and Public Policy Issues*, ed. Debra Mathieu (Boulder, CO: Westview Press, 1988), p. 94.

to different patients suffering from organ failure, each nevertheless has equal need for the organ if he or she is to survive; each equally faces certain death, and thus loses everything, without it.

We can say a bit more about this claim grounded in justice or fairness. It is often argued that justice requires taking account of the personal perspective of each individual affected by a distributive scheme, and not simply maximizing the overall benefits as determined from an impersonal perspective. From the personal perspective of an individual with organ failure, the loss of his or her own life dwarfs differences in expected benefits that he or she would gain from being saved compared with what others would gain if they were saved instead. To return to the National Legal Center's case, the fact that Treatment B would sustain B's life and fully restore function, while Treatment A would sustain A's life but leave A unable to walk, would not make treating B more important to A than treating A. Although treating B would produce a greater benefit from an impersonal perspective, treating A would nevertheless be more important to A from his or her personal perspective. We would not normally think that A would be morally required to sacrifice his own treatment for the sake of B's treatment, and would not criticize A morally for failing to do so.[18] To favor B merely because a larger benefit, more QALYs, would be produced if we treat him, is unfair to A, who would by that distributive principle have no chance to be saved. Moreover, if medical care should be distributed on the basis of need, then on one natural sense of "need," each has an equal need—the same need—for the lifesaving treatment, because each faces certain death without it. It seems unfair to favor the patient who will recover normal function over the patient who will have a residual disability, when each will die without treatment.

In my earlier essay, which discussed this conflict in the context of organ transplantation, I argued that most of us are unwilling to give sole moral weight to either of these conflicting considerations—maximizing benefits or ensuring fair chances. Few people would be willing, for example, to give equal chances to receive a scarce organ to these two patients, each of whom will die very soon without it:

> an otherwise healthy twenty-five-year-old who is expected to have a normal lifespan without any significant disability if she receives a transplant; [and] a seventy-five-year-old patient who is expected to die from unrelated medical conditions within one to two years whatever is done, who has a low probability of a successful transplant, and who will have a severely compromised quality of life for her remaining one to two years even if the graft succeeds. Even the hardiest of egalitarians and the strongest proponents of fairness are

[18] Frances Kamm, *Morality, Mortality: Volume I, Death and Whom to Save from It* (Oxford: Oxford University Press, 1993).

> very unlikely to be willing to support a random selection process between these two patients.[19]

But it also seems wrong to decide who gets this scarce resource solely by very small differences in the benefits expected from giving it to one or the other, as in a case where

> two relatively young patients appear otherwise identically good prospects for transplant, except that one has a life-expectancy with transplant only slightly greater than the other, say forty years instead of thirty-seven years. If being fair to both requires giving each an equal chance to be selected for transplant, then there is not a large enough difference in the expected good that would be produced by preferring the one with the slightly greater life expectancy to outweigh fairness and thereby to justify not treating them fairly.[20]

In my earlier essay, I argued that in the case of organ transplantation we are faced with independent conflicting moral considerations or principles – maximizing benefits and ensuring fair chances – in determining how to distribute this benefit. Neither principle is plausibly held always to override the other; instead, they must be balanced against each other. I used the example of a weighted lottery to illustrate one way that balancing might be achieved in organ transplantation.[21]

How does this conflict between maximizing benefits and ensuring fair chances apply to prioritization of resources for nondisabled and disabled persons? Its most direct application is that using the maximizing-benefits or best-outcomes principle to select recipients for organ transplantation would systematically disadvantage disabled persons, because they would have a lower quality of life than nondisabled persons after a successful transplant because of their disability. That seems to value the lives of disabled persons less than the lives of nondisabled persons. Moreover, it is not just quality-of-life differences that would disadvantage the disabled. Many disabilities, though of course not all, are associated with reduced life expectancies such that for two otherwise similar patients in need of a life-sustaining transplant, greater life years, apart from the quality adjustment, will be produced by favoring the normal person. But the indirect implication for disabled persons of prioritizing by best outcomes is more far-reaching. As illustrated in the National Legal Center's second scenario, in which one injured patient would survive with normal function and the other with a loss of the ability to walk, disabled persons

[19] Brock, "Ethical Issues in Recipient Selection for Organ Transplantation," p. 94.

[20] *Ibid.*

[21] Roughly speaking, the weighted lottery would give a greater probability of being selected to receive a scarce organ to patients likely to benefit more from it, but would also give all in need at least some chance of being selected.

would be systematically disadvantaged in the prioritization of all life-sustaining treatment because their disability reduces their quality of life.

Does prioritizing health-care services in terms of their relative benefits disadvantage the disabled only in the case of life-sustaining treatments, or does the same disadvantage arise with non-life-sustaining treatments? In most cases in which one of two patients needing the same treatment already suffers from a disability that diminishes quality of life, the disability will produce no difference in their benefits from treatment. For example, if two patients needed an artificial hip replacement, there is no reason to believe that if one was deaf she would for that reason receive any less benefit from the hip replacement; the benefit of improved function from the hip replacement would not be affected by the presence or absence of deafness. This will be true for many, probably most, non-lifesaving treatments for disabled and nondisabled persons.

In other cases, however, the disability may act as a co-morbid condition, making the benefit from treatment of the new condition less likely and/or less full. Suppose again that two patients need an artificial hip, but one of them suffers from Chronic Obstructive Pulmonary Disease (COPD). The COPD patient's mobility and physical function are not likely to be as fully restored by the hip replacement, because those functions will still be limited by the COPD. While the public may be unaccustomed to thinking of diseases like COPD as disabilities or handicaps, I believe the ADA properly defines "disability" very broadly so as to include all chronic medical conditions, such as COPD, that seriously limit function. Any chronic medical condition, physical or mental, "that substantially limits one or more of the major life activities of [an] individual" is a disability under the ADA.[22]

In still other cases, the disability is not present at the outset, but is an outcome of treatment. Consider two patients, neither of whom is disabled and who more generally have roughly comparable levels of function and quality of life before becoming ill. Suppose it is predictable (or becomes clear in the course of treatment) that one of them is likely to emerge from treatment with a higher level of function than the other. Treating the one who will emerge with the disability, or with the greater disability, will produce less benefit and be given lower priority.

Thus, for both life-sustaining and non-life-sustaining treatments, prioritization of treatments based on the extension of life and on the improvements in quality of life or level of function they produce for patients will often disadvantage disabled persons because of their disability. If we return now to Oregon's actual prioritization process, the seventeen prioritized categories of treatments into which Oregon placed specific treatment/condition pairs are shot through with distinctions based

[22] Public Law 101-336 (*supra* note 10).

on the improvement in the quality of life of patients with treatment. For example, category one is "[a]cute, fatal conditions for which treatment prevents death and provides full recovery," whereas category three is "[a]cute, fatal conditions for which treatment prevents death but recovery is limited."[23] But it is not just in the highest categories, where it could be argued that all services will be covered and thus that a prioritization into category three instead of category one does not result in any denial of services, that differences in quality of life are important. The definition of category ten is "[a]cute, nonfatal conditions for which treatment is likely to bring a return to previous health," whereas the definition of category twelve is "[a]cute, nonfatal conditions for which treatment is unable to fully restore previous health"; treatments in category twelve will be ranked lower than those in category ten because they leave patients with an impairment that category ten treatments do not. If maximizing benefits must be balanced against giving patients equally in need of a treatment a fair chance of receiving it, then prioritization of treatments based solely on the extension of life and improvement in the quality of life is ethically unacceptable. Such prioritization would not give disabled persons a fair chance of receiving treatment, because their disability would often result in their receiving less benefit from treatment than an otherwise similar person without the disability. Whether the disadvantage that disabled persons suffer in the prioritization of health-care services according to their relative benefits is unjust depends, in part, on how we resolve the more general conflict between maximizing benefits and ensuring fair chances.

Before pursuing that issue further, it is worth noting that I have focused up to this point entirely on the benefit side of cost-benefit analysis, in significant part because the method of prioritizing used by Oregon—the method which drew criticism for discriminating against the disabled—essentially prioritized only according to benefits, not costs. Appeal to costs can also result in additional disadvantaging of the disabled, however. It will do so in those cases in which it is more expensive to provide treatment for a given medical condition as a result of an individual's disability. This can occur in a number of ways, such as when the disability acts as a co-morbid condition making the treatment in question more complex or lengthy than it would otherwise be.

III. Could Maximizing Benefits Be Compatible with Ensuring Fair Chances?

If maximizing benefits is sometimes in conflict with ensuring fair chances, a central issue is how they are to be weighed or balanced against

[23] Garland, "Justice, Politics, and Community," p. 70.

each other in particular cases, given that it seems implausible to treat either as always overriding the other. We need a principled basis for these trade-offs, a general account of how maximizing benefits and ensuring fair chances should be weighed against each other in different contexts, but I cannot pursue that general problem here. I do want at least to mention, however, a line of argument that might be thought to show that in fact there is no conflict between maximizing benefits and treating all in need fairly.[24] That argument seeks to reinterpret what fairness requires in a manner that removes the conflict with maximizing benefits. Recall the National Legal Center's second scenario, in which lifesaving treatment returns one patient to normal function and leaves the other unable to walk. Maximizing benefits favors the former patient, while giving each a fair chance at the benefit seems to require some method of random selection. But perhaps the requirement of fairness has already been satisfied, because each had an equal chance of turning out to be the one who could be restored to full function, and it was only bad luck in the accident that left one unable to regain his ability to walk.

In this interpretation of the requirement of fairness, the process of giving each an equal chance at the benefit through randomization took place in the accident itself, which determined who could be most benefited; to randomize again, when we know which patient will benefit more, would be to unnecessarily repeat the process of giving each an equal chance to get the benefit—which is not required by, but indeed in conflict with, ensuring fair chances. Likewise, if Patient A was disabled before the accident, then perhaps the biological and/or social lottery that led him or her to be disabled, and Patient B not to be, is sufficient for each to have had a fair chance at being the one who would benefit most from getting the treatment. The difficult question is whether "nature's randomization" satisfies the demands of fairness—or whether, instead, real historically situated individuals with all their contingent differences must, at the time they need a scarce benefit, be given a fair chance to get it. Would it matter if Patient A had lost the use of his legs before the accident, so that the lifesaving treatment would be equally effective for each patient, although greater QALYs would be produced from the patient returned to normal function?

Individuals should agree on distributive principles *ex ante*, as it is sometimes put, before they know how their own particular interests would be affected by different principles. This is necessary to satisfy the moral requirement of impartiality, which precludes adopting principles of distributive justice specially tailored or selected to favor one's own interests.

[24] Brock, "Ethical Issues in Recipient Selection for Organ Transplantation"; Daniel Wikler, "Equity, Efficacy, and the Point System for Transplant Recipient Selection," *Transplantation Proceedings*, vol. 21 (1991), pp. 3437–39.

There is a temptation, at least among consequentialists, to think that if people must select principles *ex ante*, all will support the distributive principle that favors the alternative that maximizes benefits to all affected. Having no knowledge of what position one will fill in any distribution, it is argued, it is reasonable to assume that one has an equal chance of filling any position; if so, then one will maximize one's expected benefits under this uncertainty by maximizing the total benefits to all.

We know from general work in justice and moral theory, however, that this reasoning is much too quick. For example, in John Rawls's version of selecting principles of justice *ex ante*—that is, under a veil of ignorance in the original position—he argues that the nature of the choice is such that it is reasonable to be conservative and to select the difference principle, which requires maximizing the expectations of the worst off.[25] There are some things which it is, at least sometimes, not reasonable to put at risk, even for the sake of possibly greater overall gains; the most obvious example is one's life, which, once lost (if the gamble turns out badly), cannot be won back on later "rolls of the dice." Under Rawls's scheme for choosing principles of justice which are to govern the circumstances and institutions that will determine people's overall life prospects, individuals know that they will have one and only one life to live; a gamble with those prospects that turns out badly would never allow them to recoup the loss. The worst-off members of society would reasonably regret accepting principles *ex ante* that permit significant sacrifices in their expectations for the sake of greater benefits for others already substantially better off.

How does this apply to resource distribution between the disabled and the nondisabled? The disabled are by definition individuals who suffer significant functional disadvantages compared with nondisabled persons. Disabilities, as defined by the ADA, are chronic physical or mental conditions that cause limitations in one or more major life activities, such as caring for oneself, performing manual tasks, walking, seeing, hearing, speaking, breathing, learning, and working. As a chronic condition, a disability affects significant portions of one's life. Should both the disabled and nondisabled agree *ex ante*—that is, before anyone knows whether he or she is or will become disabled—that under conditions of resource scarcity, distributions should favor the nondisabled over the disabled whenever greater QALYs will be produced by doing so? This would seem to be a choice that the disabled would reasonably regret for just the same reasons that persons in Rawls's original position would reasonably regret accepting trade-offs between persons in the service of utilitarian maximization, if they turned out to be among the worst off whose prospects were substantially sacrificed for greater gains to the already better off.

[25] Rawls, *A Theory of Justice*, section 29.

IV. Do Disadvantages of the Disabled in Prioritizing Health Care Constitute Unjust Discrimination?

How did Oregon avoid the conflict with the ADA in order to secure the federal waivers needed under Medicaid law? Recall that Oregon, quite plausibly, prioritized not treatments, but treatment/condition pairs. A particular treatment can appear more than once on the list of prioritized services, because when given to patients in significantly different conditions it can have substantially different expected benefits. One example in the original list of 709 treatment/condition pairs that attracted the attention of disability-rights organizations, and was specifically criticized by Health and Human Services Secretary Sullivan in his initial denial of Oregon's request for Medicaid waivers, is the medical treatment of low-birth-weight newborns. The secretary specifically noted that ranking at number twenty-two the treatment of newborns over twenty-three weeks gestation, while ranking next to last at number 708 the treatment of newborns under twenty-three weeks gestation, raised concerns under the ADA. His letter did not make the precise nature of the concern clear, but it appears to be that differentiation in the ranking between otherwise similar patients, either on the basis of a disabling condition or on the basis of a likely resultant disability from treatment, would violate the ADA. Oregon's apparently ad hoc response was to combine treatment of all premature newborns with birth-weights below twenty-five hundred grams; this new combined category received a ranking of number forty, presumably reflecting the much larger number of newborns between five hundred and twenty-five hundred grams (most of whom will have good outcomes) than below five hundred grams (nearly all of whom will have very poor outcomes).

Although this new combined category removed the putative discrimination on grounds of disability to which the secretary had objected, it is important to understand that combining the two groups of premature newborns was flatly in conflict with Oregon's methodology of ranking treatments in terms of their benefits for patients in particular conditions. What that methodology requires, and what Oregon did at other places in its ranking, was to *differentiate*, not *combine*, treatment/condition pairs when the same treatment produces substantially different overall benefits for patients in different conditions. The separation of newborns under and over twenty-three weeks gestation in the earlier ranking was the result of correctly following that methodology. More generally, in any of the kinds of cases that I have discussed, in which the presence of a disability pre- or post-treatment causes an important reduction in the benefits provided to the patient by that treatment, the methodology in principle requires separation into more than one treatment/condition pair, with the resulting disadvantage to patients with the disability. The methodology will frequently be in conflict with the ADA so long as the ADA is understood as barring appeal to "quality of life" and "ability to function," which, Secretary Sullivan indicated, "place importance on 'restored' health and functional 'independence' and thus expressly value a person without a disability more highly than a person with a disability in the allocation of medical treatment."[26]

In two of the most detailed and explicit defenses of Oregon's plan against the charge that it wrongly discriminates against people with disabilities, David Hadorn and Paul Menzel both acknowledge that using quality of life and ability to function to evaluate treatment outcomes does sometimes disadvantage persons with disabilities, but they argue in effect that we must accept that result as the cost of a rational priority-setting process. For example, Hadorn writes:

> Banning consideration of quality of life and ability to function is, as I have argued above, counterproductive; moreover, it is inconsistent with the massive effort to facilitate and fund health outcomes research – the lion's share of which deals with quality of life and ability to function.[27]

Hadorn seeks to minimize the extent to which such consideration would, in practice in the Oregon list, result in significantly lower priority to care for the disabled. Even if he is correct about Oregon's revised list, however, that is in part because of ad hoc departures from the methodology (such as in the case of premature newborns) which were undertaken to avoid the apparent conflict with the ADA. The Oregon methodology of prioritizing by relative benefit is incompatible with a prohibition on giving weight to quality of life and ability to function in assessing the relative benefits of treatment outcomes. Moreover, if the methodology is openly employed at the policy level in prioritizing health-care services, it will be difficult at the clinical level to convince physicians that they should not take similar account of quality of life and ability to function in recommendations about treatment for individual patients, with the result that patients with disabilities do not receive treatments that do go to non-disabled patients.

Menzel, too, bites the bullet in accepting that priority setting cannot avoid disadvantaging the disabled:

> Quality of life considerations as well as likelihood of medical success sometimes do get associated with disabilities (though not *only* with disabilities). Such considerations must not be seen as biased against persons with disabilities just because they catch disabilities in their net. They ought to be regarded as inconsistent with the ADA only

[26] Sullivan, unpublished letter.
[27] Hadorn, "The Problem of Discrimination in Health Care Priority Setting," p. 1459.

> if we would reject them as legitimate considerations at all were they not sometimes to deny care to persons with disabilities. This is a tough distinction for many to accept, for it means that even with the ADA, particular disabled individuals will end up disadvantaged. It is, however, a distinction utterly essential to maintain if we are going to have any significant rationing at all. . . . Rationing that considers quality of life must be allowed to go forward even if at times it happens to disadvantage persons with disabilities. Indeed, it is questionable whether we could ever devise a system of priority setting that was not informed in some measure by assessments of quality of life.[28]

In this view, quality-of-life considerations are inconsistent with the ADA only if we would systematically reject them, quite apart from their sometimes resulting in disadvantages to disabled persons. Menzel is correct, I believe, when he says that the conflict between rational prioritizing by relative benefit and disadvantaging the disabled is ineliminable. Such prioritizing does seem to place less value on the lives of the disabled, and on some treatments provided to disabled patients as opposed to otherwise similar nondisabled patients.

A measure of benefits like QALYs will, in certain cases, favor a nondisabled person over an otherwise similar disabled person. But perhaps it does not follow from this that the use of that measure unjustly devalues disabled people's lives, despite the disadvantage the disabled are placed at by this method of prioritizing. Perhaps this disadvantage no more unjustly devalues the lives of, or discriminates against, the disabled than giving a scarce intensive-care-unit bed to a more critically ill patient, rather than to another patient who can be managed with less risk without intensive care, discriminates against the less ill patient. Giving preference in circumstances of scarcity to patients for whom treatment will do the most good or prevent the greatest harm does not imply that the person who is thereby favored is judged of greater value, or that the patient who is not favored has been the subject of unjust discrimination.

This defense of relative-benefit prioritizing seems least convincing in the case of life-sustaining treatment. Though it is the lesser benefit from treatment, not an explicit judgment that disabled people and their lives are of less value, that is the basis for the priority, it is precisely the lower quality of the disabled person's life (which is produced by his disability) that makes the life-sustaining treatment for him less beneficial. A significantly disabled life is a life of fewer QALYs, other things being equal, than a nondisabled person's life. Moreover, this is not an implication only of the QALY measure, since no plausible measure of treatment benefits could entirely ignore effects on quality of life. This prioritization does

[28] Paul T. Menzel, "Oregon's Denial: Disabilities and Quality of Life," *Hastings Center Report*, vol. 22, no. 6 (1992), pp. 21–25.

seem to imply that it is a less good outcome if the disabled person survives than if the nondisabled person survives, because the disabled person has a less good life.

This implicit devaluing of a disabled life, and in turn of the disabled person, may be worse than an apparently similar devaluing implicit in another practice which has received stronger and more explicit criticism from disability-rights groups. Genetic screening for a variety of fetal abnormalities is typically undertaken with the intent of aborting the fetus if a serious abnormality is found to be present. In a few cases the abnormality is so serious as to plausibly make the prospective life not worth living—for example, in the case of Tay-Sachs disease. In most cases, however, the abnormality screened for is not that serious; for example, most persons with Down's syndrome, one of the most common conditions screened for, can have satisfying though limited lives with appropriate support. Disability groups and individual advocates for the disabled have protested that these screening programs carry an implicit devaluation of disabled individuals' lives.[29] More specifically and seriously, it is charged that genetic screening seems implicitly to say to a disabled person that it is better if people like you never are born, and do not exist, and thus that it would have been better if you in particular had not been born, and if you did not exist.

To this charge, however, there is at least a partial response. The judgment implicit in the practice is that it is better if serious disabilities are prevented, if people do not have serious disabilities. If a woman takes steps before becoming pregnant to ensure that her child will not have some disability, she implicitly acts on that judgment. If she judges her fetus at the time of screening to be not yet a person with the moral standing and protections that persons have, then her abortion of an affected fetus in effect prevents there being a person with a serious disability. This is fully compatible with accepting that a person with that disability is no less valuable in the sense of having the same moral standing, with no less moral protection, as a normal person. While it would be better if people did not have this disability, it does not follow of any existing person with this disability that it would be better if he or she did not exist, or that it would be morally permissible to terminate his or her existence. Thus, this case only implies that it is better to create people without disabilities than with disabilities, and therefore is unlike allocating a scarce lifesaving treatment according to a measure such as QALYs, where it is said that it is better for an actual nondisabled person to live than an actual disabled person, because that disabled person's disability makes his life a less good or less valuable life.

[29] See, e.g., Adrienne Asch, "Can Aborting 'Imperfect' Children Be Immoral?" in *Contemporary Issues in Biomedical Ethics,* 4th ed., ed. Tom Beauchamp and Leroy Walters (Encino, CA: Wadsworth Publishing, 1987).

V. Compensation for Handicaps

Until now, I have been considering whether prioritizing health-care resources so as to maximize their benefits disadvantages, and in turn devalues, disabled persons. This issue could be recast in terms of whether disabled persons receive the equal concern and equal treatment with nondisabled persons that justice requires in the allocation of health-care resources. However, it is a considered part of many people's moral and political beliefs, and in particular a part of most egalitarian theories of justice, that individuals should receive compensation, not just equal consideration and treatment, to make up for disabilities or handicaps (I shall use these terms interchangeably here) that they suffer through no fault of their own. For example, in the important "equality of what" debate within political philosophy over the past decade, among the alternatives which have been both defended and criticized have been equality of welfare, of resources, of primary goods, of capabilities, of opportunity for welfare, and of access to advantage.[30] The proponents of each of these conceptions of the requirements of equality have argued that it is a strength of their conception that it properly compensates individuals for their handicaps, and have often criticized other conceptions for failing to properly compensate individuals for their handicaps. The debates have concerned what compensation for handicaps a particular account of equality implies, and what compensation for handicaps the best theory of justice requires, but not whether compensation for handicaps is morally required at all. The general issues of the extent and ways in which justice requires compensating individuals for handicaps and disabilities is complex and cannot be pursued here. Nevertheless, I want at least to suggest why just treatment of the disabled in prioritizing health-care resources might require not only that they suffer no disadvantage from their disability, but also that at least some positive moral priority be given to treatment that compensates for their disability, in comparison with treatment that produces equal benefits for the nondisabled. This will be a higher moral priority than treatment of the disabled would otherwise receive on either relative-benefit or cost-benefit grounds.

One common reason for the moral belief that disabilities and handicaps require compensation is to provide equality of opportunity for the disabled and handicapped. Whatever weight equality of opportunity is given

[30] See, e.g., Rawls, *A Theory of Justice* (endorsing primary goods as the relevant comparison); Amartya Sen, *Commodities and Capabilities* (Amsterdam: North Holland, 1985) (endorsing equality of capability); Ronald Dworkin, "What is Equality? Part I: Equality of Welfare," *Philosophy and Public Affairs*, vol. 10 (1981), pp. 185–246 (criticizing equality of welfare); Ronald Dworkin, "What is Equality? Part II: Equality of Resources," *Philosophy and Public Affairs*, vol. 10 (1981), pp. 283–345 (endorsing a particular interpretation of equality of resources); Richard Arneson, "Equality and Equality of Opportunity for Welfare," *Philosophical Studies*, vol. 56 (1988) (endorsing equality of opportunity for welfare); and G. A. Cohen, "On the Currency of Egalitarian Justice," *Ethics*, vol. 99 (1989), pp. 906–44 (endorsing equality of opportunity for advantage).

in a full moral or political theory, its proponents agree that it can require measures that do not constitute the most beneficial, or cost-effective, use of resources. Securing equality of opportunity justifies at least some moral priority, for example, to providing access to public buildings and transportation for disabled persons both over other uses of those resources that would provide greater benefits to the nondisabled, and even over other uses of the resources that might satisfy stronger preferences of the disabled, but that would not improve their opportunity. If we are concerned only with the cost-effective use of resources, then apart from concerns about the distribution of income, we could look to a market in services like transportation to determine whether and where there was sufficient effective demand from the handicapped for special transportation services accessible to them to make it profitable to offer those services.

The moral and political requirements of equality of opportunity (as well as the legal requirements of the ADA) do not leave the availability of transportation services, which have a fundamental impact on people's opportunities, to the workings of the market precisely because the market will not ensure the services necessary for equality of opportunity. In the area of employment, the ADA's requirement that employers make "reasonable accommodations" for disabilities in employment decisions also does not leave this aspect of equality of opportunity to the market. Norman Daniels has argued that health care's importance for justice lies in its effects in preserving or restoring equality of opportunity.[31] More specifically, different health-care services gain their relative moral importance in Daniels's view from their relative effect on opportunity. I have argued elsewhere that the effect on opportunity is only a part of health care's moral importance,[32] but even if health care's moral importance is only in substantial part its impact on equality of opportunity, then prioritizing health-care services on either relative-benefit or cost-benefit grounds is not morally justified. Doing so fails to give positive priority to health-care services that compensate the disabled and handicapped for their undeserved diminished opportunity.

A second way of bringing out the special moral claims on health-care resources of the disabled or handicapped appeals to the moral priority of improving the condition of the worst off. For the sake of making the point succinctly, assume we can measure people's quality of life (QL) on a scale from 0 to 1. Serious disabilities or handicaps will, by definition, typically reduce a person's quality of life. Suppose individuals A and B have equal life expectancies of twenty years, and A has a QL of 1, and B has a QL of .5 because of a serious disability. If A needs treatment *m* to avoid a

[31] Daniels, *Just Health Care*, chs. 1–4.

[32] Dan W. Brock, "Justice, Health Care, and the Elderly," *Philosophy and Public Affairs*, vol. 18, no. 3 (1989), pp. 297–312.

reduction in her QL to .75 and B needs treatment *n* to avoid a further decrease in her QL to .25, prioritizing treatments on the basis of their relative benefits (or on cost-benefit grounds if they are equally expensive) would rank these treatments as of equal priority, because each treatment produces a .25 quality increase for twenty expected life years. If we could only provide one treatment because of resource scarcity, then presumably a random selection of who to treat and who to leave untreated would be morally required. Yet at least if B is worse off through no fault of her own—for example, because she has a genetically transmitted disability—many people would give priority to B on grounds of justice. With a QL of .5, B is now worse off than A, who has a QL of 1, and the inequality between them would be widened to .75 if A is treated instead of B; if the worse off should have any (not absolute) priority, then B should at least have a greater chance of getting treatment than A. In one sense of need, B's need for treatment is greater than A's, because B will be worse off without treatment than A. This example is, of course, oversimplified and does not readily fit real-world priority-setting exercises like Oregon's. Nevertheless, it makes the important theoretical point that to justly distribute scarce benefits such as medical treatment, it is often not enough to know only the relative amounts of benefits from different treatments. We must also know who will receive the particular benefits in order to give appropriate moral priority to improving the condition of the worst off. Serious disabilities and handicaps are one important source of disadvantage to which health-care resource prioritization must attend.

VI. The Perspective Problem—Normal or Disabled?

I have argued that no simple policy of maximizing benefits with limited health-care resources will secure justice to disabled persons. Nevertheless, any more-complex prioritization that is appropriately responsive to the claims of the disabled will almost certainly have to give some weight to the relative benefits of health-care services that prevent the loss of, or restore, function from various disabilities. Assessments of relative quality of life with various disabilities will be necessary even if we reject simple relative-benefit or cost-benefit prioritization. What I will call "the perspective problem" is the question of whose perspective should be used in evaluating a person's quality of life with a particular disability—the perspective of the person with the disability, or that of a nondisabled person? The problem was characterized as follows by Secretary Sullivan:

> There are substantial indications in the material Oregon has provided that the quality of life data derived from the Oregon telephone survey quantifies stereotypic assumptions about persons with disabilities. Scholars who have examined quality of life surveys have concluded that as compared to persons who have the disabilities in

> question, persons without disabilities systematically undervalue the quality of life of those with disabilities.[33]

It is unclear to what extent Oregon's prioritized list was affected by this difference in evaluations of the quality of life of disabled persons, but that is not my concern here. Rather, my question is how we should resolve this issue of perspective for the purpose of priority setting. At the very least, justice to the disabled requires not basing their treatment on stereotypes held by the nondisabled. The nondisabled not only must refrain from imposing their own perspective on the condition of the disabled, but must attempt to be responsive to disabled people's own perspectives on their lives. It is not clear, however, whether or when the perspective of the disabled about their quality of life is the correct perspective for priority setting and rationing. There is a practical version of this problem, as well as a deeper theoretical version.

The practical version holds that the views of participants in the telephone surveys were based on stereotypes and other false beliefs about the lives of disabled persons. This shortcoming could be remedied, at least in principle, by correcting the false beliefs of those surveyed and then asking for evaluations based on their new true beliefs about living with disabilities. No doubt it would be difficult or impossible in practice fully to locate and correct all the false beliefs and stereotypes of participants in a survey, and attempting to do so would inevitably raise doubts about whether the survey had been illegitimately manipulated. There is no theoretical difficulty raised by this version of the problem, however, since evaluations of people's quality of life should be based on true beliefs about the nature of their lives.

The deeper theoretical version of the problem concerns determining the correct evaluative standpoint for estimating the effect of a particular disability on quality of life. Here is the problem as I see it. Assume that both the nondisabled person and the disabled person have the same correct beliefs about what differences in functional capacities exist between a nondisabled person and, say, a person who is unable to walk, and assume as well that the result noted by Secretary Sullivan still obtains—"as compared to persons who have the disabilities in question, persons without disabilities systematically undervalue the quality of life of those with disabilities." The question then is what degree of reduction in quality of life the disability creates. Why should there be any difference in the perspectives of nondisabled and disabled persons on quality of life with a disability, once any stereotypes and false beliefs have been removed? The nondisabled person is being asked to evaluate the degree to which he believes his quality of life would be reduced by the disability. The natural way to do so is by estimating the degree to which his ability success-

33 Sullivan, unpublished letter.

fully to pursue his aims, ends, and activities, or to carry out his plan of life, would be decreased by having the disability. Why would this evaluation by a nondisabled person be different from that of the person who actually has the disability?

A disabled person will likely have adjusted his plan of life to accommodate his disability in two respects. First, he will have given up the aims and activities that are now much more difficult or impossible as a result of his disability, and substituted new aims that he can now achieve, but that he would likely have considered less valuable before becoming disabled. As a result of this change in his life-plan and values, the degree to which he successfully achieves his aims will likely be higher than the nondisabled person *correctly* judges his would be if he were disabled but still retained his original life-plan and values. The second accommodation of the disabled person to his condition is in his subjective satisfaction or happiness with his life. Individuals who suffer serious disability often come to accept their limitations in function in a way that makes possible a higher level of satisfaction or happiness than the nondisabled person correctly expects that he would have, given his current aims and expectations, if he suffered that same disability. In the extreme case of complete accommodation to the disability, disabled persons may have sufficiently changed their aims and values so as to have as high a degree of success (or even higher) in pursuing their new aims as they had with their old aims before becoming disabled, and to have as high a level of satisfaction or happiness (or even higher) as they had before becoming disabled. Should we then say that the disability has produced no reduction in their quality of life? What is the correct value of the quality of life with the disability?

Two points need underlining. The nondisabled person is correct about how his quality of life would decline judged from his current aims and values. The disabled person is also correct that his quality of life is not less, judged from his current aims and values, which he has adapted to accommodate his disability. The standpoint of the nondisabled person seems correct for the evaluation of how bad it would be for him to become disabled, and thus for determining the value of health care that protects against that disability, or restores function after he has been disabled but before he has adjusted to his new condition. On the other hand, the perspective of the disabled person seems correct, for example, about the evaluation of treatment that preserves his life, or about the increase in quality of life that restoring him to normal function would bring about. The two different standpoints yield conflicting evaluations of the quality of life with a given disability, whereas either a relative-benefit or cost-benefit methodology for prioritizing treatments requires that a determinate value be assigned to the quality of life with a given limitation in function.

Suppose we could show the nondisabled person that were he to suffer the disability in question, he too would almost certainly revise his aims and values over time to accommodate his disability, and would in turn come to share the higher evaluation of his quality of life that the already-disabled person now has. Would that be enough to justify setting aside the lower evaluation of the quality of life of that disabled state that he has now from the perspective of his nondisabled state? I believe that it would not and that these are two irreducibly different evaluative standpoints, neither of which is correct for all evaluations of the quality of life with a given disability. We would be justified in setting aside the nondisabled person's evaluation of life with a disability if the evidence about how he would change his evaluation gave him reason to conclude that his present evaluation of that disabled state was mistaken. That conclusion would be unwarranted, however. Rather, what happens is that in response to his new condition, his aims and values evolve in accommodation to that condition; he loses aims that are no longer feasible and gains new feasible ones, with an attendant gain in satisfaction from his success in his new aims. In the absence of a disability, many of us undergo more-limited changes of this sort as a result of changes in opportunities which accompany such major life changes as a move from city to rural life, taking up a very different occupation, and so forth. Looking back, we view ourselves as having changed our aims and values, and in the loose, everyday sense we view ourselves as having become very different persons than we once were, but not as having been mistaken in our earlier aims and values. The correct conclusion is only that we have changed, not that we have corrected our earlier mistaken aims and values. The disabled person is in an epistemically privileged position with regard to facts about the experience of having his disability, but not with regard to how that condition should be evaluated. Thus, even if the nondisabled person became convinced that, were he to become disabled, he would in time come to give up the evaluation which he now has of the quality of life of that disabled state, and would in time come to share the higher evaluation of it that the disabled person now makes, I believe that is not reason for him now to change his current evaluation of the quality of life in that disabled state.

Another related aspect of the complexity of the perspective problem is the degree to which quality of life in various impaired states should be evaluated on objective or subjective grounds. By "objective grounds," I have in mind here the degree to which normal human function is in fact impaired by disease. An objective evaluation requires the specification of a range of normal human functions, giving a rough weighting to the different functions according to their role and importance in carrying out normal human life-plans, and from this constructing a scale or measure of overall functional capacity. Some such objective evaluation of functional capacity will be appropriate, for example, if we want to measure the degree of opportunity, or impairment of opportunity, an individual has in pursuing a normal range of life-plans in her society.

By "subjective grounds," I have in mind the degree to which a particular individual's quality of life or well-being is impaired by disease. Subjective grounds will differ from objective grounds in at least two respects. First, the degree to which disease impairs an individual's quality of life—and, in turn, the degree of benefit from treatment that prevents that disease and impairment—should be measured principally in terms of the effects of the disease and treatment on that particular individual's pursuit of her own specific life-plan. The standard is the particular individual's life-plan, not a general range of normal human life-plans. Second, a part of an individual's quality of life or well-being is the subjective satisfaction or happiness she has with how well the pursuit of her life-plan is going. An individual's subjective satisfaction or happiness is to some degree independent of her success in pursuing her aims, and thus neither of these subjective grounds of quality of life can serve as a surrogate for the other. Because of this partial independence, the relative weight to be given to these two subjective grounds in overall quality-of-life judgments is important, but also ethically controversial. Some appeal to these subjective grounds seems unavoidable if we are concerned with the relative benefits of medical treatments on the quality of life of the individuals who receive the treatments. It is unavoidable as well if we are to take account of the different impacts that particular health-care services can have on the lives of nondisabled and disabled persons. And it is the use of these subjective grounds which gives rise to what I have called the perspective problem.

We began this brief discussion of the perspective problem with the objection that appeal to preference weightings of various disabled states by nondisabled persons fails to reflect the different, and usually higher, preference weightings of those states by disabled persons. This objection turns out to reveal two deeper and more general theoretical difficulties. First, there appear to be two diverse and irreconcilable perspectives for evaluating quality of life with a specific disability, neither one of which seems to have a clear claim to be the correct perspective for prioritizing health-care treatments and their benefits for both nondisabled and disabled persons. Second, the perspective problem raises the general difficulty of the place and weight of objective versus subjective grounds in evaluating the effects of disease and its treatment. While there may be strategies that will minimize the practical effects of these difficulties, their theoretical solution is not yet clear.

VII. Conclusion

Both in health policy and in the clinical care of patients, we have been able largely to ignore the issues about justice and the disabled that I have discussed in this essay, because we have clung to the illusions that we neither do nor should limit access to beneficial care, and that prioritizing care is therefore unnecessary. Instead, both physicians and third-party payers have generally used a standard of "medical necessity" and accepted that all medically necessary care should be provided and funded. Very roughly, "medically necessary care" has been understood to be any and all care that makes a significant contribution to the effective treatment of a patient's disease, but with little if any regard to its cost. Cost-effectiveness has generally entered in only when the same or comparable benefits could be obtained with less costly means. Under this standard of medical necessity, the additional medical needs of disabled persons should receive all effective treatment, without regard to whether there are more beneficial uses of resources for nondisabled as well as disabled persons either within or outside the area of health care. The illusion in the United States that it is possible to provide to everyone all beneficial care, no matter how small the benefit and how high the cost, will continue to erode as the health-care system is transformed by both private and governmental efforts to control costs. All health-care systems always have and always will confront resource limits. Open, fair, and accountable prioritization in the use of health-care resources is desirable to the extent that it contributes to creating a health-care system that is more economically rational and more just. That prioritization will force us to confront the issues I have discussed here, and others, in order to clarify our moral responsibilities to disabled persons; and we have seen that these issues concerning the disabled turn out to raise deep and difficult, more general issues about just health-care prioritizing and rationing.[34]

Philosophy, Brown University

[34] See Norman Daniels, "Rationing Fairly: Programmatic Considerations," *Bioethics*, vol. 7, nos. 2 and 3 (1993), pp. 224–33; and Dan W. Brock, "Some Unresolved Issues in Priority-Setting of Mental Health Services," in *What Price Mental Health? The Ethics and Politics of Setting Priorities*, ed. P. Boyle (Washington, DC: Georgetown University Press, 1995).

THE DEMOCRATIC UNIVERSITY: THE ROLE OF JUSTICE IN THE PRODUCTION OF KNOWLEDGE*

By Elizabeth S. Anderson

What is the proper role of politics in higher education? Many policies and reforms in the academy, from affirmative action and a multicultural curriculum to racial and sexual harassment codes and movements to change pedagogical styles, seek justice for oppressed groups in society. They understand justice to require a comprehensive equality of membership: individuals belonging to different groups should have equal access to educational opportunities; their interests and cultures should be taken equally seriously as worthy subjects of study, their persons treated with equal respect and concern in communicative interaction. Conservative critics of these egalitarian movements represent them as dangerous political meddling into the disinterested pursuit of knowledge.[1] They cast the pursuit of equality as a threat to freedom of speech and academic standards. In response, some radical advocates of such programs agree that the quest for equality clashes with free speech, but view this as an argument for sacrificing freedom of speech.[2]

Liberals rightly feel uneasy over the framing of these disputes as a conflict between freedom and equality. This framing challenges the premises behind sphere differentiation, the traditional liberal strategy for securing freedom and equality in society. The liberal separation between public and private spheres aims to secure individual freedom and equality by insulating citizens' practices from political intervention and state favoritism.[3] When the state withdraws from higher education, individuals are supposedly left free to pursue knowledge according to autonomously devised standards of academic excellence. But the strategy does not work if some groups exercise politically consequential power over others even when the state withdraws from the sphere in question. Racist, sexist, and intolerant cultures can sustain themselves through private actions with-

* I thank David Hills, Don Herzog, Ellen Frankel Paul, Justin Schwartz, Cass Sunstein, and the other contributors to this volume for helpful comments.

[1] See, for example, Allan Bloom, *The Closing of the American Mind* (New York: Simon and Schuster, 1986); and Dinesh D'Souza, *Illiberal Education* (New York: Free Press, 1991).

[2] See, for example, Mari Matsuda, Charles Lawrence III, Richard Delgado, and Kimberle Williams Crenshaw, *Words that Wound* (Boulder, CO: Westview Press, 1993).

[3] Don Herzog, *Happy Slaves* (Chicago: University of Chicago Press, 1989), pp. 173–74; Michael Walzer, "Liberalism and the Art of Separation," *Political Theory*, vol. 12 (1984), pp. 315–30.

out state enforcement of their norms, and these actions can interfere with the freedom of others to learn and inquire.

Some liberals are sensitive to this problem. John Stuart Mill saw threats to freedom from private intolerance as even more dangerous than state coercion.[4] Once we see these issues as cultural rather than legal, however, the standard liberal legal categories which were devised to prevent state censorship, such as viewpoint neutrality, appear inadequate. It is one thing to define state toleration of speech in terms of viewpoint neutrality, quite another to define individual toleration this way. Campus groups are legally free to invite or disinvite any speakers they want. But does allegiance to a culture of toleration and academic freedom demand that they heed or ignore others' arguments that some speakers are unworthy of invitation because of their hateful views? Does heeding such arguments imply that they have properly left themselves open to persuasion on the merits of the case, or that they have caved in to the intolerant demands of "political correctness"? Some viewpoints are deeply wrapped up with contempt for or indignation toward others. All sides agree that expressing such attitudes through vilification, denunciation, and ridicule silences others' speech. They disagree only on who is silencing whom. Campus conservatives complain that they are being silenced by charges of racism and sexism against them. Students of color, women students, and gay and lesbian students complain that they are being silenced by racist, sexist, and homophobic speech. Liberal theory needs to return to the task of articulating a model of a culture of free, open, and tolerant discussion, suitable to higher education, that goes beyond the juridical categories used to define the state's role in regulating speech.

I shall propose a liberal democratic model of a culture of free expression that reconciles the tensions in liberal theory between freedom and equality, sphere differentiation (represented as political withdrawal) and political intervention to promote justice. Contrary to appearances, the liberal strategy of sphere differentiation, according to which different spheres of legitimate human endeavor must be free to pursue their internally defined aims, *supports* liberal demands for equality in higher education. This is because the equality of speakers is a background condition for free and open discussion, which in turn is a condition for successful inquiry. Contemporary conflicts over higher education policy can be understood as conflicts over the relations of cognitive authority among inquirers that are required to successfully produce and disseminate knowledge. Relations of cognitive authority determine who gets to participate in inquiry, who listens and defers to whom, who claims authority to speak on a given subject matter, and on what grounds, how the community of inquirers decides what (who) is a worthy subject of study, and what (whose) questions about it are worth taking seriously. The libertarian

[4] John Stuart Mill, *On Liberty* (London: J. W. Parker and Son, 1859).

model of the academy accepts whatever relations among inquirers result from the unregulated expression of "ideas" and unregulated competition for access to public forums. I shall argue that this model fails to secure the conditions for objective justification of knowledge claims and for free inquiry. The best model of academic relations is a democratic one that enforces relations of equality among inquirers. This model imposes certain content and viewpoint constraints on expression in the academy, but in ways required by academic freedom itself. Before we explore these rival models of inquiry, however, I want to explain the sense in which they all involve making political demands on the academy.

I. Political Epistemology and the Social Character of Inquiry

The claim that higher education is subject to "political" demands suffers from a fundamental ambiguity. Conservatives and some liberals use it to express the complaint that higher education is being held hostage to a narrow partisan agenda, imposed either by state coercion or the intimidation of radical students and faculty who tolerate no dissent.[5] Certainly such a state of political intervention would be incompatible with freedom of inquiry and undermine confidence in the objectivity of research results. But left-wing liberals (among whom I count myself) and radicals use the claim that education is "political" to express the view that to each epistemology there corresponds a sociology, an account of the sort of social organization that best realizes the goals of inquiry and education. In this usage, the "political" refers to the ways power relations structure social practices. It need not refer specifically to state power, to narrow partisanship, or to the use of raw coercion when reason gives out. It refers to a dimension of analysis, which may be contrasted with viewing a social practice through the ways geographical, ecological, or neurological factors figure in it. Thus, in claiming that education is and must be "political," leftists are not urging what conservatives understand by this claim—that the state, narrow partisan interests, or sheer force should determine what universities do. They are calling attention to the political content of epistemology, to the ways relations of cognitive authority do and should determine who gets to speak, who listens to whom, and how people respond to what others say.

Call the study of the political order best suited to academic inquiry "political epistemology." We cannot produce a theory of inquiry without a political epistemology because inquiry is a social practice governed by social norms. The social dimensions of inquiry are a product of our mutual

[5] See David Bromwich, *Politics by Other Means: Higher Education and Group Thinking* (New Haven: Yale University Press, 1992); D'Souza, *Illiberal Education*; and Roger Kimball, *Tenured Radicals* (New York: Harper and Row, 1990).

epistemic dependence on one another. No individual is a self-sufficient investigator. She relies on the language and conceptual resources developed by others in disciplines and traditions of study to undertake her own research. Most of the tools and methods she uses—from microscopes and interviews to regression analysis and iconography—were developed by others. Most of the beliefs on which she relies to draw inferences to new beliefs are ones she acquired not through personal investigation but through the testimony of others. These traditions, tools, and beliefs crucially influence what further claims an individual will come to accept. In all these ways, *what one believes crucially depends on whom one believes*. Because of our epistemic dependence on others, we cannot isolate the logic of inquiry from the politics of epistemic authority. We cannot determine the warrant of knowledge claims without consulting social norms that tell us whose testimony is credible or authoritative, whose testimony is to be distrusted or discounted, whose criticisms should be taken seriously and whose ignored. We cannot evaluate the reliability of the social practices producing such claims without seeing whether they are living up to those same norms. Do their rules of membership exclude those who have brought or could bring information, tools, skills, or critical perspectives relevant to inquiry? Do their norms of conversation and critical exchange silence, marginalize, distort, or discount the contributions of those entitled to participate in inquiry?

These questions about membership and communication lie at the core of present controversies over affirmative action, sexual and racial harassment codes, pedagogy, and civility in higher education. Rival answers to these questions depend upon rival models of the proper organization of cognitive authority in the university. These answers involve political values because they concern relations of authority. Since any university must at least implicitly presuppose some model of inquiry, no university can escape commitment to some political order or other, that is, to some organization of power. Our choice is not between a university that transcends politics and a university submerged in it, but between universities embodying different types of political regime.

The individualist models of inquiry popular in epistemology and the philosophy of science might challenge this claim.[6] These models concede that due to our limited time, energy, and resources, no individual can ever gather all the data needed to justify her beliefs; and thus they concede that we must rely on others for information. But they relegate this

[6] See, for instance, Fred Dretske, *Knowledge and the Flow of Information* (Cambridge, MA: MIT Press, 1981), which takes the paradigm of communication to be between an instrument and an observer, not between people; W. V. Quine, "Epistemology Naturalized," in *Ontological Relativity and Other Essays* (New York: Columbia University Press, 1969), which assumes that science should regard knowers as isolated organisms interacting with the world; and Bayesian theories in the philosophy of science, such as John Earman, *Bayes or Bust?* (Cambridge, MA: MIT Press, 1992), which define rational belief revision in strictly individualist terms.

fact to the context of discovery. In the context of justification, all of an individual's beliefs can in principle be tested monologically, by one mind alone. Dialogue or interaction with others forms no necessary part of the justification of knowledge claims. Bayesian theory provides the most sophisticated attempt to develop procedures of justification on this individualistic assumption. It depends upon the possibility of developing a theory of justification that works monologically, by means of procedures available to an isolated inquirer.

The key intuition that underwrites individualism is that with sufficient training, any competent observer can in principle go and check for herself whether the facts are as a witness says they are. Call this the "checking principle." Leaving aside the question of testimony about past events, for which corroborating evidence usually fades, this principle is true. But the ways it fits into our actual epistemic practices reinforce a social, not an individualist, account of epistemic justification. The principle shows us that rational inquiry never ultimately rests on the authority of any *particular* individual—but it does not show that it is in principle possible for a single rational inquirer to dispense with reliance on *everyone* else in justifying claims.

This is true for at least three reasons. First, individuals rely on others' testimony to interpret the evidence they gather in checking any given person's claims. In checking another's measurements with a ruler, one relies on the testimony of the ruler manufacturer that the ruler is calibrated to the official standard.[7] Individual perceptions cannot be separated from interpretations of them that rely on the testimony of others. Second, the checking principle lays down a social criterion of publicity for what counts as a reason for belief. It expresses a norm for the autonomy of theoretical reason. It denies any individual the authority to command others to believe her controversial claims just on account of her avowal of them. She must be able to defend her claims with reasoning and evidence accessible to others: divine revelation, mystical inspiration, occult insight, and other essentially private sources of "evidence" do not count toward the justification of claims, any more than raw appeals to authority do. Third, new or controversial claims, or claims that purport to mark significant advances in theoretical knowledge, are not accepted as justified and are not incorporated into the body of knowledge upon which inquirers may rely until they have been checked by more than one person. New results are not generally accepted by scientific communities until they are *replicated* by other researchers.[8] Even mathematical theorems do not count as justified until their proofs have passed scrutiny by more than one math-

[7] The arguments and observations in this paragraph are indebted to C. A. J. Coady's fine book, *Testimony* (Oxford: Clarendon Press, 1992).

[8] Helen Longino, "Essential Tensions—Phase Two: Feminist, Philosophical, and Social Studies of Science," in *A Mind of One's Own*, ed. L. Antony and C. Witt (Boulder, CO: Westview Press, 1993), p. 264.

ematician. Thus, the checking principle does not prove that individual reasoning and observation hold a justificatory priority over testimony by others, as individualists hold. It proves that the evidence of testimony and of personal observation stand on a par. It shows that one's own reasoning and perceptions are just as susceptible to correction by the testimony of others as others' testimonies are susceptible to correction by one's own reasoning and perception.

Our need for external confirmation even for matters of reasoning that seem most amenable to a purely internal logic of justification reflects the fact that individuals on their own are unreliable thinkers, subject to numerous cognitive biases.[9] Even the most highly trained scientists are as prone to the same cognitive biases as people are in ordinary life. For example, scientists are prone to assign greater evidential weight to evidence produced by themselves than by others, evidence produced within their specialties than evidence generated by other specialties, and evidence that supports their research programs than evidence that undermines it.[10] Our unreliability as individual cognizers provides further grounds for emphasizing the importance of epistemic dependence for practices of justification. Even if no individual can transcend her cognitive biases and limitations, collectively we may be able to do so, *provided our social practices of inquiry stand us in relations of cognitive authority that enable us to correct or balance our individual biases*. Theorists may each weigh evidence they have produced more heavily than evidence produced by others, but if they stand in relations of equality to one another (that is, if their influence on inquiry is not suppressed or discounted on account of cognitively irrelevant factors such as country of origin), no one theorist's bias toward her own evidence will unduly influence the *community's* acceptance of the theory supported by that evidence.[11]

This social perspective on justification enables us to evaluate rival proposals for the organization of cognitive authority in the university. Given that everyone has biases, and that we all depend on others' testimony to justify our own beliefs, we cannot identify a logic of justification independent of a theory of testimony and its credibility, which is essentially tied to the cognitive authority of persons. Whether a theory is justified is not only a function of its relation to a given set of data, but also a function of who provided the data and on what terms it was received. These terms—for example, the degree to which testimony is spoken or suppressed, recognized or ignored, understood or misinterpreted, credited or discounted, due to the cognitive authority ascribed or denied to its providers—must

[9] See Daniel Kahneman, Paul Slovic, and Amos Tversky, eds., *Judgments under Uncertainty: Heuristics and Biases* (Cambridge: Cambridge University Press, 1982).

[10] Miriam Solomon, "Social Empiricism," *Noûs*, vol. 28 (1994), pp. 325–43, has documented the influence of these biases in scientists' evaluations of the theory of continental drift.

[11] *Ibid.*, pp. 18–20. See also Helen Longino, "Essential Tensions," pp. 266–67.

themselves be subject to critical scrutiny, to determine whether the theories that come to be accepted by a community of inquiry are warranted. For suppose we find that the data offered in support of a theory was produced by dishonest or unskilled researchers, or by researchers with uncorrected cognitive biases, or that the theory has been protected from critical scrutiny by silencing those likely to produce disconfirming evidence or rival theories. Such facts give us reason to think that we lack credible evidence, or a sufficiently wide-ranging or unbiased sample of evidence, in favor of the theory, that we are ignorant of the theory's weaknesses, and that the theory has not been subjected to critical tests. And no theory can be warranted or justified, no theory can merit acceptance, on the basis of discredited data, biased samples, and inadequate testing. Thus, the fact that a theory appears to be justified relative to the data a community is willing to take seriously does not of itself establish the warrant of the theory. The justification will be spurious if the community's relations of inquiry systematically exclude or discount the testimony of rational inquirers who have access to a different set of evidence, or who would provide alternative critical perspectives that correct the biases of the community's membership.

I propose that we view the rival camps in the debates over "political correctness" as articulating rival theories of the social relations of inquirers needed to secure full-blooded justification of knowledge claims. These theories are all *political*, because they concern the distribution of cognitive authority among inquirers. They are political also in the sense that they model their conceptions of cognitive authority after different types of political regime. The party of *aristocracy* is represented by proponents of a Great Books curriculum and "traditional" standards of merit, such as William Bennett, and the National Association of Scholars, and advocates of Straussian interpretation, such as Allan Bloom.[12] This party offers us a hierarchical model of cognitive authority in the university: transcendent truth or supreme cognitive authority is accorded to various authors of Great Books, to whom living teachers and researchers are supposed to defer, to whom students, in turn, are supposed to defer.[13] The party of *nationalist communitarianism* is represented by certain postmodernist multiculturalists, such as Richard Rorty, Afrocentrists such as Molefi Asante, and separatist students who express skepticism about the prospects for successful cross-cultural communication.[14] This party offers us a frag-

[12] William Bennett, *To Reclaim a Legacy* (Washington, DC: National Endowment for the Humanities, 1984); Symposium on the Great Books, *Academic Questions* (a publication of the National Association of Scholars), vol. 2 (1989); and Bloom, *The Closing of the American Mind*.

[13] Leo Raditsa, "On Sustenance: Teaching and Learning the Great Works," *Academic Questions*, vol. 2 (1989), pp. 30–39 (arguing that "it is essential that the teacher subordinate himself . . . to the texts [of the great books]," p. 34).

[14] See, for example, Richard Rorty, "Feminism and Pragmatism," *Tanner Lectures in Human Values*, vol. 13 (Salt Lake City: University of Utah Press, 1992), pp. 1–38; and Molefi K. Asante, *The Afrocentric Idea* (Philadelphia: Temple University Press, 1987).

mented, Balkanized model of cognitive authority, according to which different social and cultural groups may claim separate, autonomous departments and other organizations, which operate according to communally specific standards of inquiry, without expecting any time soon to share the fruits of their inquiry with others. The party of *libertarianism* is represented by First Amendment absolutists such as Nat Hentoff and Jonathan Rauch, who hold that truth is the product of a "free market of ideas."[15] On this view, relations of cognitive authority should not be fixed by any preconceived pattern, but should be whatever emerges from the free, unregulated speech interactions of inquirers. Finally, the party of *liberal democracy* is represented by egalitarian theorists of rational autonomy such as Cass Sunstein and Onora O'Neill, and some feminist epistemologists such as Helen Longino.[16] This party holds that equality in the relations among inquirers, enforced by norms of mutual recognition and respect in communication, is a prerequisite to autonomous and objective inquiry. In this essay, I shall compare only the last two political epistemologies, because I regard them as the most serious contenders. I shall argue that liberal democratic epistemology is superior to libertarian epistemology, for much the same reasons that liberal democracy is superior to a libertarian political regime.

II. The Free Market of Ideas: Libertarian Political Epistemology

Civil libertarians offer two arguments connecting speech with rational inquiry to support freedom of expression. The first claims that freedom of expression is instrumental to the production of truth or justified belief. The second claims that freedom of expression is demanded by the autonomy of theoretical reason. Both arguments understand inquiry as a social practice, requiring the interaction of many individuals on noncoercive terms. Familiar civil libertarian rhetoric expresses this understanding in a particular institutional model of open inquiry, known as "the free market of ideas."[17]

[15] See, for example, Nat Hentoff, *Free Speech for Me, but Not for Thee* (New York: HarperCollins, 1992); and Jonathan Rauch, *Kindly Inquisitors* (Chicago: University of Chicago Press, 1993).

[16] See, for example, Cass Sunstein, *Democracy and the Problem of Free Speech* (New York: Free Press, 1993); Onora O'Neill, *Constructions of Reason* (Cambridge: Cambridge University Press, 1989), chs. 1–2; and Longino, "Essential Tensions."

[17] Use of this model by civil libertarians does not imply that they also support free markets in commodities, as political libertarians do. Most civil libertarians are liberals, not political libertarians. My target is all libertarians, whether civil or political, who are attracted by a market model of free speech. In drawing attention to some of the disturbing implications of this model for speech, I aim to persuade liberal civil libertarians that the same reservations they typically have about free markets in commodities apply to free markets in speech. I also aim to persuade political libertarians that free markets in speech are not sufficient to ensure freedom of speech for all, and can even reinforce cultures inimical to free speech.

John Stuart Mill made famous the instrumental case for freedom of expression.[18] He argued that the truth would most likely be discovered, disseminated, and entrenched in a society that permitted all points of view to be expressed and criticized. In such a regime, false or inadequate conjectures will be refuted, and only the unfalsified theories will survive. By contrast, we cannot be confident in the conclusions reached by a community if it punishes people for criticizing those conclusions, or for defending different beliefs. Even if these conclusions are true, those who believe them will lack good grounds for believing them if they are not aware of and capable of responding to criticism. Truth is the product of a regime in which everyone is maximally free to voice her own opinions and criticize the opinions of others. This view fits neatly with research into individual cognitive biases undertaken by cognitive psychologists.[19] Individuals are biased in numerous ways, both "hot" (influenced by interests and values) and "cold" (influenced by value-neutral cognitive limitations). They are prone to regard their own experiences as representative of everyone's experiences, to weigh evidence in favor of their pet theories more heavily than evidence against it, to believe theories that advance their interests over theories that undermine them. Bias and error can be best corrected in public forums in which all views can be freely expressed and offered up for everyone's acceptance, forums where all views are subject to public scrutiny and criticism.

Theorists in the Kantian tradition see freedom of expression as the institutional embodiment of rational autonomy. Reason is the power to frame and change one's beliefs or intentions in response to considerations offered for and against them. The autonomy of reason consists in the fact that reason accepts no other authority than itself. This implies that no one may be rationally compelled to accept any belief just because some authority orders her to do so or punishes her for disobeying. Reason acts autonomously when it governs itself solely in accordance with principles that all rational beings can endorse. Considerations of autonomy provide a particularly powerful argument against state censorship of speech on grounds of its dangerous or corrupting influence. Such censorship rests on the principle that one may refuse to be influenced by considerations that one would find persuasive were one exposed to them. Reason cannot endorse such a principle, since acting on it amounts to abandoning rational autonomy itself. Citizens must always reserve to themselves the power to judge what beliefs to accept and what not; they destroy their rational autonomy in delegating this authority to third parties.[20]

Some civil libertarians take unregulated markets as their model for a

[18] Mill, *On Liberty*, ch. 2.

[19] See Kahneman, Slovic, and Tversky, *Judgments under Uncertainty*.

[20] Thomas Scanlon, "A Theory of Freedom of Expression," *Philosophy and Public Affairs*, vol. 1 (1972), pp. 204–26.

regime of free expression.[21] In the free market of ideas, beliefs are the commodities put up for "sale" (acceptance) by speakers. Just as the state should not try to force individuals to buy any particular brand of commodity, regulate the prices of commodities, or ban whole classes of commodities, it should not try to engineer the outcomes of public discussion by enforcing an official truth, limiting the supply of certain viewpoints, striving for balance in the viewpoints expressed, or prohibiting whole subjects from being discussed. The analogy thus supports a strong presumption against speech regulations, especially those that lack viewpoint and content neutrality. Individuals must be free to speak about any topic and express any viewpoint on it. The market analogy also supports a strong distinction between negative and positive liberties. Market freedom is the freedom to sell what one owns and purchase what one wants with the wealth in one's possession, without interference by others. It does not include the right to obtain what one needs if one lacks the resources to pay for it. Similarly, freedom of speech is the freedom of speakers to convey ideas in public forums or in private forums that they own. It does not include the right to command an audience to listen, or to express one's ideas in someone else's newspaper.

These analogies between freedom of expression and free markets are well known. They emphasize the relations between individuals and the state, which are mediated by legal norms backed up by formal sanctions. Another dimension to the market analogy is less often considered. This concerns the relations between speakers that are mediated by cultural norms enforced by informal sanctions. Many free markets are not genteel places. They are ruthlessly competitive and show no mercy for fainthearted, diffident, and even polite people. Car salesmen routinely exploit norms of civility to gain bargaining power over customers: those who think it rude to disparage the qualities of a car so as to bargain down the price will end up paying more for it than those who skillfully play the haggling game. Libertarians view the free market of ideas as similarly free-wheeling, competitive, raucous, and uncivil, strongly marked by emotion, invective, put-downs, and jockeying for prestige. Discussion of controversial ideas often gets heated and personal. Thus, they are suspicious of calls to enforce norms of civility in conversation, whether by formal or informal sanctions. Informal sanctions, such as shouting down racist speakers or pressuring groups to rescind invitations to such speakers, interfere with listener's rights to hear what is being said and chill speech that should be protected. The fact that some speech is offensive to others is no reason to punish the speaker, formally or informally. Libertarians advise those who feel psychically wounded by racist or sexist

[21] Oliver Wendell Holmes, joined by Louis Brandeis, promoted the analogy most vividly: "The best test of truth is the power of the thought to get itself accepted in the competition of the market." And: "The ultimate good desired is better reached through free trade in ideas." *Abrams v. United States*, 250 U.S. 630, 616 (1919) (Holmes and Brandeis, dissenting).

insults to toughen up, develop thick skins, and fight fire with fire. The only legitimate way to counter false or obnoxious speech is more speech. One should not use informal sanctions to prevent certain things from being said or heard in the first place. This is the source of many libertarians' sneering disparagement of calls for civility and "sensitivity" in campus discourse.[22]

Civil libertarians developed their conception of freedom of expression to apply to citizens at large, interacting in public forums or outside of institutional contexts. Few see a significant distinction between universities and public forums. On this view, faculty and student rights to academic freedom are derived from and coextensive with citizens' First Amendment rights to freedom of speech in the world at large. The thought that libertarian analysis can be applied without modification to the university context is reinforced by the fact that two of the most compelling arguments for a libertarian regime of freedom of speech rest upon its role in rational inquiry, which is the distinctive mission of the university.

I shall argue that the defects of libertarianism as a social epistemology correspond to the defects of libertarianism as a political philosophy. Where libertarian political theorists are insensitive to systematic failures of commodity markets, libertarian epistemologists are insensitive to systematic failures in free markets of ideas. Some civil libertarians, sensitive to this charge, remedy this defect by repudiating the market model of political epistemology; but they continue to analyze free speech issues in the university as on a par with free speech issues in public arenas. This reflects a subtler problem with libertarian political theory: its inadequate provisions for social sphere differentiation. I shall argue that freedom of inquiry in the university requires a more robust system of sphere differentiation than is available within a libertarian framework.

III. Market Failure in Libertarian Epistemology

Libertarian epistemology represents the free market of ideas as instrumental to knowledge and constitutive of rational autonomy. Let us then define failures in markets of ideas as occurring when spontaneous speech interactions in such markets systematically propagate false or unwarranted beliefs, or undermine the conditions of rational autonomy. I shall argue that both types of failure occur in free-speech regimes characterized by (1) no positive rights to access to forums and resources for inquiry, (2) a lack of norms of civility that enforce the equality of speakers, and (3)

[22] See, for example, Hentoff, *Free Speech for Me, but Not for Thee*, p. 152 (chiding "the Jacobins" for their lack of humor); Rauch, *Kindly Inquisitors*, p. 130 (arguing that calls for civility lead people to "go into the business of professional offendedness"); and John Taylor, "Are You Politically Correct?" in *Are You Politically Correct?*, ed. Francis Beckwith and Michael Bauman (Buffalo, NY: Prometheus Books, 1993), p. 23 (complaining that "joking isn't allowed!").

prohibition of content- and viewpoint-constraints on speech. These are the three features that distinguish the market model from other models of free expression.

Just as free markets in commodities systematically produce massive inequalities in income, free markets in ideas systematically produce massive inequalities in access to forums and resources for inquiry. The two inequalities are linked, since it takes income to get access to higher education, both because of high tuition and because admission to college is partly a function of the quality of one's high school, which in turn is partly a function of the prosperity of the community that supports it. Thus, the proportion of poor and working-class people in the academy is far lower than in the population. Moreover, since income inequalities in the United States partly track racial identity, the proportions of African Americans, Latinos, and Native Americans in the academy are also far lower than their proportions in the population.

Barriers preventing the entry of oppressed groups into the academy cast doubt upon the objectivity of knowledge claims produced by members of the dominant groups who prevail in the academy. One does not have to accept a radical perspectivist epistemology to believe that one's racial and class identity influence one's circumstances and hence one's experiences. This is a truism in any society in which power relations track race and class. Barriers preventing the entry of oppressed groups into the academy therefore insulate knowledge claims from criticism by people with different ranges of experience than those possessed by dominant groups. Dominant groups may conduct inquiry informed by questionable unarticulated background assumptions, which, because they are taken for granted by inquirers with common experiences, escape critical scrutiny.[23] Members of subordinate groups are often in a better position to detect the ways theories developed by dominant groups ignore or misrepresent them, and usually have a greater interest in correcting these biases as well.[24]

This claim is not merely hypothetical. The history of the entry of members of oppressed groups into inquiry offers numerous illustrations of enhanced objectivity in research. For example, it took African American

[23] Longino, "Essential Tensions," pp. 265–66.

[24] This is not to defend "standpoint theory." Standpoint theorists claim that the position of subordinate groups offers an epistemically privileged perspective on social phenomena. See Nancy Hartsock, "The Feminist Standpoint," in *Feminism and Methodology*, ed. S. Harding (Bloomington: Indiana University Press, 1987). Our thoroughgoing epistemic interdependence implies that no particular subject position can claim epistemic privilege over all the rest. The argument for diversity need claim no more than symmetrical cognitive biases on everyone's part. If no one has a perfectly representative sample of experiences, and everyone generalizes from his or her own experiences, then everyone will be biased. If the research community consists of a demographically unrepresentative sample of people, biases will remain that can be corrected by expanding its representativeness, even if the new members are just as biased in their own way as the old ones are.

scholars such as Aldon Morris to criticize the dominant theories of the civil rights movement, which represented black masses as either mob-like or else passively led about by outside elites. Such representations reflected the difficulty many white scholars had in grasping lower-class blacks as rational agents, capable of high degrees of planning and organization. Morris advanced the objectivity of knowledge of the civil rights movement by theorizing it from the point of view of grass-roots activists.[25] For similar reasons, the pervasive sexism and androcentrism of scholarship in such varied fields as biology, psychology, and law were not exposed and criticized until women scholars entered these fields and saw that they ignored or misrepresented the characteristics, contributions, and interests of women.[26]

A knowledge claim gains objectivity and warrant to the degree that it is the product of exposure to the fullest range of criticisms and perspectives. Resource-based barriers to entry into communities of inquiry pose a threat to the objectivity of their research by blocking the potentially transformative criticisms that could be developed and articulated by those kept out. The internal knowledge-promoting aims of the university thus call for measures to promote equality of access by all groups in society to membership in its ranks. This is an argument for affirmative action in university admissions and faculty hiring that recognizes the positive contributions that members of oppressed groups can and do make to enhancing the objectivity of research. Equality of access through affirmative action policies is not, therefore, an external political goal that threatens to compromise the quality of research. It is a means to promote the objectivity of that research.

Free-speech theorists such as Joshua Cohen and Cass Sunstein emphasize the importance of equality of access in any institutional embodiment of freedom of expression that aims to promote informational and deliberative interests.[27] For this reason, both reject the market model of free speech. But mere membership in the university is not sufficient to ensure that all can participate effectively in research and learning. Nor, if toleration means nothing more than the cessation of hostility, is mere toleration of their presence in the university enough.[28] Their criticisms and perspectives must be taken seriously by all inquirers. This means that the academy must structure its communicative relations by norms that ensure that inquirers have their say, that encourage them to pay attention to

[25] Aldon Morris, *The Origins of the Civil Rights Movement* (New York: Free Press, 1984).

[26] See, for example, Ruth Bleier, *Science and Gender* (New York: Pergamon, 1984); Carol Tavris, *The Mismeasure of Woman* (New York: Simon and Schuster, 1992); and Catharine MacKinnon, *Toward a Feminist Theory of the State* (Cambridge, MA: Harvard University Press, 1989).

[27] Joshua Cohen, "Freedom of Expression," *Philosophy and Public Affairs*, vol. 22 (1993), pp. 215–17; Sunstein, *Democracy and the Problem of Free Speech*, chs. 2, 3.

[28] O'Neill, *Constructions of Reason*, pp. 30–31; Longino, "Essential Tensions," p. 267.

what other members say, that discourage them from systematically discounting or distorting what others say, and that urge them to actively respond to criticisms and alternative perspectives by appropriately modifying the content and methods of their studies. These are norms of civility and mutual respect, by which inquirers recognize each others' cognitive authority. Objectivity of research requires an effective recognition of the equal status of inquirers—in the sense that all are equally entitled to speak, to be heard, and to be respectfully responded to.

Currently entrenched informal norms of communicative interaction in the university and in society at large fail to meet these norms of civility and equality. Instead, they systematically suppress or discount the voices of women of all racial groups and of men and women of color. Teachers at all levels of education ask more, and more challenging, questions of men than of women. Men talk more often and at greater length than women in the hierarchically and competitively structured classrooms that are the norm in higher education. They influence the topic of conversation more than women do. They interrupt women more often than women interrupt them, and do so more often by making inappropriate personal comments that shut women up. Teachers pay more attention to white men than to women, more attention to white students than to students of color, and least attention of all to female students of color. They also offer more encouragement to white men than to women, and expect them to achieve more, especially in subjects such as mathematics that are coded "masculine." Similar patterns of interaction occur among faculty members, and disadvantage male and female students and faculty of color as well as white women.[29]

Even when members of oppressed groups manage to get a word in edgewise, others discount the quality of their contributions because of their group identity. Psychologists M. A. Paludi and W. D. Bauer found that a group told that a paper's author was "John T. McKay" assigned it a much higher average ranking than a group told that the same paper's author was "Joan T. McKay." A group told that its author was "J. T. McKay" rated the paper between the other groups' evaluations, reflecting its suspicion that the author was a woman trying to conceal her gender identity.[30] L. S. Fidell sent vitae identical in all but name to heads of psychology departments that advertised open-rank positions. The psychologists said they would offer higher-ranking jobs to the purportedly

[29] Roberta Hall, "The Classroom Climate: A Chilly One for Women?" (Washington, DC: Association of American Colleges, 1982); Myra Sadker and David Sadker, *Failing at Fairness* (New York: Charles Scribner's Sons, 1994); Wellesley College Center for Research on Women, *How Schools Shortchange Girls* (Washington, DC: American Association of University Women, 1992); J. R. Becker, "Differential Treatment of Females and Males in Mathematics Classes," *Journal for Research in Mathematics Education*, vol. 12 (1981), pp. 40–53.

[30] M. A. Paludi and W. D. Bauer, "Goldberg Revisited: What's in an Author's Name," *Sex Roles*, vol. 9 (1983), pp. 287–390.

male applicant than to the purportedly female applicant.[31] When the Modern Language Association reviewed papers submitted for their meetings with authors' names attached, men's submissions were accepted at significantly higher rates than women's. After they instituted blind reviewing of papers, women's acceptance rates rose to equality with men's.[32]

Norms of deference and arrogance structured along race, class, and gender lines influence the seriousness with which participants in inquiry take the observations and arguments of others. Studies of mock juries find that people systematically confuse the social rank of the speaker with the merits of her arguments, and that they tend to defer to the opinions of higher-status individuals. Higher-status individuals—those who are white, male, and/or professionals or managers—are more likely to presume that their opinion is correct and to try to impose their views through browbeating, without seriously engaging in dialogue with lower-status individuals or entertaining the possibility that they could be mistaken.[33] These differences in the cognitive authority ascribed to speakers thus feed into a structure of communicative interaction that limits the responsiveness of communities of inquiry to the contributions of oppressed speakers, and thereby reduces the objectivity of the knowledge claims such communities produce.

I analyze these failures of objectivity as failures of civility. By civility I mean not merely politeness or decorum, but a system of norms that upholds civic equality, by requiring each person to treat everyone else with respect. To interrupt, ignore, and discount what others say on account of their subordinate social status is to refuse to recognize them as equal participants in inquiry. It is to treat them with contempt. What people believe crucially depends on whose words they take seriously. Failures of civility therefore influence the claims that research communities accept. Since many of our background norms of contempt and respect allocate cognitive authority independently of the cognitive worth of speakers' contributions, they undermine the objectivity of inquiry. A thorough restructuring of informal norms of communication that promotes equal respect of inquirers in the university is therefore in order. The informal norms of speech proper to the university are not those of the used-car lot.

So far I have considered norms of communication that need not be embodied in speech acts with any distinctive content or viewpoint. To ignore what others say, or to defer to what they say, need not involve saying anything oneself. One can even interrupt others without speaking oneself, by turning off a microphone. But individuals can also be effectively silenced, their claims to cognitive authority stripped away, by

[31] L. S. Fidell, "Empirical Verification of Sex Discrimination in Hiring Practices in Psychology," *American Psychologist*, vol. 25 (1970), pp. 1094–98.

[32] M. R. Lefkowitz, "Education for Women in a Man's World," *Chronicle of Higher Education*, August 6, 1979, p. 56.

[33] Lynn Sanders, "Against Deliberation," *Political Theory* (forthcoming).

speech that ridicules, demeans, or harasses others on account of their subordinate social status. At my institution, the University of Michigan, an African-American medical student reported to me that he and his peers are still routinely called "boy" by some members of the medical staff. Flyers advocating the lynching of African Americans have been posted on campus and slipped under students' doors. Asian and Asian-American students have been verbally and physically assaulted while walking on campus or attempting to join parties to which all students had been invited. Some students have circulated the *Protocols of the Elders of Zion*. During a statistics class, a professor compared the shape of a graph he had drawn on the board with the shape of one of his students' breasts. Another professor told a student that she could be identified by her "Latino smell." A student showed a pornographic film to his visual-arts class in which he had grafted a photograph of another film student's head onto the body of a naked woman. Incidents like these shape the daily experiences of students of color, Jewish students, and women of all racial and ethnic identities.

Considered in isolation, any one of these speech acts might be considered merely offensive. But they do not occur in isolation. They are part of a systematic pattern of abuse by which members of oppressed groups are constituted as the proper objects of others' contempt, derision, and mistrust.[34] The public meaning and effect of such patterns of discriminatory verbal harassment in a campus context is to attack the recipient's legitimacy and power to engage in inquiry on terms of equality with others in the university. It is to attack her ability to command the respect of others, an ability that is a prerequisite for her contribution to be taken seriously. A natural response to such systematically contemptuous treatment is silence. If what one says is ignored or ridiculed on account of one's social status, why bother talking? This response is reinforced by the fact that people view themselves in terms of the dominant categories used to characterize them; they internalize the contempt others express for them. Discriminatory harassment tends to cause a collapse of the self-confidence and self-respect people need to get on with their projects.[35]

Civil libertarians respond to these problems by recommending that the victims of discriminatory harassment toughen up. This is psychologically unrealistic. Individuals are not self-sufficient in their capacity to summon up a sense of self-respect and self-confidence. This capacity requires social bases of support, including most importantly the recognition and respect of others.[36] Discriminatory harassment constitutes a direct assault on the

[34] Numerous surveys of other campuses reveal similar patterns across the country. See The National Council for Research on Women, *To Reclaim a Legacy of Diversity* (New York: NCRW, 1993), and the reports in each issue of *The Journal of Blacks in Higher Education*.

[35] Matsuda et al., *Words that Wound*.

[36] Charles Taylor, *Multiculturalism and the Politics of Recognition* (Princeton: Princeton University Press, 1993).

social bases of self-respect of its victims. Civil libertarians also recommend that victims should respond with more speech, rather than try to silence speech that mocks and demeans them. But discriminatory harassment is a form of speech that itself silences speech, either by literally shutting other people up, or by reinforcing norms of interpretation whereby what the victims of harassment say is ignored, discounted, or dismissed as "hypersensitivity," evidence of a lack of humor, of a contemptible "victim's mentality," of a "culture of complaint"—or, indeed, of "political correctness." These are all ways of labeling what people say so as to discredit their claims to be taken seriously as speakers.

Self-respect and the recognition of others are conditions for taking one's own speech seriously and for having others take one's speech seriously. To take one's own and others' speech seriously is to interpret their words as offering *reasons* for belief and action, rather than as mere *symptoms* of defects in the speaker. It is to recognize them as bearers of cognitive authority. Given our profound epistemic interdependency, social conditions in which we recognize one another as capable of offering one another reasons for belief constitute a prerequisite for autonomous inquiry for everyone. Given our individual cognitive biases and limitations, which are influenced by several dimensions of social inequality, social conditions in which we recognize all communicatively competent members of society as bearers of cognitive authority constitute a prerequisite for exposing our knowledge claims to the widest range of criticisms and perspectives, and hence for crediting our knowledge claims with objectivity. In a society in which profound inequalities of social status are constructed along lines of race, class, gender, and ethnicity, those in dominant positions will use spoken and nonspoken means to exclude individuals from access to education and public forums and to establish informal norms of communication that constitute individuals as lacking cognitive authority on account of their social status. A libertarian free market of ideas leaves people free to establish their communicative domination over others in this manner. Hence, the libertarian free market of ideas undermines the social conditions for autonomous and objective inquiry in societies such as ours. It is a regime of systematic market failure.

One defect in the market model that accounts for this failure lies in its inadequate conception of the sphere differentiation required to secure freedom. Political libertarians in the United States, who accept the market model for virtually all social interactions outside a minimal state, hold that the most extensive freedom for all can be secured in a society that recognizes only two social spheres: the state and the private sphere. The state has a monopoly on violence, which it needs to prevent individuals from reducing freedom by invading others' rights. If we minimize the role of the state to preventing force and fraud, and maximize the scope of the private sphere, where everyone is presumed to enjoy perfect freedom, we get a maximally free society. This picture forgets that private interactions can generate systems of domination that do not require the use of state power to sustain themselves. Cultures of class-based, racist, and sexist domination can and do persist without laws that require discrimination, and without market competition putting discriminators out of business. When these cultures are allowed free rein in all private social spaces, there are no social spaces left where all persons can interact as equals.[37] A minimal condition for freedom of citizens is a third sphere of interaction: what we know as civil society. Civil society consists of those social spaces which are universally accessible to citizens, and in which citizens ideally interact as equals, on terms acceptable to all. Public parks and other spaces designated as public forums are among the institutions of civil society, which is why they have traditionally been considered so crucial for the protection of freedom of speech. Market models of inquiry fail because they do not secure the social spaces for interaction among equals that objective and autonomous inquiry requires.

IV. The Democratic University: Liberal Democratic Epistemology

A characteristic response to market failure is to introduce democratic constraints on the background conditions under which people interact. Let us explore, then, the prospects for a democratic epistemology. Democracies are characterized by universal citizenship, equality among citizens, and publicity of operation. All competent adults are entitled to have a say in a democratic institution's activities. A democratic model of higher education would thus require universal access on the part of communicatively competent adults, who engage in inquiry on terms of equality. Universities would recruit students and faculty to ensure broad representation of people from all walks of life, so that the products of inquiry are open to critical scrutiny and influence from the widest range of viewpoints, and so that the subjects and direction of inquiry are responsive to the widest range of interests. Background norms of communication that express the equality of inquirers (their common status as persons entitled to speak, to be heard, and to be respectfully responded to) would be enforced. Inegalitarian social relationships of domination, contempt, and marginalization undermine the academic freedom of mem-

[37] Some of the most interesting cases of a free-market-driven abolition of civil society appeared in the nineteenth-century company towns of the United States. They embodied a culture of class-based inequality incompatible with the egalitarian demands of civil society. George Pullman, the owner of the company town Pullman, Illinois, owned all spaces of public and private association—including church buildings, schools, parks, businesses, municipal buildings, and houses—and asserted the property right to determine what went on in them. Company towns are a social order likely to return in the kind of free-market regime endorsed by political libertarians. On Pullman, see Michael Walzer, *Spheres of Justice* (New York: Basic Books, 1983), pp. 295–99.

bers of subordinate groups and thereby suppress the full critical scrutiny of knowledge claims in the academy. The point of a democratic model for the university is to highlight the need to abolish these inegalitarian relationships so as to promote free and objective inquiry.

But isn't the very idea of a democratic epistemology absurd? After all, truth is not determined by majority vote. Yet democracy does not have much to do with the majority voting rule either. Democracies use a variety of voting rules, none of which mark anything particularly democratic about their operation. (All multimember decision-making bodies, however autocratic, need voting rules that guarantee a unique decision.) Democracy is better conceived as government by discussion among equals. Democratic epistemology, therefore, should be seen as inquiry by discussion among equals. Our epistemic interdependence ensures that successful inquiry requires an exchange of views among researchers. Truth may not be defined as the product of consensus, but our only reliable access to theoretically significant, objectively justified knowledge is determined by the consensus of inquirers who have exchanged their views and responded to each other's criticisms and proposals.

The part of the democratic model of inquiry that is harder to accept is the claim that inquirers should be recognized as equals. Don't learning and progress in research require deference to the opinions of experts? Actual communities of inquiry contain hierarchies of cognitive authority. Democrats tend to be hostile to hierarchies of authority, and I am no exception. The hierarchical structure of cognitive authority in universities today is thoroughly corrupt. I have already documented one dimension of corruption: people ascribe cognitive authority to individuals partly on the basis of their ascribed social status, independently of the content of their contributions. They pay more attention to the opinions of white middle-class men, defer to their opinions more, allow them to control agendas of discussion, habitually yield them the floor, and evaluate what they say more highly, simply on account of their dominant social status. They ignore what working-class people, persons of color, and women of all racial and ethnic identities say, if they get the floor at all; assign their opinions the greater burden of proof when they disagree with what white men say, if anyone listens to them; and have a lower opinion of what they say, simply on account of their subordinate social status. Other corrupt hierarchies of cognitive authority are built around researchers' disciplinary affiliations, subfield specialties, methodological commitments, and the like.[38] One might reply that perhaps race, gender, and class should not be the basis of a hierarchy of cognitive authority, but mustn't students, in order to learn, defer to the opinions of their instructors, who have more expertise? I would have thought that the shut-up-and-listen

[38] Kathryn Addelson, "The Man of Professional Wisdom," in *Discovering Reality*, ed. S. Harding and M. Hintikka (Dordrecht: D. Reidel, 1983), pp. 165–86.

school of pedagogy was dead, but sycophantic schools are not, so the question deserves further exploration.

Expertise does, of course, matter in inquiry. Since what we believe depends on whom we believe, the certification of inquirers as experts (through awards of degrees and honors, citations of research, hiring and promotion to faculty ranks) is of very great importance. But nothing in these facts is incompatible with a democratic model for epistemology. Consider the parallel claim in politics: what we do depends on whom we must obey, and thus the assignment of political office to individuals is of very great importance. Democrats do not deny that social order requires some hierarchies of *office*; they deny the need for hierarchies of persons. Upon vacating their offices, persons must lose the powers of office; while in office, their special powers must be limited to what they do in their official capacities. A general can order his soldiers into battle but cannot order his wife (or his soldiers) into bed. In epistemology, too, we should recognize a person/office distinction: considerations of classroom order may obligate students to refrain from usurping their professor's plans, but this does not mean they cannot think that their professor is an idiot. Democracy is also compatible with honoring *merit* in persons, with recognizing that some people are more skilled, accomplished, intelligent, persuasive, interesting, and trustworthy than others, and with supporting them for these reasons. In a democracy, however, *merit must be demonstrated to the satisfaction of those who offer their support*: they must be persuaded by arguments and evidence, not bullied into submission by those who claim epistemic superiority as a birthright.

The kind of equality required by democracy is equality of citizenship or status, not of merit, of the influence that comes with merit, or of office. In political democracies, equality of citizenship means that all citizens are equals in respect of their rights, and entitled to demand a justification of public policies which are open to their scrutiny. In epistemic democracies, equality means that all communicatively competent persons are acknowledged as having the status of inquirers: they must be regarded as reason-givers and reason-takers, and their speech interpreted accordingly. All inquirers have a status that entitles them to call upon others to explain and justify their beliefs, and to offer reasons for them to change their beliefs, which means that others are obliged to listen and respond in kind. No one is assigned a second-class form of cognitive authority, or deprived of cognitive authority altogether, on account of his or her race, gender, class, ethnicity, or other ascribed social status.

Democracy is a response to the inequalities among inquirers that arise from a libertarian model of freedom of speech. When individuals are free to use speech and informal norms of communication to deprive others of the status of inquirers, or to turn them into second-class speakers, on account of their class, race, or gender, they undermine the objectivity of research and the autonomy of inquiry. Objectivity and autonomy, the same values that underwrite freedom of expression, also underwrite the equality of inquirers. To exercise one's rational autonomy, one must be free to engage in the communicative interactions with others that constitute inquiry. This requires, however, that one be treated by others as a reason-giver and a reason-taker, that one enjoy the same status as a bearer of cognitive authority that everyone else has. Equality of status, therefore, is a prerequisite to freedom of inquiry. To attack a person's status as an inquirer on account of her ascribed social status is therefore to attack her freedom of inquiry.

To adopt a democratic epistemology is not yet to possess all the elements needed for a *liberal* theory of freedom of expression. Liberalism is a response to the inadequate sphere differentiation of libertarianism. Liberalism enhances freedom by distinguishing civil society from the private sphere, and protecting it from invasions by private power. This creates space for people to exercise the kinds of freedom that require universal access on terms of equality. Let us generalize this freedom-creating strategy with respect to speech. Freedom of expression serves a wide range of interests: inquiry and democratic deliberation are rightly seen as central, but selling products, venting emotions, entertaining audiences, arousing or soliciting sexual interest, and seeking religious converts are others. All of these activities take place in civil society, but they cannot all be pursued, or be pursued equally well, in the same social settings in which the other expressive interests are being pursued. Liberalism enhances our freedom to pursue these varied expressive interests by creating further social differentiations within civil society. *It creates social settings in which, to enable some expressive interests to be freely pursued by all, the pursuit of other expressive interests is precluded*. This does not inhibit freedom of expression: if you want to pursue the other expressive interests, you are free to do so in another social setting, in which your doing so does not interfere with others pursuing the expressive interests proper to the setting at hand. Consider policies against sexual harassment in the university. These policies prevent faculty members from using the classroom or office to engage in certain sorts of sexually titillating conversations with students, especially when they single out certain students for unwanted sexual attention. One of their functions is to *enhance* students' freedom of inquiry, by ensuring that no one makes it a condition of their pursuing their studies that they become someone's sexual plaything, and that their status as inquirers is not undermined by speech that invites others to regard them as mere objects of sexual fantasy. Freedom of inquiry needs social settings where freedom of sexual expression is constrained.

I propose, then, that we view the university as the social setting liberalism sets aside for the free pursuit of disciplinary inquiry. Other expressive interests may be pursued in this setting only on condition that they not interfere with this primary freedom. This provides a basis for distinguishing between the freedom of speech we enjoy as citizens, and the freedom of inquiry we enjoy as members of a university. Call the latter "academic freedom." The content of our academic freedom rights is derived not from the First Amendment of the United States Constitution,[39] but from the basic mission of the university, which is research, learning, and the public dissemination of knowledge. The expressive freedom we enjoy in the university is to use our speech to engage in inquiry, under the constraint that we accord equal academic freedom to others. This implies that some other expressive freedoms people enjoy outside the university may be constrained within it for the sake of protecting academic freedom. Freedom of speech within the academy is not coextensive with freedom of speech outside it. Let us explore the structure of expressive freedoms proper to an academic setting, then, given a liberal democratic epistemology.

V. Academic Freedom and Democratic Civility

The primary function of speech in the academy is the development and public dissemination of disciplinary knowledge. The norms regulating academic speech are tailored to this end. These norms give us the best institutional model yet instantiated for promoting knowledge. They support nothing like a libertarian free market of ideas. On the contrary, the academic "market" is the most extensively regulated idea market in civil society. We could not be confident that the claims it generated were worthy of the name "knowledge" if it were not so extensively regulated. Consider the fact that researchers can be expelled from the academy for publishing fraudulent research. This is viewpoint discrimination: the academy punishes the expression of viewpoints the speaker knows to be false. In the rest of civil society, people are free to express many kinds of deliberate lies and nonsense—just read the tabloids, or listen to almost any politician speak. But this kind of viewpoint discrimination within the academy is clearly justified. Given our epistemic interdependence, we need mechanisms to ensure the reliability of others' testimony. Dishonest researchers threaten this reliance, so sanctions are needed to prevent their claims from disrupting the quest for knowledge. Faculty and student speech is also minutely regulated for content and quality, and subject to a complex system of rewards and punishments. Grades, honors, probation, diplomas, employment, pay, promotion, tenure, letters of recommendation, grants and scholarships all hang on what students and faculty say, and how well they say it. This is what maintaining academic standards is all about.

Although universities as we know them today provide the most successful model yet devised for advancing objectively justified knowledge, they do not fully live up to their own ideals of promoting free and open

[39] "Congress shall make no law . . . abridging the freedom of speech, or of the press. . . ."

inquiry and objective justification. I have traced this failure to the racist, sexist, and class-based speech norms that currently govern the interaction of inquirers. Much of the attention devoted to these issues has focused on formal codes against hate speech. We should focus instead on the informal norms of civility and communication that govern our interactions. For overt, hateful harassment, while deeply damaging and distressing, is the smallest part of the problem. Much racist and sexist speech is coded and thus impossible to regulate by formal means without chilling speech clearly entitled to protection.[40] Moreover, much is racist or sexist in ways that escape the consciousness of the speaker, for example, by promulgating insulting stereotypes or by assuming that a single person can speak for a whole group. Besides, much more of the racism and sexism in communication is due to background norms for assigning credibility and access to the floor rather than to the content of speech itself. These norms are ingrained in habits that work behind people's backs more than in hateful emotions harbored in their hearts, or contemptuous thoughts lodged in their heads.[41] The key problems are thus much more widespread and deeply entrenched than formal codes could ever address. Their correction requires a comprehensive reform of the pedagogical habits and informal norms of civility that prevail in universities today.

For example, rules for getting access to the floor must change to ensure that opportunities to speak are allocated fairly. Many a class discussion or faculty forum could better foster free and open inquiry if those present enforced elementary rules of civility—forbidding people to usurp the floor by interrupting those presently holding it, insisting that all have an opportunity to speak once before anyone gets to speak another time, setting limits on the time any single speaker has the floor. We should not think that such rules are objectionable because they require shutting people up. *All* norms for the allocation of the floor silence some speakers so that others may be heard. The norm of tolerating interruption permits interrupters to silence those they interrupt. There is no trade-off between equality and liberty in this case. On the contrary, the most free and open discussions are those in which opportunities to get the floor are allocated widely and equally.

Many civil libertarians would gladly concede this point. They might argue, however, that the norms just discussed for constraining access to the floor are legitimate only because they do not discriminate against any

[40] Henry Louis Gates, Jr., "Let Them Talk," *New Republic*, September 20 and 27, 1993, p. 45.

[41] For example, Sadker and Sadker (in *Failing at Fairness*, pp. 46–48) report that most teachers who are shown through videotapes how they pay more attention to boys than to girls are surprised and hurt to discover this fact about themselves. Most genuinely like their female students, and sincerely profess belief in the equality of the sexes. People are unaware of many of their habits, which can persist even when they do not cohere with consciously held beliefs and attitudes.

speakers on account of what they have to say. Content- and viewpoint-neutrality are necessary features of any speech norm that can lay a claim to enhancing free and open discussion. This principle is mistaken. Content discrimination is clearly in order in classrooms and public presentations. We may require speakers to address the topic at hand, and questioners to get to the point. A content-neutral norm would allow a group to effectively shut down discussion of a topic they want to suppress by packing the room and having each of their members speak off-topic when each gets his turn to have the floor. Perhaps, then, we should draw the line at viewpoint discrimination. Speakers may be required to speak on topic, but must be permitted to take any position on this topic.

This proposal is far too crude to guide the construction of informal norms of speech that promote free and open discussion. In the first place, the content/viewpoint distinction is not robust. Someone might think that an entire field of study is misguided from the start, as creationists think of evolutionary theory, and evolutionary theorists think of creationism. These are viewpoints about the intellectual merits of whole contents or fields of thought. What's worse, whether one sees the distinction between them as one between content or viewpoint itself depends upon one's viewpoint: creationists are more likely to see themselves as taking different viewpoints about the same content, evolutionary biologists are more likely to see the case as one in which the disputants are engaged in entirely different fields, one scientific, the other theological. The standard content/viewpoint distinction cuts no ice here.

In the second place, the more important concern of the academy is not the stand one takes but the manner in which one defends one's stand. Individuals often overtly or covertly attempt to gain an edge in debate by pulling rank on their opponents, or through browbeating, bullying, arrogant posturing, and similar tactics. Here again the content/viewpoint distinction does not help us identify the dimension of speech that is of concern. The expression of some viewpoints, such as conservative defenses of aristocratic hierarchies, is intimately connected to a contemptuous tone of voice toward those regarded as inferior. Yet a democratic culture must be free to chastise such arrogance and put those who presume their own superiority in their place, which is no higher than anyone else's. Thus, norms concerning the proper tone of voice in communication—who may address whom with a patronizing, overbearing, or dismissive tone—cannot be viewpoint-neutral. We can adopt democratic or aristocratic norms here, and which we choose will both presume the validity of the viewpoint in question and have a significant impact on the influence each viewpoint will have, when expressed in accordance with the prevailing norms.

Finally, the academy may properly distinguish between speech that constitutes inquiry, and speech that, although expressing a "viewpoint," constitutes a disruption of inquiry. Consider the following case, which occurred in a political science class at the University of Michigan. A black student asked a question about the matter under discussion. From the back of the room, a white student loudly and sneeringly commented, "That's what you get with affirmative action." His implication was that the question was a stupid one to ask, but of a level only to be expected from black students, who are presumptively unqualified to be present. Is his "contribution" entitled to a respectful discussion on its merits, on the ground that it expresses a legitimate "point of view"? The suggestion is absurd. The student was not engaged in an inquiry into the merits of affirmative action programs. He was ridiculing another student for asking a question, and attacking her right to participate in class on account of her race. Should his comment, then, simply be passed over in silence, as not germane to the discussion at hand? This permits the attack to stand unchallenged, which amounts to complicity in its effects. The white student's message deters inquiry on the part of black students by sending the message that they may ask a question only at the risk of public ridicule. Furthermore, it instantiates a norm for interpreting what black students say: instead of treating their speech as an inquiry deserving of response on its own terms, treat it as evidence of the mental inferiority of the speaker. To follow this norm, or be complicit in its invocation, is to fail to treat black students as participants in inquiry; it is to strip them of recognition and hence of membership in the community of inquiry.

The white student's speech, then, was not an inquiry deserving of protection. It was an assault on freedom of inquiry itself. One is not free to ask a question if the threatened cost of doing so is being stripped of one's dignity. The student's words called for immediate, harsh, unequivocal, indignant rebuke on everyone's part, but especially on the professor's part. And the proper response in this context is *denunciation*, not a dispassionate discussion of the propriety of the remark, with rival sides allowed to debate the question. To treat this question as up for grabs is to treat it as up for grabs whether it is all right to ridicule this student for asking a question. This is itself to deprive her of recognition. Respect for others is *constituted* by a determination to regard certain matters concerning their status as closed.[42]

The rebuke called for here is speech that aims to silence abusive speech. There is no cause for hand-wringing in a case such as this, no reason to think the student's speech is on a par with the speech he silenced, no reason to regard his academic freedom as squelched by rebuke. We must distinguish between speech that deters or discredits people's inquiry by personally attacking them through ridicule or harassment, and speech that contributes to inquiry itself. Where one kind of speech can be protected only by rebuking and thereby silencing the other, the ideal of aca-

[42] See John Rawls, *Political Liberalism* (New York: Columbia University Press, 1993), p. 152 n. 16.

demic freedom is unequivocal. In a campus context, the interest in protecting freedom of inquiry trumps other expressive interests.

As a first step toward sorting out the informal speech norms that best promote free and open inquiry, let us distinguish between (a) speech that argues for an impersonal claim of general intellectual interest, and (b) speech that seeks to discredit a person. Along these lines, it might be suggested that we should adopt a rule against ad hominem attacks—attempts to discredit a claim by attacking the speaker. The rule tells us to regard all claims of type (b) as strictly irrelevant to assessing claims of type (a). This rule could be informally promulgated through logic classes, where the ad hominem fallacy is repudiated, and informally enforced through grading practices—marking down student work for employing it—and group expression of disapproval (hissing, booing, chastising) for those who invoke it in public forums. This rule, effectively ruling all attacks under (b) out of order, is too sweeping. Since what we believe depends on whom we believe, it is important for the academic community to reserve for itself the power to discredit unreliable speakers and to assess the credibility of testimony by considering the intelligence, credentials, expertise, honesty, and achievements of the speaker. "He's a charlatan" is a claim of type (b) that, if true, gives us a perfectly good reason for doubting claims of type (a) that we are asked to accept on the charlatan's word. The ad hominem fallacy is no fallacy, if we take it to be arguing to the credibility, rather than directly to the truth, of the claims in question.

A better rule would repudiate attacks on speakers that either are made for some other purpose than assessing the credibility of testimony (as is true for the white student's remarks above), or that attack the credibility of a speaker on cognitively irrelevant grounds. It makes sense to doubt a person's announcement of a surprising finding from a delicately rigged experiment on the ground that he's clumsy. His lack of skill with the experimental apparatus makes it more likely that his observation was a mere artifact of a contaminated experiment than that he discovered a novel phenomenon. It does not make sense, however, to doubt a person's testimony on account of his or her race, gender, or ethnicity, for these are cognitively irrelevant factors that have no bearing on the person's cognitive authority. The general rule seems right, but the particular conclusion drawn from it is not. Depending on the subject, the race, class, gender, or ethnicity of the speaker may be cognitively relevant for evaluating his or her testimony. It matters for testimony concerning *what it is like* to be "marked" as of a particular race, class, gender, or ethnicity. Facts of this sort are essentially perspectival, and the people with primary authority to testify about them are those who first-personally occupy the perspectives in question. People who are not marked in the same way can take up these perspectives, but only vicariously, second-hand, only by accepting the cognitive authority of first-hand witnesses, and never transparently or innocently. I propose, then, that the best rule of civility for academic discourse is to rule out of order all overt or covert mockery, ridicule, put-downs, or stigmatization of a person on account of race, class, gender, or ethnicity, and to adopt a strong presumption against more civil ways of questioning his or her credibility on such grounds, rebuttable only by a careful defense of the cognitive relevance of such status to the topic at hand.

Civil libertarians are often rightly suspicious of calls for civility in discourse. Often they are covers for the suppression of legitimate dissent. William Chafe, in his masterful *Civilities and Civil Rights*, documents how genteel white southern racists in North Carolina manipulated norms of civility so as to characterize black calls for desegregating schools as rude, unruly, and irresponsible.[43] The "responsible" blacks who were accorded "credibility" by the white power-structure were the ones who spoke in deferential and understated tones, who dared not openly challenge the plans whites made for the schools. They were forced to frame their claims in such mild, indirect, and apologetic terms that whites could characterize their own behavior as accommodating expressed black concerns, when in fact they were ignoring them. Calls for civility provided an excuse for endless stonewalling: in the face of any dispute over real change, the solution was to talk things over in a patient, civilized manner. The norms of civility were so structured that there was no *polite* means by which blacks could express their legitimate demands.

In the face of civility systems like this, there is no way to achieve justice except by being rude. Today as in the past, simply to point out another's unjust behavior is seen as unconscionably rude, even threatening to the accused person's freedom. The creation of a democratic culture of discourse in the face of aristocratic norms of civility in earlier centuries required numerous transgressions of then-prevailing norms of civility. It required calling out aristocrats and men of leisure for pulling rank on the lower classes, and loudly and openly repudiating deference to social rank.[44] The work of creating a democratic culture of discourse was not completed once those of noble birth could no longer get away with claiming superior cognitive authority on account of their ancestry or social class. The aristocracy of birth is not dead in this culture, it is simply reconfigured. Blue blood doesn't count anymore, but white blood still does. Open assertions of white male privilege don't figure in polite discourse among sophisticated academics, but covert assertions, whether through coded language or double standards for assigning cognitive authority and access to the floor, are pervasive. Moreover, elite colleges and universities still function to acculturate the children of the wealthy to display the exclusive markers of class privilege, in ways that marginalize students of poor and working-class backgrounds.

[43] William Chafe, *Civilities and Civil Rights* (New York: Oxford University Press, 1980).

[44] See, for example, Gordon Wood, *The Radicalism of the American Revolution* (New York: Vintage Books, 1993), ch. 15.

Here, too, there is no way to achieve justice in communicative relations without calling attention to the racism, sexism, and class bias that presently inform these relations. Those who have raised alarms about "political correctness" on college campuses characterize such activity as rude and threatening to academic freedom. Within the terms of present norms of civility, which demand polite deference to those in authority, such behavior is certainly rude. Whether it threatens or rather enhances academic freedom depends on whether it hits its target more often than not, and on a broader plain, whether academic freedom is best achieved in a democratic or an aristocratic culture. The transition from an aristocratic to a democratic culture requires rude behavior to shift norms of discourse to an egalitarian footing. This does not represent a repudiation of civility itself, but rather a reconstruction of its terms on a democratic basis.

VI. The Question of Discriminatory Harassment Codes

So far I have focused on informal norms of discourse, which are mainly enforced through speech on the part of people acting in an unofficial capacity. Is there any legitimate role in the academy for formal discriminatory-harassment codes, enforced through administrative sanctions such as letters of reprimand, expulsion, and fines? Such codes cannot be expected to reach to the heart of the problem. Controversy surrounding them may well distract from the larger task of reconstructing the ordinary norms of communicative interaction by falsely suggesting that the source of injustice lies in the hateful attitudes of a few bigots. Nevertheless, a principled case can be made that such codes, carefully drafted and confined to the most blatant and egregious examples of racial and sexual harassment, can play a legitimate role on college campuses.

Inquiry can flourish only in a culture of free and open discussion, equally accessible to all members of the university. Academic freedom requires that all claims made in the course of inquiry that are relevant to the development or justification of impersonal knowledge claims of academic interest be protected. Neither their controversial nature, their political unpopularity, their offensiveness, nor their tendency to arouse discomfort provide grounds for punishing academic speech, for truth may lie in places that are unpopular or that hurt people's feelings. People are entitled to argue that affirmative action programs are unjust, that homosexuality is a disease, that poverty is due to personal irresponsibility. Individuals pursuing all manner of politically controversial and offensive research programs—for instance, those that try to prove that women are biologically incapable of successfully competing with men for prestigious positions, or that blacks have lower intelligence coded into their genes—must be protected from being punished on account of the obnoxious political implications of their research. They may, however, be punished for pursuing their research dishonestly—for example, for fabricating data. In addition, departments and disciplines are free to judge on the evidence that such research programs have come to naught, that only cranks take them seriously, and hence that they shall not recruit individuals pursuing these research programs into their faculties, or grant tenure to researchers whose work is stuck in these ruts. History departments need not hire or tenure Holocaust-never-happened fanatics any more than geology departments need hire flat-earthers, or biology departments creationists. This is an expression of academic freedom, which includes the freedom to maintain academic standards. Furthermore, individuals are free to criticize research programs for being racist and sexist, to argue that the vicious motives of researchers cast doubt on the credibility of their testimony, and to urge that researchers choose research programs that promote rather than undermine important human interests. The freedom to conduct controversial research is not the freedom to be insulated from criticism.

Not all speech put forth in an academic context constitutes inquiry. Some speech has no rational bearing on the assessment of academic ideas, but consists simply in a vicious personal attack on other persons that deters or discredits their participation in inquiry on cognitively irrelevant grounds, through ridicule, haranguing, or insults. Such speech constitutes an attack on others' academic freedom and on the social conditions necessary for justifying knowledge claims. Consider, in this light, Stanford University's discriminatory-harassment provision, which regulates expression that (a) is *intended* to stigmatize individuals on account of race, gender, ethnicity, or sexual orientation, (b) is *directly* addressed to its victims, and (c) makes use of insulting or *"fighting words"* that convey hatred or contempt for others on account of their social identity.[45] This narrowly drawn conjunction of criteria captures a class of expression that has a damaging impact on others' freedom of inquiry by depriving them of the social bases of self-respect and recognition they need to participate effectively in it. At the same time, provisions (a) and (c) guarantee that the expressions in question do not function as contributions to inquiry, and thus restricting them does not in any way undermine academic freedom. Provision (c) limits sanctions to the most crude and egregious cases. Insults through subtle insinuation, such as that expressed by the white University of Michigan political science student discussed above, would not be covered, since they do not involve racial epithets or comparable fighting words.[46] The expressions covered by Stanford's policy are therefore properly subject to formal sanctions in the interests of protecting an atmosphere of free and open *academic* discussion.

[45] See Cohen, "Freedom of Expression," p. 208.

[46] U.S. constitutional doctrine defines "fighting words" as speech that is not an essential part of the expression of ideas and that is so insulting that it provokes the average person to fight. *Chaplinsky v. New Hampshire*, 315 U.S. 568 (1942).

No defense of discriminatory-harassment codes can be satisfactory that does not respond to several fundamental civil libertarian objections to the regulation of speech on account of its "viewpoint." Where regulation is defended as a response to market failure, skepticism may always be raised as to whether administrative solutions can be trusted to deliver better results than admittedly inefficient markets operating on their own. I shall argue that the case I have made for speech regulation in and by the academy, within a framework of strong sphere differentiation, is not vulnerable to the standard civil libertarian criticisms of speech regulation that envision enforcement by the state across all social spheres. Civil libertarians fear that, given the heated nature of political disputes, speech essential to democratic deliberation could be chilled if one of the parties could threaten a civil suit whenever the other side was provoked to an angry outburst. Where speech regulations are confined to academic contexts, these fears are not warranted. The conditions required for free-wheeling political campaigns are not the same as those required for effective learning in the university. In classrooms, labs, and offices, faculty are educators, not political agitators. Their role is not to hound out political enemies, but to promote free, open, and reasoned discussion of conflicting views. If they cannot control their tempers with students, that is evidence of pedagogical incompetence that could justify administrative intervention, with or without a speech code. If students prove themselves incapable of maintaining a reasoned and civil discussion with their classmates without resorting to "fighting words," this is also reason to question their competence to perform responsibly in academic settings. Other expressive interests in other social settings might require freedom from discriminatory-harassment regulations—but within the academy, these interests properly take a back seat to expressive interests in inquiry, the protection of which may require a more restrictive policy. The liberal strategy of sphere differentiation reminds us that our expressive interest in inquiry needs its own protected spaces subject to its own norms of communication, which may not be the same as those governing interactions of individuals in the rest of civil society.

Civil libertarians worry that any discriminatory-harassment policy is bound to be vague and overbroad.[47] In addition, the state is not in a good position to be an arbiter of truth, or to discriminate between speech that contributes to inquiry and speech that undermines it. These objections carry considerable weight against certain grounds for upholding hate-speech codes, especially when applied in society at large. For example, that speech is offensive or even deeply emotionally hurtful provide worrisome grounds for censoring it, given that the scope of these charges is potentially unlimited. Some people feel almost any expression of dis-

[47] This was the opinion Judge Avern Cohn correctly reached about the University of Michigan's student speech code in *Doe v. Michigan*, 721 F. Supp. 852 (E.D. Michigan, 1989).

agreement with their views to be wounding. The promotion of academic freedom and sound inquiry supply different grounds for restricting discriminatory harassment in academic settings. The academy can make a clear, principled, and narrowly tailored distinction between offensive or discomforting speech and discriminatory harassment—that is, speech that ridicules, slanders, or stigmatizes other members of the university on discriminatory grounds. Such attacks undermine their participation in educational activities, and serve no redeeming educational or cognitive function. It is not hard to tell the difference between personal discriminatory attacks on university members and offensive claims that may be of general academic interest. "Die, Nigger"[48] is easily distinguished from "Black poverty is due to rampant black teenage sexuality." Nor is there sound reason to doubt the capacity of academic institutions to make such distinctions responsibly. Academics routinely make much tougher distinctions, such as that between superior and shoddy research, or between original and plagiarized work, which carry consequences as great as any that could arise under a policy against discriminatory harassment. Any grounds for skepticism about the capacity of academic institutions to make the discriminations necessary to enforce a suitably narrowly tailored discriminatory-harassment policy are grounds for skepticism about the capacity of academic institutions to promote reasoned inquiry altogether.

The critical race theorists, who support state restriction of hate speech in civil society, rest their case for regulation on the legal precedents of group defamation and the "fighting words" doctrine.[49] Neither precedent is a promising one for civil rights activists.[50] It is unclear whether the Supreme Court's *Beauharnais* decision on group defamation remains good law; and the record shows that the state cannot be trusted to enforce the "fighting words" doctrine in a manner that promotes racial equality. Neither doctrine offers the best grounds for regulation of discriminatory harassment within the academy. The better analogies to discriminatory harassment in the academy are to (a) sexual harassment in the workplace and (b) academic sanctions against fraudulent research. Discriminatory harassment is like sexual harassment in that it unjustly undermines the ability of individuals to participate on terms of equality in a cooperative enterprise, and unjustly constrains their freedom there by imposing unconscionable costs on their participation. It is like fraudulent research in that it constitutes an assault on academic freedom, which carries with it the responsibility to use speech to promote, not

[48] Spray-painted on the office walls of an African-American student and secretary at the University of Colorado, Denver; see *The Journal of Blacks in Higher Education*, vol. 1 (1993), p. 107.

[49] Matsuda et al., *Words that Wound*. An Illinois law against group defamation was upheld by the U.S. Supreme Court in *Beauharnais v. Illinois*, 343 U.S. 250 (1952). The "fighting words" doctrine is articulated in *Chaplinsky v. New Hampshire*, 315 U.S. 568 (1942).

[50] Gates, "Let Them Talk," pp. 39–40.

undermine, objective inquiry. Both analogies are based on sound and just laws. Sexual-harassment law remains good law, and it is difficult to turn the law against those it is meant to protect. (A boss can be charged with sexual harassment for firing a worker who refuses a sexual advance, but the worker is in no position to be so charged, since she cannot fire her boss.) Moreover, no one thinks twice about the compatibility of the First Amendment with university sanctions against fraudulent research, even though this constitutes a violation of viewpoint neutrality.

The critical race theorists' justifications of discriminatory-harassment provisions pit the ideals of freedom and equality against one another. They therefore pit civil rights activists against civil libertarians, splitting progressives who could make more progress if they united in a common cause.[51] The justification for altering speech norms in an academic context highlights the unity of freedom and equality. The liberal democratic model of epistemology shows how equality of recognition is a prerequisite to free and autonomous inquiry. No adequate understanding of academic freedom can countenance its use as a cover for the assertion of race- and gender-based domination of others through personal abuse.

Civil libertarians worry about the loss of truth or conviction that can arise from viewpoint censorship. The academic case for regulating discriminatory harassment recognizes that not every expression of a "viewpoint" constitutes a cognitively relevant contribution to inquiry. There is no loss to knowledge from restricting expressions that have no bearing on the assessment of the impersonal knowledge claims of concern to the academy. This point also responds to Thomas Scanlon's worry that the restriction of speech that is apt to influence people's beliefs and attitudes constitutes a violation of autonomy.[52] Discriminatory hate-speech does influence people's beliefs and attitudes, but it does so behind their backs, for reasons that cannot be reflectively endorsed on any model of autonomous inquiry. It manifests its influence through its reinforcement of cognitive biases, not through rationally endorsable channels. Reason is powerful and can lead to objective knowledge, but it works reliably only under conditions where irrational influences are kept out. One of those influences is speech that insulates claims from criticism by attacking potential critics on discriminatory grounds. The objectivity of knowledge claims and the autonomy of inquiry are undermined when they are protected from criticism by social norms that enforce the inequality of speakers. Academic constraints on discriminatory harassment may thus be viewed as on a par with Ulysses-style strategies for rationally constraining irrational tendencies in ourselves. They help block the operation of cognitive biases due to widespread social contempt for individuals of low social rank, which leads us to ignore or discount what they say. In this

[51] *Ibid.*, p. 49.

[52] See Scanlon, "A Theory of Freedom of Expression" (*supra* note 20).

respect, they are like academic constraints on the publicity of authorship in the referee process of blind-reviewed journals: they help us focus on the merits of what is said, apart from prejudices that may attach to the author.

Civil libertarians may object that the threat of false accusations by hypersensitive people will chill the legitimate speech of others. But student and faculty speech is already chilled by discriminatory harassment. This creates an atmosphere of distrust that disrupts educational activities, and that can only fester in the absence of institutionalized means of dispute resolution. Nevertheless, the worry points to the advantages of designing a discriminatory-harassment policy to emphasize nonpunitive and educational means of dispute resolution that help restore the conditions for effective learning and research. This parallels the evolution of academic policies toward sexual harassment, most of which emphasize dispute resolution over punishment, in the recognition that most victims simply want abusive behavior to stop and are typically uninterested in punitive measures.

Although I have defended the propriety of formal discriminatory-harassment codes in academic contexts, I do not believe that much weight should be placed on them in comparison with movements to change pedagogical techniques and norms of civility. They are far too crude a tool to attack the deepest and most pervasive inequalities among inquirers, which are reproduced more through informal cultural norms than through overtly hateful acts. Codes tailored narrowly enough to meet common civil libertarian objections are likely not to cover many harmful but coded personal attacks. Formal sanctions cannot perform the hard work of creating a culture of democratic equality.

VII. The Role of Justice in the Production of Knowledge

Conservatives have cast contemporary struggles for justice in higher education as political interventions, external to educational aims, that threaten freedom of thought and the integrity of academic institutions. My defense of a liberal democratic political epistemology responds to this charge by showing how demands for justice—that is, for equality of persons in the academy—are generated internally to the aims of higher education itself. Freedom of thought in the academic context, what we call "academic freedom," is conditioned by its constitutive aim, the production of objective knowledge. That aim, and hence academic freedom itself, has the equality of inquirers as its political prerequisite. This aim cannot be achieved in a libertarian "free market of ideas," which succeeds only in reproducing an undemocratic culture of discourse marked by sharp inequalities along lines of race and gender. It can be achieved through democratic regulation of the "market of ideas." Our exploration of norms of civility and access to forums exposes the illusion behind the idea that unregulated speech maximizes freedom of speech. All norms of speech, however they arise, enable some speech by silencing other speech. Liberal sphere differentiation offers us an alternative model for enhancing freedom of speech. Instead of trying to "maximize" freedom of speech, we can create a variety of social spaces in which many different kinds of expressive freedom can find a home. Academic freedom is one such expressive freedom, the flourishing of which requires social spaces of universal access on terms of equality. Thus, the demand for justice, understood as equality of respect in the academy, cannot be seen as an external political demand threatening academic freedom. It is a political demand generated internally by the aims of the academy itself.

Philosophy and Women's Studies, University of Michigan, Ann Arbor

DETERRENCE AND THE JUST DISTRIBUTION OF HARM*

BY DANIEL M. FARRELL

It is extraordinary, when one thinks about it, how little attention has been paid by theorists of the nature and justification of punishment to the idea that punishment is essentially a matter of *self-defense*. H. L. A. Hart, for example, in his famous "Prolegomenon to the Principles of Punishment," is clearly committed to the view that, at bottom, there are just three directions in which a plausible theory of punishment can go: we can try to justify punishment on purely consequentialist grounds, which for Hart, I think, would be to try to construct a purely utilitarian justification of punishment; we can try to justify punishment on purely retributive grounds; or we can try to justify punishment on grounds that are some sort of shrewd combination of consequentialist and retributive considerations.[1] Entirely absent from Hart's discussion is any consideration of the possibility that punishment might be *neither* a matter of maximizing the good, nor of exacting retribution for a wrongful act, nor of some imaginative combination of these things, but, rather, of something altogether different from either of them: namely, the exercise of a fundamental right of self-protection. Similarly, but much more recently, R. A. Duff, despite the fact that he himself introduces and defends an extremely interesting fourth possibility, begins his discussion by writing as though, apart from his contribution, there are available to us essentially just the options previously sketched by Hart.[2] Again, there is no mention here, any more than in Hart's or any number of other recent discussions, of the possibility that we might be able to justify the institution of punishment on grounds that are indeed *forward-looking*, to use Hart's famous term, but that are not at all *consequentialist* in any ordinary sense of the word.

* Earlier versions of this paper were read at Stanford University and at the University of St. Andrews, and I am grateful to my listeners on each of these occasions, and to the other contributors to this volume, for helpful commentary. This paper is a continuation of a project on which I have been working for some time, and hence I am grateful, as well, to all the people thanked in previous papers (see note 7 below), who have been so kind as to help this project along with their comments and criticisms. Finally, I would like especially to thank Ellen Paul, of the Social Philosophy and Policy Center, for a long set of enormously helpful editorial suggestions.

[1] H. L. A. Hart, "Prolegomenon to the Principles of Punishment," in Hart, *Punishment and Responsibility* (New York: Oxford University Press, 1969), pp. 1–27.

[2] R. A. Duff, *Trials and Punishments* (Cambridge: Cambridge University Press, 1986).

Now, I shall not have a great deal to say about punishment, at least explicitly, in what follows. Instead, I am going to be talking about deterrence, and about how threats of harm, as well as the subsequent infliction of harm when those threats have been ignored, can be justified by an appeal to certain principles of distributive justice[3] – principles that themselves underlie, I believe, many of our most deeply felt convictions about the justification of self-defense. I hope it will be obvious as I proceed, though, that the account of deterrent threats and harms that I am developing here, if essentially correct, ought to be able to be developed fairly readily into a comprehensive theory of punishment – a theory in which punishment is viewed neither as an institution for the overall advancement of the social welfare, nor as an institution designed to concern itself solely with matters of retribution, nor as an institution designed to accomplish some subtle combination of these ends. My reason for presenting here my theory of the justification of deterrent threats (and enforcements), instead of elaborating my views about the implications of this theory for the problem of punishment, is simply that I believe the theory of deterrence that I develop to be both more fundamental and of considerably wider application than the theory of punishment that it entails.

I. Self-Defense, Deterrence, and Some Principles of Distributive Justice

To deter someone from doing something, I shall suppose, is to induce him not to do it for fear of the consequences that are likely to ensue if he does it. One way of effecting deterrence thus conceived, of course, is by means of threats: I judge that someone is about to harm me in some way, and, in hopes of inducing him not to do so, I threaten him with retaliatory harm in the event that he in fact attacks; if he takes me seriously, and refrains from attacking because of my threat, I have deterred him from doing what he otherwise would have done.

It is deterrence effected in this way that will be the principal object of my attention in what follows. It is worth noting, though, as I begin, that deterrence does not, as such, *require* threats: simply warning another of

[3] We ordinarily think of principles of distributive justice as principles that tell us how various *goods* are to be distributed, when some distribution or other must be made and we want the distribution to be a just or fair one. As I show below, however, we sometimes have to distribute *undesirable* items (or outcomes) as well – "evils" or "harms," as we might say – and, clearly, we need principles governing the justice or fairness of these distributive choices too. Note that these latter principles will, if I am right, be quite distinct from so-called "retributive" principles: the latter require harm to be imposed on those who have done wrongful harm to others and to be so imposed *simply* because the agent chose to do that wrong; principles of *distributive* justice, by contrast, tell us how to distribute harms, justly or fairly, when, regardless of what we do, someone will be harmed (or subjected to an increased probability of being harmed) by our action (or inaction) – see below for examples.

the natural consequences of doing what he is about to do might in some cases be enough to induce him not to do it.

Despite the fact that deterrence does not require threats, however, I think it is clear that attempts at deterrence that involve threats are of special interest, both morally and philosophically. For one thing, of course, to threaten another, in order to control his conduct, is to subject him to a form of coercion, and coercion is something that most of us believe needs to be justified. The point is not that we believe coercion can never *be* justified, but that we believe that those who engage in it bear the burden of showing why we should suppose their use of it *is* in fact justified in any given case.

Another reason deterrence through threats is of interest is this: Typically, it is not enough merely to *threaten* another with harm in order to deter him from doing what we want him not to do. We must be prepared actually to inflict that harm, if our threat is to be effective, and, in many cases, we must in fact inflict it in the event that our threat is ignored. This, of course, is because our threats will deter only if they are credible and because credibility often requires both a readiness to act on one's threats and actually acting on them once they have been ignored. Thus, those who issue deterrent threats must not only be able to justify making those threats, they must also be prepared to justify actually enforcing them once they are ignored. They must be able to do this, that is to say, or else either forswear protecting themselves with threats (and occasional enforcements) or continue doing so while admitting that they can provide no justification for their practice.[4]

Now, it would be a mistake to suppose that deterrence is always a matter of defending oneself (or others) from possible aggression on the part of the person whose conduct one is attempting to deter. A scoundrel might well attempt to deter others from acting to protect their savings from him, and a concerned parent might well attempt to deter a child from doing what the parent believes will not be in the child's best interest. In neither case would we be dealing with threats aimed at protecting the innocent from aggression, and in both cases the question of whether the attempt at deterrence is morally justifiable is independent of the question of whether it is an attempt to prevent wrongful aggression. However, despite the fact that deterrence can be sought in contexts other than those that involve appeals to the idea of self-defense, cases where such appeals are possible are a good starting-point, I believe, for a theory of when deterrent activities are and are not justified. I shall begin my account, therefore, with a discussion of cases of this sort, leaving for

[4] I assume that threats, including deterrent threats, must be justified—to the person against whom they are being made—because threats, at least in the present context, are made in an attempt to control the behavior of the person threatened, and because I believe that such attempts, being attempts to limit another's choices, are justifiable only in special circumstances.

another time an elaboration of this account that will allow us to extend it to cases of other sorts.

Imagine a case, then, where the conduct one hopes to deter is conduct that would clearly constitute a serious instance of wrongful aggression if one were unable to deter it: temporarily stranded on a desert island with me, let us suppose, another person has made it clear that he is prepared to do whatever he has to do, including murdering me, if need be, in order to gain sole control of the resources we both need in order to survive. I could, of course, wait until this person actually commences his attack before attempting to defend myself from him. Suppose, though, I have reason to believe that by threatening him with certain harms in the event he attempts an attack, I can significantly lower the probability that he will in fact attempt an attack. In such a case, it seems to me, it is tempting to think that the use of deterrent threats is justifiable and that it is justifiable entirely on grounds of self-defense. After all, in threatening my fellow islander in such a case, I am simply attempting to keep him from wrongfully harming me. If anything qualifies as justifiable self-defense, one is tempted to say, surely this does.[5]

There is a problem here, however—one that it is easy to overlook. No doubt one's aim in such a case is perfectly blameless: one merely wants to protect oneself from wrongful harm. What is not yet clear, though, is why we should suppose that this particular way of achieving that end is morally tolerable. After all, one is not *simply* acting to avoid being wrongfully harmed, if one makes the requisite threats. One is doing so by trying to create sufficient fear in the mind of one's potential antagonist as to make an attack seem to him a less promising course of conduct than it might otherwise have appeared to be. The question is: Exactly how is the argument for the justifiability of doing this best made out?

The answer to this question, I believe, must begin with an analysis of a slightly different kind of case: a case of what we might call "direct self-defense," where one protects oneself from an actual assault by responding to the attacker's use of force with force of one's own. Cases of this sort, given the right details, constitute a kind of paradigm of what we mean by justifiable self-defense. But why? What is it about cases of this sort that makes the defensive actions they involve seem so clearly justifiable?

Some philosophers would say that there is no answering a question like this: either we accept the right to self-defense as a kind of fundamental moral axiom, or we do not accept it at all.[6] I think this view is mis-

[5] See, for example, Warren Quinn, "The Right to Threaten and the Right to Punish," *Philosophy and Public Affairs*, vol. 14 (1985), pp. 327–73.

[6] Thomas Hobbes, of course, is the classic example—see especially *Leviathan*, ed. Michael Oakeshott (New York: Macmillan Publishing Co., 1962), ch. 14. Locke too, though, like many who have followed him, appears to think of the right to (rightful) self-defense as simply *given* by the law of nature—see especially *Two Treatises of Government*, ed. Peter Laslett (New York: New American Library, 1963), Book II, ch. II.

taken, though. I think that our right to direct self-defense is itself best conceived, at least in a critically important class of cases, as a corollary of the following principle for the just distribution of harm (as a corollary of the following principle of *distributive justice*, in other words):

(P_1) When someone knowingly brings it about, through his own wrongful conduct, that someone else must choose either to harm him or to be harmed herself, the latter is entitled to choose that the former shall be harmed, rather than that she shall be harmed, at least if the harm thereby inflicted on the former is not radically disproportionate to the harm that would otherwise be inflicted on the latter.[7]

The central ideas behind this principle are the ideas of fairness and of individual responsibility for the consequences of one's informed, voluntary actions. In a case where someone's informed, wrongful choices have led to the necessity of *someone's* suffering certain harms, the principle says, and where one of those who could be harmed is the person who has culpably brought this state of affairs about, it is only fair that the person who is responsible for this situation should suffer rather than that some other, "innocent" individual should suffer.[8]

To be sure, thus conceived, this way of understanding our putative right to (direct) self-defense has no immediate application to the problem that currently interests us—that is, the problem of justifying, on grounds of self-defense, the threats we might be tempted to make in cases of the

[7] A principle similar to this is defended by Phillip Montague in "Punishment and Societal Defense," *Criminal Justice Ethics*, vol. 2 (1983), and I am indebted to the spirit of Montague's argument in what follows. For more detailed remarks on aspects of the argument that follows, but without reference to the theory of punishment, see my "The Justification of Deterrent Violence," *Ethics*, vol. 100 (1990), pp. 301–17. An early (and quite inchoate) version of the line I try to develop here was sketched in my "The Justification of General Deterrence," *Philosophical Review*, vol. 94 (1985), pp. 367–94. Also relevant, in connection with the theory of punishment, is my "Punishment without the State," *Noûs*, vol. 22 (1988), pp. 437–53. I should note, in connection with the principle introduced in the text, that I am aware that there are cases where self-defensive violence would appear to most of us to be justifiable and yet would not be justified by a principle like P_1: a case, for example, in which my "attacker" is himself innocent of any wrongful intent (he has been ruthlessly brainwashed, let us suppose, and is under the control of someone who is using him to harm me), but where, unless I seriously harm him, he will seriously harm me. Obviously, if self-defense is justified in such cases (and I think it sometimes is), P_1 is not the principle that justifies it. However, far from thinking that the existence of such cases threatens the account I offer below (of a very different type of case), I think further reflection on such cases in fact supports the view defended here. But limitations of time and space preclude further discussion of this issue at present.

[8] I say that the relevant wrongful choice must be an *informed* choice because the principle I wish to defend is plausible, in my view, only when the situation that results from the agent's wrongful choice is one he knew, or had good reason to believe, would likely result from that choice. In cases where an agent acts wrongfully, but without knowing (or having good reason to believe) that a choice-of-harms situation is likely to ensue (for another agent), P_1 does not apply.

sort described above (cases where we want to prevent the initiation of an attack by making a verbal threat). After all, in the case of a decision that falls naturally under a principle like P_1, we are dealing with a decision that we have been forced to make precisely because of the wrongful actions of another. In cases of the sort that currently interest us, by contrast, we are supposing that there has as yet been no wrongful action; the point is rather to prevent someone from acting as he might otherwise act.

Despite the fact that it provides no immediate solution to our present problem, though, I think the realization that P_1 can be used to ground our putative right to self-defense is an important step in the resolution of that problem (the problem of justifying anticipatory *threats*, that is to say, as well as self-defensive actions that are consequent to an already initiated attack). For one thing, it enables us to see that the right to self-defense can indeed be *grounded*—on independent and quite plausible moral considerations—rather than simply having to be accepted as a moral axiom of some sort, with nothing to be said for it except that it is an element in our moral thinking that most of us find impossible to resist. For another thing, it shows us the direction in which such an independent justificatory enterprise might plausibly go: it underlines a point which is likely to seem obvious once reflection has brought it to our attention—namely, that self-defense is typically a matter of the distribution (or redistribution) of harm, or of the probability of harm, and hence that the justification of self-defense must at some level involve, even if only implicitly, an appeal to considerations of distributive justice.[9]

We can now return to the problem that actually interests us, and we can notice, to begin with, that cases where I must decide whether to threaten another, in order to try to deter him from wrongfully harming me in some way, are certainly cases where I am faced with a problem about how I should, or at least may, rightly, distribute certain harms. For in such cases I must choose between making the threat, thereby at least trying to burden my potential antagonist with the evil of restricted choice, or not making the threat, thereby leaving myself burdened with the evil of continuing to face (and therefore fear) an attack which I have reason to believe would have been less likely to occur if I had made the threat. The question, therefore, is not whether cases of the sort that currently interest us are, in this respect at least, analogous to cases of direct self-defense, but whether the idea of individual responsibility, or something like it, can be linked to the idea of a just or fair choice among a constrained set of options, to support a principle of the relevant sort—that

[9] In "The Justification of General Deterrence," and in "The Justification of Deterrent Violence," I show that a principle like P_1 can be used to justify deterrent violence in certain cases, *independently of any antecedent threats*, and hence can be used to justify "making an example" of someone in such cases, absent prior threats, without at the same time making oneself liable to the charge that, in so acting, one has "used" the person in question in a morally objectionable way.

is, a principle that gives one a right to try to put the burden of evil on one's potential antagonist in cases of the appropriate sort rather than leaving it on oneself.[10]

The answer, I think, is that these ideas can indeed be linked in the desired way. To see how, it will be useful to digress for a moment, in order to reflect on a related problem of justification. Suppose that on my desert island I have at my disposal a device of the sort that a number of writers have recently introduced into discussions of the justification of punishment: a so-called "automated retaliation-device," which will automatically inflict on anyone who wrongfully attacks me, whatever penalty I have previously programmed it to inflict.[11] (Suppose for the sake of discussion that the device is "foolproof" in the following sense: it never harms anyone "by mistake"—it harms only those who have wrongfully harmed me, and it does to them only what I have previously programmed it to do.) Obviously, I could use such a device to try to deter my fellow islander from attacking me, in much the same way I might have used an ordinary threat for this purpose in our original example: I program the device to harm him in some way, in the event that he wrongfully attacks me, telling him, while I do so, that this is what I am doing, and explaining why I am doing it (that is, strictly for the sake of inducing him not to attack me).

Justifying the use of such a device for deterrent purposes confronts one with all sorts of difficulties—many more, in fact, than we face in the justification of a deterrent strategy that relies only on ordinary threats.[12] My interest here, though, is not in the details of an account that might justify the use of such devices, much less in the special difficulties such an account would face, but in the general form a justification for using such a device must take. The answer to this question, it seems to me, is obvious enough: the most plausible line of argument in favor of using such devices for the stated end would be one that appeals to a principle of choice for the just distribution of harm analogous to the one I used above for the justification of the right to self-defense. Very roughly, I think, that argument would go as follows. By using the device, under circumstances where I correctly believe that by using it I can significantly reduce the probability of a wrongful attack, and where I believe that *only* by using

[10] I am using "evil" here, of course, simply to refer to undesirable outcomes, as explained in note 3 above.

[11] See, especially, Lawrence Alexander, "The Doomsday Machine: Proportionality, Punishment, and Prevention," *Monist*, vol. 63 (1980), pp. 199–227; and Quinn, "The Right to Threaten and the Right to Punish," pp. 327–73.

[12] One of these problems, of course, is that in actual practice no such device would ever harm *only* those who have wrongfully (and willfully) harmed others. What's more, everyone would know that this is so. Hence, we would have to justify both the wrongful harms the device does, if it does some, *and* the antecedent risk and fear of such harms, which we impose simply by constructing and activating the device. This is not the place, though, for a proper discussion of these problems.

it can I achieve this end, I am choosing to place the burden of evil on my antagonist in order to reduce the burden of evil for myself. After all, by using it I am, by hypothesis, making one of his options less desirable, we may suppose, against his will; and I am also raising the probability of harm to him—in the event that he wrongfully harms me—to close to 1 (that is, to as close to certainty as I can make it). If I choose not to use the device, on the other hand, I am in effect choosing to take the burden of evil upon myself, inasmuch as I then have to continue to live with an avoidably high probability of wrongful harm. Under these circumstances, it seems reasonable to suppose, I could argue in favor of using the device as follows. If I use it, I leave it *to him* to decide whether or not he will be harmed, burdening him, as I do so, only with the evil of constrained choice, where, by hypothesis, the choice I am attempting to constrain is one he has no right to make. If I choose not to use the device, on the other hand, I am choosing to leave the question of whether I will be harmed in *his* hands, at least to a degree, even though I know that self-protection was available to me at the price just described. Given these circumstances, I might well suppose, it is surely fair to act to put the burden of evil on him in order to reduce the burden on myself. For, as we have seen, if I so act, he will be harmed—apart from the harm or evil of being constrained not to do what he has no right to do—only if he does what, by hypothesis, he has no right to do, in circumstances where he knew that this is what would happen to him if he did it and where he knew that this had been arranged solely in order to induce him not to attack.

Suppose that, at least as a schema for an argument of the requisite sort, these remarks are sound. The principle they are designed to support might then be summarized as follows:

> (P_2) When my situation is such that either I resort to the use of an automated-retaliation strategy, as a way of protecting myself from wrongful harm, or I do not resort to such a strategy, thereby leaving myself significantly more vulnerable to that harm than I otherwise would have been, I am entitled to choose the former alternative over the latter, at least if the relevant device is certain to harm only those who have wrongfully harmed me and to do to them only what I have previously programmed it to do.[13]

Could an analogous principle be justified that would ground the use of ordinary threats, when the latter are made in an attempt to protect one-

[13] A fuller discussion of automated-retaliation strategies would have to include a discussion of an analogue to the "proportionality requirement" that was included in P_1. I omit this here, for the sake of brevity, because I am introducing the notion of an automated-retaliation strategy only as a heuristic: the point is to show that if such strategies can be justified, then what we might call "ordinary-threat strategies" can be justified as well. It is the latter point that is elaborated below.

self from wrongful harm? [14] In this latter case, all we are trying to justify, at this stage of our inquiry, is the *making* of the threat. Thus, in this respect at least, our justificatory task would appear to be easier than the one we have just discharged. Notice, though, that the similarities between the two sorts of strategies are significant: in both cases we are faced with the need to justify an attempt by one person to induce another person not to act in a certain way—an attempt which involves convincing the latter that the costs of acting in that way are greater than the gains, and in which those costs are not costs that are "naturally" connected with the behavior one is trying to constrain. In both cases, in other words, one is faced with justifying the imposition of two independent but related "evils" on the person with whom one is interacting: the evil of constrained choice and the evil of living with the fear of what will happen to him if he acts as one wants him not to act. But, then, surely my remarks about the justification of automated retaliation-devices, if sound, will apply in the case of ordinary threats as well. For here, as there, it appears that I can argue, in support of my defensive actions, as follows. Either I make the relevant threats or I do not. If I make them, I am disburdening myself of a certain amount of evil by imposing certain evils on my fellow islander. If I do not make them, on the other hand, I am choosing to retain the burden I would otherwise not have to bear, in order to refrain from burdening him with the evils he would otherwise have to bear. Given the nature of the evils involved, it seems fair to choose to burden my fellow islander rather than to continue to be burdened myself. For his burden is simply to be constrained from doing what he has no right to do in the first place and to live with the fear of what he will likely suffer if he nonetheless does it, whereas my burden is to live with the fear of what *he* will do *to me*, unjustifiably, in the event that he chooses to do it. In such a case, as in the case of my choosing to use the automated retaliation-device, it seems more reasonable, because it seems more fair, for him to bear the relevant burden rather than for me to bear the alternative burden that I would otherwise have to bear.

II. Justifiably Enforcing Justifiable Threats

Suppose my argument thus far is sound: at least some deterrent threats can be justified on grounds of self-defense, where the latter is conceived as constituted by a set of rights that are themselves grounded on a set of assumptions about the justice, or *fairness*, of distributing harms and other evils in one way in certain types of situations rather than in another. Our next first-order normative question would then presumably be the follow-

[14] By an "ordinary" threat I mean a verbal (or written) threat that the threatener implies will be carried out by him or his agent(s), at will, rather than by a machine, automatically.

ing: Just *how much* may one threaten, in any given case, in order to attempt to deter a prospective act of aggression of a given sort? In answer to this question, of course, any number of views might be defended. Someone might argue, for example, that in defending oneself against what one correctly believes to be the prospect of wrongful harm, one may threaten whatever it is reasonable to believe one has to threaten in order to deter that harm, but no more. We might say that while this view does indeed set a limit on what one may justifiably threaten in any given case, the limit it sets is a purely "a posteriori" one, inasmuch as the limit depends entirely on the contingent features of each case: as long as one does not threaten more than it is reasonable to believe one has to threaten in order to deter the relevant harm, one has not threatened too much. On another, much stronger view, by contrast, one must observe both this a posteriori limit and another limit as well – what I shall call an "a priori" limit on what one may justifiably threaten in an attempt to deter a given wrong. An a priori limit is one that depends on the exact nature of the harm one is attempting to deter, the general idea being that the harm one threatens must not be radically worse than the harm one is attempting to deter. On this latter view, there are certain harms one may not threaten in an attempt to deter a given harm, even if one reasonably believes one has to threaten them if one is to deter those harms. (One cannot threaten someone with death, for example, as a way of keeping him off one's lawn, even if one correctly believes that this is the only threat that is going to keep him off one's lawn.) Finally, it might be argued – against both these views – that there are no limits at all on what one may justifiably threaten in a legitimate attempt to protect oneself against wrongful harm: if one is justified in threatening anything at all, on this view, one is justified in threatening whatever one would like, since, as we have seen, all one is doing in making the threat is attempting to prevent someone from doing something he has no right to do in the first place.

These and a number of other possible views would have to be considered at this point if I were going to proceed in what would seem to be the natural way: namely, by following up my brief discussion of the justification of deterrent threats with a discussion of how much one can justifiably threaten in any given case, supposing for the sake of argument that at least some threats would be morally justifiable in at least some cases. However, despite the fact that this appears to be the most natural way of proceeding at this point, I am not going to proceed in this way. Instead, I want to take up the question of when a person is justified in *enforcing* a threat she has previously and justifiably made. For in answering this question, which I believe to be the most difficult question a theory of deterrent violence has to answer, we will naturally be led to introduce a set of considerations which will make it considerably easier to answer, at least in outline form, the question that I am now proposing to skirt: that is, the question of what limits there are, if any, on what one may justifiably threaten in a case where one has a presumptive right to use threats in defending oneself from the prospect of unjust aggression.

Our question, then, is this: Of the deterrent threats one can justifiably make, which can one justifiably enforce, and why? Here, of course, as in the case of our question about the possible moral limits on justifiable threats, any number of different answers might be defended. Notice at once, though, that this new question is a pressing one precisely because it seems implausible to suppose that one very simple answer is correct: namely, that any threat one was justified in making is a threat one may justifiably enforce. For one thing, this simple answer seems clearly implausible for cases where threats to harm the innocent are involved. Under certain circumstances, someone might say, one may well be justified in threatening harm to the innocent as a way of protecting oneself from wrongful harm from someone else, especially if the innocent parties need not even know about one's threats. (Imagine a case where the only way you can protect yourself and your family from wrongful death is to threaten to kill your potential murderer's children if he attempts to kill you and your family and fails.) Obviously, it is not at all clear that the justifiability of such threats, supposing they are sometimes justified, entails anything whatsoever about the justifiability of enforcing them in the event that they are ignored.

It is possible, of course, that the simple view I am here rejecting is meant to apply only to justifiable threats to harm those whose misconduct we are attempting to deter. Even in that case, though, it is not at all clear, it seems to me, why we should suppose that any such threat one was justified in making is a threat one may justifiably enforce. Suppose, for example, that the harm one has to threaten is in some intuitive sense vastly disproportionate to the harm one is attempting to deter: in order to keep someone from allowing his dog to foul my front yard, let us suppose, I have had to threaten him with death in the event that he fails to see to it that this shameful practice is curtailed. If, despite my threat, he continues to fail to control his dog's behavior, do we really want to say that I am justified in killing him, and that I am justified in doing so *simply* because I was justified in making the relevant threat in the first place (supposing, for the sake of argument, that I was justified in making it)?

It might be replied that it is ludicrous to suppose that a threat of this magnitude could possibly be justified in the circumstances just imagined: no threat that is so far out of proportion to the harm it is intended to deter could possibly be justified, someone might say. For reasons that will be explained below, I think this line of argument would be mistaken. Here, though, I shall simply note that there is another, completely independent reason for being suspicious about the view that we may justifiably enforce any threats we have justifiably made—at least if the latter are threats to harm those whose wrongful behavior we are trying to control. Imagine that what I have had to threaten in a given case is not at all out of proportion, in the relevant sense, to the harm I am trying to deter: in order to prevent someone from attempting to kill me, let us suppose, I threaten to kill him if he makes the attempt and fails. (Assume that this is the only threat that is even remotely likely to deter him from making a murderous attack on me.) If, despite my threat, this person attacks, I must decide, in the event that I manage to repulse his attack, whether or not to enforce my threat. We shall consider in a moment circumstances that would tend to make plausible the claim that I may rightly enforce it. Suppose, though, that in the case we are imagining, the circumstances subsequent to his failed attack are these: so far as the need to protect myself from similar attacks is concerned, I have no reason whatsoever to enforce my earlier threat. (My attacker has been permanently incapacitated as a result of my defense, let us suppose, and no one else even knows I made the threat, much less whether or not I will subsequently enforce it.) On the view we are now considering, I nonetheless have a right to enforce that threat, and I have this right simply because it was a threat I was justified in making at the time it was made. The problem is: it is not clear why we should suppose this is so. We could, of course, bring in retributive considerations at this point: we could argue that while the threat was justified on grounds of self-defense, enforcement is justified because of the wrong that was done in the ignoring of that threat.[15] In that case, however, the simple view would no longer be so simple, for one thing, and an entirely new burden of argument would have to be met, for another—one that the history of our subject suggests it is quite difficult to bear. (I refer to the need for a philosophically compelling defense of retributivism.) To be sure, it is possible that this burden can be borne, and that the resulting view, while not so simple as the earlier version, would strike us as quite compelling. I want to leave the discussion of this possibility for another time, however, since I think we have another option, one which, superficially, at any rate, is far more plausible: we can abandon the simple view and return to our original question, hoping to find some alternative view that will strike us as a more tenable starting-point for answering that question in a compelling way.

Our question, it will be recalled, was this: Of the threats one has previously and justifiably made, which may one justifiably enforce, and why? One very tempting answer, once we have rejected the simple view, is the following: The justification of enforcements can be grounded upon exactly the same considerations as the justification of direct self-defense—namely, the considerations that underlie a principle like P_1 above. The general idea here is simple enough. P_1 tells us that when someone

[15] This may be Quinn's position in "The Right to Threaten and the Right to Punish," though this is not entirely clear from the text. It is also very likely J. D. Mabbott's position in his famous paper "Punishment," *Mind*, vol. 48 (1939), though this too is not entirely clear from the text.

knowingly brings it about, through his own wrongful conduct, that someone else must choose either to harm him, or be harmed herself, justice allows the latter to choose that the former shall be harmed, rather than that she shall be harmed, at least if the harms thereby inflicted on him are roughly proportionate to the harms that would otherwise be inflicted on her. Suppose, then, that a purely defensive threat of the sort discussed above has been made and then ignored: having been told what I would do to him if he wronged me in a certain way, my fellow islander nonetheless attempts to wrong me in precisely that way. It is possible, of course, as we have already seen, that I will have no forward-looking reasons to enforce this threat once it has been ignored. In that case P_1 does not apply. It is also possible, though, and much more likely, that I *will* have forward-looking reasons for enforcing my threat—both in a two-person case of the sort we are currently imagining and, quite clearly, in a multi-person case where there are other potential attackers in addition to the one we have been imagining. This, of course, is because once one has made a deterrent threat, one will typically be at risk of losing one's credibility if one does not enforce that threat in the event that it is ignored. And to lose one's credibility is to lose the capacity, at least in circumstances of the relevant sort, to continue to protect oneself with deterrent threats: it is to be put at risk of further harm, either from one's current attacker or from other, like-minded individuals, if such exist. In circumstances where this is so, it appears that P_1 will apply and will justify enforcement. For in such circumstances one is indeed in a situation where, as a result of another's wrongful conduct, one must choose either to harm him or to be harmed oneself. Or, to put the point a bit more carefully, one is, as a result of his wrongful conduct, in a position where one must choose either to harm him or to suffer the evil, oneself, of being more vulnerable to harm, from him or from others, than one otherwise would have been (that is, than one would have been had he not attacked one in defiance of one's previous threat). And P_1 tells us that in such circumstances one is entitled to act to protect oneself by seeing to it that, if someone must be harmed, it is the person who has created the necessity of choice who should be harmed, rather than some other, innocent party such as oneself.

One problem with this line of argument, of course, is that it presupposes the validity of P_1. Another problem is that even if we accept the validity of P_1, the principle's application to cases of the sort that now interest us is problematical in a way the argument just sketched ignores. To see this, imagine the recipient of the enforcements this argument aims to justify arguing as follows. No doubt, he observes, each of us has the right accorded to us by P_1—the right to see to it that the responsible party suffers, in cases of the sort that interest us, rather than that we should suffer as a result of that party's wrongful choices. In a case where a distribution of harms is made necessary, however, by virtue of someone's having ignored someone else's self-defensive threat, it would be implausible to say that the person who ignored the threat is alone responsible for the fact that there are now harms to be distributed that we were not faced with distributing prior to his wrongful act. For if the threat to retaliate had not been made in the first place, there would be no question of someone's having to suffer, for the sake of the threatener's continued credibility, once that threat was ignored. Thus, the fact that unsuccessful threateners face credibility problems is due not (merely) to the fact that their threats have been ignored, but rather to the fact that they were made in the first place. And this means that an appeal to P_1 is not sufficient, by itself, to justify enforcement in cases of the sort that currently interest us.

This objection is not a frivolous one: it does indeed show that the justification of enforcement is not as easy as the preceding argument suggests. It will perhaps be obvious, though, how an amended argument must go. It would begin, I take it, by noting that in situations of the sort that interest us, a person is faced not merely with the question of whether she can justifiably enforce a previously justifiable self-defensive threat *in some one case*, but rather with the question of whether she can justifiably adopt and implement a certain self-defensive *policy* or *strategic plan* for the conduct of her relations with others over a certain period of time. After all, if we suppose that a person may not (rightly) enforce her threats in cases of the relevant sort—cases where the credibility of those threats will be undermined if she does not enforce them—we are in effect saying that her right to defend herself with threats is so severely limited as to be almost worthless so far as her actual strategic situation is concerned. For, from the standpoint of a person committed to acting only as she may rightly act, threats she may not rightly enforce are as good as no threats at all.

Suppose, then, that we introduce the notion of a self-defensive *strategic plan*: an overall plan of action for defending oneself from others' potentially aggressive actions—one which includes plans for what one will do in the event that others react in one way rather than another to one's previous defensive moves. And suppose we call a plan that is morally defensible in its own right, *and* that contains no projected actions that would not themselves be morally defensible as well, a "morally tenable" plan. A morally tenable self-defensive (strategic) plan, then, would be a self-defensive plan of the sort just described which is itself morally defensible and which contains no elements which are not morally defensible as well, including any instances of threat-enforcement the plan happens to require. It is possible, of course, that no actual plan that requires enforcements would in fact be morally defensible. This, I take it, is precisely the possibility that is raised by the objection to the argument for justifiable enforcements that was just sketched. It is also possible, however, as I shall now try to show, that a plan that would not *seem* to be defensible, if we considered its prospective actions entirely in isolation from one another, could in fact be shown to be defensible when viewed *as a plan*, in the sense defined above, and in relation to the alternative plans that are available to the agent.

Consider again the situation of the person who not only has reason to believe that she must *make* retaliatory threats, if she is significantly to reduce the probability of unjust attacks against her, but who also correctly believes that she must regularly enforce those threats, if this end is to be achieved, when her threats have been ignored. We saw that, despite initial appearances, such a person could not justify enforcing previously justifiable threats *simply* by appealing to a principle like P_1 on a case-by-case basis. Obviously, though, she could justify enforcement, at least in a restricted class of cases, if we could show that the following principle is at least as plausible as P_1 and is plausible for exactly the same kinds of reasons:

(P_3) When one's situation is such that either (a) one adopts and acts on a plan of making and enforcing threats of a certain sort, thereby protecting oneself from wrongful aggression on the part of those against whom those threats are addressed, or (b) one does not adopt such a strategy, thereby leaving oneself subject to an avoidably high probability of being attacked by those individuals, one is entitled to choose the former alternative over the latter, provided that (i) one's threats are within certain limits, and (ii) they are threats to harm those, and only those, whose wrongful conduct one is trying to deter.

The question, of course, is whether this principle is as plausible as P_1.

To see why I think it is, it will be useful to return for a moment to our discussion of the use and potential justifiability of so-called "automated retaliation-devices" ("ARDs" for short). Though at best incomplete, my remarks did, I believe, show how an argument justifying the use of such devices might go and how that argument might be grounded on considerations closely related to those involved in the justification of a principle like P_1. The basic idea was that when my situation is such that either (a) I resort to the use of an ARD, thereby lowering the probability that I will be harmed by ensuring that anyone who harms me will be harmed himself, or (b) I do not resort to the use of an ARD, thereby leaving myself more vulnerable to harm than I would otherwise have to be, it is fair for me to choose the former option over the latter, at least if the harms my device is programmed to inflict are in some sense roughly proportionate to the harms that will otherwise be inflicted on me. After all, the argument went, if I do not use the device, I am leaving the question of whether *I* shall be harmed, to a certain degree at least, in the hands of my potential attacker, while if I do use the device, I am protecting myself from this harm by burdening him with "harms" it appears he cannot reasonably object to, given the assumptions embodied in the case.

Suppose this discussion was on the right track. It is obvious, I think, that exactly analogous considerations can be used in defense of a principle like P_3. For in a real-world situation where my options really are just those identified in the antecedent of P_3, and where this is clear not only to me but to my potential antagonists, I can presumably defend adopting the one strategy over the other by arguing as follows. Either I adopt the relevant threat-and-enforcement strategy or I do not. If I do, I protect myself at the cost of burdening my potential antagonists with the evils of constrained choice and of knowing that they will be harmed if they ignore my threats and wrong me in the relevant ways. If I do not adopt that strategy, on the other hand, I refrain from burdening my potential antagonists in this way, but only at the cost of retaining the burden of probable wrongful harm that I otherwise would have avoided. In such a situation, as in the situation where my choice is between utilizing or not utilizing an ARD, it seems reasonable to suppose that I am entitled to choose to put the relevant burden on my potential antagonists rather than to continue to bear it myself. For, as in that earlier case, I am in effect choosing between leaving the question of whether I will be harmed entirely in the hands of my potential attackers, or taking that question out of their hands, at least to a degree, by imposing on them harms of the sort just discussed (that is, constraint of a choice they have no right to make and reasonable fear of harm should they nonetheless make it). In this sort of situation, as we have seen, it is hard to see how they could reasonably object if I choose to subject them to the relevant evils as a way of protecting myself from the alternative evils I would otherwise have to endure. They certainly cannot object to the fact that I am attempting to restrain them from making a choice they have no right to make; and as for the evil of knowing that they will be harmed if they wrongfully harm me, it seems fair to impose this burden on *them* rather than continuing to live, myself, with an increased burden of fear of being harmed by them. After all, it is they who will decide if they are to be harmed, if I use the strategy, while it is they, and not I, who will decide if *I* will be harmed, if I do not use it.[16]

[16] My argument here is analogous to a famous argument of Hart's in "Punishment and the Elimination of Responsibility," in *Punishment and Responsibility*, pp. 158–85; my argument differs from Hart's, however, in at least one crucial respect: while he uses the value of "choice" as one among many goods that must figure in an adequate *utilitarian* defense of the system he is defending, I am using it as part of an argument based entirely on the concepts of fairness and individual responsibility for the consequences of one's informed decisions.

III. The Problem of Limits

Suppose the argument thus far is right: threats can be justified by appeal to an argument analogous to the argument for the in-principle justifiability of using ARDs in certain circumstances, and a threat-and-enforcement strategy can be justified by appeal to a principle like P_3. One question that remains unanswered, even if we suppose there are no major problems with our argument so far, is the question of *how much* one can justifiably threaten, in any given case, as a way of protecting oneself from wrongful aggression that one reasonably believes one will otherwise suffer. This question, it will be recalled, was tabled at the start of Section II, so that we could consider the question of when, if ever, one was justified in enforcing threats one had previously and justifiably made.

One reason for tabling it should now be clear: while it would perhaps be interesting to know exactly which threats one could justifiably *make*, independently of whether one could ever justifiably enforce them, a more pressing matter is the question of what threats one could justifiably make *and then enforce*, as part of a morally tenable strategic plan of the sort described above. It is to a brief consideration of this latter question that I now want to turn, therefore, before bringing the present discussion to a close.

I should begin by noting that it would be foolish to be at all ambitious at this point: even on the question of what one can justifiably do in direct self-defense, there is enormous disagreement among people who have reflected seriously on these matters. Nearly everyone agrees that one may do no more than one has to do in order to prevent a given wrong, but there is wide disagreement about whether there are limits of another sort on one's right to direct self-defense. Some hold that regardless of the degree of harm one is attempting to prevent, one is entitled to do whatever one has to do in order to prevent it, so long as it is reasonable to believe that the latter really is required. Others hold, by contrast, that there are what I shall call "a priori" limits on what one may do in direct self-defense, limits that depend on the nature of the harm one is attempting to prevent and that must be respected even in cases where one will not be able to protect oneself unless they are exceeded.

A conservative strategy for dealing with the question that now concerns us would be the following. Assume that there are both "a posteriori" limits, as I shall call them, on what one may justifiably do in direct self-defense—limits that arise from the fact that one may never do more than it is reasonable to believe one has to do in order to prevent the harm at hand—and a priori limits of the sort just described. Then ask, with this in mind, what sorts of cognate limits it is reasonable to suppose there might be on what one may justifiably threaten *and do* in a morally tenable self-defensive strategic plan of the sort that interests us.

Suppose one wanted to follow this conservative strategy. How exactly would one proceed? I suggest the following approach. First, let us return to the imaginary world in which I defend myself with ARDs, and let us ask, about that world, a question analogous to the one that actually interests us here. Let us ask what programming limits it is reasonable to suppose one must accept, if the use of ARDs is to be morally defensible given our conservative assumption above (the assumption that there are both a priori and a posteriori limits on what one may justifiably do when acting in self-defense). Then, having answered this question (supposing an answer is possible), let us return to the question that actually interests us, to see whether our reflections about the limits it seems reasonable to suppose we would have to honor if we were to use ARDs have any relevance for the question with which we are actually concerned: namely, the question of just how much one may justifiably threaten and then do in the course of pursuing a self-defensive strategic policy of the sort defended above – an "ordinary-threat strategy," as I shall call it.

Some writers have suggested that it is unreasonable to suppose that there would be any moral limits at all on what one could rightly program an ARD to do in the sorts of circumstances that interest us: since anyone who does wrongful harm to me will have been warned of what would happen to him if he did so, he can have no reasonable objection to what I program the device to do to him.[17] I have no argument against this view. However, since at least as many people would reject it as would accept it,[18] I suggest the following move here, in line with the conservative strategy we are now pursuing (whereby we attempt to find those assumptions that are most broadly appealing and least controversial, while at the same time being assumptions that, like those suggested above, will give us far-reaching and seemingly quite important theoretical results). Let us suppose there *are* limits on what one may program an ARD to do and that they are analogous to what one may do in direct self-defense: one may not program the device to do any more than one reasonably believes one has to program it to do in order to deter the wrongful actions one is attempting to deter, and one may not, in any case, program it to do, for any given wrongful act, more than what one could justifiably do to prevent that particular act in a case of direct self-defense. The question, of course, is not whether the imposition of these limits will seem reasonable to those who accept no limits – obviously, it will not – but whether programming an ARD to act *within* these limits is something one can defend against a potential wrongdoer's claim that even *that* is more than one has a right to do in order to protect oneself against him.

[17] See Alexander, "The Doomsday Machine," pp. 199–227.

[18] See Farrell, "The Justification of Deterrent Violence"; and Quinn, "The Right to Threaten and the Right to Punish."

The answer to this last question, it seems to me, is that it clearly *is* something one can defend doing. To see this, recall that we are assuming that the use of ARDs is something that is in principle morally defensible. The question is merely whether we can say anything at all useful about the limits within which one must stay in using them. We are assuming for the sake of argument, of course, that there are some such limits. The question before us now is simply whether it is reasonable to suppose we have not gone beyond those limits if, in programming an ARD in any give case, we allow ourselves to go at least as far as we would feel entitled to go in an analogous case of direct self-defense, given conservative assumptions about what one is entitled to do in cases of that sort. I claim that it is reasonable to suppose that we have not. For suppose the likelihood of a successful attack is roughly the same, in the absence of a suitably programmed ARD, as would be the likelihood of attack in an analogous case of direct self-defense. If an attacker could not reasonably object, in the latter case, to being treated in a certain way—a way one reasonably believed it necessary to treat him if one were to repulse his attack—why should he be entitled to object to being treated in that same way by means of an ARD? Why, that is to say, should the harm one is entitled to inflict on another in defending oneself from him with an ARD be any different from that which one is entitled to inflict on him in a relevantly similar case of direct self-defense?

Suppose this line of argument is right. The next question is whether it is reasonable to believe that what is true of programming limits for ARDs is also true of the limits on what we may threaten and then do in the implementation of an ordinary-threat strategy. The answer to this question, it seems to me, is obvious enough: one ought to be allowed to threaten and then if necessary do, in the latter case, at least as much as one would be allowed to program an ARD to do in an analogous case. After all, the only difference, so far as our present interests are concerned, is that in the one case the device does the enforcing and in the other case one does it oneself. And surely this is not a difference that ought to make a difference, morally.[19]

IV. Concluding Remarks

Suppose what I have been saying is essentially correct. One important consequence is this: it at least *seems* that an account like the one I have

[19] Note that the account sketched above needs to be extended in a number of obvious ways. For example, the probability of attack is apparently not an important element, morally, in self-defense, or in the case of a threat-and-enforcement strategy, if we are imagining just a two-person world. However, in multi-person worlds, probabilities appear to be quite important, at least in the case of threat-and-enforcement strategies, so far as the justifiability of various penalties is concerned. Unfortunately, discussion of these and a number of related problems must await another occasion.

sketched would be able to provide a very solid basis indeed for an account of an institution very much like the institution of punishment—an institution whose raison d'être is the prevention of wrongful harm to the innocent, but whose moral basis is neither the utilitarian consequentialism rightly condemned by Kant and his twentieth-century followers, nor the compromised or "constrained" consequentialism adopted by Hart and his followers. Its moral basis is, rather, a fairly straightforward set of principles of distributive justice of the sort discussed and briefly defended above. Much more would need to be said, of course, in order to show how such a theory of punishment could be systematically and coherently worked out. Here I claim only to have provided at least a general outline of how such a theory might ultimately look, and to have provided, as well, at least some reason for thinking that a successful theory of this sort is a genuine possibility. Further development of these ideas would be worthwhile, I believe, precisely because (among other reasons) the account suggested here is so unlike most other accounts of punishment, both classical and modern: it avoids the seemingly very telling objections to both utilitarian and retributive approaches to punishment, while at the same time exploiting the idea that nearly all of these other theories systematically ignore—namely, that, at bottom, punishment is essentially a matter of justifiable self-defense.

Another interesting feature of the present account of the justification of deterrent activities, though, is this: it suggests, it seems to me, that a moral account of the use of threats, not to mention enforcements, in international relations must be based on principles importantly different from those on which the present account is based. This is because the principles on which the present account is based are principles that depend crucially on the fact that the threats it justifies are threats to harm those who would *themselves* otherwise wrongfully harm the threateners, while the enforcements it justifies are enforcements of threatened harm that are imposed solely on those who have wrongfully harmed those threateners despite antecedent warnings of what would be done to them if they so behaved. While such principles would be relevant *in a theoretical way* to conceivable strategies for dealing with potential international aggression, on a practical level they are bound to be of very limited use in this latter context. For in international relations it is almost inevitable that deterrent threats will involve threats of harm to the innocent—either directly and intentionally, as in certain strategies for nuclear deterrence, or indirectly and arguably unintentionally, as in certain "limited war" strategies. Thus, a great deal more work would need to be done before the present account could be applied, in a useful, realistic way, to the moral problems of international deterrence.

In the case of our ordinary institution of punishment, by contrast, the present reflections seem likely to be of far more practical relevance, as I have indicated; for here—at least for the most part[20]—we *threaten* to harm only those who knowingly and willingly choose to do wrongful harm to others. Hence, the preceding account of the justification of self-defensive threats and enforcements seems promising as a possible moral basis for an institution that has proven remarkably resistant, over the centuries, to a settled and generally accepted moral grounding. To be sure, much more needs to be said, even in general terms, before the present account can claim to constitute an interesting and compelling alternative to traditional accounts. In particular, the problem of unintended harm to the innocent, which is unavoidable in the real-world institution of punishment, remains to be discussed, as does the problem of how an essentially individualistic, state-of-nature account, like the one sketched above, can be reshaped as an account of how a real human community might decently attempt to constrain harmful wrongdoing by its members. Still, it seems reasonable to me to suppose that further reflection along the lines pursued above will, in the end, enable us to solve these and a host of other outstanding problems. Such, at any rate, is my present hope.

Philosophy, Ohio State University

[20] Crimes governed by laws of "strict liability" are an exception. This is as it should be, however, since many writers find such laws to be morally objectionable, while others, though finding them ultimately justifiable, admit that their justification requires an appeal to principles that are not required for the justification of the rest of the criminal law. For useful discussion, see Hart, *Punishment and Responsibility*, especially essays II, V, VI, VII, and IX.

THREE PROBLEMS WITH CONTRACTARIAN-CONSEQUENTIALIST WAYS OF ASSESSING SOCIAL INSTITUTIONS*

BY THOMAS W. POGGE

We can look at the events of our social world in two ways. On the one hand, we can see them interactionally: as actions, and consequences of actions, performed by individual and collective agents. On the other hand, we can see them institutionally: as effects of how our social world is structured—effects of our ground rules, practices, or social institutions. These two ways of viewing events lead to different descriptions and explanations of social phenomena. I will here discuss how they can also lead to different moral assessments.

I. INSTITUTIONAL MORAL ANALYSIS

During the last few decades, political philosophy has drifted from interactional toward institutional viewing. We ask less frequently how governments and their agencies and officials (as well as other agents in the political arena) ought to conduct themselves, and more frequently how social institutions ought to be designed. In the English-speaking world, this shift is largely due to John Rawls, who has reconceived justice as "the first virtue of social institutions."[1] It is worth noting, however, that the same shift shows up elsewhere as well—for example, in the German "critical theory" tradition. Having been an enthusiastic supporter of this shift, I will here examine some of its problems.

Talk of social institutions does not refer to organized collective agents such as General Motors or the Environmental Protection Agency; a focus on institutions in this sense would exemplify interactional moral analysis. Rather, institutions are a social system's practices or "rules of the game," which govern interactions among (individual and collective) agents as well as their access to material resources. Institutions define and regulate property, the division of labor, sexual and kinship relations, con-

* Work on this essay was supported by a Laurance S. Rockefeller fellowship at the Princeton University Center for Human Values. Many thanks also to Marko Ahtisaari, Richard Arneson, Christian Barry, Hilary Bok, Tony Coady, Peter de Marneffe, Amy Gutmann, Alan Houston, Hidé Ishiguro, Yasuo Iwata, Francis Kamm, George Kateb, Bonnie Kent, Andrew Koppelman, Arthur Kuflik, Sidney Morgenbesser, Liam Murphy, Thomas Nagel, Takeshi Ohba, Debra Satz, Ling Tong, and the editors of this volume for all their critical help.

[1] John Rawls, *A Theory of Justice* (Cambridge, MA: Harvard University Press, 1971), p. 3.

trol over and responsibility for children, as well as political and economic competition; and they govern how collective projects are undertaken and executed, how conflicts are settled, and how social institutions themselves are created, revised, interpreted, and enforced. The totality of the more fundamental and pervasive institutions of a social system may be called its basic structure (as Rawls calls it) or institutional scheme.

Later we will need the distinction between the rules of the game as it is supposed to be played, according to some ideal blueprint laid down perhaps in the law books, and the rules of the game as it is actually played. Of course, these two need not diverge, but they generally do—as when particular conduct is in theory to be punished, but in practice generally ignored by the relevant authorities. I will use the term "ground rules" to refer to the official rules of the game, and "practices" or "institutions" to refer to how such ground rules are actually understood, implemented, and followed.

The concern with social institutions is motivated by an increasing appreciation of their importance—and of their *increasing* importance—for human welfare. We have gradually come to understand how deeply the structure of our society shapes our conduct—not merely by determining in large part a person's menu of options and the various incentives and disincentives attached to them, but also by influencing rather profoundly what interests, desires, and abilities persons develop in the first place. Moreover, human lives are increasingly interdependent, affecting one another through highly complex networks of interrelations. This trend is well illustrated by our modern practices of economic cooperation, with their extended markets for goods, services, and capital, through which our decisions may intensely affect the livelihoods of unknown others over great distances. Because such effects result from the confluence of decisions made independently by a multitude of agents, it is unfeasible to hold such agents morally accountable for those effects; we cannot plausibly blame particular market participants for widespread homelessness and unemployment. Yet we also cannot plausibly view these as natural calamities on a par with the striking of a large meteorite. A straightforward solution to this dilemma is to view the participants in an institutional scheme as having not merely an individual moral responsibility for their conduct within it, but also a shared collective moral responsibility for its terms. If a laissez-faire market scheme tends to produce more severe and more widespread poverty than some feasible alternative ways of arranging the economy, and if this poverty is morally regrettable, then, other things equal, we should support institutional reforms toward such an alternative. It is our common moral task and duty as citizens to set and reset the institutional parameters of our society in light of their foreseeable morally relevant effects. Moreover, this is not part of a wide-ranging and weak positive duty to do something to improve the world, but a sharp and strong negative duty not to collaborate in the imposition of an unjust institutional scheme without working toward institutional reform or at least helping the victims of injustice.

What this negative duty comes to more concretely depends on a variety of factors: Which institutional schemes can I be said to participate in—for example, am I a participant in a global scheme of trade and diplomacy, and thus co-responsible for its effects? How do we assess institutional alternatives in order to determine whether an existing scheme really is unjust? What reforms of any unjust institutional scheme I participate in are feasible? What can I do to promote such reforms, and what can I do to support the victims of those unjust institutional schemes?

Institutional viewing, though suggested by cases like that of complex economic interrelations which resist interactional moral analysis, is not confined to cases of that sort. If a legal requirement of regular safety-inspections of automobiles tends to reduce the incidence of serious traffic accidents, and if the burdens imposed by the requirement are of comparatively minor moral significance, then we ought to institute this requirement. Here it is not implausible, when the requirement is absent, to attribute moral responsibility to individuals: those who own or operate unsafe automobiles can quite plausibly be held morally accountable for any resulting accidents. One can nevertheless locate an additional, shared moral responsibility at the collective level. One can say that the citizenry at large is responsible for imposing a scheme that, without offering important compensating benefits, foreseeably produces an excessively and avoidably high rate of traffic casualties.

Saying this seems compelling: for why should it matter whether harm we could prevent by changing the rules can or cannot also be seen as the responsibility of agents? Compare a fair tax code that does not work well because it is too complex for people to follow correctly with another one that works equally poorly because it is difficult to monitor and thus leads to widespread noncompliance. Ought we not change each of these codes, and for the same basic reason?

II. The Contractarian-Consequentialist Approach

Once we view our social world institutionally, we will be drawn to a broadly consequentialist mode of assessment: an institutional scheme is just, or good, if it is on the whole better for the persons living under it than its alternatives would be.[2] In the case of conduct, such a "recipient-based" mode of assessment is at least problematic, if not implausible:

[2] Such formulations can be found not only in Rawls and in utilitarian authors, but also on the Continent—for example, in Jürgen Habermas, *Moralbewußtsein und kommunikatives Handeln* (Frankfurt: Suhrkamp, 1983), pp. 75f., where Habermas proposes that social norms should be assessed by reference to the interests of all those affected by them. (For an English translation, see Jürgen Habermas, *Moral Consciousness and Communicative Action*, trans. C. Lenhardt and S. W. Nicholsen [Cambridge, MA: MIT Press, 1990].)

most would want to bring in the standpoint of the agent as well, and make morally significant the distinctions between harms she intends and harms she merely foresees, between harms she brings about and harms she merely allows to happen, and/or other distinctions concerning how an agent is related to the effects of her conduct.[3]

This agent's standpoint seems to have no analogue when the assessment is not of conduct but of ground rules or practices or institutional schemes. The latter are mere means for regulating our interactions so that we all have a better life; thus, there seems to be no reason for giving moral significance to any distinctions between different classes of effects that ground rules might have—for example, to the distinction between the benefits and burdens specifically called for by an institutional scheme, and others that merely foreseeably come about under it. The moral assessment of ground rules should then be entirely recipient-based—a point nicely expressed in the contractarian image of an ideal institutional scheme chosen prudentially by its prospective participants.[4] Such prospective participants (or their representatives) will be interested exclusively in results: in the quality of life they can expect under this or that institutional scheme. They will not care how these results come about: through desert or luck, through decree or voting, through birth or the market—except insofar as these mechanisms themselves affect the quality of their lives.

Adopting a prospective-participant perspective, we will take the justice (J) of institutional schemes to be a function of the quality of the individual lives (Q_i) each tends to produce: $J = f(Q_i)$. Much of the discussion in political philosophy in the English-speaking world these days is about how—perhaps through some hypothetical-contract story—to fill in the two key terms (Q_i and f) in this broadly consequentialist equation: Should the relevant notion of the good for individuals be specified in subjective terms (human happiness, desire fulfillment, preference satisfaction, pain avoidance, or opportunity for welfare) or in objective terms (human rights, resources, social primary goods, capabilities, or the fulfillment of human needs)? And should social institutions maximize the sum total, the arithmetic or geometric mean, the bottom level (Rawls's maximin), or equality in the distribution, of quality of life? I will not worry here about which of the many possible combinations within and across

[3] We generally do not believe, for example, that neglecting to save someone is morally on a par with killing her. Nor do we think that one ought to kill whenever doing so will save a larger number from being killed. We admit that it might be better for people in general if we accepted these principles. The disposition to kill one for the sake of saving several may be desirable from the standpoint of others at large. But we do not let the recipients' standpoint alone settle the matter.

[4] I use "contractarian" in reference to the idea of a *hypothetical* social contract (as opposed to, e.g., a historical one). Though my primary example is Rawls, I mean to include more thinly veiled social contracts as exemplified by David Gauthier, *Morals by Agreement* (Cambridge: Cambridge University Press, 1987).

clarity of my challenges by making them more concrete and by placing them in a familiar setting. My claim is, however, that the difficulties I discuss arise for almost any presently proposed moral conception that focuses on appraising social institutions in a contractarian or broadly consequentialist way.

III. The Problem of Natural Inequalities

Rawls's conception of justice has been criticized for being insensitive to natural differences among persons—to the greater health-care needs of the sickly, the greater textile needs of the tall, and the greater food needs of those with higher metabolic rates, for example.[10] This criticism can be presented as an internal critique of Rawls's position: what quality of life each participant can attain under any institutional scheme depends not only on her share of the benefits and burdens whose distribution is regulated by this scheme (her rights and duties, income and wealth, powers and opportunities), but also on her natural (genetic) features. Prospective participants therefore have reason to want the institutional scheme that takes account of these features in an optimal way. If they use Rawls's maximin rule, for example, they have reason to insure themselves against natural handicaps by preferring schemes under which the naturally handicapped are favored in the distribution of social goods.[11]

At first blush, this critique looks like a friendly amendment which Rawls should welcome with open arms. After all, aren't decent people agreed that (at least in a wealthy society) social institutions should favor those born with physiological handicaps? But then there are other dimensions of natural difference with regard to which the consensus would seem to go the other way: A homely physique, for example, or a disposition toward melancholy, clearly reduce quality of life; few believe, however, that justice mandates social institutions that favor persons with *these* natural features. Yet such institutions are exactly what prospective participants would prefer, if the internal critique of Rawls is valid.

Here is a simple illustration. Imagine a society with three social classes. Higher education is free, but scarce: 50 percent of each age cohort are admitted by lot. Those so educated will—depending on their endowments, motivation, and luck—end up in one of the top two classes. Those

[10] Amartya K. Sen is the most prominent of these critics. See "Equality of What?" in his *Choice, Welfare, and Measurement* (Cambridge: Cambridge University Press, 1982), esp. p. 366; and his *Inequality Reexamined* (Cambridge, MA: Harvard University Press, 1992), esp. pp. 79–87.

[11] Someone using the maximin rule of decision making strives to *max*imize her *min*imum pay-off. In the case at hand, prospective participants using the maximin rule would rank alternative institutional schemes by the worst social position each would produce: if one institutional scheme produces a superior bottom position than another, then the former is preferred to the latter because it secures a higher minimum.

not so educated will—depending on the same factors—end up in one of the bottom two. There are then four segments: the fully educated in the top class (FT), the fully educated in the middle class (FM), the less educated in the middle class (LM), and the less educated in the bottom class (LB). Each segment contains a quarter of the population.

Sixty percent of the population have attractive natural features (A), while the remaining 40 percent are unattractive (U).[12] While the unattractive bear some genetic handicap, which reduces the quality of their private lives (love and friendship, self-respect), they are not sick or otherwise dysfunctional. Nor does their handicap result in any economic disadvantage: since the unattractive do not differ from the attractive in regard to talents, motivation, and luck, and are not treated any worse in the public sphere, they are proportionately represented in all four segments. There are then altogether eight relevant groups: FTA (15 percent), FTU (10 percent), FMA (15 percent), FMU (10 percent), LMA (15 percent), LMU (10 percent), LBA (15 percent), and LBU (10 percent).

The following reform is proposed. The unattractive should be entitled to automatic admission to college, and only the remaining openings should be filled by lottery. Given our stipulation, this reform would not affect economic performance (the unattractive are just as talented and motivated as the population at large), so incomes in all segments would remain the same. The only change would be in how the attractive and the unattractive distribute over the four segments: FTA (5 percent), FTU (20 percent), FMA (5 percent), FMU (20 percent), LMA (25 percent), and LBA (25 percent). Groups LMU and LBU would not exist.

Rational prospective participants using the maximin rule would, on the face of it, choose principles that support this reform. For the worst-off group under the reformed scheme is either FMU or LBA; and both of these groups are clearly better off than LBU under the unreformed scheme.[13]

This result would be welcomed by those who believe that the institutions of a just society must compensate persons not merely for severe handicaps that affect health, but also for all other involuntary factors neg-

[12] We can specify this notion in various ways, for example, as physical attractiveness, as being disposed toward a cheerful temper, or as some combination of the two.

[13] Variants of this example work for CC conceptions that use an aggregation function other than maximin. If a CC conception specifies f as averaging (conceives prospective participants as maximizing probability-weighted expectations), for instance, the example could stipulate (as seems plausible empirically) that the attractive and the unattractive differ in the extent to which education and income differentials affect their quality of life: a given advantage in education or income means more to the unattractive, because it contributes more to their chances of achieving rewarding personal lives. As in the example in the text, institutions should then be designed so as to favor the unattractive in the distribution of such advantages. For the sake of simplicity, the examples are somewhat crude. The same point could be made through illustrations involving more fine-grained or even scalar dimensions, more dimensions than our three (education, class, genetic attractiveness), or correlations between class and talents or class and motivation.

atively affecting quality of life, such as homeliness, cheerlessness, and low intelligence.[14] But most of us do not share this belief. If we are committed to the CC approach nevertheless, we must explain why prospective participants would *not* find it rational to adopt principles that take account of *all* natural handicaps and deficiencies.

Rawls does not give any such explanation. He presumes that prospective participants have three higher-order interests.[15] Though the extent to which a person can fulfill her third higher-order interest—can "protect and advance some determinate (but unspecified) conceptions of the good over a complete life"[16]—is clearly affected by her natural features, including attractiveness, Rawls concludes that the parties would adopt a criterion of justice (the "two principles") that is formulated in terms of (social) primary goods among which attractiveness is not included.[17] He leaves unexplained why the parties do not choose natural attractiveness as a primary good to be incorporated into their criterion. Why do they not

[14] See, for example, Richard Arneson, "A Defense of Equal Opportunity for Welfare," *Philosophical Studies*, vol. 62, no. 2 (May 1991); G. A. Cohen, "On the Currency of Egalitarian Justice," *Ethics*, vol. 99, no. 4 (July 1989); and John Roemer, *A Future for Socialism* (Cambridge, MA: Harvard University Press, 1994), especially the section on what socialists want. Amartya Sen (*supra* note 10) may not belong on this list. To me, at least, his examples suggest that he envisions a conception of justice that is not sensitive to *all* natural inequalities that affect quality of life (as colloquially understood).

[15] See John Rawls, *Political Liberalism* (New York: Columbia University Press, 1993), pp. 74f., 106.

[16] *Ibid.*, p. 74. The other two higher-order interests are the interests in developing and exercising the two moral powers (*ibid.*), namely,

> a capacity for a sense of justice and a capacity for a conception of the good. A sense of justice is the capacity to understand, to apply, and to act from the public conception of justice which characterizes the fair terms of social cooperation. Given the nature of the political conception as specifying a public basis of justification, a sense of justice also expresses a willingness, if not the desire, to act in relation to others on terms that they also can publicly endorse. . . . The capacity for a conception of the good is the capacity to form, to revise, and rationally to pursue a conception of one's rational advantage or good. (*Ibid.*, p. 19)

[17] In *Political Liberalism*, Rawls formulates his two principles of justice as follows. First principle: "Each person has an equal claim to a fully adequate scheme of equal basic rights and liberties, which scheme is compatible with the same scheme for all; and in this scheme the equal political liberties, and only those liberties, are to be guaranteed their fair value" (*ibid.*, p. 5). Second principle: "Social and economic inequalities are to satisfy two conditions: first, they are to be attached to positions and offices open to all under conditions of fair equality of opportunity [the opportunity principle]; and second, they are to be to the greatest benefit of the least advantaged members of society [the difference principle]" (*ibid.*, p. 6). The first principle is to have lexical priority over the second and, within the second principle, the opportunity principle is to have lexical priority over the difference principle (Rawls, *A Theory of Justice*, p. 302f.). The word "lexical" is short for "lexicographical" (*ibid.*, p. 42f.). The paradigm case of a lexical priority is this: when arranging words alphabetically, as in a lexicon, one gives priority to the first letter over the second, to the second over the third, and so on. For example, one lists all words beginning with an "a" ahead of all words beginning with a "b" regardless of the second and subsequent letters—as when "azure" is listed ahead of "baal." Rawls conceives the priority of one principle over another along the same lines: in the comparison of basic structures, an advantage in terms of a lexically prior principle overrides any disadvantage in terms of lexically subordinate ones.

insist that poor and unattractive persons should count as worse off than equally poor but attractive ones, seeing that the former clearly face inferior prospects of fulfilling their third higher-order interest than the latter do?

One might base such an explanation on pragmatic grounds: The proposed reform would make being-naturally-unattractive socially more salient and thereby render the handicap more hurtful (imagine tax forms inquiring about ugliness as they now do about blindness). The reform would be socially divisive, because there are no clear and generally acceptable standards by reference to which citizens could be graded for natural handicap in a publicly accessible way, and also because citizens are liable to disagree about how significantly such handicaps reduce one's quality of life and about what would constitute adequate compensation. Finally, the reform might lead to perverse incentives: to persons (being suspected of) pretending to be naturally handicapped by altering their appearance and/or conduct. These pragmatic considerations cannot be lightly dismissed. Still, I wonder whether enough pragmatic arguments can be found to convince prospective participants that they should not take account of *any* natural inequalities beyond the uncontroversial ones involving serious physical handicaps. Moreover, such pragmatic arguments seem to involve a distortion of the grounds on which it is widely believed that our social institutions need not favor the homely and the cheerless in order to compensate them for their handicap: people see no *moral* reason why citizens should have to compensate one another for such misfortunes.

For these reasons, I have previously tried to explain in a principled way why only *social* goods and their distributions should be deemed relevant to the comparative assessment of alternative institutional schemes.[18] This strategy now strikes me as ad hoc, however: in order to derive the contract we want, we would have to tell the hypothetical contracting parties what is blatantly false—namely, that natural (genetic) differences among persons do not, under any circumstances, affect their quality of life. Without this disinformation, rational parties would demand that, insofar as quality of life *is* affected by differentially distributed natural features, a basic structure should be considered more or less just depending on how well the distribution of social goods it generates fits the distribution of natural features—with fit measured by reference to the distribution of overall quality of life that arises from the superimposition of the two (the social upon the natural) distributions.[19]

[18] See Thomas W. Pogge, *Realizing Rawls* (Ithaca: Cornell University Press, 1989), pp. 44–47, 114–16, 183–89. I also show there that CC conceptions meeting this constraint (I called them "semiconsequentialist") can accommodate our conviction that the distribution of health care should favor those with greater health problems by defining the relevant social good as "access to health care when needed."

[19] This demand would generally lead to institutions favoring the naturally handicapped, even if the parties do not employ the maximin rule. But there could be exceptions. It might

IV. The Problem of Group Inequities

While the CC approach would seem to be too sensitive to certain natural inequalities, it may not be sensitive enough to group inequities. CC conceptions assess institutions in terms of their effects upon individual persons: if two alternative institutional schemes would generate identical distributional profiles, then they are equally just. Intuitively we are convinced, however, that the justice of an institutional scheme also depends on the extent to which it allows certain involuntary and morally arbitrary factors (such as gender, race, the status of one's parents) to influence who ends up where on the distributional scales—the greater this influence, the more unjust (*ceteris paribus*) the scheme. This moral conviction cannot be reaffirmed within a CC conception. A prospective participant cares solely about the share she can expect under each scheme (that is, about the distributional profile it produces) and not about how these shares (distributional profiles) are produced. Rawls, of course, has a principle of fair equality of opportunity that forbids some group inequities (those based on initial social class—the status of one's parents);[20] but I see no way of supporting anything like his opportunity principle through the original position.

Let me give an illustration which involves the choice of a basic structure for a relatively simple society.[21] We take for granted that Rawls's first principle and *formal* equality of opportunity must be satisfied. Applying the difference principle within the remaining option space, we get a society with two classes: the more privileged (P) and the less privileged (L). As children, persons belong to the class of their parents; as adults, their class is determined by their professional position. Thus, there are four possibilities: PP (born among the privileged and holding a privileged position as an adult), LP, PL, and LL. Talents, motivation, and luck are roughly equally distributed among children of the two classes. The top-flight education necessary for a privileged position is expensive, however, and only very few less-privileged parents make the sacrifices necessary

---

be argued, for instance, that lack of access to higher education generally reduces the quality of life of gifted persons more dramatically than, and (other things equal) below, that of the less gifted. Contracting parties presumed to know this would then have reason to prefer institutions under which the naturally *better* endowed are favored in the distribution of the social good education.

[20] The principle requires that "those who are at the same level of talent and ability, and have the same willingness to use them, should have the same prospects of success regardless of their initial place in the social system, that is, irrespective of the income class into which they were born" (Rawls, *A Theory of Justice*, p. 73, cf. pp. 275, 301). Does fair equality of opportunity rule out group inequities involving race and gender as well? Rawls does not incorporate this constraint—perhaps because he believes that formal equality of opportunity (together with the first principle of justice) suffices to wash out race-induced and gender-induced inequalities over time.

[21] This illustration uses class-induced inequalities in order to stay as close as possible to Rawls's formulation of fair equality of opportunity.

to give their children such an education. This basic structure (S_1) engenders the following income distribution:

S_1:	Average Annual Income over Lifetime[22]	Percentage of Population
PP_1	180	9%
LP_1	170	1%
PL_1	110	1%
LL_1	100	89%
Weighted Average	108	

S_1 violates *fair* equality of opportunity. Those born into less privileged families—though they exhibit the same distribution of natural talents, motivation, and luck—have much less of a chance (one in ninety) to attain a privileged position than those born into privileged families (nine in ten). Nevertheless, S_1 satisfies economic efficiency and the difference principle: enough children are born into privileged families and well educated at their parents' expense to ensure that leadership positions (including those that require not only a superior education but also exceptional talents and motivation) are filled well.

Fair equality of opportunity could be achieved by reforming the education system so that the same limited number of superior educations are provided at public expense and distributed through a lottery scheme. This reform will have some economic cost, as people would have less of an incentive to work hard to attain privileged positions: one advantage of occupying such a position—the freedom to guarantee a superior education to one's children—would be absent.[23] Applying the difference principle within this much narrower option-space (readjusting tax rates, etc.), we get an alternative basic structure (S_2) which engenders the following income distribution:

[22] I have designed the example so that the inequality in average annual incomes is very modest indeed (compared to present realities), in order to reassure the reader that the fair value of the political liberties is really being maintained and that the difference principle is really satisfied.

[23] It may be said that I have not told a plausible story showing that the maintenance of fair equality of opportunity can have net costs; if so, another such story can be substituted. One might further object that the difficulty I indicate cannot arise at all, because maintaining fair equality of opportunity has important benefits that will *always* outweigh any costs. This strikes me as unlikely. Even if it were a fact, however, it would not support the *inherent* moral importance that Rawls (and most of us) attach to the avoidance of class inequities. Fair equality of opportunity would not be demanded in its own right by justice (by prudent prospective participants), but would come about as a merely contingent by-product of the realization of economic efficiency or the difference principle. This scenario would confirm, not defeat, my claim that CC conceptions cannot explain why fair equality of opportunity should have any moral standing in and of itself. I am indebted to Ling Tong for this objection and subsequent discussion.

S_2:	Average Annual Income over Lifetime[24]	Percentage of Population
PP_2	162	1%
LP_2	153	9%
PL_2	99	9%
LL_2	90	81%
Weighted Average	97.2	

The reform eliminates the intuitive injustice Rawls meant to rule out with his requirement of fair equality of opportunity. It ensures that those similarly endowed and motivated have similar chances of success irrespective of their initial social class. But why in the world should rational prospective participants care about this effect of the reform? Who benefits from the elimination of class-induced inequalities?

Rawls is specially constrained in answering this question: given that his parties use the maximin rule, he must be able to say that the worst off benefit. Now the worst off under both basic structures are the members of LL. Comparing across schemes, we must conclude that the members of LL_2 are surely worse off than the members of LL_1: they are just as much excluded from a superior education and their income is lower by 10 percent.

One might say that under S_2 at least there are fewer persons in LL. This will not help, however, because group PL_2 is also worse off than LL_1; thus, the union of LL_2 and PL_2 is both larger and worse off on average than LL_1.

It might also be said that prospective participants would care not about lifetime income (*ex post*), but about expected lifetime income (*ex ante*).[25] But this suggestion does not work either: it entails that prospective participants would not care how unequally given benefits and burdens are distributed so long as the distribution is based on a fair neonatal lottery (so that everyone has the same *expected* pay-off); this is absurd. Moreover, it does not even support the desired conclusion. For the expected lifetime income of those born less privileged under S_1 is $(170 \times 1\% + 100 \times 89\%) \div 90\% = 100.78$. Under S_2 it would be worse, namely $(153 \times 9\% + 90 \times 81\%) \div 90\% = 96.30$.

Another tack is to say that group LL_2 is better off than LL_1 because they live in a society without class inequities, but this just begs the ques-

[24] To ensure comparability between this and the previous table, let us assume that any expenditures for education are counted not as income of those adults who pay them (parents under S_1, and taxpayers under S_2), but as income of the youngsters who are receiving the educational benefit.

[25] Rawls explicitly repudiates this idea. See John Rawls, "Social Unity and Primary Goods," in *Utilitarianism and Beyond*, ed. Amartya K. Sen and Bernard Williams (Cambridge: Cambridge University Press, 1982), p. 164.

tion: a society should maintain fair equality of opportunity because that way its members will enjoy the benefit of living in a society that maintains fair equality of opportunity. The stipulation that the parties to the social contract care very much that life prospects not be influenced by initial social class simply builds the desired conclusion into the premises. I will say more about such "gimmicky"—as Robert Nozick likes to say[26]—argumentative strategies below (Section VC, penultimate paragraph).

Perhaps this stipulation can be defended in a more empirical way, however. Perhaps it is true that the members of LL_2 derive considerable comfort and self-respect from the knowledge that others, born into the same class as themselves, do and will receive a superior education and lead a life of privilege. It is clear why the members of LP_2—and today's beneficiaries of affirmative action—should like to think so. Nevertheless, it is an empirical question: Are the lives of ordinary workers from working-class backgrounds really improved by the knowledge that others from a working-class background succeed in becoming doctors, lawyers, and executives? Do black cleaning ladies, for example, really gain (or might they even *lose*) self-respect from knowing that other blacks, and women, ascend through the glass ceiling?[27] And is the benefit conferred by this knowledge sufficient to support a preference for LL_2 over LL_1?

CC conceptions other than Rawls's focus not only on the least advantaged but on other social groups as well. Still they all face the same difficulty and challenge. To be able to reaffirm the deep and widespread commitment to fair equality of opportunity, a CC conception must show how the required elimination of group inequities benefits individuals and how the benefits for those who gain outweigh both (a) the burdens on those who lose and (b) the general burdens on the economy. One can see most clearly how my example is troublesome for *all* CC conceptions, if one divides the populations under each of our two basic structures into percentiles and then compares down the list, percentile by percentile, across the two schemes. While there is no difference in education and relative incomes, absolute incomes are smaller under S_2 at each and every percentile.

It may be thought that my discussion of the moral comparison between S_1 and S_2 should carry no weight because I have freely stipulated the

[26] Robert Nozick, *Anarchy, State, and Utopia* (New York: Basic Books, 1974), p. 157n.

[27] The answer may well depend on whether they have offspring or not. Those who do will probably care about their children's and grandchildren's chances of occupying privileged positions. Interestingly, this offspring argument could work only for race and class, but not for gender: in the first two cases, fair equality of opportunity benefits the offspring of the worst off—those from the lowest class or of the currently most disfavored race. Fair equality of opportunity for women, by contrast, benefits one's offspring only if one's offspring are predominantly female. Assuming zero correlation between social disadvantage and predominantly female offspring, and assuming also that disadvantaged mothers do not care more for their daughters than for their sons, we cannot then argue that fair equality of opportunity for women is in the interest of the worst off because it benefits their offspring.

empirical facts that lead to the numbers presented in the two tables to suit my convenience. But then Rawls's thought experiment is supposed to give plausible guidance for institutional comparisons under *all* reasonably possible empirical assumptions about the net costs of maintaining fair equality of opportunity. This universal claim can be defeated by producing *one* set of assumptions under which it does not give plausible guidance. As to whether my empirical assumptions are reasonably possible for at least some societal context, see footnote 23.

A last remark: Even if, as I have tried to show, CC conceptions fail to reaffirm our convictions about how social institutions should accommodate natural inequalities, and also fail to reaffirm our commitment to fair equality of opportunity, their adherents may still claim that the fault lies not with the CC approach, but with our convictions. I will come back to this point in Section VI.

V. The Problem of Noncompliance

I have so far briefly discussed two problems that arise within the CC approach: the problem of natural inequalities and the problem of group inequities. The third and final problem—which is actually a set of related difficulties involving noncompliance—will be discussed at greater length. If Rawls himself has not run up against these difficulties, it is perhaps because he has largely and increasingly confined his attention to a rather ideal version of ideal theory. In this first approximation to a full theory of justice, the choice, specification, and application of a criterion for the comparative assessment of institutional schemes is based upon the unrealistic assumption that any chosen ground rules will be fully complied with by every participant at all times. The difficulties I will now discuss arise in what Rawls calls "partial-compliance theory," where the comparative assessment of sets of ground rules begins to take account of the extent to which each set of rules would actually engender compliance. The rules prospective participants would prefer given universal compliance may not be the ones they would prefer once they consider the degree of compliance each set of rules would actually engender. Rawls has largely neglected this important topic,[28] and the advocates of competing CC conceptions have followed him in this.

Rawls holds that prospective participants (characterized by the three higher-order interests) would be primarily concerned to enjoy certain basic freedoms, such as liberty of conscience, freedom of movement, and

[28] He envisions a second stage, after ideal theory, in which the preferred conception of justice and the ground rules it selects are tested for stability. This test is conceived as an either-or affair and is never integrated with the results of the first stage. Rawls never aims for an *overall* appraisal of alternative institutional schemes, an appraisal that would take account of how each would actually work in practice (degree of stability, incidence of noncompliance, etc.). See, for instance, his *Political Liberalism*, pp. 64, 133f., 140f.

integrity of the person. Guaranteeing the enjoyment of these freedoms is then the preeminent task of social institutions, as laid down in his first principle of justice.

Once we bear in mind that full compliance with legal norms is not a universal feature of human societies, it is clear that prospective participants would not settle for a written commitment to these freedoms in assorted legal documents. They care not about legal rights *as such,* but about their objects: about whether they will actually enjoy the freedoms in question. Legal enumeration is a means to this end—perhaps a necessary means under modern conditions, but certainly not a sufficient one, as is demonstrated by various "showcase" constitutions around the world.[29] Rawls himself has made this point on occasion: "Whether the basic structure guarantees equal liberty of conscience, or freedom of thought, is settled by the content of the rights and liberties defined by the institutions of the basic structure and how they are actually interpreted and enforced."[30] What matters in regard to the first principle, then, is not whether a citizen is legally entitled to certain freedoms on paper, but whether she securely enjoys these freedoms themselves.

While it is quite clear—textually and systematically—that this is his view, Rawls has paid far more attention to the scope of these freedoms than to the security of their enjoyment. He thereby bypasses a crucial problem for the lexical priority he postulates for his first principle. The problem is this. There is no realistic hope for a human society in which basic freedoms are absolutely secure, yet Rawls wants it to be realistically possible for his first principle to be fully satisfied. Therefore, this principle must be read as requiring that the basic freedoms it covers merely be *reasonably* secure. The principle will then have a clear meaning, will fulfill its intended function within a standard for assessing social institutions, only if, for each basic freedom, some security threshold is specified—a threshold one can refer to in order to judge whether the enjoyment of some particular basic freedom by some particular participant under some particular institutional scheme is reasonably secure or not.[31] Without such thresholds, the theory is overly vague. But with such thresholds it involves a highly implausible discontinuity. Insecure enjoyment below the threshold is an injustice of the first order, and societies must enhance security through institutional reforms regardless of the economic cost. Insecure enjoyment above the threshold is a matter of moral indifference,

[29] I have in mind constitutions whose words are highly protective of civil rights and democratic procedures but bear little or no relation to the realities in the relevant country. The successive constitutions of the USSR are a clearcut example, as are many constitutions in present and former Third World dictatorships and one-party regimes.

[30] Rawls, "Social Unity and Primary Goods," p. 163.

[31] Such a security threshold would presumably be defined in terms of frequency-based probabilities. Here one may need to take account of various personal characteristics. Thus, it is quite possible that a certain basic freedom is reasonably secure for some citizens (defined by wealth, geography, race, gender, or age, for example) but not for others.

and societies need not achieve greater security even when doing so is cheap and easy.[32] However the requisite security thresholds may be defined, it is unclear why we, or prospective participants, should attach such tremendous importance to them.

Rawls does not specify or envisage security thresholds, and so his conception faces the problem of excessive vagueness. Every institutional scheme leaves citizens' basic freedoms insecure to some extent, and we have no way of judging whether it nevertheless satisfies the first principle or not. This is not merely a philosophical point, but also an eminently practical and political one. What must a society be like to secure the freedom and integrity of the person,[33] for example? What if opponents of government policies are occasionally roughed up by police when they demonstrate for their convictions; how often can this happen without contradicting the justice of a society's basic structure? What if 20 percent of all women are raped, or 1 percent of all black men murdered, within ten years of reaching age sixteen? Without answers to such questions, the consensus around Rawls's first principle of justice is in large part deceptive: it is unclear what it would mean to apply or realize this principle.

The partial-compliance problem I have just described is specific to Rawls's CC conception—it arises from his postulate of the first principle as both satiable and lexically prior. The related difficulties I shall now discuss arise for any CC conception. Citizens' quality of life—however conceived—may be affected by the government and its officials on the one hand and by other (individual and collective) agents on the other. Citizens are roughed up by the police and by gangsters, killed by executioners and by drunk drivers, imprisoned in jails and in basements, tortured by secret services and by private death squads.

In aiming for institutions that minimize such abuses, a CC conception will treat both kinds of abuses as on a par; that is, it will be insensitive to how given effects of social institutions come about. Taking the perspective of a prospective participant, one will consider social institutions under which one's physical integrity is endangered by crime to be, other things equal, just as bad as ones under which one's physical integrity is equally endangered through government officials. And this leads to the final problem I shall discuss: a CC conception of justice may require social institutions that permit and even encourage government officials to invade citizens' basic freedoms or fundamental interests, if these institutions minimize such invasions overall. It is quite likely that such trade-offs

[32] The discontinuity could be somewhat mitigated: justice demands, one might say, that the basic liberties be made more secure than the first principle mandates, and this demand is on a par with, and to be balanced against, the demands of either the opportunity principle or the difference principle.

[33] This is said to include that one be free "from psychological oppression and physical assault." See John Rawls, "Reply to Alexander and Musgrave," *Quarterly Journal of Economics*, vol. 88, no. 4 (November 1974), p. 640.

would be worthwhile in our own social world. I will illustrate this claim in regard to three topics within the criminal law.

A. The definition of criminal offenses

For the first topic, we can begin with an example Rawls gives in a brief foray into partial-compliance theory:

> Suppose that, aroused by sharp religious antagonisms, members of rival sects are collecting weapons and forming armed bands in preparation for civil strife. Confronted with this situation, the government may enact a statute forbidding the possession of firearms. . . . And the law may hold that sufficient evidence for conviction is that the weapons are found in the defendant's house or property, unless he can establish that they were put there by another. Except for this proviso, the absence of intent and knowledge of possession, and conformity to reasonable standards of care, are declared irrelevant. . . . Now although this statute trespasses upon the precept ought implies can it might be accepted by the representative citizen as a lesser loss of liberty, at least if the penalties imposed are not too severe. . . . Citizens may affirm the law as the lesser of two evils, resigning themselves to the fact that while they may be held guilty for things they have not done, the risks to their liberty on any other course would be worse.[34]

Rawls refers to cases of this sort as "extreme eventualities,"[35] but they are not so far from our reality today. With firearms being used in the United States to wound and kill tens of thousands of persons each year, it may certainly seem that it would be, on balance, a gain for the representative citizen, if possession of firearms were prohibited with the kind of strict-liability statute Rawls contemplates.

What is at stake in his hypothetical example is the venerable precept that *mens rea* (a "guilty mind") ought to be a necessary condition of criminality and hence a prerequisite for any severe punishment. This precept does not require that the defendant must have intended or foreseen the harm she is to be held legally accountable for, or a significant probability of such harm (as in recklessness). Even merely negligent conduct is normally deemed sufficient to satisfy the *mens rea* condition: agents *can* act without negligence. The problem with the strict-liability law Rawls entertains is that even those who take great care to abide by it, and thus

[34] Rawls, *A Theory of Justice*, p. 242. The quote shows nicely how his commitment to the prospective-participant perspective attenuates the uplifting idea (chosen for the cover of the paperback) that "[e]ach person possesses an inviolability founded on justice that even the welfare of society as a whole cannot override" (*ibid.*, p. 3).

[35] *Ibid.*, p. 242.

are not even ever so slightly negligent, may be convicted under it—for example, a woman who searched her house and grounds frequently for weapons and, though she knows someone else must have put the weapon on her property, cannot prove that this is so.

Once we countenance the broadly consequentialist reasoning suggested by a prospective-participant perspective, we are likely to find ourselves attracted to strict-liability laws in cases where criminal conduct with *mens rea* can be significantly reduced through the extra deterrence that comes from the general knowledge that pretending to lack *mens rea* will be to no avail.[36] Cases in which such pretensions are hard to refute are many: speeders often claim that their cruise control or speedometer malfunctioned; drunk drivers claim that they had no idea the punch contained (so much) alcohol; drug runners claim not to know how the drugs got into their luggage; rapists claim that they honestly thought their victim had consented; and killers claim that their victim's death was accidental (for example, "during rough sex"). In some of these cases, of course, the extra deterrence gained may not be worth the cost in terms of having to find persons guilty who genuinely lacked *mens rea* and who constitute no abnormal danger to others. In other cases, however, it will be worth it—it will be rational for prospective participants to run a certain risk of being convicted of some crime without *mens rea* in exchange for reducing more significantly their risk of being harmed through crimes of this type.

B. The apprehension and judgment of suspects

We are quite firmly convinced that it is much more important, morally, to avoid convicting the innocent than to avoid acquitting the guilty. We impose very high standards of evidence ("beyond a reasonable doubt") in criminal cases, especially where severe punishments are at stake. We categorically reject imposing lower standards ("clear and convincing evidence," say, or "preponderance of evidence") that might significantly reduce the number of false acquittals at the cost of only a few more false convictions.[37] Once we adopt the institutional view, however, such a categorical stance is hard to justify: it may lead to a society in which many crimes are committed by persons who have been falsely acquitted and many crimes are encouraged by the well-grounded belief that, with a resourceful lawyer, one has an excellent chance of escaping conviction even if caught. Prudent prospective participants would not impose this requirement for social worlds in which the additional crimes engendered

[36] One may also be attracted to strict-liability laws that criminalize harmings through clumsiness, mental confusion, and the like, where the main benefit is not deterrence but prevention of like harms caused by the same offender.

[37] There is a similar categorical commitment to various other procedural safeguards—for example, to the prohibition of double jeopardy (Fifth Amendment to the U.S. Constitution) and to the prohibitions on informing the jury about the accused's prior convictions.

by the higher standard of evidence do more to reduce the citizens' quality of life than the additional false convictions engendered by the lower standard.[38]

Analogous reflections apply to apprehension work by the police. The incidence of crime may well be higher when the police must not conduct so-called unreasonable searches and seizures and when any evidence so acquired is inadmissible in court: as a consequence of this constraint, some criminals are never caught and others cannot be convicted. Thus, even if freedom from unreasonable searches and seizures counts as a basic freedom, it is still arguable that the objects of all basic freedoms would on the whole be better protected if the relevant restraints upon the police were somewhat looser.

C. *The punishment of convicted criminals*

Our current punitive practices are still, by and large, informed by the value of proportionality: the severity of punishment[39] should match the culpability of the offender, with culpability a function, mainly, of the magnitude of the harm (or risk of harm) inflicted and of the offender's state of mind. Prospective participants, by contrast, would want punitive practices to be informed by the idea that harms overall should be kept to a minimum; hence, they would want the severity of punishments to be justified by their (negative) impact on the rate of incidence of the offense. According to CC conceptions, the punishment (type) fits the crime (type) when there exists no alternative punishment offering either (1) a decrease

[38] In nonideal theory, we must settle what kinds of abridgments of basic liberties are called for when it is impossible to safeguard all basic liberties for all. What sorts of abridgments of the basic rights of the accused would the contracting parties countenance for the sake of reducing to a certain extent the excessive incidence at a certain level of crimes of a certain kind? It may be said that we are not (yet) in a nonideal situation, that current crime rates are not excessive, do not undermine the claim that the basic right to physical integrity is fulfilled for all; and it may then be concluded that the first principle prohibits the lower standards of evidence, assuming it mandates evidence beyond a reasonable doubt in ideal theory. The issue cannot be so easily avoided, however. For we must also justify how, in ideal theory, the *basic* liberties are carved out of a much wider domain of candidate freedoms, how one particular design of a universalizable scheme of basic liberties is chosen. This involves showing that the parties would indeed consider the existing insecurity of the right to physical integrity consistent with the first principle being fully satisfied, thereby protecting the basic rights of the accused from abridgment. At some level, the parties must trade off between citizens' freedom from being innocently convicted and citizens' freedom from being innocently victimized by crime. For some reflections about this trade-off, see Jeffrey Reiman and Ernest van den Haag, "On the Common Saying that It Is Better that Ten Guilty Persons Escape than that One Innocent Suffer: *Pro* and *Con*," *Social Philosophy and Policy*, vol. 7, no. 2 (Spring 1990).

[39] A punishment is more or less severe (as I use this term) the more or less it hurts the person punished. In many jurisdictions, rich persons receive larger fines than poor ones for the same offense. This does not mean that the severity of punishment varies with wealth. To the contrary, those differentials accommodate the concern that severity should *not* vary with wealth. Only a larger fine can punish a rich offender as severely as a smaller fine punishes a poor one.

in expected punishment costs that outweighs any decrease in expected crime-reduction benefits, or (2) an increase in expected crime-reduction benefits that outweighs any increase in expected punishment costs.[40] Consider two types of crime which, in accordance with the prevailing proportionality standard, draw roughly equivalent punishments. Suppose their rates of incidence differ significantly in how elastic they are vis-à-vis the severity of punishment: the rate of incidence of the first crime would rise/drop by several percentage points for every 1 percent decrease/increase in punishment (jail time, say) from the prevailing level, while the rate of incidence of the second would be affected only minimally if at all. Rational prospective participants would want prevailing punishments to be revised so that the first crime is punished more severely than the second.[41]

I will here focus on high-elasticity crimes, with respect to which more severe punishments work especially well—generally by being especially effective in deterring potential offenders and/or in taking would-be repeat offenders out of circulation. To avoid the problem of heterogeneity of costs and benefits, I consider the death penalty for offenses that result in deaths.[42] Here we might ask whether prospective participants, guided solely by rational prudence, would mandate the death penalty for murder if this minimizes premature deaths overall. Let me entertain, however, another death-penalty proposal which, though in a sense perfectly plausible, is also rather wild. In the U.S., drunk driving causes at least ten thousand premature deaths per year.[43] A practice pursuant to which

[40] The word "expected" is to serve as a reminder that costs and benefits have to be assessed from the perspective specified by the relevant CC conception. If the hypothetical contracting parties use the maximin rule, for example, they define the *expected* net benefit of a punishment scheme in terms of its impact on the quality of life of the worst off (in comparison with the quality of life that the worst off under alternative schemes would enjoy).

[41] I assume that, for CC conceptions, the imposition of punishments will involve expected costs in terms of quality of life. (Otherwise prospective participants would want equal, namely maximal, punishments for *all* crimes, and the prospective-participant perspective would be in even greater trouble than I allege.) This assumption is plausible, because prospective participants run some risk of being (correctly or falsely) convicted and subjected to any punishment they authorize, and may have to pay a share of the cost of inflicting punishments. It does not follow, however, that *more severe* punishment for a particular crime will entail *greater* cost. When elasticity is high, the opposite may be true: though each person convicted of the crime receives more jail time (say), the crime is less frequent and fewer persons are punished for it. Since the increase in the first factor may be overwhelmed by the decrease in the second, total jail time imposed for the crime may actually decline.

[42] I assume, as seems inevitable, that any reasonable CC conception counts involuntary premature death as a major evil.

[43] The figures provided by the American Automobile Association are as follows: The annual death toll on U.S. highways hovers around forty-three thousand. About half these deaths are caused by accidents in which at least one intoxicated person is relevantly involved (i.e., involved not merely as passenger, but as driver or pedestrian). Of course, in some of these cases there is no drunk *driver*, and in others the intoxication of one or more drivers did not contribute to the accident. There is some dispute over what the death toll on U.S. highways would be if there were no drunk driving, but the lowest estimate seems to be that ten thousand premature deaths (plus one hundred thousand injuries and one billion dollars in property damage) would be avoided every year. For these figures, see H. Laurence Ross, *Confronting Drunk Driving* (New Haven: Yale University Press, 1992), pp. 35–38. Over

some two hundred of the worst offenders are executed annually would presumably have a tremendous deterrent effect and thus would greatly reduce the frequency of the offense. No one knows how great this reduction would be. Still, I am quite confident that it would vastly exceed 2 percent and that the total number of premature deaths would decline.[44] Here we have, then, a draconian proposal that looks quite mad and yet would seem entirely plausible under institutional viewing.

We can render the "reform" even madder: to maximize the deterrent effect, the law should be that anyone repeatedly caught heavily intoxicated at the wheel of an automobile is subject to the death penalty, but that only a fraction of those so caught, selected by lottery, will actually be executed. The percentage to be executed is adjusted so as to minimize the overall loss of lives: executed offenders plus vehicular-homicide victims plus killed police officers.[45] This idea of an execution lottery, by the way, goes back to the ancient Romans, who punished cowardliness on the part of whole armed units with a one-in-ten chance of execution. We still have the word—"to decimate"—but the practice has long since gone out of fashion.

Can adherents of the CC approach stick to their respective CC conceptions of justice and yet consistently reject the mad reform? They might propose that the optimal punishment for drunk driving lies somewhere between our current practices and the death penalty regime I have entertained: repeat offenders should, perhaps, receive multi-year jail sentences. This proposal runs into two difficulties, however. First, it does not detach the CC approach from the view that the death-penalty regime, though perhaps not optimal, is at least morally preferable to the status quo. This view is a considerable embarrassment. Second, it is doubtful whether the proposal is empirically sustainable. For suppose multi-year jail sentences would reduce drunk-driving fatalities to an annual rate of three thousand. It would seem likely, once again, that the execution of sixty of the worst offenders every year could further reduce this annual rate by well over 2 percent.[46]

---

a period of seventy years, then, a U.S. resident's chance of death due to drunk driving works out to about one in four hundred.

[44] We must consider that the projected "reform" would increase the killing of police officers: notorious drunk drivers, when flagged down, may believe that they have little left to lose. I owe this point to Michael Levin.

[45] Note that the argument for using the death penalty here extends, for purposes of assessing social institutions, the same concern and respect to all citizens—criminals and innocents alike. It counts the execution of a guilty person as no less bad than the vehicular death of an innocent. A higher execution rate would be called for, if the lives of innocents were weighted more heavily.

[46] For the record, let me say that—though I am unconvinced by the draconian practices that (I have argued) are entailed by the CC approach—I do believe that punishments for grave and repeated drunk-driving offenses ought to be significantly more severe than they currently are and than they ought to be according to Douglas Husak, "Is Drunk Driving a Serious Offense?" *Philosophy and Public Affairs*, vol. 23, no. 1 (Winter 1994), pp. 52–73. But then this essay is not about appropriate punishments for the various drunk-driving offenses.

Adherents of the CC approach might also claim that deaths by execution are worse than traffic deaths. But how can this claim be supported? Morally, the opposite would look more plausible: most of those executed for drunk driving would have inflicted serious harms or risks of harm on others, while those killed by drunk drivers are mostly innocents.[47] Prospective participants, too, might have the opposite valuation: one can gain a good deal of security against the risk of being executed by leaving one's car at home when going out for entertainment; but one cannot, without enormous losses in quality of life, attain the same degree of security against the risk of being killed by a drunk driver. Here it might be said that a premature death with social stigmatization is worse than an otherwise similar death without. But how much worse? Is it so much worse as to make it rational to prefer our current one in four hundred chance of premature death through drunk driving to a one in one thousand chance, say, of death by execution for drunk driving?

A third strategy for blocking the mad conclusion stipulates that prospective participants are strongly averse to living in a society with extensive use of the death penalty. This stipulation is entirely ad hoc, however, unless one can connect the stipulated aversion to interests that members of modern societies can plausibly be assumed to have. Without such a connection, the stipulation tends to trivialize and undermine the contractarian thought experiment: in this manner we can, after all, derive anything we like simply by stipulating that the hypothetical contractors like it as well. The core idea of modern contractarianism is to subject our moral judgments to an independent test by comparing them to the prudential judgments that rational persons would reach in a fair initial situation. And why should it be *prudent* to prefer a greater risk of premature death through drunk driving to a significantly smaller risk of premature death through execution for drunk driving?

While it is difficult, if not impossible, for CC conceptions to avoid endorsing the mad reform, it can easily be rejected on interactional viewing. Here we can distinguish, in good old deontological fashion, between deaths that we, acting through the state, bring about and deaths that merely come about as a consequence of what we, through legislation, do. "Excess" homicide deaths are, on this account, still morally regrettable, but we simply must not kill even a few to save a greater number. (This claim is often embellished by the Kantian thought that, insofar as we impose superproportional punishments in order to sustain deterrence, we are illicitly using convicted criminals merely as means.) The paradoxical implications of the CC approach are then connected to the fact that it focuses not on actors (the people or the government), but on the societal basic structure which produces various good and bad events in particular frequencies and is to be held morally responsible for them: for execu-

[47] A good many victims of drunk driving are, of course, victims of their own drunk driving.

tions as well as for traffic deaths, for punishments as well as for crimes, for taxes as well as for bankruptcies.

D. *Summary*

With each of our three criminal-law topics—defining offenses, apprehending suspects, and establishing punishments—we feel, I believe, strong moral resistance to the idea that our practices should be settled by a prospective-participant perspective. This becomes quite clear when we look at how the "reforms" suggested by institutional viewing might combine once we consider all three topics together: imagine a more extensive and swifter use of the death penalty in homicide cases coupled with somewhat lower standards of evidence; or think of backing a strict-liability criminal statute with the death penalty.[48] Of course, such "reforms" would increase the execution of innocents; but, their proponents will tell us, any penal system involves the punishment of some innocents, and, if it provides for the death penalty, the execution of some innocents. Moreover, why is it worse for innocents to be punished than for innocents to suffer an equivalent harm in some other way? Formulated from a prospective-participant perspective: Why not run a small risk of being innocently executed in exchange for reducing, much more significantly, the risk of dying prematurely in other ways?

While the criminal law in the countries of the developed West is clearly concerned to enhance citizens' quality of life, it is also informed by a plurality of further, conflicting and competing values and principles which, from a prospective-participant perspective, deserve no independent weight. Examining our three topics in the criminal law, it does not appear that these further principles are in decline. While strict liability is important, and increasingly so, in tort law, there is still great reluctance to use it within the criminal law. In the second topic, the picture is similar: the standards of proof protecting criminal defendants ("beyond a reasonable doubt") are virtually unchallenged, and the protections of suspects have even been significantly expanded over the past thirty-five years, despite the evident negative impact of this expansion upon crime rates. In the third topic, the prospective-participant perspective seems to have made some inroads.[49] Nevertheless, our penal institutions on the whole

[48] In the long passage I quoted from Rawls at the beginning of Section VA, he writes that the representative citizen can accept the strict-liability statute "at least if the penalties imposed are not too severe." But whence this limitation? The harms at stake ("civil strife") are very serious, and, if only the death penalty can avert them, then it is possible that the death penalty is called for to protect optimally the representative citizen's right to life.

[49] For the United States, witness, for example, punishments of so-called "accessories after the fact" and punishments under the Racketeer Influenced and Corrupt Organizations (RICO) statute. In both cases the punishment for given criminal conduct can become much more severe on account of circumstances beyond the offender's knowledge and control (an element of strict liability) and can become grossly disproportionate to the offender's culpability.

diverge dramatically from what a plausible CC conception of social justice would presumably require, and we seem to be quite strongly committed, morally, to maintaining this divergence.

It may be said, of course, that there is no such divergence, that our criminal law does correspond, reasonably closely, to the hypothetical preferences of a prospective participant. More specifically, it may be said that the penal reforms we have looked at would have negative collateral effects outside the penal system and thus would lose their plausibility once we compare, as we certainly should, entire institutional schemes in light of their likely overall effects. I have not considered this objection for two reasons. I do not believe it has a chance of being true, and I do not believe that complex empirical considerations reconciling our current practices with a prospective-participant perspective can possibly lie behind our strong and unhesitating moral condemnation of the penal "reforms" I have entertained. Most people think that imposing the death penalty even for the most notorious drunk drivers is absurd, and they think this without having remotely studied the relevant statistics, thought through deterrence effects, or the like. This firm conviction may well be a deontological hang-over of interactional viewing, which has long been in decline in political philosophy but appears to be alive and well in the subfields of political philosophy connected with the criminal law. This hang-over leads us to think of ourselves as much more responsible, morally, for harms we impose through the state than for harms that merely come about as a consequence of our social institutions. We say: "People driving while intoxicated surely deserve punishment; but they do not deserve to die for it. So we simply cannot kill them, no matter what good this might do." When pressed, we readily acknowledge that those who die on our roads because we fail to impose a death penalty for drunk driving do not deserve to die either. We do not feel morally responsible for these excess road deaths, however, or at least we feel much less responsible than we would for the proposed executions.

VI. Conclusion

Political philosophy today stands before the following tetralemma:

1. We can bite the bullet by following the CC approach, which seems so attractive under institutional viewing, wherever it may lead. But this option runs into the problems discussed in Sections III through V: it could well force us to accept social institutions that compensate persons for unattractiveness, institutions that violate fair equality of opportunity, and various draconian revisions of our criminal-law system.

2. We can abandon institutional viewing, go back to the old ways of interactional moral analysis, and then make morally significant the distinctions between what we, as a society, intend and what we merely foresee—and between what we, through the state, do and what merely

comes about as a consequence of our legislation. But this option abandons the great moral and explanatory advantages (briefly sketched in Sections I and II) of institutional viewing in the modern world.

3. We can try to find some plausible rationale for delineating the spheres of institutional and interactional viewing so as to block the difficulties. Thus, one might say, as Thomas Nagel has suggested to me, that in the criminal-law domain the burden of intending and producing a particular outcome falls on particular persons—police officers, judges, executioners—who must enforce the optimal ground rules against particular defendants. This is not the case in the economy, where people can be poor or unemployed without anyone having intended and produced this outcome. That is why it is appropriate to view legal and economic institutions differently: the former interactionally and the latter institutionally. But this option, whatever its merits in regard to the set of difficulties discussed in Section V, would not seem to work for the problems discussed in Sections III and IV.

4. We can search for a principled way of reconciling our considered convictions about natural inequalities, group inequities, and the criminal-law domain with institutional viewing by abandoning the CC approach to the moral assessment of social institutions. To make this work, one could consider a backward-looking account à la Nozick, which assesses an institutional scheme through an appraisal of its history. One could also aim for a forward-looking account that breaks out of the $J = f(Q_i)$ mold, as Thomas Scanlon seems to do—though so far his conception is still rather sketchy.[50]

On the face of it, a resolution exemplifying the third or fourth option (or some combination of these) would seem most appealing. The task is, however, to formulate a plausible resolution of this sort in detail. This is one project, I think, that political philosophy should now undertake.

Philosophy, Columbia University

[50] See Thomas M. Scanlon, "Contractualism and Utilitarianism," in Sen and Williams, eds., *Utilitarianism and Beyond*, esp. pp. 110–28.

JUSTICE, SELF-OWNERSHIP, AND NATURAL ASSETS*

BY MICHAEL GORR

A question that has recently attracted considerable attention is this:

> What is the nature and significance of the *normative* relationship a person bears to herself (where the self is understood to include the whole embodied person)?

On one view, it is held that persons are *self-owners*: as Locke put it in one of the more famous passages in the *Second Treatise*:

> [E]very man has a *property* in his own *person*: this no body has any right to but himself. The *labour* of his body, and the *work* of his hands, we may say, are properly his.[1]

It has usually been thought that, for Lockeans, the importance of such a claim was as a premise in an argument designed to establish the legitimacy of private property rights in external objects.[2] Some contemporary libertarians, jettisoning the crucial theological substratum of Locke's own account, have even suggested that the labor theory of property is no more than a corollary of the right of self-ownership.[3] By contrast, a number of leftist philosophers[4] have argued that, even if self-ownership is con-

* For their helpful comments and criticisms, I am grateful to David Anderson, Sterling Harwood, Kent Machina, Daniel Shapiro, Mark Siderits, and Thomas Pogge. I also wish to acknowledge the generous financial support provided by the Earhart Foundation.

[1] John Locke, *Second Treatise of Government* [1690], ed. C. B. Macpherson (Indianapolis: Hackett, 1980), ch. 5, section 27.

[2] The literature on this issue is quite large. Three representative attempts to carry out at least part of the Lockean project are Robert Nozick, *Anarchy, State, and Utopia* (New York: Basic Books, 1974), pp. 167–82; Anthony Fressola, "Liberty and Appropriation: Reflections on the Right of Appropriation in the State of Nature," *American Philosophical Quarterly*, vol. 18, no. 4 (October 1981), pp. 315–22; and Eric Mack, "Self-Ownership and the Right of Property," *The Monist*, vol. 73, no. 4 (October 1990), pp. 519–43.

[3] See, for example, Murray Rothbard, *The Ethics of Liberty* (Atlantic Highlands, NJ: Humanities Press, 1982), chs. 6–8.

[4] See G. A. Cohen, "Self-Ownership, World-Ownership, and Equality: Part I," in Frank Lucash, ed., *Justice and Equality Here and Now* (Ithaca, NY: Cornell University Press, 1986); Cohen, "Self-Ownership, World-Ownership, and Equality: Part II," *Social Philosophy and Policy*, vol. 3, no. 2 (Spring 1986), pp. 77–96; and Richard Arneson, "Lockean Self-Ownership: Towards a Demolition," *Political Studies*, vol. 39, no. 1 (March 1991), pp. 36–54. Further criticism along these lines may be found in Andrew Levine, "Capitalist Persons," *Social Philosophy and Policy*, vol. 6, no. 1 (Autumn 1988), pp. 39–59; Andrew Kernohan, "Capitalism and Self-Ownership," *Social Philosophy and Policy*, vol. 6, no. 1 (Autumn 1988), pp. 60–76; and John Christman, "Self-Ownership, Equality, and the Structure of Property Rights," *Political Theory*, vol. 19, no. 1 (February 1991), pp. 28–46.

ceded, one cannot derive anything like the full panoply of capitalist property rights.

In this essay I propose to ignore the highly contentious issue of what implications a principle of self-ownership has for the theory of property rights and to focus instead on the principle itself. I shall begin by contrasting and evaluating a number of attempts to define self-ownership, one of which, I shall argue, is significantly more perspicuous than its rivals. In the second and longest part of the essay, I shall take up the charge that John Rawls's theory is premised upon a rejection of self-ownership because of his insistence that the distribution of natural talents ought to be treated as a collective asset.[5] I shall argue that the critique of Rawls on this issue put forward by Robert Nozick and Michael Sandel involves some serious misunderstandings, and that Rawls's theory (particularly in its most recent, avowedly "political" interpretation) carries with it a deep commitment to an important form of self-ownership. Finally, I shall conclude with some brief general observations on the rationale for recognizing a right of self-ownership and on the extent to which it is useful or illuminating to premise an account of justice on claims about the moral relations that people bear to themselves.

I. Defining Self-Ownership

G. A. Cohen has suggested that the right of self-ownership may be explicated as follows:

> (1) Each person is the morally rightful owner of himself. He possesses over himself, as a matter of moral right, all those rights that a slaveholder has over a complete chattel slave as a matter of legal right, and he is entitled, morally speaking, to dispose over himself in the way such a slaveholder is entitled, legally speaking, to dispose over his slave.[6]

The main problem with this principle is that it is largely indeterminate in the absence of an account of what precisely *are* the legal rights of a slaveholder with respect to his slave. Clearly this may vary considerably from one slaveholding society to another (as may be seen if we contrast, say, antebellum Virginia with ancient Greece, or either of these with a hypo-

[5] John Rawls, *A Theory of Justice* (Cambridge, MA: Harvard University Press, 1971), esp. section 17. Similar sentiments are expressed in Ronald Dworkin, "What is Equality? Part I: Equality of Welfare," *Philosophy and Public Affairs*, vol. 10, no. 3 (Summer 1981), pp. 185–246; and Dworkin, "What is Equality? Part II: Equality of Resources," *Philosophy and Public Affairs*, vol. 10, no. 4 (Fall 1981), pp. 283–345. The suggestion that this view seems to deny self-ownership is most vigorously pressed in Nozick, *Anarchy, State, and Utopia*, pp. 213–31; and in Michael Sandel, *Liberalism and the Limits of Justice* (Cambridge: Cambridge University Press, 1982), chs. 1–2.

[6] Cohen, "Self-Ownership, World-Ownership, and Equality: Part I," p. 109.

thetical socialist society which permitted the enslavement of members of a particular ethnic group). Even less satisfactory would be the following:

(2) Each person has a fundamental right that neither physical force nor coercion be used against her except in response to certain proscribed acts on her part or as a means of preventing such acts under circumstances where they would be reasonably anticipated.

Since this formula leaves open what counts as a proscribed act, it is not so much a statement of *the* self-ownership principle as a schema for generating a whole host of such principles, many of which would have little plausibility for anyone. (What kind of self-ownership principle, for example, would permit the use of force or coercion to prevent a person from scratching her head?)

Libertarians have usually argued, plausibly enough, that self-ownership provides you with protection against other persons so long as, and only so long as, you do not engage in activities prejudicial to *their* self-ownership.[7] This suggests recasting (2) to read:

(3) Each person has a fundamental right that neither physical force nor coercion be *initiated* against him.

One difficulty with this way of explicating self-ownership (which, it should be noted, is pretty standard among libertarians) is that there is considerable controversy over the analysis of coercion, particularly with respect to the question of whether or not it must be defined in a way that includes ineliminable reference to moral concepts.[8] Even if we leave this issue aside, however, there is the further problem of what would count as *initiating* force or coercion against someone. Since libertarians generally hold that I do *not* violate any of your rights if I use force or coercion to prevent you from violating one of my *property* rights, it follows that to use force or coercion under such circumstances is not to be guilty of initiating its use. But this in turn implies that (3) *presupposes* a substantive theory of property rights, which thereby disqualifies it from serving as the general foundation for such a theory.

More promising is Richard Arneson's suggestion that self-ownership is best explicated in terms of the following pair of principles:

(4a) People should be left free to do whatever they choose unless their actions cause (or threaten to cause) harm, in specified ways, to nonconsenting others.

[7] See, for example, Rothbard, *The Ethics of Liberty*, p. 51.

[8] For opposing views on the question of whether coercion must be defined moralistically, contrast my *Coercion, Freedom, and Exploitation* (New York: Peter Lang, 1989), with Alan Wertheimer, *Coercion* (Princeton, NJ: Princeton University Press, 1987).

And:

(4b) Each person has the right not to be harmed by others (in specified ways) without prior consent, in one range of cases, or without full compensation, in another range of cases.[9]

However, in the absence of a specification of what types and ways of harming are proscribed, this is only a marginal improvement over (2). After all, if harm were construed very broadly—say, as any measurable loss of utility—the attempt to enforce the rights specified by (4a) and (4b) would create a society in which people's freedom to act would seem far too circumscribed for us to ascribe to them a substantive right of self-ownership.

I think we can do at least somewhat better if we reflect on what appears to be the guiding intuition behind theories of self-ownership, namely, that each person (except perhaps children and the manifestly incompetent) should ordinarily have the dominant say in how to live his or her life. This would imply that the bundle of rights that would be definitive of a defensible notion of self-ownership would at least include positive agent rights (rights to perform certain kinds of actions), negative agent rights (rights not to perform certain kinds of actions), and negative recipient rights (rights that persons other than the right-holder not perform certain kinds of actions). This is because rights of these three sorts seem necessary to provide an individual with the social freedom to decide what use she will make of her life. Whether self-ownership would also include positive recipient rights[10] (rights that persons other than the right-holder perform certain kinds of actions) is more controversial. Most libertarians argue that it would not, since they claim that to acknowledge rights of this sort would in effect be to give the right-holder some say in what use the person against whom the right is held can make of her life (and would thus seem incompatible with *her* self-ownership). While the soundness of such an argument is certainly debatable, any attempt to deal with it here would take us too far afield. If, therefore, we bracket this issue, as well as the question of what specific implications self-ownership has for the theory of property, can we say anything useful about what a principle of self-ownership would look like?

I think we can. I suggest that the following is a reasonably apt expression of the intuitions of those who have used the language of self-ownership:

[9] Arneson, "Lockean Self-Ownership," pp. 36 and 37.

[10] What is controversial, of course, is only the possibility of there being *natural* positive recipient rights, i.e., rights that people possess simply in virtue of being persons. Obviously no plausible view would deny the legitimacy of *acquired* positive recipient rights (e.g., those created by valid contracts).

(5) Each person has a fundamental right[11] to have a significantly stronger say than anyone else in how she chooses to live her life and in what may be done to her, a right that is normally forfeitable only if she acts in ways that are prejudicial to the exercise of this right on the part of others.

Of course, this principle (which I shall term the "Moderate Self-Ownership Principle" or "MSOP") requires considerably more fleshing out, since as it stands we are not told either *how much* stronger that say should be or how such a right should be institutionalized. Still, I think that the MSOP is not wholly empty, since it plainly asserts a fundamental asymmetry between *my* right to control how I choose to live my life and the rights of everyone else to do this. A potentially more serious objection is that the MSOP is less an expression of the thesis that persons are self-*owners* than of the view that they are *majority shareholders* in themselves. This is apt to be troubling to those who believe that the ideal of self-ownership requires that each person's rights over herself are not just quantitatively but qualitatively different from those of anyone else. Unfortunately, without some explanation as to what such a qualitative difference would consist in, I feel more comfortable in sticking with the MSOP (which would, in any event, be compatible with a stronger claim of this sort, since it expresses only the minimal requirements of a principle of self-ownership).

An important advantage of the MSOP is that, in all but its most extreme versions, it is immune to a series of important objections that have recently been urged by leftists who are critical either of the neo-Lockean project or of the thesis of self-ownership in general. Nothing in the MSOP requires, for example, the recognition of unlimited rights of appropriation. Indeed, it seems capable of being interpreted in a way that is compatible with (for example) Hillel Steiner's view that each person has a natural right to a per-capita share of the (unimproved) resources of the earth.[12] Nor need the MSOP be vulnerable to Andrew Kernohan's charge that it may lead to a situation in which some persons, because they lack access to the means of production, are effectively denied their self-ownership. If, as he argues, (i) robust self-ownership requires not only ownership of one's skills but ownership of the exercise of those skills, (ii) ownership of the exercise of one's skills requires access to the physical means of their exercise, and (iii) the recognition of universal self-ownership could lead to a situation in which some persons lack such access, then it follows that

[11] As I have just indicated, such a right will actually be quite complex, consisting in a bundle of appropriately related agent and recipient rights.

[12] See Arneson, "Lockean Self-Ownership," pp. 50–53. Steiner's proposal is explained and defended in his "The Natural Right to the Means of Production," *Philosophical Quarterly*, vol. 27, no. 106 (January 1977), pp. 41–49.

"[s]elf-ownership is led to justify its own negation."[13] But of course nothing in the MSOP requires us to affirm the third premise in this argument. It certainly seems possible to allow each person to exercise dominant control over her own life without permitting the sort of appropriations that would preclude some persons from having any significant legal access to the physical prerequisites of purposeful behavior.[14] Finally, consider an objection that Arneson apparently believes would tell against any form of self-ownership:

> [Suppose that] by forgoing a minor pleasure I could act to save someone's life. Self-ownership entails the extreme denial that any genuine enforceable obligation to aid is ever generated even by the most favourable ratio of benefit to loss.[15]

On the contrary: a defender of the MSOP might, for example, support Good Samaritan laws, with or even without a requirement that the person who is rescued compensate his benefactor. Moreover, the MSOP can certainly be interpreted in ways which would permit welfare legislation of various sorts.

Of course, it will no doubt have occurred to the reader that the intuitive attractiveness of a view like the MSOP, together with the facility with which it sidesteps many of the objections to more traditional notions of self-ownership, might well be "partly a function of [its] vagueness."[16] After all, just what significant moral or political view does the MSOP rule out? Well, as Cohen has observed, a theory which called for joint ownership of the external world would seem to be precluded, since a person could hardly be said to be a self-owner in any substantive sense if she could literally do nothing without the consent of everyone else.[17] More importantly, as I noted at the outset, it has been argued that the version of liberalism defended by Rawls is explicitly opposed to self-ownership of any sort, inasmuch as it is one of the fundamental claims of justice as fairness that the distribution of natural talents ought to be treated as a collective asset. If such a charge is correct, wouldn't that by itself be a powerful reason to reject Rawls's theory? Or does he supply us with a countervailing reason to give up the MSOP? Or, alternatively, is it just a mistake to think that there is anything in Rawls's theory that is incompatible with some plausible version of self-ownership? In the next section

[13] Kernohan, "Capitalism and Self-Ownership," p. 76.

[14] It is worth noting, of course, that nothing in the MSOP requires that such access be equal.

[15] Arneson, "Lockean Self-Ownership," p. 54.

[16] *Ibid.*

[17] Cohen, "Self-Ownership, World-Ownership, and Equality: Part II," p. 83.

I shall take up these and related questions as part of my inquiry into the meaning and normative significance of the self-ownership thesis.

II. Rawls and the Principle of Redress

Rawls's account of the moral status of a person's *natural assets,* i.e., her hereditary or biological endowments,[18] is unfortunately still a matter of some controversy. The radical attack on this view by such well-known critics as Nozick[19] and Sandel[20] has itself been challenged, by Thomas Pogge,[21] on the grounds that it is premised upon a serious misunderstanding of what Rawls is up to. It may be useful, then, if I begin by briefly summarizing the interpretation of Rawls's views that I have myself defended in an earlier essay,[22] an interpretation that is closely allied with—but in some ways goes further than—that of Nozick and Sandel. I can then take up the issue of how defensible this interpretation is in the light of Pogge's criticisms. When all of this has been hashed out, I will try to determine to what extent, if any, Rawls's views (particularly in their new political guise) pose a challenge or alternative to the thesis of self-ownership.

According to Rawls's contractarian (or, in the terminology he now seems to prefer, *constructivist*) account of justice, the most adequate principles of justice (at least for inhabitants of liberal democracies)[23] are those that would be unanimously agreed to under a set of conditions, which he terms the "original position," which ensured that the choice of such principles would be rational and fair. Probably the most distinctive and controversial element of the original position is the veil of ignorance, the requirement that the parties choose principles without any knowledge of, among other things, the details of their own rational plan of life, their socioeconomic status, or their share in the distribution of natural advantages and disadvantages. But why think a fair and reasonable procedure for choosing principles of justice would involve such a constraint? Rawls's answer is that the derivation of the principles of justice presupposes a

[18] I shall ignore here questions about exactly how "natural" assets are to be defined and whether there may be morally significant differences between different kinds of natural assets; for a very insightful treatment of these and related issues, see Alexander Rosenberg, "The Political Philosophy of Biological Endowments: Some Considerations," *Social Philosophy and Policy,* vol. 5, no. 1 (Autumn 1987), pp. 1–31.

[19] Nozick, *Anarchy, State, and Utopia,* pp. 213–31.

[20] Sandel, *Liberalism and the Limits of Justice,* chs. 1–2.

[21] Thomas W. Pogge, *Realizing Rawls* (Ithaca, NY: Cornell University Press, 1989).

[22] Michael Gorr, "Rawls on Natural Inequality," *Philosophical Quarterly,* vol. 33 (1983), pp. 1–18. All page references are to the reprint of this essay in J. Angelo Corlett, ed., *Equality and Liberty* (London: Macmillan, 1991).

[23] For the new, more "political" understanding of Rawls's theory, see his *Political Liberalism* (New York: Columbia University Press, 1993).

"Kantian interpretation" of justice as fairness, i.e., a set of "deeper" precontractual principles which supply the moral rationale for the various elements of the original position. Among those principles is one which he terms the "principle of redress,"[24] and which, in a section of *A Theory of Justice* revealingly entitled "The Tendency to Equality," he summarizes as follows:

> This is the principle that undeserved inequalities call for redress; and since inequalities of birth and natural endowment are undeserved, these inequalities are to be somehow compensated for. Thus the principle holds that in order to treat all persons equally, to provide genuine equality of opportunity, society must give more attention to those with fewer native assets and to those born into the less favorable social positions. *The idea is to redress the bias of contingencies in the direction of equality.*[25]

Where does the principle of redress come from? According to the Kantian interpretation, the fundamental right of all persons is to act autonomously by giving expression to their essential nature as rational agents. To help explain what this involves, Rawls introduces the notion of a *range* property, that is, a general property which characterizes all entities that exemplify any one of a specified range of fully determinate properties. As an example, he suggests:

> the property of being in the interior of the unit circle. . . . All points inside this circle have this property although their coordinates vary within a certain range. And they equally have this property, since no point interior to a circle is more or less interior to it than any other interior point.[26]

Similarly, what is essential to persons is just their (equal) possession of such range properties as rationality and moral personality—hence, their basic right to give expression to their essential nature as persons involves a right (if not a duty) to act in accordance with principles which reflect

[24] Pogge has suggested (in conversation) that Rawls may endorse not the principle of redress in its entirety, but only some weaker principle, as a basis for the design of the original position. However, I do not see how to reconcile this interpretation with what Rawls says in section 17 of *A Theory of Justice*, especially the following passage:

> Now the principle of redress has not to my knowledge been proposed as the sole criterion of justice. . . . It is plausible as most such principles are only as a prima facie principle, one that is to be weighed in the balance with others. . . . But whatever other principles we hold, *the claims of redress are to be taken into account*. (p. 101, emphasis added)

[25] Rawls, *A Theory of Justice*, pp. 100–101 (emphasis added).

[26] *Ibid.*, p. 508.

only their equal possession of these range properties. These principles, of course, are just those that would be chosen in the original position, the hypothetical choice situation which models persons' possession of (and only of) those range properties. The *degree* to which I am rational or possess the requisites of moral personality, insofar as this exceeds the bare minimum necessary for me to possess the corresponding range properties, is *not* essential to my being a person, and hence is not something I have a basic right to express. As Rawls puts it, "any variations in ability within the range are to be regarded as any other natural asset,"[27] that is, are to be "nullified" or "compensated for" by treating their distribution as a collective asset in accordance with the principle of redress.

In my earlier essay I argued that such a view seems open to a number of objections, among the most important of which are these: (i) the principle of redress appears to embody an extreme and highly counterintuitive form of egalitarianism; (ii) it is not clear how plausible or even intelligible it is to suppose that persons have a right to give expression to their range properties without having a right to give expression to the determinate properties in virtue of which those range properties are instantiated; and (iii) it is difficult to see how any such principle can be squared with Rawls's insistence on "tak[ing] seriously the *distinction* between persons."[28]

What positive arguments does Rawls offer in support of the principle of redress? I believe there may be as many as four, though none is more than briefly sketched. First, he appears to hold that in a world like our own, in which the "distribution" of natural assets is both unequal and undeserved, it would be unfair to award goods and positions on the basis of actions (e.g., displays of entrepreneurship) the possibility of which is importantly affected by the nature and extent of one's natural assets. This "argument from desert," however, has been extensively criticized by others,[29] and thus I shall say no more about it here. A second response is that the kind of compensation called for by the principle of redress is necessary in order to provide what Rawls terms "genuine" equality of opportunity.[30] But the short answer to this contention is that the requirements of a defensible conception of equality of opportunity are a matter of intense dispute. Alan Goldman, for example, defends the more orthodox view that equal opportunity consists in "roughly equal *socially* imposed

[27] *Ibid.*

[28] *Ibid.*, p. 27. For an elaboration of these criticisms, see Gorr, "Rawls on Natural Inequality," pp. 30–35.

[29] See Nozick, *Anarchy, State, and Utopia*, pp. 213–31; Alan Goldman, "Real People (Natural Differences and the Scope of Justice)," *Canadian Journal of Philosophy*, vol. 17, no. 2 (June 1987), pp. 377–94; Rosenberg, "The Political Philosophy of Biological Endowments" (*supra* note 18), passim; and Alan Zaitchik, "On Deserving to Deserve," *Philosophy and Public Affairs*, vol. 6, no. 4 (Fall 1977), pp. 370–88.

[30] Rawls, *A Theory of Justice*, pp. 100–101.

obstacles to the attainment of desirable educational and career positions"[31] and goes on to deny that it requires compensation for natural inequalities. In the absence of an independent reason for rejecting such an alternative construal, this argument for the principle of redress seems plainly question-begging.

The third approach is suggested primarily by what Rawls says in the notorious section 40 of *A Theory of Justice,* where he claims that to act autonomously is to realize one's "true" self by acting on principles which reflect "the point of view from which noumenal selves see the world" and which "reveal [one's] independence from natural contingencies and social accident."[32] The problem here, however, is that it is far from clear how we are supposed to interpret such claims. If they are meant to invoke a Kantian theory of the metaphysical nature of persons, then, even leaving aside obvious questions about the plausibility of such an account, Rawls would be contradicting one of the central contentions of his most recent work, namely, that the argument for the principles of justice must not be premised upon controversial philosophical claims about the nature of persons. But if his remarks in section 40 are not intended to be taken literally, then it is unclear just what they do mean and how they could provide the needed support for the principle of redress.[33]

There is, however, a fourth, more radical argument which is at least suggested by what Rawls says and which, to my knowledge, has not been explicitly addressed by any of his critics. The principle of redress is concerned not just with the fact that it is morally arbitrary that people differ in the extent to which they possess particular biologically based *traits* but also with the fact that *which* of those traits are *advantageous* (i.e., which constitute *assets* rather than *disabilities*) is a matter of what characteristics happen to be socially valued.[34] As Alexander Rosenberg has pointed out, being well-coordinated and seven feet tall are considerable advantages in a society which prizes basketball, but would be of little or no benefit in a different sort of society (e.g., one which scorns athletics and treasures only poetry and mathematics).[35] But if assets are complexes of both biological endowments and values (those of the possessor of the trait as well as of other members of his or her society), the way is open for a defender of the principle of redress to argue as follows:

> If whether or not a biological trait constitutes an asset for its possessor were an objective fact independent of anyone's preferences or

[31] Alan H. Goldman, "The Justification of Equal Opportunity," *Social Philosophy and Policy,* vol. 5, no. 1 (Autumn 1987), p. 102 (emphasis added).

[32] Rawls, *A Theory of Justice,* p. 255.

[33] For further criticism along these lines, see my "Rawls on Natural Inequality," pp. 29–30.

[34] Sandel explicitly notes this but makes use of it only in considering a version of the desert argument; see his *Liberalism and the Limits of Justice,* ch. 2.

[35] Rosenberg, "The Political Philosophy of Biological Endowments," pp. 6–7.

> choices, then Nozick's charge that the considerations which underlie the principle of redress "embody or are based upon envy"[36] might have to be conceded. However, as we have just seen, whether or not a trait is an asset depends on social choices which could have been different. Hence, those persons in any given society whose biological traits cause them to be relatively disadvantaged in that society have grounds for complaint that need not be mere expressions of spite or envy: had society chosen instead to place a premium upon traits which they possess, then *they* would have been relatively advantaged. Therefore, to secure their acquiescence in a social scheme in which their traits are not so prized, *some* sort of compensation would seem appropriate—and that, of course, is precisely what the principle of redress calls for.

To assert that "society" values or disvalues a particular trait is, however, normally just shorthand for the claim that a majority of the individuals within the society in question have such an attitude. But surely the fact that the utility functions of most people in a particular society include a preference for basketball and an aversion to poetry would hardly seem sufficient by itself to sustain the charge that (say) short people with a bent for verse were being treated unfairly. Why should I be thought to have a legitimate complaint just because the particular biological endowment that I possess is not the basis for attributes that are highly valued by those around me?

Perhaps it will be argued that what may involve unfairness is not people valuing or disvaluing particular attributes per se (something which, in any event, is largely beyond their direct control) but the choice to set up a society structured in accordance with certain rules (particularly *economic* rules) which *promote* the positive evaluation of certain traits to the detriment of others. Consider, say, the activities which serve to establish and maintain a market society. Is it not reasonable to suppose that a predictable consequence of this will be a tendency on the part of most people in such a society to value (at least instrumentally) the sorts of personality traits that are generally conducive to success in the marketplace? If so, would this be fair to those who lack the biological basis for such attributes, but who possess instead the biological basis for the sort of attributes that would be rewarded under alternative social arrangements (say those characteristic of feudalism or socialism)?

One who raises this kind of objection is, however, making a tacit but crucial assumption, namely, that no principles of justice can be satisfactory unless they afford compensation for those whose natural attributes will tend to be disvalued in a society informed by those principles. But to assume that is simply to beg the question against critics of the princi-

[36] Nozick, *Anarchy, State, and Utopia*, p. 215.

ple of redress! Nozick, for example, would argue that there are grounds for accepting his entitlement theory of justice which imply the falsity of the principle of redress. Without some independent reason for rejecting such alternatives, this last argument seems no more persuasive than any of the others.

Even if we have not found any positive reason for endorsing the principle of redress, however, it is also true that we have not shown conclusively that it is unacceptable.[37] Given, therefore, that Rawls apparently remains committed to it, we need to look much more closely at the nature of its relationship to the MSOP. Nozick and Sandel, of course, have argued fairly vigorously that Rawls's commitment to the principle of redress (as one of the considerations that should be used to shape the original position) virtually ensures that the resulting principles of justice will be inimical to self-ownership, grudgingly permitting it only insofar as doing so is required, in virtue of the infirmities of human motivation, to satisfy the requirements of the maximin principle. By way of a response to this general line of reasoning, Pogge makes a series of claims, the most important of which I shall now discuss.

First, he notes that since the writing of *A Theory of Justice*, Rawls has categorically denied that his account of natural assets implies the permissibility of such nightmarish possibilities as involuntary organ transplants or a head tax on superior abilities. Pogge points out that Rawls goes so far as to insist that "[w]e have a right to our natural abilities,"[38] which suggests that he (Rawls) is explicitly endorsing something like a version of the self-ownership doctrine. Indeed, Pogge adds that Rawls "has no reason to deny" that persons are self-owners:

> Within the option space available in a just social system, persons should have the right to develop or not to develop, to exercise or not to exercise, their endowments as they wish and should be entitled to the full benefits offered for their efforts in this regard.[39]

The crucial question, of course, is whether the right to utilize one's talents in accordance with principles that are explicitly designed to "[give] . . . weight to the considerations singled out by the principle of redress"[40] could plausibly be thought of as a genuine, substantive right of self-ownership.

[37] For a careful critique of a whole range of redress principles, see Allen Buchanan, "Equal Opportunity and Genetic Intervention," elsewhere in this volume.

[38] John Rawls, "The Basic Structure as Subject," in A. I. Goldman and J. Kim, eds., *Values and Morals* (Dordrecht: Reidel, 1978), p. 65.

[39] Pogge, *Realizing Rawls*, p. 75.

[40] Rawls, *A Theory of Justice*, p. 100. It should be noted that Pogge's quote of Rawls's claim that "[w]e have a right to our natural abilities" (*supra* note 38) is incomplete. The sentence in question continues: "and a right to whatever we become entitled to by taking part in a fair social process."

As part of his effort to defend an affirmative answer to this question, Pogge tries to explain why, contra Nozick and Sandel, Rawls is not committed to the following sort of anti-self-ownership argument:

(1) Natural endowments may be regarded as a common asset.
(2) Hence, the talents and abilities of (or "residing in") the exceptionals may be used as a means.
(3) Hence, the work and efforts of the exceptionals may be used as a means, or harnessed.[41]

Pogge maintains that this argument is thoroughly mistaken and that in fact Rawls does not endorse any of the three propositions in it. With respect to (1), the sole premise of the argument, he claims that Rawls's view is not that natural talents per se are to be regarded as collective assets, but only their *distribution* within society. He immediately concedes that making such a distinction "may seem to have an air of sophistry," so he attempts to illustrate its significance by the following example.

> A travel company operating with run-down accommodations, unsafe flights, hidden charges, and the like may be said to use the needs and desires of its customers as means for its own enrichment. This use may well be, as Nozick and Sandel would insist, tantamount to using the customers themselves merely as means. By contrast, consider a travel company that charges different prices for identical services provided at different times of the year (off-peak, high season, etc.), so as to equalize demand. In this case it is the distribution of customer interests and desires, the fact that customers are different in various relevant respects, that is used as a means. Though the end motivating the policy may be the same in both cases (maximization of profit, say), it seems clear that only the first policy can reasonably be said to use customers as means.[42]

I am afraid I do not find this very helpful at all. For one thing, basing an explanation of anything on an appeal to the notoriously elusive distinction between treating someone as an end in himself and treating him as a mere means risks the danger of explaining the obscure in terms of the even more obscure. In any event, the *obvious* explanation of why the first travel company is treating its customers as mere means is that it is *cheating* them! The second company is not engaged in anything remotely like this, but is simply following a reasonable business policy—a policy of which its customers are presumably fully aware—of adjusting its prices to reflect seasonal differences in demand. While I suppose that one could

[41] Pogge, *Realizing Rawls*, p. 69.
[42] *Ibid.*, p. 74.

describe its activities as "using the distribution of customer interests" as a mere means to its objectives, this fact seems irrelevant to an explanation of the legitimacy of those activities.[43]

Pogge, however, also denies that Rawls endorses (3)—thereby, he claims, "destroy[ing] the ordinary rationale for attributing (1) and (2) to him."[44] Again, he charges Nozick and Sandel with a misinterpretation of Rawls's argument. As they see it, according to Pogge, Rawls is claiming that

> the exceptionals, if they want to exercise their special talents, must "help" the [disadvantaged], must "improve their situation" and "give them compensating advantages." . . . And does this requirement not presuppose that we *do* know what flows from their work and efforts, namely their entitlements under [a situation in which the difference principle is satisfied] *plus* whatever "help" was diverted to [the disadvantaged]?[45]

Pogge maintains, however, that a more careful reading of Rawls discloses that

> the implicit reference of such comparative expressions as "gain," "improve," "help," "giving compensating advantages" is *not* to the

[43] Pogge has attempted (in a private communication) to further explain this distinction in the following way. If people's talents were themselves a collective asset, then it would be legitimate for society to determine how they are to be utilized (e.g., by assigning persons to particular jobs in order to produce the optimal social output). Rawls, however, clearly does not hold a view of this sort. Rather, he claims that what society is entitled to determine is only what *rewards* are to be associated with various contributions to overall social output. A system of differential rewards, however, would make sense only if people differed in their talents and preferences—hence, what Rawls regards as a collective asset is only the *distribution* of talents. But, Pogge goes on to claim, virtually everyone (even libertarians) would regard the distribution of talents as a collective asset in this sense. Where real disagreement arises is only at the *further* step in Rawls's argument: his contention that social reward schedules must be constructed so as to satisfy the requirements of the difference principle.

Pogge's suggestion (if I have understood him correctly) that what is controversial is not the claim that the distribution of talents is a collective asset but only Rawls's account of *how* that distribution is to be utilized by society does not seem to square very well with what Rawls himself says. In *A Theory of Justice*, Rawls states: "[T]he difference principle *represents*, in effect, an agreement to regard the distribution of natural talents as a common asset . . ." (p. 101, emphasis added). This strongly suggests that, contra Pogge, it is the difference principle which is the *basis* for claiming that the distribution of natural talents is to be regarded as a collective asset, and that, consequently, Rawls would *not* make a similar claim about alternative social arrangements (such as the libertarian ones favored by Nozick) in which the difference principle plays no role. Furthermore, even if Rawls believes that society should assign only rewards rather than specific persons to social positions, this would obviously cede to society enormous power that seems capable of being utilized in ways that would seriously undermine any substantive form of self-ownership. The alleged difference between treating talents per se as collective assets and treating only their distribution in this way remains, I am afraid, a very elusive one.

[44] Pogge, *Realizing Rawls*, p. 69.

[45] *Ibid.*

> (smaller) share the [disadvantaged] would have if the exceptionals did less work. . . . Instead, the implicit reference is to the smaller share of the [disadvantaged] *as it would exist under alternative schemes*.[46]

Pogge is surely correct in defending what he calls the *inter*schemic interpretation of the difference principle: what is required (roughly) is that we choose *whichever* economic system has the highest income floor. What is not so clear is the validity of his further contention that the Nozick-Sandel "harnessing" charge *presupposes* the mistaken *intra*schemic interpretation. Pogge claims that this is the case because, on the interschemic construal, such a charge loses its intuitive punch inasmuch as it "reduces to the commonplace that some schemes are better for some groups and others for others."[47] But what Nozick would surely reply is that he rejects the underlying assumption of *both* the interschemic and intraschemic interpretations, namely, that an economic system must be *designed* so that the talents, efforts, and achievements of some groups must make a *specific, determinate* contribution to the welfare of *other* particular groups. This much, at least, seems to be implied by Nozick's rejection of "patterned" conceptions of justice.

An assessment of this reply, however, would necessitate an inquiry into the details of Nozick's general attack on patterned and end-state principles of justice, an attack which has itself been the subject of some powerful criticisms (not the least of which are those advanced by Pogge himself).[48] Instead, let us consider Pogge's further contention that what Rawls is claiming is not that "endowments are to be equalized or that an economic system must not offer greater rewards to those better endowed," but only that

> the better endowed have no special claims upon the construction of the criterion of social justice. . . . [W]hen the appropriate terms of economic cooperation are negotiated (for example, in the original position), it is morally inappropriate for endowments to be a factor in the participants' bargaining position.[49]

The first of these claims seems correct. The second, however, is more contentious. Libertarians (as well as neo-Hobbesians such as Gauthier)[50] would reject it, since they hold that people do have a precontractual entitlement to their natural assets. Furthermore, Nozick's contention (and

[46] *Ibid.*, p. 70.
[47] *Ibid.*, p. 72.
[48] *Ibid.*, ch. 1.
[49] *Ibid.*, p. 73.
[50] David Gauthier, *Morals by Agreement* (Oxford: Clarendon Press, 1986).

Rawls's as well?) is that preventing one's endowments from being a bargaining chip via the veil of ignorance is *tantamount* to treating them as collective property. Again, this is hardly surprising in light of the fact that much of the rationale for including the veil of ignorance among the constraints of the original position is its efficacy in satisfying the requirements of the principle of redress.

I conclude that, despite his ingenuity, Pogge has not demonstrated his contention that the "starting points of Rawls's argument are quite mainstream and hardly warrant the surprise and hostility they have evoked."[51] On the contrary, the principle of redress seems to me a very radical principle indeed, and one that is decidedly *not* part of the mainstream. It is an element in an extreme Kantianism that, at least in *A Theory of Justice*, appears to run quite deep. Rawls maintains there that a person's fundamental right qua person is to act on principles expressive of her "true" self, and that that true self is (at least something like—this remains *very* obscure) a *noumenal* self which is characterized by its "independence from natural contingencies and social accident."[52] Insofar as this is intelligible, it seems to lead directly to the view that, at least at the fundamental level, a person lacks any *special* rights over those of her determinate characteristics which are essential to her identity as the particular distinct individual that she is.[53] Indeed, in Rawls's earlier attempts to reply to Nozickean objections concerning the possibility of forced organ transplants and the like, he had a distressing tendency to emphasize either the practical difficulties in implementing such schemes or the obstacles this would place in the way of the efficient social exploitation of the full range of human abilities.[54] It is thus unsurprising that at least one important left-wing defender of Rawls, Andrew Levine, has suggested not only that Rawls's theory is based on assumptions incompatible with self-ownership but that it implies that "[w]e ought . . . to work to transform our natures, the better to realize the egalitarian vision Rawls's theory of justice articulates."[55] Levine maintains that insofar as Rawlsian principles permit practices that seem expressive of self-ownership (such as material incentives that result in differential rewards for efforts), this is merely a concession to the sorts of motivational structures alleged to be so prevalent in our society, structures whose potential malleability warrants the most careful scrutiny. On his interpretation, the Rawlsian ideal, if only it were

[51] Pogge, *Realizing Rawls*, p. 86.

[52] Rawls, *A Theory of Justice*, p. 255.

[53] I develop this line of argument in more detail in "Rawls on Natural Inequality," pp. 32–34.

[54] See, for example, John Rawls, "Some Reasons for the Maximin Criterion," *American Economic Review*, vol. 64, no. 2 (May 1974), pp. 144–45. Only toward the end of his discussion does Rawls go on to mention that "another difficulty is the interference with liberty" (p. 145).

[55] Levine, "Capitalist Persons" (*supra* note 4), p. 49.

attainable, would seem to be a society in which self-ownership would have disappeared both in theory and in practice.[56]

There is, then, strong evidence that there are fundamental features of Rawls's theory that seem decidedly inimical to self-ownership. This suggests that we consider the possibility that there are *other* aspects of justice as fairness which would prove *supportive* of self-ownership. An argument to this effect might go as follows:

> At the deepest level of his theory, Rawls does not accept a right of self-ownership. Indeed, his acceptance of the principle of redress makes it clear that *at that level* he explicitly repudiates any such right. However, those in the original position would choose at least one principle which, by guaranteeing to each person "an equal claim to a fully adequate system of equal basic rights and liberties,"[57] would justify a set of rights that are equivalent to at least one credible version of a right of self-ownership.

This response invites at least three further questions: (1) Do the rights and freedoms called for by Rawls's first principle of justice really imply a right of self-ownership? (2) Even if they would imply such a right when considered in isolation, would the requirements imposed by Rawls's second principle (which mandates both "fair" equality of opportunity and a socioeconomic system that maximizes the expectations of the least advantaged) serve to so constrain the exercise of those freedoms that self-ownership would be effectively eviscerated? (3) If a derivative right of self-ownership is implied by Rawls's principles, just how secure would it be? (How would its status compare, for example, with the status, under a utilitarian system, of the right of the innocent not to be punished?)

A definitive answer to these queries would require a lengthy examination of Rawls's two principles (and of what would be required for their implementation) that is far beyond the scope of this essay. Still, by way of a preliminary response to the first two questions, I would note that, as Rawls himself has conceded, his principles could be realized in a capitalist welfare state whose basic structure would bear more than a passing resemblance to that of many contemporary Western democracies. And surely there is no doubt that the legal systems of all these countries are compatible with a fairly robust version of the MSOP. Most of their citizens, for example, enjoy considerable freedom not only to choose their government but also to decide for themselves what occupation they shall

[56] This may be something of an overstatement, since Levine is not always careful to distinguish a view like the MSOP from more debatable interpretations of self-ownership that serve to support inegalitarian economic arrangements.

[57] This quote is from Rawls's most recent formulation of his first principle of justice in *Political Liberalism*, p. 5.

enter, where they shall live, who they shall marry, how they shall dispose of their income, how they shall spend their leisure time, etc. While those freedoms may fall short of what some would favor, that does not imply that such regimes fail to recognize a right of self-ownership, but only that there may be room to complain about the *kind* and *degree* of self-ownership that is permitted. In any event, I shall assume that, at least under anything like present circumstances, the instantiation of Rawlsian justice would be strongly supportive of some significant form of self-ownership.

The third question, however, is more interesting (and disturbing). If Levine is right, Rawls's endorsement of self-ownership is largely contingent on certain features of human psychology that may at least someday be open to alteration. If so, the recognition of self-ownership within a Rawlsian society would simply be an artifact of our relatively undeveloped technologies of genetic engineering and behavior control. It is natural, then, to consider whether Rawls's theory has the resources for generating a right of self-ownership that is "deeper" and less of a hostage to fortune. Given our previous account of the role of the Kantian conception of the person that is at the root of justice as fairness, this may seem an impossible task. If the principle of redress implies that the *differences* between persons are of no moral significance for the purposes of determining principles of justice, and if any plausible principle of self-ownership gives people special control over the use to which their own unique natural assets are put, then how can such a right be anything more than a concession to expediency?

I believe this objection rests upon a tacit but highly dubious inference, namely, that because a *knowledge* of which specific determinate characteristics we possess is denied to those in the original position, it follows that the fact that we *have* such fully determinate characteristics is *also* irrelevant—at least for the purposes of constructing principles of justice. But this is plainly mistaken. That we possess *some* determinate degree of rationality, intelligence, moral personality, etc., in virtue of which we exhibit the corresponding range properties, is something that of course is known behind the veil of ignorance. Indeed, such knowledge plays a crucial role in Rawls's argument for his two principles, as is illustrated by the following passage in defense of the priority of liberty:

> [I]t seems evident that the parties [in the original position] must choose principles that secure the integrity of their religious and moral freedom. They do not know, of course, what their religious or moral convictions are, or what is the particular content of their moral or religious obligations as they interpret them. . . . *All they know is that they have obligations which they interpret in this way.*[58]

[58] Rawls, *A Theory of Justice*, p. 206 (emphasis added).

More generally, while the parties in the original position do not know what their talents are or what their conception of the good is, they do know that they have *some* determinate share of talents and *some* determinate conception of the good. They do not reason on the assumption that they possess only range properties, for not only would that undercut the argument for the two principles (as I have just noted) but it also would be plainly false—indeed, incoherent. But if the veil of ignorance does not screen out the knowledge that we are distinct and determinate individuals with a desire to do what we can to protect our distinct and determinate interests (even if it does prevent us from knowing *what* those distinct and determinate interests are), then isn't it possible that the parties in the original position would select principles with an eye toward guaranteeing themselves some measure of self-ownership? And if this is so, then isn't there reason to believe that Rawls's theory does recognize a right of self-ownership that, even if derivative, is far better entrenched than would be (say) the sort of "rights" that utilitarians might be willing to countenance?

Furthermore, since Rawls now conceives of justice as fairness as a theory which is "political, not metaphysical"[59]—i.e., which is primarily intended to express and systematize the fundamental values of contemporary liberal democracies—there is a strong presumption that it would accord considerable weight to some form of self-ownership, since that is clearly among the foremost of those values. There is thus good reason to think that a principle of self-ownership may not be merely derivative, but, rather, may be one of the "fixed points" in our deliberations about justice—a principle which, like the principle of redress, must itself be reflected in the very structure of Rawls's constructivism. Our representatives in the original position, that is, would recognize and desire to protect not only our religious and moral interests but also our interests in having special and extensive control over how we shape the contours of our own lives and over what may be done to us by others (particularly the state). How such control is to be reconciled with—and balanced against—other fundamental liberal values (particularly the egalitarian ones typified by the principle of redress) is, of course, precisely what Rawls hopes to explain via the elaborate theoretical artifices of justice as fairness. The extent to which he succeeds in such a daunting enterprise is a question that cannot be addressed here. For our purposes, I think, all that needs to be noted is that there appears to be a strong presumption within Rawls's theory (especially as it has been developed in his later writings) that a just society will recognize some substantive form of self-ownership.

Whether Rawls himself would endorse everything I have said here is

[59] See John Rawls, "Justice as Fairness: Political, Not Metaphysical," *Philosophy and Public Affairs*, vol. 14, no. 3 (Summer 1985), pp. 223–51, and *Political Liberalism*, passim.

not entirely clear. In his later writings he has taken pains to emphasize that justice as fairness involves a purely political conception of the person in that its central construct, the original position, is a device that is intended to represent only those aspects or characteristics of persons that are crucial to conceiving of them as potential citizens of a well-ordered liberal society.[60] Paramount among these characteristics are a conception of the good and a sense of justice. Rawls explicitly denies, however, that justice as fairness involves commitment to any of the *comprehensive* moral ideals, such as autonomy or individuality, that have traditionally been associated with liberalism.[61] Perhaps, then, he would make a similar claim about self-ownership, which would appear to be closely connected with both of these more comprehensive ideals. If so, however, his view is open to the charge that it arbitrarily favors one conception of the person that is (arguably)[62] embedded in the political culture of liberal democracies—the Kantian conception—over other incompatible conceptions that have at least an equal claim to this status, one of which—the Lockean—clearly does endorse self-ownership.

To assess this charge, we must consider more carefully just what goes into the selection of principles of justice in the original position. The parties there are assumed to be motivated by a desire for primary goods. In the revised, political version of Rawls's theory, the latter are defined as means for advancing the "higher-order" interests of persons qua citizens of liberal democracies. He identifies three such interests: the first two involve developing one's two moral powers (a capacity for a sense of justice and for forming and revising a conception of the good), and the third is a desire to advance one's determinate conception of the good.[63] Thus, if the principles of justice can be said to embody a firm, noncontingent commitment to some form of self-ownership (i.e., a commitment which is not simply a matter of efficiency or the like), it would have to be the case that an interest in self-ownership is a corollary of one or more of these three fundamental interests.

[60] See especially "Justice as Fairness: Political Not Metaphysical," section VI. It should be noted that the most extreme statements of the Kantian interpretation—including the only explicit discussion of the principle of redress—occur in *A Theory of Justice*; on the other hand, Rawls has never explicitly disavowed any of these views. For an interesting defense of the "political" Rawls against the "Kantian" Rawls, see Charles Larmore, *Patterns of Moral Complexity* (Cambridge: Cambridge University Press, 1987), pp. 118–30.

[61] Rawls, *Political Liberalism*, p. 99f.

[62] The charge that there are rival, incompatible ideals of the person entrenched in the culture of democratic liberalism is powerfully defended in Gerald Doppelt, "Is Rawls's Kantian Liberalism Coherent and Defensible?" *Ethics*, vol. 99, no. 4 (July 1989), pp. 815–51; and in Patrick Neal, "Justice as Fairness: Political or Metaphysical?" *Political Theory*, vol. 18, no. 1 (February 1990), pp. 24–50. (I should note here that, while I am conceding otherwise for the sake of argument, I very much doubt that there is any substantial commitment in our culture to all of the features of the Kantian conception of the person. In particular, as I have already noted, I think very few people even implicitly endorse the extreme sort of egalitarianism exemplified by the principle of redress.)

[63] Rawls, *Political Liberalism*, pp. 73–77.

The most obvious candidates are the two higher-order interests concerned with one's conception of the good. Rawls has argued that a person's good consists in the fulfillment of a rational plan of life.[64] But if the parties in the original position are concerned not only to advance the good (so understood) of those whom they represent, but also to protect the latter's power to *form* and *revise* their conceptions of the good, then it seems that they would necessarily be concerned to ensure a degree of personal freedom that would be tantamount to a form of self-ownership. If this is correct, then we are again driven to the conclusion that there are deep reasons internal to Rawls's theory which support a principle like the MSOP, and the acknowledgment of the corresponding right would be much more than a grudging concession to the infirmities of human motivation under capitalism.

If this argument is correct, then the interpretation of Rawls championed (in different ways and for quite different purposes) by Nozick, Sandel, and Levine is mistaken in at least one crucial respect. Rawls's commitment to the sort of rights expressive of self-ownership is considerably deeper than these writers have acknowledged. In particular, it is certainly not the case that the "tendency to equality" is tempered *only* by considerations of efficiency. As Rawls himself has been careful to point out, the principle of redress is but a prima facie principle:

> Thus, even if an equal distribution of natural assets seemed more in keeping with the equality of free persons, the question of redistributing these assets (were this conceivable) does not arise, since it is incompatible with the integrity of the person.[65]

And for those who count egalitarian ideals as well as a principle of self-ownership among their intuitive commitments, the procedure Rawls suggests for resolving disagreements as to how these should be balanced against one another—namely, choosing the appropriate regulative principles in a hypothetical situation designed to ensure fairness and rationality—may well have considerable appeal.

To sum up: I have argued that the apparent tension between the MSOP and the principle of redress is significantly alleviated if we distinguish (in a way that has become quite common in ethical theorizing)[66] between

[64] Rawls, *A Theory of Justice*, ch. 7. This view is reiterated in *Political Liberalism*, pp. 176–78.

[65] John Rawls, "A Kantian Conception of Equality," in Virginia Held, ed., *Property, Profits, and Economic Justice* (Belmont, CA: Wadsworth Publishing Co., 1980), p. 205.

[66] R. M. Hare has argued that many of the common objections to utilitarianism can be satisfactorily answered if we distinguish between the *critical* and the *intuitive* levels of moral thinking; see his *Moral Thinking* (Oxford: Clarendon Press, 1981). Analogously, it has been suggested that the apparent dispute between moral impartialists and moral partialists can be largely dissolved if we distinguish between the level at which basic principles are chosen (which is the level at which impartiality is required) and the level at which such principles are applied in the actual making of decisions (which is the level at which partiality

the deeper theoretical level at which basic principles are *chosen* (for Rawls, this would be the level at which the design of the original position is determined) and the practical level at which such principles are *applied*. It seems certain that the basic structure that would serve to instantiate the principles chosen in the original position would require a substantive form of self-ownership in any society remotely like our own. However, this concession still leaves Rawls's theory open to Levine's charge that since "Kantian persons do not own themselves,"[67] and since the limits of human motivation in capitalist democracies may not be coextensive with the limits of human motivation in all conceivable societies, the principles of Rawls's deep theory require that we take whatever steps are feasible to bring about a more radically egalitarian society in which self-ownership would play a considerably diminished role. In response, I have argued that the principle of redress is but one component of a deep theory which also includes a concern to protect the interests of persons to form, promote, and revise their own conceptions of the good. But this latter, strongly individualist commitment ensures that a significant form of self-ownership is firmly anchored at the most fundamental level of the theory. What the principle of redress does (via the veil of ignorance) is to impose significant *constraints* on the ability of persons to advance their interests in pursuing and revising their conceptions of the good. The really important question, I believe, is whether the rationale for imposing such constraints is a compelling one. While I argued in my earlier essay that it is not, that position is compatible with holding that Rawls's theory is nevertheless a genuinely liberal one (and not a disguised form of radicalism) that incorporates a healthy, well-grounded commitment to self-ownership.

III. Self-Ownership, Autonomy, and Identity

The question as to why we should be concerned with self-ownership—at least of the moderate sort I have been discussing—may seem no more difficult to answer than the question as to why we should be concerned with freedom. For surely it is just a basic fact about human beings that, all else equal, they prefer to have the dominant say in how their own lives are to be run. Although I am sympathetic to this sort of response, it is vulnerable to the charge that self-ownership may be only an artifact of some (primarily Western) philosophical traditions and that, in any event, a society which failed to recognize self-ownership is not inconceivable. Indeed, it is often remarked how many people in our own society prefer authoritarian social structures (such as the military) precisely because they wish to be relieved of the burden of making the crucial decisions about how

is permitted). For an excellent discussion of this approach, see Marcia Baron, "Impartiality and Friendship," *Ethics*, vol. 101, no. 4 (July 1991), pp. 836–57.

[67] Levine, "Capitalist Persons," p. 51.

their lives are to go. Unfortunately, I am not sure to what extent one can provide an argument for self-ownership that is not ultimately either question-begging or dependent upon assumptions that may seem no better entrenched than the thesis of self-ownership itself. If that is so, then perhaps the principal value of the considerations I shall sketch below is simply the fact that they foster a greater appreciation of just what self-ownership involves and of what would be lost if it were given up.

First, and probably fairly obviously, anything like what is usually termed the right to autonomy presupposes the MSOP. While there is considerable dispute as to exactly what autonomy involves, the core idea is that of *self*-government.[68] But the latter surely requires some significant degree of self-ownership, since a person cannot have the right to exercise his powers of autonomous choice unless he has a substantive right to decide how he shall act, and he cannot have the latter right unless he is a self-owner.

A second consideration is this. A principle like the MSOP would seem to be required if we are to give appropriate normative expression to the fact that the metaphysical relationship a person bears to herself is far different from—and much closer than—the metaphysical relationship she bears to anyone else.[69] I am, after all, *identical* with only one person—me. While you can sometimes have knowledge of what I am thinking, feeling, and experiencing, only I can *have* those thoughts, feelings, and experiences. Each of us, as Thomas Nagel has so eloquently noted, has a particular perspective on the world that no one else can share simply in virtue of *being* the particular, separate individuals that we are.[70] Only the thesis of self-ownership, I am suggesting, provides us with a normatively adequate accommodation of these facts.

Wojciech Sadurski has urged the following objection to this kind of argument:

> Cutting your finger against your will causes you pain and discomfort; it is wrong because it harms and hurts you. To say that the wrong of it consists in removing part of your identity sounds odd. If we have rights not to have our fingers removed against our will it is because we value them (the fingers, that is) where they presently are; not because they are part of our separate identities.[71]

[68] See the essays collected in *The Inner Citadel*, ed. John Christman (New York: Oxford University Press, 1989).

[69] This remains true even if Parfit's reductionist account of personal identity is correct; see Derek Parfit, *Reasons and Persons* (Oxford: Oxford University Press, 1984).

[70] Thomas Nagel, *The View from Nowhere* (Oxford: Oxford University Press, 1986), passim.

[71] Wojciech Sadurski, "Natural and Social Lottery, and Concepts of the Self," *Law and Philosophy*, vol. 9, no. 2 (May 1990), p. 163.

But a defender of the argument in question need not hold that my fingers are a part of my identity in the sense that they are *essential* to my being the particular person that I am. All that needs to be maintained is that my fingers are a part—albeit an incidental, nonessential part—of the particular embodied person who is me. Furthermore, it is not clear just what Sadurski means when he asserts that my rights with respect to my fingers are grounded not in any relationship between my fingers and my identity but only in the fact that I normally value my fingers "where they presently are." For where they presently are is *attached to my hand*—hence, what I value about them is largely the fact that they are a *part of me*.

As I noted at the outset, I think that much of the apparent hostility to self-ownership is really directed at some of the questionable claims that have been made concerning its implications for a defensible system of property rights. Other complaints may seem to cut more deeply, however. Andrew Williams has complained that it is often supposed that unless a commitment is made to a doctrine of self-ownership (thus providing a wedge for anti-egalitarian forms of Lockeanism that he apparently finds objectionable), one must endorse the highly counterintuitive view that persons are collectively owned. But such an inference is invalid, he maintains, since "it ignores the possibility that persons might not be treated as subject to any *ownership* rights whatsoever."[72] Hence, the egalitarian denial of self-ownership need not rely upon the supposition that people are collectively owned:

> Rather it may rely, as for example does Rawls's theory, upon asserting a right to the existence of a basic structure of entitlements and incentives, which operates so that inequalities exist only if they benefit the least advantaged. Hence it becomes incumbent upon the anti-egalitarian to explain why the assertion of *this type of right* should be regarded as morally equivalent to that of a *property right* in other people.[73]

One can only wonder just how Williams understands the notion of self-ownership. If, as I have argued, it is best explicated by the MSOP, then it seems clear that, unless we suppose that *no one* has any rights over how people live their lives, a rejection of self-ownership *does* commit one

[72] Andrew Williams, "Cohen on Locke, Land, and Labour," *Political Studies*, vol. 40, no. 1 (March 1992), p. 64. No doubt there are others who might be tempted to take this line because they regard *all* talk of owning persons as morally inappropriate. But this would be a muddle since, on the standard legal analysis, to own something is just to have a certain bundle of rights with respect to that thing (primarily rights to control what is to be done with it). To endorse self-ownership, then, is to do nothing more than ascribe to persons certain control rights over themselves. For a summary of the standard analysis of ownership, see Lawrence C. Becker, *Property Rights* (London: Routledge and Kegan Paul, 1977), ch. 2.

[73] Williams, "Cohen on Locke, Land, and Labour," p. 65 (emphasis in original).

to the view that people are owned by other people. As we have seen, Rawls's theory does not involve an endorsement of collective ownership precisely because—and only because—it does involve an endorsement of self-ownership.

By way of conclusion, I would reiterate that the MSOP is so deeply rooted in our shared moral consciousness that any account of justice incompatible with it would have little intuitive appeal. Furthermore, I think it is fairly evident that acknowledging a principle of self-ownership has significant implications for a wide range of moral issues, most notably those concerned with paternalism.[74] I am less confident, however, that it can by itself provide us with much assistance in resolving broader questions such as the choice between libertarian and egalitarian theories of property and distribution. This is because, if I am correct in supposing that the source of much of the appeal of the self-ownership principle is the *special* relationship that people bear to themselves, it is very unclear how such a principle could be supposed to have direct implications for the rights of persons over parts of the world to which they are *not* so intimately related.

Philosophy, Illinois State University

[74] This would explain why a recent film dramatizing a struggle over a person's right to die was titled *Whose Life Is It Anyway?*

DESIGNING DEMOCRATIC INSTITUTIONS AND THE PROBLEM OF EVIL: A LIBERAL CHINESE PERSPECTIVE*

By Baogang He

Chinese liberals have been searching for a just society, one regulated by democratic institutions and rules—a society where the human potential for evil is properly controlled. It is in this context that Chinese liberal intellectuals such as Yan Jiaqi,[1] Hu Ping,[2] and Liao Xun,[3] drawing on

* I feel much indebted to Andrew Nathan, Ellen Frankel Paul, Barry Hindess, and Lucien Bianco for their useful comments, and to the participants in the seminars given at the Department of Political Science, Research School of Social Sciences, Australian National University, Canberra; the Institute of East Asia, Columbia University, New York; and Ecole des Austes Etudes en Sciences Sociales, Paris. I would also like to thank Rosemary Smuts for her assistance in formatting the manuscript of this essay.

[1] Yan Jiaqi, born in 1942 in Jiangsu Province, has lived as an exile in Paris since 1989. Yan was elected Director of the Institute of Political Science in Beijing's Academy of Social Sciences in 1985. In October 1986, he was assigned to former Party General Secretary Zhao Ziyang's Central Research Group for Reform of Political Structure, a government organization headed by Zhao's trusted aide Bao Tong. In 1989, Yan played a major role as one of the leaders of the Association of the Intellectual Circle in Beijing. He was a member of a group of intellectuals who, in May 1989, issued a sharply worded statement attacking Deng Xiaoping as "China's uncrowned Emperor and a senile, muddle-headed dictator," and demanding his resignation. After the June 1989 Beijing Massacre, Yan and his wife Gao Gao fled to Paris, and, on July 20, 1989, co-founded the Federation Democracy of China, of which he was later elected chairperson.

His writings include: Yan Jiaqi, "Tizhi gaige shi dui chuantong wenhua de zhongda tupo" (Political reform makes a great breakthrough in traditional culture), *Shenzhen quingnianbao* (Shenzhen youth news), December 5, 1986; Yan Jiaqi, *Wode sixiang zichuan* (My intellectual autobiography) (Hong Kong: Sanlian shuju, 1988); for the English translation of *Wode*, see David S. K. Hong and Denis C. Mair, *Toward a Democratic China: The Intellectual Autobiography of Yan Jiaqi* (Honolulu: University of Hawaii Press, 1992); and Yan Jiaqi, *Zouxiang minzhu zhengzhi* (Toward democratic politics) (Teaneck, NJ: Global Publishing, 1989). See also *Yan Jiaqi and China's Struggle for Democracy*, ed. and trans. David Bachman and Dali Yang (Armonk, NY: M. E. Sharpe, 1991).

[2] Hu Ping was born in Sichuan Province in 1947. He was admitted to Beijing University in 1978 as a graduate student in European philosophy, specializing in Hobbes, Locke, and Hume. He became a contributor to the unofficial periodical *Wotu* (Fertile), in which he published his long essay "Lun yanlun ziyou" (On freedom of speech), defending the thesis that freedom of speech benefits society. He was voted into office as a representative in December 1980 in the county-level elections, during which he had campaigned for freedom of speech, obtaining 57 percent of the vote. His political stance made him so controversial that, after he obtained his M.A., the university was unable to find him a job. He remained unemployed for five years—the price he paid for having actively championed freedom of speech. In 1987, he enrolled in Harvard University in the U.S. to obtain a Ph.D. in Western political thought. He gave up his academic work when he was elected chairman of the Chinese Alliance for Democracy (CAD) in New York a year later—a position he held from January 1988 to June 1991. He is currently an editor for *Beijing Spring* in New York.

His writings include: Hu Ping, *Gei wo yige zhidian* (Give me a fulcrum) (Taiwan: Lianjing their respective experiences of the tragedies in China, have taken the idea that there is always a potential for evil in human nature as a starting-point for a just society and for designing democratic institutions.[4]

Thus, the topic of the evil side of human nature, which has been discussed through the centuries by Western theorists such as Marcus Aurelius, Augustine, Niccolò Machiavelli, Thomas Hobbes, David Hume, and James Madison, has come to be relevant to Chinese liberal thinkers.[5] The ideas of these Western theorists have some interesting new implications in a Chinese context. There has also been discussion of the Chinese legalist Han Fei-tzu (280?-233 B.C.),[6] whose doctrine of evil constituted the basis of his design for autocratic institutions.[7] It was often believed that Confucius (551–479 B.C.) ignored the issue of evil, but now scholars have argued that Confucius acknowledged the evil side of human action, although his acknowledgment of it is incomplete, secondary, and inconsistent.[8] There is, moreover, some debate on whether the Confucianist

chuban Gongshi, 1988); this is a collection of his essays which includes his writings before he went to the U.S. My citations of this collection refer in the main to his early works, such as "On Freedom of Speech" (1979). See also Hu Ping, "Bolinqiang suixiang" (Short notes on the Berlin Wall), *Democratic China*, no. 1 (Paris, April 1990), pp. 38–43; and Hu Ping, "Rujia renxinglun yu minzhu xianzheng" (The Confucian view of human nature and democratic constitutionalism), *China Tribune*, no. 374 (Taibei, 1991), pp. 111–18.

[3] Liao Xun, born in Beijing in 1950, is now a research fellow in economics, and the Vice Director of the Research Center of Social and Economic Development under the government of Hannan Province. He was a member of the Institute of Industry Economics in the Chinese Academy of Social Sciences and took part in economic reform in the early 1980s. He gained his reputation from his earlier advocation of the idea of "small government and large society," which was adopted by provincial leaders in Hannan in the mid-1980s. Since 1985, he has played a major role in designing the institutions of Hannan Province according to his liberal idea of limited government.

His writings include: Liao Xun, " 'Fange yuanze' yu zhengzhi minzhu" (Political democracy and the principle of preventing evil), *Zixue* (Self-learning), no. 1 (1987), pp. 6–9; and Liao Xun, *Xiaozhengfu dashehui* (Small government and large society) (Beijing: Shanhuan Press, 1991).

[4] Evil is only one of the central themes of Chinese liberals' thinking on democracy. Other important themes include human rights, procedures, and ways of infusing rights-based moral principles into democratic institutions. See Baogang He, "Democracy as Viewed by Three Chinese Liberals: Wei Jingsheng, Hu Ping, and Yan Jiaqi," *China Information*, vol. 6, no. 2 (Leiden, Autumn 1991), pp. 23–43.

[5] In this regard, Yan Jiaqi has been influenced by Machiavelli and Madison (see Yan, "Tizhi gaige"); Hu Ping has been influenced by Hobbes and Hume (see Hu, "Bolinqiang suixiang"); and Liao Xun has been influenced by Madison (see Liao, " 'Fange yuanze' yu zhengzhi minzhu").

[6] *Fajia* was the Chinese legalist or realist school, which emphasized strict control of the people by harsh laws, encouraged agriculture and aggressive warfare, and emphasized the need to preserve and strengthen the state. Like Machiavelli's famous treatise, to which it has often been compared, Han Fei-tzu's work is a handbook for the prince; see *Han Fei-tzu: Basic Writings*, trans. Burton Watson (New York: Columbia University Press, 1964).

[7] See Baogang He, "Han Fei quanli lilun tanwei" (An investigation of Han Fei-tzu's power theory), *Zhexue yu wenhua* (Monthly review of philosophy and culture), vol. 17, no. 3 (Taibei, March 1990), pp. 242–48.

[8] See, e.g., the introduction of Zhang Hao, *Youan yishi yu minzhu chuantong* (The sense of dimness and democratic tradition) (Taiwan: Lianjing chuban Gongshi, 1989).

idea of human nature hindered the development of democratic institutions in China. Zhang Hao, a scholar specializing in Chinese political thought, argues that the Confucianist overestimation of the good side of human nature, and underestimation of the evil side, were an intellectual hindrance to democracy in China.[9] Hu Ping, on the other hand, believes that Zhang's argument misses the point, and argues for the compatibility of Confucianism's positive view of human nature with the design of democratic institutions.[10]

My aim in this essay is to discuss the emerging Chinese liberal view of democracy. The view's central theme, as Yan Jiaqi argues, is that the idea that human nature is potentially evil is the starting-point for the rule of law and procedural justice.[11] Or in Liao Xun's words, the principle of preventing evil is a theoretical basis for democracy.[12] (I should make it clear here that the theorists I am discussing view evil as universal only in the sense that everyone could potentially be evil; this does not mean that all people are actually evil.) I shall attempt to describe, discuss, and develop this central theme and to provide a reliable theoretical foundation for the Chinese liberal arguments for the design of democratic institutions.

I characterize Hu Ping, Yan Jiaqi, and Liao Xun as liberals on the basis of the following criteria: they look for moderate, nonviolent avenues of reform; they exhibit a genuine concern about protecting basic civil liberties such as freedom of speech and of the press; and they favor a constitutional government designed to support the democratization process and provide institutional checks on authoritarianism.

I have selected Yan Jiaqi and Hu Ping as representatives of Chinese liberals' thinking on evil and democracy because their works are relatively systematic and well argued and have greatly influenced today's China. I have selected Liao Xun, a less well-known scholar, because he is the author of a 1987 article[13] which specifically discusses the issue of evil and democracy and raises a number of interesting points. I have refrained from discussing the leading thinkers of democratic theory and practice in post-Mao China, such as Wang Ruoshui, Su Shaozhi, and Hu Jiwei, because their commitment to, and discussion of, the Marxist theory of alienation presupposes an ideal of the goodness of human nature which causes them to pay less attention to the problem of evil than the three writers I have selected. Moreover, their understandings of democracy fall into the Marxist framework, which has been declining. Finally, although I focus on three main Chinese liberals, I will broadly refer to and discuss

[9] *Ibid.*, ch. 1 and conclusion.

[10] Hu Ping, "Rujia renxinglun," p. 111. A more detailed discussion of this subject is beyond the scope of this essay.

[11] Yan Jiaqi, "Tizhi gaige"; Yan, *Wode sixiang zichuan*; and Bachman and Yang, eds., *Yan Jiaqi and China's Struggle for Democracy*, pp. 54–58.

[12] Liao Xun, " 'Fange yuanze' yu zhengzhi minzhu," p. 7.

[13] *Ibid.*

the ideas of a group of other liberal writers such as Jin Guantao, Su Wei, Ding Xueliang, and Ding Chu.

I should acknowledge that although Hu Ping, Yan Jiaqi, and Liao Xun share some views on evil, they have different arguments (which I will discuss in this essay) and they will play different political roles (which are beyond the scope of my discussion here). I should also note that although political thought about institutional arrangements depends on certain suppositions about human action, institutional design in political life also depends on culture, technology, economics, and the details of particular situations.

The remainder of this essay is divided into five sections. Section I describes the emergence of the discourse of evil and institutional design—that is, the shift from the notion of goodness to the concept of evil as a starting-point in Chinese political thought on democracy. Section II discusses Chinese liberal views of evil and specifies the Chinese liberal concept of evil in terms of the violation of basic rights. Section III offers a justification for taking the supposition of potential evil as a starting-point for the design of liberal democratic institutions and briefly discusses the limits and problems associated with that approach. Section IV criticizes neo-authoritarian institutional design, which is based on the concept of the evil of people. Section V argues for the establishment of democratic institutions which would provide for a guarantee of individual rights, a division of power, and restrictive and regulative institutions to deal with the problem of evil.

I. The Emergence of the Discourse of Evil and Institutional Design

I should say right at the beginning that the emergence of the discourse of evil in China does not imply that the idea of goodness has disappeared or that it no longer plays a role in political thinking. Furthermore, when I observe that the Maoist project is largely based on the idea of the goodness or perfection of human nature, and that Chinese liberals' institutional design is largely based on the idea of evil, I do not mean to imply that the Maoist project does not incorporate the idea of evil and that the liberal project does not incorporate the idea of goodness.

The revolutionary and romantic project designed and guided by Maoism, which follows the Enlightenment tradition of Rousseau and Marx, can be seen as an attempt to design and create the best economic, political, and social institutions, and to transform the egoistic and self-interested human into "a new socialist man"[14] in order to achieve the

[14] This was borrowed from the idea of the "new Soviet man," which dominated political thought in the Soviet Union in the 1920s and 1930s.

ideal of a communist society. The Maoist project involves the following assumptions:

1. It assumes that humans, lacking innate defects, are thoroughly malleable and perfectible through a public-ownership system and education. This assumption makes it possible for Maoism to favor a moral-educational approach to reform. The Maoist "moral approach" to politics stresses the exemplary virtues of uprightness and benevolence as the essential ethical bases of social and political order, and denigrates written laws, regulations, and punishments as ineffective and even counterproductive. As Yan Jiaqi points out, the notion of the goodness of human nature is a starting-point for Mao Zedong's efforts toward "choosing a perfect successor" and launching movements aimed at "self-criticizing selfishness and fostering public spirit."[15] Here I should stress that the Maoist moral-educational approach should be distinguished from the rule-following educational approach to politics, which is based on the idea that politics is about devising the proper procedure to deal with conflicts, and that rule-following is a necessary condition for the operation of democratic institutions.

2. The idea that people are "perfectible" unavoidably implies that they are currently imperfect. In this respect, Maoism, according to Hu Ping, distrusts people and regards them as immature and unable to distinguish good from evil. Some Chinese communists inwardly believe that human nature is inferior and liable to be seduced by evil so as not to be interested in virtue.[16] Moreover, as American sociologist Andrew Walder observes, Maoism has a history of seeing hidden enemies and traitors within Chinese intellectual circles and within the Party. The proclaimed purpose of the Cultural Revolution was to unmask these hidden traitors, drag them out of their hiding places, and save socialism from domestic and international forces of subversion.[17] However, I should stress that the Maoist view of evil did not constitute an intellectual starting-point for Maoist institutional design, although it played a role in decision making. This contrasts with the case of Chinese liberals, who have different conceptions of evil and have taken the notion of evil as a normative premise (see Sections II and III below).

3. The Maoist project assumes that revolutionary elites have the capacity to master truth and science, to tell good from evil persons, to know what is a worthwhile project and how to carry it out. It is this assumption that makes the romantic revolutionary project feasible.

4. Points 1 and 2 show the Maoists' two-sided view of human nature—as both perfectible and imperfect. These aspects seem to be contradictory,

[15] Yan Jiaqi, "Tizhi gaige," p. 2.

[16] Hu Ping, "Bolinqiang suixiang," pp. 39–40, and "Rujia renxinglun," pp. 117–18.

[17] Andrew Walder, "Cultural Revolution Radicalism: Variations on a Stalinist Theme," in *New Perspectives on the Cultural Revolution*, ed. William A. Joseph (Cambridge: Harvard University Press, 1991), pp. 43–46.

but are consistent in that both are compatible with the premise that social relationships are determinants of human nature. Maoism also sees human nature as class-differentiated. During the period of the early Cultural Revolution (1966–1976), a vulgar class analysis had defined the goodness of the proletariat, and the incorrigible evil of the "bad classes" on the basis of bloodlines. Further, it was thought that economic and educational environments determined whether human beings would be good or evil. On the Maoist view, it is private ownership that makes people selfish; and public ownership, if it is set up, can help human beings to be altruistic.

5. The Maoist project assumes that, for thousands of years, human beings have been slaves of private ownership, and that selfishness has taken root in their hearts. Consequently, when public ownership is established, selfish human nature will not be automatically eradicated. The solution to this problem is to carry out moral education which demands of the Chinese that they be moral sages, or achieve the highest ideal state. This requirement of being sages denies the legitimacy of individual self-interest: to be a sage is to break totally with the fundamental instinct of self-interest.

6. Economic institutional arrangements such as public ownership are important to the Maoist project in the sense that these arrangements are conceived of as useful tools to mold human nature, and as instruments to achieve the ideal of a communist society. At the same time, the idea that state institutions can be used to perfect people unavoidably implies that the state is better than and should be above the people. In political terms, institutional checks on top leaders are thought to be of little importance, because it is assumed that the first-generation revolutionary leaders are intellectual masters and moral sages. This assumption creates and supports the idea that revolutionary leaders such as Mao Zedong are so good that they do not need to be checked, or at least that we can trust them generally without checking them. As a result, as Liao Xun observes, the principle of preventing evil through the division of power was overlooked by the Chinese communists.[18]

In the early 1930s, Reinhold Niebuhr identified the errors of the communist project in the following terms: the communists found the Kingdom of God in history, and regarded humans as perfectible; and communist economic reorganization gravely jeopardized the condition of freedom. Niebuhr also predicted that the destruction of economic privilege could hardly be expected to alter human nature to the degree that no one thereafter would desire to make selfish use of power. Moreover, the attempt to establish an economic equilibrium through public ownership might create new inequalities in the distribution of power. Finally, the abuse of power was bound to grow as the pure revolutionary ideal-

[18] Liao Xun, " 'Fange yuanze' yu zhengzhi minzhu," p. 8.

ists were supplanted by those who consciously sought the possession of power.[19]

Writing in the 1980s, fifty years after Niebuhr's remarkable criticisms of communism, Chinese liberals began to arrive at the same conclusions. The difference is that the Chinese liberals' works have been written not only in words but also in tears, suffering, and even blood; that is, Chinese liberals have witnessed and suffered from the failures of the Maoist project in practice, while Niebuhr successfully predicted them. The Great Leap Forward of 1958, which aimed at the establishment of a "People's Commune," resulted in the end in the deaths of millions from hunger. The failure of the Great Leap Forward caused the first crisis in Mao's authority and shook the faith of the peasantry in the Party and in Mao himself. Even more disillusioning were the consequences of the Cultural Revolution, which led the masses, intellectuals, ordinary Party members, and bureaucrats to doubt Maoism's official ideology and its final goal, and to become more pragmatic and individualistic. Post-Mao China has been marked by open disbelief in the superiority of socialism, widespread contempt for those wishing to join the Party, a view of officials as a self-seeking exploitative class, and pervasive political indifference. In the 1980s, what Chinese officials called a crisis of faith, confidence, and trust reflected not only the lingering disillusionment of the Maoist era but also problems generated by the emerging post-1976 policies.

In particular, the Cultural Revolution, as Hu Ping argues, created the following forms of evil.[20] It encouraged ordinary people to derive pleasure from the misfortune of others, and to become free-riders, seeking advantages from their community while not doing their share. It encouraged them to be filled with envy, or hostility, at the greater good of others, and to be willing to deprive them of their greater benefits. High officials such as Marshal Lin Biao, who strove for supreme power, willingly practiced deception and hypocrisy, and even attempted to assassinate Mao Zedong in 1971. Lin Biao said clearly that one who attempts to be ambitious has to lie in political life. In factional fights during the Cultural Revolution, evildoers were happy to dehumanize their victims before destroying them, with or without disguising the act under a cloak of morality. It is because of this historical and intellectual background that Chinese liberals take the problem of evil seriously and attempt to redefine politics and human nature.

[19] Reinhold Niebuhr, *Moral Man and Immoral Society: A Study in Ethics and Politics* [1932] (New York: Charles Scribner's Sons, 1948), pp. 61, 222; see also Charles W. Kegley and Robert W. Bretall, *Reinhold Niebuhr: His Religious, Social, and Political Thought* (New York: Macmillan, 1956), pp. 15, 139, 302.

[20] Hu Ping, writing in the periodical *China Spring*, July 1988, p. 50. See also Jin Guantao, "Zhongguo wenhua de wutoubang jinsheng" (Utopianism in Chinese culture), *Twenty-First Century*, vol. 2 (December 1990); Yan Jiaqi, "Tizhi gaige"; and Bachman and Yang, eds., *Yan Jiaqi and China's Struggle for Democracy*.

I turn now to the Chinese liberals' redefinition of human nature, their ideal of politics, and their solution to Chinese political problems, focusing on the following three developments. First, liberal-minded Chinese intellectuals have rejected the Marxist belief that human nature can be molded at will by exposing it to proper external conditioning; in this they agree with Hobbes that humans possess ineradicable selfish instincts. They seem to have arrived at the same conclusion as social scientists in the former Soviet Union in the 1960s—the conclusion that human nature cannot be completely changed.[21] To say that human nature cannot be completely changed is misleading (as I argue below); but what matters here is the underlying effort of Chinese liberals to legitimize individual interests, and the recognition that the design of political institutions has to meet basic individual needs, both physical and social. Moreover, the question concerning the wickedness of humans has led Yan Jiaqi to address the related question concerning the design of institutions, the finest and most subtle of human inventions. Yan Jiaqi seeks an external remedy; that is, he seeks to focus on how to change external conditions and how to systematically establish institutional constraints on evil. This, I observe, is very close to Hume's idea that since it is impossible to change or correct anything material in our nature, the most we can do is attempt to change our circumstances and situation, so that we find the observation of the laws of justice to be our nearest interest, and their violation our most remote interest.[22]

Chinese liberals are also rethinking the role of economic institutions in molding human nature. In contrast to the Maoist view that public ownership can eradicate selfish human nature, Chinese liberals argue that the power of economic institutions is limited: such institutions might influence human actions in various ways, but we cannot expect that sound institutions can actually extinguish selfish tendencies. Chinese liberals provide a further argument against the Chinese Marxist environmentalist view of human nature: it can lead to the development of either autocratic or democratic political institutions. This ambiguity in the environmentalist view of human nature does not allow for a solid intellectual foundation for democracy. However, although some liberals, such as Jin Guantao, reject the economic environmentalist view, they fall ironically into, to some degree, a cultural environmentalist view—the view that traditional Chinese culture necessitated Mao's effort to look for a utopian society.[23] Further, the rejection of Marxist economic determinism does not imply that the environmentalist view of human nature is totally wrong. In fact, institutional design does presuppose elements of the environmentalist view

[21] James Davis, *Human Nature in Politics: The Dynamics of Political Behavior* (New York: John Wiley and Sons, Inc., 1963), p. 1.

[22] David Hume, *A Treatise of Human Nature* (London: J. M. Dent and Sons, Ltd., 1949), vol. 2, p. 237.

[23] Jin Guantao, "Zhongguo wenhua."

of human nature, in that well-established institutions can change, or at least influence, human actions.

The second development in the Chinese liberals' approach is their rejection of perfectionism. Given the pessimistic view of human beings inspired by Hobbes, the ideal of the complete perfection of a political system, or a human being, is thought by Chinese liberals such as Jin Guantao, Yan Jiaqi, Hu Ping, and Su Wei to be both impossible and undesirable; and there can be no repose for humanity in a "good society" defined once and for all.[24] Perfectionism, a teleological theory, presupposes that its proposed goal is unique and the best in the world; thus, to maintain its superiority, it denies the existence of other doctrines and the rights of dissenters. Consequently, it has led unconsciously to totalitarianism and autocracy in China.[25] Contrary to the perfectionist view of politics, the object of politics now, in Jin Guantao's view, is not happiness, but liberty; and a perfectionist goal is not necessary for the design of a rational society.[26] Human beings are not divine; therefore, their actions cannot escape the stain of self-interest and evil. Political achievements of democratic institutions must in consequence always be limited, fragmentary, and incomplete. The design of democratic institutions is not a final and perfectionist solution to the problem of evil, but it is better than the autocratic way of dealing with the problem of evil. Also, as Hu Ping argues, the democratic election system cannot ensure that the best persons are elected; however, it can ensure that people are capable of voting corrupt politicians out of office.[27] Chinese liberal-minded intellectuals, therefore, look to the democratic system as a relatively better political system—or, in Hu Ping's terms, a "possible good system" rather than "the best possibility"—to avoid the worst consequences associated with the evil of human behavior.[28]

Third, Chinese liberals have opposed the Maoist "moral approach" to politics.[29] The reason they reject Mao's "moral approach" is their shared disappointment in the social experiment in which Mao Zedong attempted to mold "the new socialist man" by mobilizing and indoctrinating the

[24] See "Tansuo weilai de daolu: Dongbailin shirentan" (Exploring the road to the future: Ten people's conversation in East Berlin), *Democratic China*, no. 2 (June 1990), pp. 42, 44, 48; and Jin, "Zhongguo wenhua."

[25] Chinese moral perfectionism can be compared with German racial perfectionism: the former provided a justification for the Party to deny the rights of those who were regarded as immoral; the latter provided a justification for the Nazis to fight to "liberate" mankind from "rule of subhumans," and to eliminate forever certain "races" such as the Jews.

[26] Jin Guantao, "Zhongguo wenhua," p. 31.

[27] Hu Ping, writing in *China Spring*, July 1988, p. 50.

[28] Hu Ping, *Gei wo yige zhidian*, p. 178; see also Su Wei's speech in "Tansuo weilai de daolu" (*supra* note 24), p. 44.

[29] In traditional China, there were various ideas of hell, which often hold, e.g., that Yarnluor, ruler and judge of the Chinese hell, can see one's sins from his terrace, or that one's sins are reflected in the mirror, etc. Thus, one can still rely on religious persuasion to control evil. However, since belief in hell has been declining in China, the institutional remedy proposed by Chinese liberals is likely to be more effective.

masses. In reality, the so-called "new socialist man" turned out to be a hypocrite: an altruist in appearance, but inwardly still predominantly motivated by innate drives such as self-interest and self-protection. And after all, this social experiment proved so cruel that it was carried out at the cost of millions of people's lives; it has totally ignored individuality, privacy, and self-respect, and has forced the Chinese to behave in ways defined by the instructions of Maoism and the Party. In this respect, Jin Guantao carefully argues that the Learning from Lei Feng Movement[30] was a moral elitism that still allowed the masses to pursue selfish interests; it consequently set a limit on utopian perfectionism. The Red Guard Movement in the 1960s, on the other hand, forced people to overcome selfishness and foster public spirit. It nevertheless failed in the end, and the result has been the destruction of moral life and the creation of a moral vacuum.[31]

Chinese liberals such as Yan Jiaqi now view the checks and balances of a democratic political system and the socially divided structure of a civil society, rather than broad ethical imperatives, as the most effective means of resolving the problem of evil and of maintaining political order.[32] They would no longer rely on human beings to do good on their own, but would restrict them in such a way that they could do only minimal harm under well-established institutions. This shift in opinion among Chinese intellectuals has been demonstrated in their strong criticisms of Li Xiangnan, a heroic, honest, and upright reformer in the *Xinxin* television series in 1984,[33] and of the emergence of neo-authoritarianism[34] between 1986 and 1989—both of which carried too many messages in favor of the traditional idea of the rule of honest and upright officials.

II. Liberal Views of Evil

I should first acknowledge the following points. The concept of evil is controversial, and it is difficult to agree on what evil is.[35] Thus, there are

[30] Lei Feng, an ordinary soldier, was praised by Mao Zedong in the 1960s as a moral hero who sacrificed himself for the public good.

[31] Jin Guantao, "Zhongguo wenhua," pp. 26–27.

[32] See Yan Jiaqi, "Tizhi gaige," pp. 54–58; Bachman and Yang, eds., *Yan Jiaqi and China's Struggle for Democracy*; and Baogang He and David Kelly, "Emergent Civil Society and the Intellectuals in China," in *The Development of Civil Society in Communist Systems*, ed. R. F. Miller (Sydney: Allen and Unwin, 1992), pp. 24–39. "Civil society" refers here to autonomous organizations that are independent of direct political control by the state or the Party.

[33] This series told the story of a reformer who served people whole-heartedly, sacrificing his own interests.

[34] Neo-authoritarian thought emerged among a group of intellectuals in both government and the academy in Beijing between 1986 and 1989, and had the attention and support of senior Party reformers, including the former General Secretary, Zhao Ziyang. See Liu Jun and Li Lin, eds., *Xinquanwei zhuyi* (Neo-authoritarianism) (Beijing: Beijing jingji xueyuan chubanshe, 1989), part 2. I will discuss the neo-authoritarian belief in the necessity of a strong government in Section IV.

[35] For example, Immanuel Kant distinguishes natural evil from moral evil in his *Religion within the Limits of Reason Alone*, trans. Theodore Greene and Hoyt Hudson (New York: Harper and Brothers, 1960), pp. 24–25. Ronald Milo distinguishes perverse wickedness from

difficulties with the slippery notion of evil when it is applied in concrete situations. Further, it is impossible to formulate a concept of human nature which can constitute an intellectual basis for institutional design. This is also true of the Chinese liberal intellectuals I discuss, who have no unified conception of evil; each usually has his own individual understanding of the idea. In order to avoid the controversy about evil, what I would like to do here is describe the Chinese liberals' views of what is and what is not evil; then I will formulate a concept of evil in terms of the violation of rights.

The Maoist communists believed that self-interest is the source of evil and that moral destruction lies deep in the individual self as a sort of "original weakness." Now, most Chinese liberal-minded intellectuals, such as Yan Jiaqi, Hu Ping, and Jin Guantao, believe that if self-interest does not take the form of self-centeredness—everyone is to serve my interests—it should not be regarded as evil. Rather, self-interest should be regarded as an undifferentiated energy which might, therefore, be seen as neutral—in the sense that it can become either a positive or a negative force, depending on the direction of the guidance provided by institutional arrangements.[36] Hence, Hu Ping believes that any revolutionary project which goes against individual interests would fail in the end. Attempts to advance personal interests are not necessarily evil; rather, those who block such attempts are doing evil.[37] Jin Guantao argues that once rules, private interests, and social differences are denied, some problems associated with self-interest might be overcome, but society itself would be destroyed. The social problems arising from concern with private interests can only be resolved through the establishment of new and fair institutions and of meta-rules which define how we change rules.[38] What is more important is that, while Maoism attempts to demolish private ownership on the ground that it creates and preserves private and individual motivations, Chinese liberals favor a privatization program on the ground that private interests are legitimate and are the source of enormous energies for productivity.

Yan Jiaqi defines evil as imperfection, corruption, weakness, and being liable to make mistakes.[39] As examples of evil, he cites abuse of power,

preferential wickedness in his *Immorality* (Princeton, NJ: Princeton University Press, 1984). Carl Schmitt regards evil not only as dangerous, corrupt, weak, cowardly, and stupid, but as rude, instinctive, vital, and irrational; see his *The Concept of the Political* [1928], trans. George Schwab (New Brunswick, NJ: Rutgers University Press, 1976), p. 96. John Rawls believes that what moves evil human beings is their love of injustice; they delight in the impotence and humiliation of those subject to them; see his *A Theory of Justice* (Oxford: Clarendon Press, 1971), p. 439.

[36] Yan Jiaqi, *Wode sixiang zichuan*, pp. 98–99.

[37] Hu Ping, writing in *China Spring*, April 1988, p. 59; June 1988, p. 52; and July 1988, p. 4.

[38] Jin Guantao, "Zhongguo wenhua," p. 31.

[39] Yan Jiaqi, *Wode sixiang zichuan*, pp. 92–98.

corruption, and uncivilized service by a bureaucrat or by a worker in a shop. Yan also cites a number of Machiavelli's ideas: that human nature is, generally speaking, evil; that people are often beset by folly, wickedness, ordinary depravity, and impulses of rage, resentment, jealousy, and avarice; that they have irregular and violent propensities; and that the Prince does not need to keep his word.[40] Yan further argues that Machiavelli revealed the absence of regularity in political behavior. Today, Yan contends, it has become increasingly possible, through the use of scientific methods, to study movements that are without regularity, and to design procedures and institutions that would make it possible to avoid large-scale, organized violence and war.[41] It was his awareness of the terrible consequences of the combination of evil behaviors and an unlimited power that led Yan to the idea of democratic institutions. Here, Yan quotes James Madison but does not mention his name: if people were angels, no government would be necessary; if angels were to govern, neither external nor internal controls on government would be necessary.[42] Yan's view of evil is that it is universal in the sense that everyone has the potential to do evil.

Liao Xun has argued that assuming that human nature is potentially evil means only that anyone who holds power will become evil if there are no built-in checks on that power. In Liao's understanding, evil applies narrowly to the power-holders rather than to the masses.[43] This is of great significance for different types of institutional design (I discuss this in Section IV).

Hu Ping emphasizes that one ought to distinguish between actual and potential evil. The Maoist communists failed to make this distinction, and therefore punished even those who were regarded only as potentially evil. For Hu Ping, liberal institutions should be designed to minimize potential evil at a psychological level, and to prevent it from becoming a destructive force in political life. However, civil and criminal penalties are not imposed on *potentially* evil persons, nor are such people denied their rights in the name of controlling potential evil.[44] This feature of liberal institutions distinguishes them from autocratic institutions, which attempt to suppress all potential evil by depriving individuals of civil and political rights.

Hu Ping also locates evil not only in human actions but in specific forms of organization and ideology. Hu regards totalitarian institutional

[40] Niccolò Machiavelli, *The Prince* (New York: Penguin Books, 1961).

[41] Yan Jiaqi, *Wode sixiang zichuan*, ch. 10.

[42] Yan Jiaqi, "Tizhi gaige"; see also James Madison, Alexander Hamilton, and John Jay, *The Federalist Papers*, introduction by Clinton Rossiter (New York: New American Library, 1961), p. 322.

[43] Liao Xun, " 'Fange yuanze' yu zhengzhi minzhu."

[44] Author's conversations with Hu Ping, January 10, 1993, and November 18, 1993. See also Hu Ping, "On Freedom of Speech," in *Gei wo yige zhidian*.

arrangements as evil because they favor a structure of overcentralized power and deny civil and political rights. The original purpose of autocracy, as Hu argues, was to do good, but it monopolized the power to do good, and prevented others from doing good. This led to the suppression of others who were willing to do good, and consequently created evils.[45] Also, as Edward Friedman correctly observes, Maoism can be understood as an attempt to avoid certain evils perpetuated under Stalinism. Maoism, however, misidentified the source of those evils: Mao saw his "opponents" as willingly taking the "capitalist road" and looking for supreme power.[46] As Jin Guantao points out, Mao even regarded political rules, regulations, and bureaucratic organs as so-called "bourgeois rights" and as sources of "revisionism"; and this led him to crack down on the Party and on governmental organizations during the early period of the Cultural Revolution.[47]

I would argue further that the overcentralized power which, in the Maoist view, is needed to demolish all evil, is nothing more than an institutionalized evil, or "evil of the Stalinist political system,"[48] in the sense that the party organization justified by Maoist ideology has at its disposal the means to carry out any immoral act and to anesthetize the moral sensitivities of those whom it makes its agents. In other words, the Party is capable of mobilizing respectable and rational actors in the service of an evil action. Worse still, people in positions of power and in public office do not feel guilty, because even if they do wrong, they take the view that if they refuse to do it, others will not refuse. Thus, they continue to do what might properly be regarded as evil. As a result, the centralization of political power provides new occasions for and temptations to injustice. This was also true of Nazi Germany: the Holocaust, as British sociologist Zygmunt Bauman notes, was a rational project of social engineering. Its evil lay not in irrational outbursts of racist feeling, but in the mobilization of bureaucracy and technology in the service of a totally evil and calculated purpose, the extinction of six million Jews.[49]

Hu Ping also identifies the evil of the official Chinese ideology. Maoism holds a perfectionist idea of goodness associated with the ideal of a communist society.[50] The pretension of scientific rationality in Maoism denies the validity of moral law and private ownership, since they are incompatible with historical materialism. Maoism prefers "substantial jus-

[45] Hu Ping, in *China Spring*, May 1988, p. 33.

[46] Edward Friedman, "Theorizing the Democratization of China's Leninist State," in *Marxism and the Chinese Experience*, ed. Arif Dirlik and Maurice Meisner (Armonk, NY: M. E. Sharpe), p. 173.

[47] Jin Guantao, "Zhongguo wenhua," pp. 29–30.

[48] This is the title of one of the wall-posters in Beijing University in 1989.

[49] Zygmunt Bauman, "The Social Manipulation of Morality: Moralizing Actors, Adiaphorizing Action," *Theory, Culture, and Society*, vol. 8 (1991), pp. 137–51.

[50] Hu Ping, *Gei wo yige zhidian*, pp. 3–8.

tice" to procedure, revolutionary cause to individual liberty and life. Consequently, it denies the rights of others to have their own dissident views of good and evil: the denial of the rights of others and even killing can be justified in terms of the revolutionary enterprise. Similarly, the failure to keep a promise can be justified in terms of substantial justice. For example, in the 1940s, the killing of Wang Shiwei, a writer and liberal-minded intellectual who attempted to maintain his own independent position, was seen as justified because Wang did not obey the Party and wanted "bourgeois freedom" in the Yanan Rectification Movement.[51] Likewise, the selling of opium by the Red Army in Manchuria in the 1930s and 1940s was seen as justified by the need to raise money in support of the revolutionary enterprise.

I would like to argue further that the evil of the official Chinese ideology is associated with the notion of salvation, and with the utopian ideal of the perfect human being. It sought a perfect system but unfortunately created evils. The Marxist and Maoist doctrine of the "dictatorship of the proletariat" led in reality to an absolute monopoly of power. Communism is in this respect more dangerous than Nazism, since its utopian illusions provide a moral facade for the most unscrupulous political policies and an opportunity for those who have evil motivations to do whatever they want.[52] Even worse, those who committed wrongs under Maoism, such as the Red Guards who beat their teachers to death during the Cultural Revolution, did not think what they did was evil; they thought it was for the good of the whole society. They should have felt very guilty indeed, but felt nothing of the sort at that time.[53] What had facilitated, justified, and even created this perverse consciousness was Mao's goal-based morality. As Richard Madsen, a specialist in Chinese culture, correctly argues, Maoism's emphasis on absolute purity and selflessness in fact precluded any kind of moral order. In the interest of absolute morality, it led to absolute immorality.[54] The history of the communist movement itself reveals that dissidents were tortured and killed in the name of defending the Marxist faith.[55] Moreover, a moral indoctrination move-

[51] The Yanan Rectification Movement (*Zhengfeng Yundong*) was launched in 1942 in the town of Yanan to remold the Party's thinking and guide its growth. It included study, discussion, criticism, and self-criticism, and involved intensive indoctrination and education in the principles of Mao Zedong's thought.

[52] Hu Ping, in *China Spring*, April 1988, p. 58.

[53] A similar case is that of Adolf Eichmann, who played a major role in Hitler's Final Solution but did not feel he was an evil-doer in the depths of his heart. He did not feel guilty before the law; rather, he declared with great emphasis that he had lived his whole life according to Kant's moral precepts, and especially according to a Kantian definition of duty. He thought he was a law-abiding citizen. Hannah Arendt comments that Eichmann gives us a lesson in the fearsome, word-and-thought-defying banality of evil. See Hannah Arendt, *Eichmann in Jerusalem: A Report on the Banality of Evil* (London: Faber and Faber, 1963), pp. 18, 120, 231.

[54] Richard Madsen, *Morality and Power in a Chinese Village* (Berkeley: University of California Press, 1984).

[55] Hu Ping, in *China Spring*, May 1988, p. 33.

ment has forced the Chinese people to confess their "sin"—that they have not yet rid themselves of their self-interest. It is this movement that serves to control evil among the populace: it makes people feel guilty; therefore, they always think that they are in error rather than that the Party makes mistakes.[56]

Drawing on the idea of organizational and ideological evils, I would like to elaborate on the idea of evil implicitly held, but not made clear, by Chinese liberals. The idea is that any doctrine, organization, or action which denies, violates, and deprives others of basic civil and political rights—except when it constitutes a reasonable limitation on rights[57]—should be regarded as evil. There are a number of reasons for characterizing the idea of evil in this way: (1) The nature of the evil of communist organizations and ideology, and the first step toward evil in Communist China, was in fact to deny, violate, and deprive others of their rights. (2) Most evil behaviors—such as arbitrary arrest and torture—involve, at the very least, the violation of rights. (3) This idea of evil is formulated in order to struggle against the tyranny of communist rule, and that is a reason why the concept of evil in terms of the violation of human rights is similar to John Locke's concept of tyranny, in which political power is said to be exercised in the absence of right.[58] Also, this understanding of evil implies and favors the idea of a rights-based morality, which I have discussed elsewhere.[59] (4) This conception of evil does not approach the Christian idea of original sin, or the Marxist ontological view of evil as the opposite of goodness. It allows for moral disagreement over the nature of evil; for example, the question of whether or not abortion is an evil is open to debate. Given the moral pluralism of modern societies, it is difficult to agree on one definition of evil. Nevertheless, a minimalist view of evil as the denial of rights has to be accepted at a meta-theoretical level, because it underlies the idea that human beings have the right to hold their own views of evil as long as they accept the overriding character of rights. If one denies the overriding character of rights, then one risks being deprived of the right to have one's own view of evil, because the official Chinese Marxist ontological view of good and evil would not allow peo-

[56] See Orville Schell, "Kafka, Kundera, Havel, and Mao," *Human Rights Tribune*, vol. 2, no. 3 (June 1991), p. 30. This movement is reminiscent of the practices of confession and penitence organized by the Christian Church in the Middle Ages. See Jean Delumeau, *Sin and Fear: The Emergence of a Western Guilt Culture, Thirteenth through Eighteenth Centuries*, trans. Eric Nicholson (New York: St. Martin's Press, 1990).

[57] On the issue of limitations on rights, see Baogang He, "Chinese Dissidents' Ideas of Human Rights: A Constructive Critique," *Thesis Eleven*, no. 30 (MIT Press, 1991), pp. 56–74.

[58] Locke states that "as usurpation is the exercise of power, which another hath a right to; so tyranny is the exercise of power beyond right, which no body can have a right to." See John Locke, *Two Treatises of Government* (Cambridge: Cambridge University Press, 1988), p. 199.

[59] Baogang He, "Infusing Morality into Political Institutions," *Journal of Contemporary China*, vol. 2, no. 1 (1993), pp. 35–52.

ple to question the doctrine itself, on the basis that the doctrine claims to be absolutely true and provides a correct answer for them. In contrast, one of the great intellectual virtues of the liberal conception of evil is that it is favorable to the institutional protection of the rights of all and is not sympathetic to despotism.

III. The Justification for Taking Evil as a Starting-Point

A. The argument against taking goodness as a starting-point

Yan Jiaqi, Hu Ping, and Liao Xun have rejected the assumption of the goodness and perfectibility of human nature which facilitated Mao Zedong's attempts to seek a perfect utopian society, and which led ironically to evil consequences during the Cultural Revolution. Their rejection of this assumption is based on their belief in ineradicable selfish instincts, the utopian nature of perfectionism, the danger of the absence of checks and balances in political institutions, and the ineffectiveness of the moral approach (all of which I have discussed above). The further question raised here concerns what is wrong with Mao's idea of the goodness of human nature as a starting-point for institutional design. There are, at least, two serious problems with the idea. First, if one thinks that goodness is the greatest and highest value, one regards it as universal; in other words, those who think that they represent goodness will require it to be increasingly accepted by members of their community. For Chinese communists the ideal of a communist society is obviously a great good for China. The Chinese Communist Party, therefore, has been imposing the value of a communist society on the Chinese both by propaganda and, when faced with resistance, by force. Forcing people to believe in this value, and to make self-sacrifices for it, is made necessary by the universalization of the goodness and is easily justified by such an apparently good intention.

Second, Mao's assumption of the goodness of human nature has led to the destruction of virtue under totalitarian institutions. Let me examine the social logic of this assertion. Mao's assumption implies a notion of hierarchical moral order in which virtuous and honest people are superior to "dishonest" people (see Section I). Hence, moral persons have a legitimate duty to enlighten these "evil" persons and deserve to rule over them. According to these ideas, totalitarian institutions are designed in favor of so-called moral persons, who are given political privileges to mobilize the masses and who have a justification for ignoring the rights of "immoral persons." That was exactly the situation under the theory of vulgar class determinism (which I mentioned in Section I) during the early period of the Cultural Revolution; that is, it was the moral obligation of members of the "good classes" to remain segregated from members of the "bad classes" and to continuously hold them suspect, even when their behavior appeared correct. Members of the "good classes" were also permitted to humiliate and physically punish members of the "bad classes" at the slightest provocation.[60] As a result, protection of the rights of everyone was ignored and even overridden, and the so-called moral persons tended to be corrupt because of the lack of any institutional checks on their behavior. In cases of this sort, a moral crisis inevitably occurs: people no longer believe in a "revolutionary morality"; a moral vacuum emerges, and virtue is destroyed. This is exactly what has happened in contemporary China.

B. The argument for taking evil as a starting-point

Having learned a lesson from Mao's attempt to use human goodness and perfectibility as the starting-point of institutional design, Yan Jiaqi, Hu Ping, and Liao Xun have taken potential evil rather than goodness as a premise for the design of democratic institutions, and have looked for a relatively better political system rather than an ideally perfect system.

However, these three writers have justified the idea of potential evil in different ways. Yan Jiaqi's justification is normatively oriented. For him, the supposition of potential evil is not a question of whether or not human beings are born evil or good; this is in fact a meaningless, old scholastic question. Indeed, the supposition of evil is more about finding a *normative starting-point* than about probing the truth of human nature, because everyday life provides evidence for both the idea that humans are evil and the idea that they are good. What matters to Yan Jiaqi is *the utility of assuming the existence of evil action as an intellectual premise*.[61] Liao Xun, in turn, provides the practical argument that the supposition of potential evil helps us question the motives and actions of all leaders, even national heroes, veteran revolutionaries of great distinction, and the "great people." The supposition also compels us to design a system of institutional checks to control evil, and fair institutional arrangements to help transform evil into a positive force in political life.[62] Hu Ping's justification of the supposition of potential evil is very careful and leads to a balanced position. On the one hand, Hu argues that the design of political offices should be based on the assumption that power-holders tend to be corrupt, rather than on the ideal of "honest and upright officials." On the other hand, he argues that to select and appoint office-holders, one needs to look at whether or not persons are honest and upright.[63] He

[60] Lowell Dittmer and Chen Ruoxi, *Ethics and Rhetoric of the Chinese Cultural Revolution*, Studies in Chinese Terminology, No. 19 (Berkeley: Center for Chinese Studies, University of California, 1981), pp. 112–13, 115.

[61] Yan Jiaqi, "Tizhi gaige."

[62] Liao Xun, " 'Fange yuanze' yu zhengzhi minzhu," pp. 8–9.

[63] Hu Ping, in *China Spring*, June 1988, p. 53.

also argues that democratic politics is based on other factors in addition to the assumption of evil (a topic I shall return to later in this section).[64]

The above justifications by these three writers are occasional and unsystematic. To reconstruct their ideas, I would like to provide the following more systematic scheme of justifications.

G. W. F. Hegel argued that the Christian doctrine which states that humans are by nature evil is loftier than the alternative doctrine which takes them to be by nature good, because the doctrine of original sin holds that humans are free agents capable of not allowing themselves to be determined by natural impulse. However, Hegel rejected the attempt to take the merely negative as a starting-point and to exalt to the first place the volition of evil, because the evil-starting-point approach is hostile to his favoring of the unification of political powers.[65] I disagree with Hegel's rejection of the approach, but agree with his idea of the strength of the doctrine of evil. Nevertheless, I use different arguments to support the supposition of universal potential evil.

The justification from formal justice. The design of liberal institutions requires the formal justice of equal treatment; that is, people should be treated as equals, not only in the sense that they have the same rights and opportunities, but also in the sense that *all* persons ought to be presumed to be potentially evil. The supposition of universal evil would lead in political practice to a complete system of checks and balances.

The justification from uncertainty. Human behavior is fundamentally uncertain and contingent in different times and contexts, and there are cognitive limits which prevent us from knowing who is evil and who is good. We also have a problem of defining a criterion for distinguishing good from evil due to our disagreement about moral issues. Given the uncertainty of human behavior, the limits of knowledge, and disagreements about moral judgments, one strategy is to assume, as Hume did, that *everyone* ought to be presumed to be a knave.[66] This strategy provides us with a simple model to address the serious and fundamental problem of evil involved in institutional design, and to help us focus on the issue of how political stability can be sustained in the worst situation. It highlights the worst possible consequences of evil, such as civil war. This awareness of the problem can force us to keep eternal vigilance over evil, because victory against evil is never final.

To illustrate the usefulness of this strategy, take the example of security checks. All people who travel by air are required to pass through

[64] Hu Ping, "Bolinqiang suixiang," pp. 42–43.

[65] G. W. F. Hegel, *Hegel's Philosophy of Right*, trans. T. M. Knox (Oxford: Oxford University Press, 1967), pp. 175, 231.

[66] David Hume, *The Philosophical Works*, ed. Thomas Hill Green and Thomas Hodge Grose (Aalen: Scientia Verlag, 1964), vol. 3, pp. 117–19. See also Baogang He, "An Analytical Investigation of Hume's Supposition of Knavery in Institutional Design," *Current World Leaders*, December 1994.

metal detectors and to allow their personal bags to be X-rayed. What does this mean? It implies that each person is assumed to be one who might carry a weapon. In fact, it is well known that only a very marginal percentage of people will do so. But technically, since we cannot readily tell those who carry weapons from those who do not, everyone is assumed to be a potential weapon carrier and all are subject to checks by a set of security arrangements.

The justification from practical value. The supposition of universal potential evil is certainly *exaggerated* in being applied to all human beings as part of the character of the race.[67] Exaggerated or not, however, the supposition has its value. Since the assumption is that even those who attempt to deal with the problem of evil could potentially be evil, there is no excuse for attempting to deprive others of their rights under the guise of resolving the problem of evil. Furthermore, the supposition of potential evil strengthens our fundamental skepticism regarding the possibility of achieving a perfect political system, and therefore helps us realize the limitations of politics. It also excludes Platonic and Confucian efforts to seek for the perfection of politics, because the evil side of human action sets powerful limits on moral and political perfectionism. Consequently, this supposition of evil leads Chinese liberals such as Ding Chu to the belief that they would rather have two evil people who check each other than an angel without check.[68] In short, the supposition of evil is reasonable and useful in democratic political thinking.

Yan Jiaqi places quotation marks around his uses of the term "human nature," indicating his reservations about using the term. Hu Ping is more explicit in arguing that the supposition of evil human nature is a necessary but not sufficient basis for democracy, although he uses the term without quotation marks in his writings. Here I would make the point clearly: the idea of potential evil does not presuppose the idea of evil human nature. Further, I would argue, the notion that the concept of human nature has value in democratic thinking should be rejected. For any intellectual foundation for democracy in terms of human nature is misleading, because the assumption that humans have an essence is unproved; there is no proof of a fixed human nature, or of a fixed correspondence between human nature and normative suppositions. It is impossible for one to sum up one or two essences of human nature and to apply these in all places and all times. Moreover, there is no need for theories of democracy to get bogged down in the hopeless morass of the question of the existence and character of human nature. To assume the potential for evil action, rather than evil human nature, is enough for us to argue for democratic institutions.

[67] Kant, *Religion within the Limits of Reason Alone*, p. 24.
[68] Ding Chu, in *China Spring*, no. 79 (December 1989), p. 37.

C. Western theorists and the problem of evil

One charge that might be brought against the above supposition of potential evil is that this supposition is based solely on an emotional reaction to communist rule. This charge might include the assertion that if Chinese communist rule were to end, the idea of evil might die away. Thus, the Chinese liberals' search for a deep foundation for democratic theory would appear problematic. A critic might even argue that the notion of human nature is an old concept and is no longer useful—drawing support for his position from the fact that the problem of evil is discussed less by current Western political theorists such as John Rawls than it once was by classical political theorists such as Hobbes, Locke, Hume, and the Federalists.

This objection is not convincing, however, because the concept of potential evil is employed by liberals such as Hu Ping not only against Chinese communist rule but against the abuse of democratic powers among democrats overseas. Moreover, the concept of potential evil is a useful tool for analyzing the serious problems associated with the process of transition to democracy. Nevertheless, the objection raises some interesting questions: If contemporary Western political theorists are less interested in the problem of evil, does this constitute a reason to reject the use of the concept of evil held by Chinese liberals? Why has Hu Ping quoted the writings of Hobbes and Locke—and why has Yan Jiaqi cited Madison—while neither has appealed to the writings of contemporary political theorists such as John Rawls? In other words, why are Hu Ping and Yan Jiaqi more interested in classical rather than contemporary Western political theories in their consideration of the problem of evil?

To understand why, consider, as an example, the limits of John Rawls's idea of the original position being applied in China. In *A Theory of Justice*, Rawls has discussed the nature of the evil man, envy, the free-rider problem, egoism, militant civil disobedience, intolerance, and deception and hypocrisy.[69] However, all consideration of the evil side of human action is excluded in Rawls's idea of the original position, because, in Rawls's theory, the choice of a conception of justice should not be affected by accidental contingencies and "certain psychological propensities."[70] For example, the issue of envy is not discussed until the two principles of justice have already been chosen.[71] As a result, Rawls rejects the place of the notion of evil in his idea of the original position and presupposes that human beings have a potential sense of justice. This rejection sets limits

[69] Rawls, *A Theory of Justice*, 124, 136 (on egoism); 267–70, 354 (on the free-rider problem); 367 (on militant civil disobedience); 388 (on intolerance); 570 (on deception and hypocrisy); 439 (on the evil man); and 530–41 (on envy).

[70] *Ibid.*, p. 530.

[71] *Ibid.*, p. 531.

on the applicability of Rawls's ideals of the person and the well-ordered society in China. If the feasibility of the ideal of the person is limited by the capacities of human nature, as Rawls argues,[72] then I would argue that Rawls's conception of the original position is limited by his failure to incorporate the idea of evil. If the psychological motive of being unscrupulously eager to excel in everything is introduced into Rawls's idea of the original position, some people might choose to be wrongdoers rather than choosing the two principles of justice. The fact that Rawls has not given enough attention to the conception of evil limits the application of his idea of the original position in the countries where the problem of evil is a pressing issue in political life. That is why Rawls has not been quoted by Chinese liberals in their consideration of the problem of evil.[73]

Conversely, on the issue of evil, classical political theories are more relevant to Chinese liberals than Rawls's theory of justice, because of the nature of the Chinese social context. There are obvious parallels between arguments against absolutism in the writings of John Locke and arguments against totalitarianism in the writings of Hu Ping, and between the Federalists' writings on how to prevent civil war and Yan Jiaqi's writings on how to establish federal democracy.

D. *Chinese liberals and the concept of virtue*

It should be made clear that the point of my discussion of the justifications of the supposition of universal potential evil is not to reject the assumption that many people will be honest and virtuous. In fact, this assumption can help to explain the feasibility of institutions designed to control potential evil.

Take the problem of the feasibility of a system of institutional checks and balances. Evil people may have an interest in obeying rules in a cooperative game, if they would otherwise suffer or somehow lose. But we cannot expect that evil persons will strictly comply with rules that they agree to set up in a noncooperative game. And nothing in the nature of evil persons will inspire conformity to normative rules. Thus, we design a coercive institution which forces evil persons to obey rules. Nevertheless, if coercers such as policemen and judges are themselves evil, how can we ensure that the coercive institutions will work, and how can we ensure that institutionally protected rights will be respected?

[72] John Rawls, "Kantian Constructivism in Moral Theory: Rational and Full Autonomy," *Journal of Philosophy*, vol. 77, no. 9 (1980), p. 534.

[73] I should note that my argument is not against Rawls's theory itself but against its application in China. It is unfair to charge Rawls with failing to take the problem of evil into account, because the issue of civil war and the danger of totalitarianism, which are major concerns for Chinese liberals, are not problems for him. Moreover, Rawls's general defense of equal liberties is relevant to Chinese debates over political values, and I have often cited it in my work.

Although this problem has no easy solution, it might be resolved, or at least reduced, as Yan Jiaqi argues, by the division of powers—a method of skillfully counterbalancing refractory and mutually antagonistic evils. This is similar to Madison's argument that ambition must be made to counteract ambition, and that the interests of human beings must be connected with the defense of constitutional rights.[74] By increasing the price of doing harm, and rewarding those who do good, democratic mechanisms indeed help to reduce evil. They also contrive an artificial identification of private and public interest. This can make conflicting private interests subservient to public interests.[75] Thus, in framing a political constitution, we can construct a relatively good whole out of bad parts.

Hu Ping and Yan Jiaqi also employ the notion of human goodness or virtue as a solution to the problem just discussed. While recognizing that the establishment of democracy in China necessitates an analysis of evil human action, they believe that human beings are also capable of goodness, and they argue that it is this goodness on which the possibility of democracy in China depends.[76] Hu Ping, who insists on a high place for noble values and goodness in democratic theory, argues that the fact that democratic institutions are devised to deal with the problem of evil does not imply that democratic politics is based solely on the supposition of evil. He contends that the idea that democratic institutions are based solely on the assumption of evil is one-sided, incomplete, and dangerous, and that those who hold this idea misunderstand the Western liberal theory of democracy and the idea of original sin. Hu is aware that under the assumption that all people are evil, and that institutions are operated by evil persons, democratic institutions cannot guarantee basic human rights, and the only choice is autocracy. Inspired by Madison, Hu favors the middle case[77] where all individuals are neither devils nor angels; it is this middle case that makes democratic institutions both feasible and necessary.[78] Thus, Hu Ping's position is in line with that of Alexander Ham-

[74] Madison, *The Federalist Papers* (*supra* note 42), p. 322.

[75] Yan Jiaqi, *Wode sixiang zichuan*, pp. 97–99.

[76] See Hu Ping, *Gei wo yige zhidian*, p. 268; Hu Ping, "Bolinqiang suixiang," p. 43; and Yan Jiaqi, "Tizhi gaige," p. 2. See also Yan Jiaqi, "Liangzhi shi shangdi de shengyin" (Conscience is the voice of God), *Democratic China*, no. 1 (1990), pp. 6–7; and "Yan Jiaqi, Zhu Gaozheng yibaifenzhong daibianlu" (A long debate between Yan Jiaqi and Zhu Gaozheng), *Zhongyang ribao* (Central daily news), Taiwan, May 15, 1990, p. 7.

[77] The idea of the middle case fits well with the Chinese people's view that the majority of human beings are good and that only a minority are evil. For example, in a survey conducted in rural Taiwan in 1983, 49.5 percent of the respondents characterized human nature as mostly good, 20.7 percent as a mixture of good and evil, 14.9 percent as all good, 11.0 percent as neutral, 4.0 percent as mostly evil, and none as all evil. See Joseph Jiang, ed., *Confucianism and Modernization: A Symposium* (Taiwan: Freedom Council, 1987), p. 241. I should acknowledge that this study of Taiwan may not represent mainland Chinese attitudes and that, to my knowledge, no such survey has been done on mainland China.

[78] Hu Ping, "Bolinqiang suixiang," pp. 42–43, and "Rujia renxinglun," p. 118. Hu also informs me of this in correspondence.

ilton, who pointed out that "the institution of delegated power implies that there is a portion of virtue and honor among mankind, which may be a reasonable foundation of confidence."[79]

Yan Jiaqi holds the same view as Hu Ping, arguing that the concept of goodness in human nature still serves as a starting-point for the advocacy of public virtue, and that an awareness of this goodness is necessary for implementing good institutions and laws. Furthermore, only through the mass media, rather than administrative power, can good public spirit be generated.[80] It should be made clear that the role of the notion of goodness employed by Chinese liberals is different from the one employed by Maoists; it does not serve as a main starting-point for institutional design, as the Maoist concept does.

IV. Evil and the Design of Neo-Authoritarian Institutions[81]

If the idea of evil is taken as a starting-point for institutional design, does this necessarily lead to democratic thinking? While Yan Jiaqi is silent on this question, Hu Ping realizes that there is no simple logical connection between the conception of evil and the design of democratic institutions.[82] Further, there is, I think, a gap between ethical foundations and practical institutions. If the concept of evil is to constitute a starting-point for institutional design, we should remember that it can lead to either autocratic or democratic institutions. As Liao Xun observes, while autocratic institutions are designed to hinder the evil of the masses, democratic institutions are designed to hinder the evil of the power-holders.[83] Here it is interesting to mention that both the idea of dictatorship and the idea of anarchy, according to the German jurist and political philosopher Carl Schmitt, also appeal to the ideas of evil and good: in the face of radical evil, the only solution is dictatorship, while if one assumes that human beings are good and government is corrupt, then all governments, as an anarchist argues, must be opposed, since every government is a dictatorship.[84]

Hobbes's absolute sovereign, Machiavelli's powerful and skillful prince, Schmitt's commissarial dictatorship,[85] and Han Fei-tzu's overcentralized

[79] Hamilton, *The Federalist Papers* (*supra* note 42), p. 458.

[80] Yan Jiaqi, "Tizhi gaige."

[81] There are many Chinese articles which have argued for and against neo-authoritarianism; see Liu Jun and Li Lin, eds., *Xinquanwei zhuyi* (*supra* note 34). Here I limit my discussion to the ways in which neo-authoritarian institutional design addresses the problem of evil.

[82] Hu Ping, "Rujia renxinglun," p. 118.

[83] Liao Xun, " 'Fange yuanze' yu zhengzhi minzhu."

[84] Carl Schmitt, *Political Theology: Four Chapters on the Concept of Sovereignty*, trans. George Schwab (Cambridge, MA: MIT Press, 1985), p. 66.

[85] *Ibid.*

government,[86] all share a common idea: given that human beings are basically evil and dangerous, a stable political order is possible only under a strong leader (or a sovereign authority) sufficiently powerful to control the evil of human behavior and to coerce free-riders into doing their part, so as to avoid the war of all against all. Today, Chinese neo-authoritarians such as Zhang Binjiu[87] follow this tradition. Zhang fears that democratic institutions may provide an open channel for civil fighting. The alternative, he says, is a neo-authoritarian government characterized as a model of semi-centralized power and designed to maintain social order in a transition toward democracy.

Zhang's neo-authoritarian project assumes that the Chinese are selfish, aggressive, destructive liars and that they tend to be free-riders; in short, it assumes that they are not ready for democracy.[88] It also assumes that cadres are willing to seek supreme power at all costs, and that only a few enlightened leaders are good. The way to resolve the problem of evil, in the neo-authoritarian view, is to centralize political power in the hands of a few enlightened leaders. This will justify depriving the masses of their civil and political rights, which is clearly part of the neo-authoritarian approach. This approach, however, is different from Maoism in the sense that neo-authoritarian institutions are designed to grant and protect people's economic rights, so as to ensure economic development.

This project of a neo-authoritarian government has serious problems. Its greatest weakness is that it invests political power in one person or a few people who are presumed to be good. As Hu Ping argues, it will certainly lead to autocracy and will not necessarily lead to enlightened rule, which in fact depends on personality and historical circumstance.[89] And if leaders become evil, people will have no rights or institutional mechanisms to resist them; under the rule of such egoists, institutions will be prone to corruption and inefficiency, and will not secure political order. The assumption that leaders will be enlightened is too optimistic: imperfection, I argue, is inherent in human action. As Hume has argued convincingly: "[T]hose whom we trust for rulers, do not immediately become of a superior nature to the rest of human beings. We may often expect, from the irregularity of human action, that they will neglect even the pub-

[86] Baogang He, "An Investigation of Han Fei-tzu's Power Theory" (*supra* note 7).

[87] Zhang Binjiu, "Jingji tizhi gaige he zhengzhi tizhi gaige de jincheng yu xietiao" (Process and coordination of economic and political reforms), and "Jijin de minzhu haishi wenjian de minzhu?" (Radical or moderate democratization?), in Liu Jun and Li Lin, eds., *Xinquanwei zhuyi* (*supra* note 34).

[88] This assumption is certainly wrong. I have examined the emergent democratic culture in China; see Baogang He, "Democratization: Anti-Democratic and Democratic Elements in the Political Culture of China," *Australian Journal of Political Science*, vol. 27, no. 1 (1992), pp. 120–36.

[89] Hu Ping, *Gei wo yige zhidian*, p. 176; Hu Ping, *Zai lixiang yu xianshi zhijian* (Between ideal and reality) (Hong Kong: Tianyuan shuwu, 1990), pp. 151–63.

lic interests in the execution of justice, and be transported by their passions into all the excesses of cruelty and ambition."[90]

Further, neo-authoritarian institutional arrangements would potentially create social and political disorder, due to their lack of institutions and proper procedures to deal with the evil of leaders. There might also be the evil of a permanent succession crisis that continually threatens chaos or even civil war when a ruler dies under a neo-authoritarian system.[91]

Furthermore, while allowing limited freedom in economic life, neo-authoritarian institutional arrangements still attempt to maintain ideological control and to suppress the aggression of the masses. Thus, there is still a lack of institutional channels to "release" this aggression. If chance allowed, as in the case of the death of Hu Yaobang and the subsequent popular demonstration in Beijing in 1989, suppressed aggression could turn out to be a destructive force.[92] As Lucian Pye, a specialist on China, points out, when disorder prevails, passion gets out of hand, aggression surfaces, and panic is likely.[93]

In short, as Yan Jiaqi argues, neo-authoritarianism is nothing but a modern version of an enlightened autocracy; the Beijing Massacre of 1989 proves the impracticality of it. What China needs is the impersonal authority of a constitution and laws which fully protect civil and political rights, rather than the personalized authority of a powerful leader.[94]

V. Arguments for Democratic Principles and Institutions

The fact that communist ideology initially attempted to resolve the problem of evil, but in the end became a new source of evil, raises the following question: How does the liberal-democratic idea or principle avoid becoming a new source of evil and overcome the problem of being abused by a despot? The principles of the priority of equal liberty and of fair procedures answer this question and serve as the best guide to the design of democratic institutions.

Hu Ping, echoing Isaiah Berlin, has argued that the Marxist idea of positive liberty is to be condemned, not only because of what it entails but also because it has been used to provide a specious disguise and a basic

[90] Hume, *Treatise*, p. 251.

[91] I acknowledge that although democracy as defined by Yan Jiaqi focuses on fair procedures, and incorporates general rules that permit a peaceful succession, the problem of succession during the process of democratization is far from being resolved.

[92] Feng Shengbao points out the negative effects of the students' demonstration in 1989 and argues against the strategy of creating "political earthquakes"; see Feng Shengbao, "Minzhu yundong yu zhongguo de zhengzhi chulu" (Democracy movement and a political breakthrough in China), *Zhishi fenzi* (Chinese intellectuals), vol. 6, no. 4 (1991), p. 56.

[93] Lucian W. Pye, *The Mandarin and the Cadre: China's Political Cultures* (Ann Arbor: University of Michigan Press, 1988), p. 128.

[94] Yan Jiaqi, *Disan gonghe – Weilaizhongguo de xuanze* (The third republic – A choice for future China) (New York: Global Publishing Co., Inc., 1992), pp. 313–17.

theoretical foundation for brutal tyranny.[95] Of course, the ideas of equal liberty and fair procedures have sometimes been used in that way as well; nevertheless, these two ideas would have their own capacity to resist being abused by troublemaking intellectuals and politicians to justify social evil, and would leave us significantly less vulnerable to such temptations. The reason is that, as Hu Ping argues, the principle of the priority of equal liberty is capable of defending the right to dissent.[96] Conversely, Chinese Marxist ideology, which claims to be a science of ideas, emphasizes the priority of truth over right, and thus is potentially capable of depriving others of their rights, particularly those who hold dissident views. Chinese Marxist ideology, therefore, has the inherent fault of hierarchy and lacks an internal mechanism against being abused by a despot.[97]

While Hu Ping often argues for the idea of the priority of liberty, Yan Jiaqi always focuses on proceduralism. For Yan, the principle of procedural fairness is capable of withstanding abuse and correcting mistakes because it contains a self-correcting procedure. Yan further argues that in order to resolve disputes, we need not appeal to the direct or strategic use of brutal force, but rather to a set of prescribed procedures within a court of appeal that is free from coercion.[98]

In short, the ideas of the priority of equal liberty and fair procedures are not compatible with any totalitarian claim to truth, or with the rule of any despot. Consequently, these ideas can help to reduce the number of cases of abuse, although there is still a possibility of abusing liberal theories at a practical level.

The poor record of Chinese communist institutions in dealing with the problem of evil raises the following question: How do liberal-democratic institutions resolve the problem of evil, in particular the problem of institutional evil, while not constituting a new evil? The design of liberal-democratic institutions, based on the minimalist conception of evil in terms of the violation of rights, meets this challenge in a number of ways.

1. Institutional guarantee of rights. The democratic way to control evil is to provide an institutional guarantee of political liberties, so as to restrict attempts to violate the liberty and lives of others. However, the difficult question is: If we know that evil persons might abuse rights in order to do evil things, do we have the right to deprive evil persons of civil and

[95] See Hu Ping, *Gei wo yige zhidian*, pp. 37–39; Hu Ping, "Bolinqiang suixiang," p. 40; and Hu Ping, "Ziyouzhuyi sichao zai zhongguo de mingyun" (The prospect for the trend of liberalism in China), *China Spring*, April 1991, pp. 51–52. See also Isaiah Berlin, *Four Essays on Liberty* (New York: Oxford University Press, 1969), p. 131.

[96] See Hu Ping's essay on the right to dissent in *Gei wo yige zhidian*. Wang Juntao has also defended the right to make counter-revolutionary statements, including statements against the Party. See John Gittings, *China Changes Face: The Road from Revolution, 1949–1989* (New York: Oxford University Press, 1990), p. 154.

[97] See also Madsen, *Morality and Power in a Chinese Village* (*supra* note 54).

[98] See Yan Jiaqi, "Tizhi gaige," p. 2; and *Wode sixiang zichuan*, ch. 10.

political rights? Should evil persons still enjoy the rights granted by a liberal constitution? Here the assumption that some people are evil and others are good does not provide a moral justification for the "good person" to deprive the "evil person" of his or her rights, because such "good people" are also presumed to be potentially evil. The claim that all human beings are potentially evil denies the right of the "good person" to deprive others of their rights. There is no legitimate reason for depriving evil persons of their rights based on their *potential* evil; to do this is to risk depriving all of us of our rights. Moreover, if potentially evil persons are granted civil and political rights, and if an evil person attempts to do bad things to other evil persons, he will be resisted by these others, who have rights to fight back. It is the institutional protection of the rights of all (including potentially evil persons) that might counterbalance the refractory and mutually antagonistic evils. The greatest source of security against evil consists in giving to good persons as well as to evil ones the basic political right to resist encroachments on their rights by other evil persons. As to the question of whether we have the right to limit the rights of *actually* evil persons, the answer is yes, because evil persons violate the principle of equal rights and do harm to others.

2. *Separation of powers.* Evil people might manipulate lawmakers to deprive others of their liberties. The state itself is potentially the greatest threat to the individual's liberty. Thus, institutional devices to separate powers are favored by Chinese liberals such as Yan Jiaqi, as means of struggling against state excesses, as well as against the evil of manipulation by elites. Charles-Louis Montesquieu, who has influenced Chinese liberal thinking, argued that political liberty is present only when power is not abused, and that liberty is secured by a certain distribution of the three types of political power (executive, legislative, and judicial), so that no single person or body can abuse power.[99] The converse of Montesquieu's thesis is true when applied to China. The Chinese Communist Party has united legislative power with executive power; thus, there are no real liberties, although liberties are granted by the constitution, because the Party that makes laws also executes them. Moreover, when the Party commands the legal power of a judge, in addition to legislative power and executive power, the power of the Party over the lives and liberty of the citizens is complete and arbitrary. It was a lack of division of power and of democratic institutions within the Party that, as political scientist Wang Huning points out, caused the Cultural Revolution.[100] That is why Chinese liberals advocate a multiparty system rather than one-party rule. That is also why Yan favors separate executive, legislative, and

[99] Charles-Louis Montesquieu, *The Spirit of the Laws,* ed. and trans. Anne Cohler, Basia Miller, and Harold Stone (Cambridge: Cambridge University Press, 1989), pp. 155, 187.

[100] Wang Huning, " 'Wenge' fansi yu zhengzhi tizhi gaige" (A reflection on the Cultural Revolution and political reform), *Shijie jingji taobao* (The world economical herald), September 29, 1986, p. 6.

judicial branches of government, and advocates four divisions of power in China as a major task of political reform: divisions between the people and the State, between the Party and the government, between the government and social organizations, and between the central government and the local governments.[101] Yan Jiaqi[102] and Hu Ping[103] have also emphasized the importance of the freedom of the press and civil society, which are seen as socially separated powers. Whether or not liberty will be preserved depends less upon the niceties of constitutional construction than upon the extent to which there are independent sources of power in civil society. As Yan realizes, the Watergate scandal in the U.S. has demonstrated that the press is capable of acting as a "fourth branch" of government, and may be more effective as a means of checking power than as a supporter of government, if freedom of the press is guaranteed.[104] In conclusion, the principle of preventing evil, as Liao Xun argues, favors a separation of powers and should be used to guide current political reforms in China.[105]

3. Restrictive and regulative institutions. Su Wei sees democracy as a mechanism to deal with or control evil.[106] This mechanism, I would argue, involves two types of institutions. Restrictive institutions attempt to control evil through the use of some form of coercion, such as civil and criminal penalties; regulative institutions attempt to have evil play a positive role and to nurture civil virtue, which helps to support the rule of law.

Restrictive institutions. The effects of some rulers' innate drives, such as the pleasure they take in aggression and destruction, and their tendencies toward corruption, can be effectively checked by the construction of a set of political institutions, i.e., through constitutional checks and periodic elections. These measures prevent these drives from "getting out of hand," and hence prevent or set a limit on the dangerous combination of evil and power.[107] Democracy limits the ability of rulers to hide their errors so as to continue in a destructive direction (thereby compounding errors into disasters). Watergate and the resignation of Richard Nixon have demonstrated that when evil people in high positions, even a U.S. president, abuse the public trust placed in them, the multiple checks built into a government of divided powers can bring such people down.

Regulative institutions or institutional guides. It is evident that we cannot eradicate potentially evil instincts, but we are capable of controlling evil by an alteration of its direction.[108] Well-established institutions can com-

[101] Yan Jiaqi, *Wode sixiang zichuan*, ch. 14.
[102] Yan Jiaqi, *Zouxiang minzhu zhengzhi*; see esp. his essay on freedom of the press.
[103] Hu Ping, "On Freedom of Speech," in *Gei wo yige zhidian*.
[104] Yan Jiaqi, *Wode sixiang zichuan*, ch. 14; see esp. p. 111.
[105] Liao Xun, " 'Fange yuanze' yu zhengzhi minzhu."
[106] See Su Wei's speech in "Tansuo weilai de daolu" (*supra* note 24), p. 44.
[107] Yan Jiaqi, "Tizhi gaige," p. 2.
[108] For the idea of an alteration, see Hume, *Treatise* (*supra* note 22), p. 197.

pel evil people to do good things. In the case of evil leaders, politically open systems of competition are so constituted that they can aggregate the self-interested rationality of nonvirtuous politicians in order to achieve virtuous ends in political life. Thus, the lust for power can be guided adroitly to serve the public under well-established institutions; and institutions can guide the fight for political achievements rather than the struggle for narrow interests. It might also be argued that although the problem of evil does pose difficulties for Chinese democratization, evil persons, under institutional constraints and historically favorable conditions, might well choose to play the democratic card and push for Chinese democratization.

I must acknowledge, however, that liberal-democratic institutional arrangements cannot guarantee the functions discussed above, because evil persons might find ways to get around the rules. Nevertheless, democratic institutions are able to provide self-correcting mechanisms which guard against abuse if this occurs. Thus, democratic institutions have the potential to avoid the possibility of becoming a new evil, or to correct mistakes if needed.

VI. Conclusion

Chinese liberals such as Hu Ping, Yan Jiaqi, and Liao Xun have identified the serious problems of evil in Chinese political life—particularly Hu Ping, who has highlighted the extent of ideological and organizational evil in Chinese communist society. These theorists implicitly hold a conception of evil in terms of the violation of rights. They have also justified the supposition of potential evil, or a principle of preventing the evil of power-holders, as an intellectual foundation for the design of democratic institutions in China.

Hu Ping and Liao Xun have realized that there is no close or direct logical link between democratic institutional arrangements and the concept of evil. There are, at least, two links between the conception of evil and the different institutional designs. The first link is based on the assumption that the Chinese people are evil, and would lead to neo-authoritarian institutional arrangements; but such arrangements, I argue, remain unacceptable. The second link draws on the supposition that all human beings are potentially evil, and Chinese liberals such as Yan Jiaqi and Hu Ping have argued for the principle of the priority of equal rights and fair procedures as a solution to the problem of official ideological evil and as a guide for the design of democratic institutions. In taking account of the conception of organizational evil, they have argued for institutional protection of liberties through the division of powers, and have argued for regulative and restrictive institutions. They have also maintained not only that democratic institutions are desirable, but that those institutions can be made to work through checks and balances and the goodness of human behavior.

Yan Jiaqi has remarked on the significance of the awareness of evil in terms of breaking with the traditional moral approach to politics.[109] This significance, however, should not be understood as a mere recognition of evil, because both Confucius and Han Fei-tzu acknowledged the evil side of human action. The significance should be understood in these terms: Chinese liberals successfully link the conception of evil, in terms of the violation of rights, to the design of democratic institutions; and this link, which I have attempted to explore and develop, represents a breakthrough in Chinese democratic thinking.

Political Science, University of Tasmania

[109] Yan Jiaqi, "Tizhi gaige," p. 2.

INDEX